EXECUTIVE MEASURES, TERRORISM
AND NATIONAL SECURITY

For Frances,
without whose loving support this book
could not have been written

Executive Measures, Terrorism and National Security

Have the Rules of the Game Changed?

DAVID BONNER
University of Leicester, UK

ASHGATE

Published by
Ashgate Publishing Limited
Gower House
Croft Road
Aldershot
Hampshire GU11 3HR
England

Ashgate Publishing Company
Suite 420
101 Cherry Street
Burlington, VT 05401-4405
USA

Ashgate website: http://www.ashgate.com

British Library Cataloguing in Publication Data
Bonner, David
   Executive measures, terrorism and national security : have
   the rules of the game changed?
   1. National security - Law and legislation - Great Britain
   - History 2. Terrorism - Great Britain - History
   I. Title
   343.4'101'09

Library of Congress Cataloging-in-Publication Data
Bonner, David.
   Executive measures, terrorism, and national security : have the rules of the game changed? / by David Bonner.
      p. cm.
   Includes bibliographical references and index.
   ISBN: 978-0-7546-4756-0
   1. War and emergency powers--Great Britain--History. 2. Executive power--Great Britain. 3. Terrorism--Great Britain. 4. National security--Great Britain. 5. Human rights--Great Britain. I. Title.
   KD6004.B66 2007
   342.41'06--dc22

2007013150

ISBN: 978-0-7546-4756-0

Printed and bound in Great Britain by MPG Books Ltd, Bodmin, Cornwall.

Contents

Foreword

One of the perennial beliefs of the human mind is that things are worse now than they have ever been. The eponymous heroine of the South African film *Yesterday* was given her name because, as her father said, yesterday is always better than today. The same is strikingly the case in relation both to terrorism and to the measures taken against it. Governments consider the terrorist threat, especially since September 2001, to be unprecedented in its nature and magnitude. Liberals consider that the measures taken to deal with it represent a wholly new degree of repression.

David Bonner's work, spanning the twentieth century and pushing forward into the twenty-first, is a factual and scholarly demonstration of how mistaken it is possible to be about these things. For a full hundred years legislation has sought to deal with the enemy within and without by handing as much power as possible to the executive and as little as possible to the courts. To lawyers, such a process magnifies the potential for injustice; to administrators and politicians, it minimises the potential for disaster.

Lord Denning, who served during World War II as legal adviser to one of the regional commissioners, later recorded:

> We detained people, without trial, on suspicion that they were a danger... I used to see the person – and ask him questions – so as to judge for myself if the suspicion was justified. He could not be represented by lawyers.... The power was discretionary. It could not be questioned in the courts.

And of one clerical suspect:

> Although there was no case against him, no proof at all, I detained him under '18B'. The Bishop of Ripon protested, but we took no notice.

It was unsurprising then, and is unsurprising now, that the courts should seek to leaven such arbitrary powers with a measure of due process. Since October 2000, when the Human Rights Act 1998 came into effect, the courts have also had a Parliamentary mandate to enforce the executive's compliance, and to oversee the legislature's compliance, with the European Convention on Human Rights.

In this situation, as David Bonner argues, some disagreement between the major limbs of the state is to be expected. But that is not to say that there are any right answers. Experience predicts, and time is bound to reveal, serious errors, whether in locking up innocent people or in freeing dangerous ones. Public dialogue will oscillate around the relative unacceptability of these respective risks, and the law will continue to insist that, while restrictions have to be accepted, they must not be inequitably distributed.

Beyond this, it may be that all one can hope for agreement on is that if measures reach the point of undermining the society they are intended to protect, they will have done some of the terrorists' work for them.

Stephen Sedley
Royal Courts of Justice
June 2007

Preface

This book is the culmination of a career-long interest in the ways in which United Kingdom Governments, both at home and in Empire, have sought to manage terrorism and other national security threats by legal means other than those in the criminal process and the criminal law. These legal means have been executive measures of internment (detention) without trial; restrictions on residence and movement; exclusion or banishment from one part of the realm or Empire; and, as regards undesirable 'aliens', denial of entry to the country or deportation from it on public good grounds. The book confirms me as a frustrated historian disguised in the garb of an academic public lawyer, fascinated by the ebb and flow in judicial supervision of executive action and the gap between the rhetoric of protecting liberty and the undue deference shown, until recently, by judges when the executive intones the mantra of emergency or national security. It also shows me as a student of human rights protection, too long disappointed by the lack of adequate European supervision afforded in this area by the European Court of Human Rights.

This book is more than a mere historical account of some interesting exercises of executive power to manage crises and threats to security and public order. After 9/11, executive measures (ATCSA detention, control orders, and public good deportations) – despite the supposed primacy of criminal prosecution – have returned to prominence in the United Kingdom's counter-terrorism strategy, after the 'blueprint' for anti-terrorism legislation for the twenty-first century – the Terrorism Act 2000 – had seemed to consign them to history. Moreover, such measures are reportedly increasingly a post-9/11 feature in a number of jurisdictions whose previous counter-terrorist strategy had been firmly founded in the criminal law and process. The book is thus also very topical.

The powers and their uses in the United Kingdom since 9/11 have proved controversial and generated equally controversial landmark judgments as judges in challenges to these powers explore the boundaries of the new constitutional settlement represented by the Human Rights Act 1998 (HRA) and the consequent emergence of a rights-based democracy. A central argument of the book is that the only 'rule of the game' that has changed (to adapt Prime Minister Blair's phrase) is the traditional one that United Kingdom courts faced with the exercise of executive powers in the 'security' sphere in reality give the executive a free hand and legitimate whatever action the executive consider necessary to deal with the threat. The hypothesis advanced here is that in this HRA era, United Kingdom courts have begun to undertake an enhanced level of scrutiny in an area they once characterized as too sensitive for judicial involvement and in which they exercised undue restraint in the face of the marked impact of the powers on the rights and freedoms of individuals. Their changed attitude has been criticized as undue 'activism', as trespassing on ground reserved for executive judgment. The rule that has changed is one that Prime Minister Blair would prefer had not. This book suggests in contrast that it is constitutionally proper that there be tensions between organs of government, that Government and judges disagree, that they are not necessarily on the 'same side'. It is the job of the courts in terms of human rights and threats to the nation in a rights-based democracy to be willing to speak truth to power, regardless of popularity.

The book thus sets counter-terrorist strategy after 9/11 in the context of the use of executive measures over the course of the preceding century, positing both that the nature of the threat is not as dissimilar to previous threats as some would have us believe and that the responses, far from being 'new', are very much a case of old wine in new bottles.

The book is designed to be read by the educated layperson as well as lawyers, historians and political scientists. To that end, it has deliberately kept footnote references short and adopted a simple referencing system. Those who wish to ignore the footnotes can readily do so. Those who wish to take things further merely have to link the footnote entry (for example, 'Simpson (1994): 1') with the corresponding entry in the bibliography to find the full title of the work referred to.

I have here deliberately chosen one of Professor A.W. Brian Simpson's fine works as an example to acknowledge a debt to his research in this field, one also acknowledged recently by Lord Bingham. This study is intended as my own small contribution to a growing literature on Law and Emergency. It is based in good part on my own research in the National Archives on control of aliens, the colonial emergencies in Malaya, Cyprus and Kenya, and counter-terrorism powers to deal with terrorism connected with Northern Ireland affairs 1971–75, both in the Province itself and in dealing with the IRA campaign in Great Britain. But the debt it owes to the work of Professor Simpson and other labourers in this increasingly rich vineyard is hopefully duly acknowledged in both footnotes and quotations.

I have endeavoured to state the law accurately in the light of the sources available to me as at 24 February 2007, but, at proof stage have been able to insert brief references to developments up to 29 May 2007.

David Bonner
Leicester
29 May 2007

Acknowledgments

I am delighted to be able to acknowledge the assistance and encouragement of a number of organizations and individuals who have contributed to bringing this project to fruition.

Particular thanks must go to the British Academy whose grant enabled me to spend some three months researching in the National Archives at Kew during a period of study leave afforded by the University of Leicester. I must also thank the University for the Special Study Leave granted me during the Autumn Term 2006, which enabled me to write this book in time to appear for the Research Assessment Exercise (RAE), which assesses Universities' research output. I am also grateful to the staff of the University Research and Finance Offices for the administration of the British Academy Grant and our Faculty Administrator, Holly Paisey, for helping me pick my way through the labyrinth of invoices.

Researchers always owe much more to library and archive staff than is realized. So I wish here to thank for their kind assistance the staff of the University Library at Leicester, of the Squire Law Library, Cambridge and of the Institute for Advanced Legal Studies in London. My biggest debt is to the very helpful staff at the National Archives at Kew.

I have been fortunate in terms of those who have read drafts of all or various parts of this work: my current colleagues, Mads Andenas, Virginia Mantouvalou and Robin White; and my former colleague, Trevor Buck, now gracing the Law School at De Montfort University. All have made encouraging comments and suggestions and some have tried valiantly, but not always successfully, to save readers from my long sentences. Unfortunately, none was prepared to accept responsibility for the errors that doubtless remain or for the views expressed herein, so, regrettably, they remain mine.

I am grateful to Alison Kirk, my commissioning editor, for having faith in the project and to the helpful comments of the anonymous referee. Thanks must also go to Carolyn Court and her editorial and production team.

Finally, but by no means least, I must acknowledge the kind permission under the waivers system of the Controller of Her Majesty's Stationery Office in respect of United Kingdom Crown copyright material in the National Archives.

List of Abbreviations

AA	Aliens Act 1905
A.C.	Appeal Cases (Law Reports)
AC	Advisory Committee
AIT	Asylum and Immigration Tribunal
AKEL	Cyprus Communist Party
All ER	All England Law Reports
ATCSA	Anti-terrorism Crime and Security Act 2001
BU	British Union
CAC	House of Commons Select Committee on Constitutional Affairs
Cm	Command Paper
CMA	Competent military authority
CND	Campaign for Nuclear Disarmament
CO	Colonial Office
DORA	Defence of the Realm Act
DORR	Defence of the Realm Regulations
DR	Defence Regulation
DTO	Detention of Terrorists Order 1972
EC	European Community
ECHR	European Convention on Human Rights and Fundamental Freedoms 1950
ECJ	European Court of Justice
EEA	European Economic Area
EHRR	European Human Rights Reports
EIJ	Egyptian Islamic Jihad
EOKA	National Organization of Cypriot Fighters
EPDA	Emergency Powers (Defence) Act
ER	Emergency Regulations
EU	European Union
EWCA Civ	England and Wales Court of Appeal, Civil division
EWHC Admin	England and Wales High Court (Administrative Court)
FAC	House of Commons Select Committee on Foreign Affairs
FCO	Foreign and Commonwealth Office
FIT	Tunisian Islamic Front
GCHQ	Government Communications Headquarters
GIA	Armed Islamic Group (*Group Islamique armé*)
GSPC	Salafist Group for Preaching and Combat
HC	House of Commons Paper

HL	House of Lords Paper
HMP	Her Majesty's Prison
HO	Home Office
HRA	Human Rights Act 1998
IANA	Immigration, Asylum and Nationality Act 2006
IAT	Immigration Appeals Tribunal
ICCPR	United Nations International Covenant on Civil and Political Rights 1966
IRA	Irish Republican Army
ISAF	International Security Assistance Force
J	Justice
JHRC	House of Commons/House of Lords Joint Committee on Human Rights
KAU	Kenyan African Union
LCJ	Lord Chief Justice
LJ	Lord (Lady) Justice of Appeal
LJKB	Law Journal Kings Bench (law reports)
MCP	Malayan Communist Party
MLJ	Malayan Law Journal
MI5	Security Service (United Kingdom)
MI6	Secret Intelligence Service (United Kingdom)
MPAJA	Malayan Peoples Anti-Japanese Army
MRLA	Malayan Races Liberation Army
NASS	National Asylum Support Service
NATO	North Atlantic Treaty Organization
NIAA	Nationality, Immigration and Asylum Act 2002
NIEPA	Northern Ireland (Emergency Provisions) Act
OASA	Offences Against the State Act
OEF	Operation Enduring Freedom
OSA	Official Secrets Act
PIRA	Provisional IRA
PLO	Palestine Liberation Organization
PM	Prime Minister
PTA	Prevention of Terrorism Act
PVA	Prevention of Violence (Temporary Provisions) Act 1939
ROIA	Restoration of Order in Ireland Act 1920
ROIR	Restoration of Order in Ireland Regulation
SASO	Special Advocates Support Office
SI	Statutory Instrument
SIAC	Special Immigration Appeals Commission
SIACA	Special Immigration Appeals Act 1997
SPA	Civil Authorities (Special Powers) Act
SPAR	Special Powers Act Regulation

SR&O	Statutory Regulations and Orders
TA	Terrorism Act
TFG	Tunisian Fighting Group
TLR	Times Law Reports
TMT	Turkish Defence Organization
TNA	The National Archives, Kew, England
UKHL	United Kingdom House of Lords (the country's highest court)
UN	United Nations
UNCAT	United Nations Convention Against Torture
UNHCR	United Nations High Commissioner for Refugees
UNMO	United Malay National Organization
UNSCR	United Nations Security Council Resolution
UPA	Ulster Protestant Association

PART I

Introduction and Overview

Chapter 1

Perspectives, Themes and Concepts

What This Book is About

This book examines the use, in the period from 1905 (the enactment of the Aliens Act) to early in 2007, of a variety of executive measures to assist in containing terrorism and to protect national security. The measures focused on are internment (indefinite detention without trial); restriction of movement and internal exile; and exclusion (keeping out) or deportation (ejection) of undesirable foreign nationals from the country. The deployment of such measures is analysed in a variety of contexts, both within the United Kingdom and by its Governmental representatives abroad in seeking to maintain its colonial empire. Part II deals with the use of such powers prior to what has been seen as a watershed in terrorism and the powers needed to counter it: the Al Qaeda attacks on the 'Twin Towers' of New York's World Trade Center, symbol of United States' economic power. This has become known by its date simply as 9/11. Part II thus examines the deployment of executive measures to deal with the 'enemy' at home in the two World Wars (chapter 2); in respect of the violent conflicts surrounding the 'Irish' and, latterly, 'Northern Ireland' questions (chapter 3); in refusing entry to or removing or deporting 'undesirable' aliens (chapter 4); and in the withdrawal from colonial empire. Malaya, Kenya and Cyprus are examined as examples (chapter 5).

It is particularly appropriate to do so at this time since two commentators have noted that counter-terrorism post 9/11 in a number of countries makes much more use of executive and even extra-legal measures than ones founded on criminal law and processes.[1] This book is thus by no means merely an historical work. It seeks through that examination of the past to contextualize the executive measures currently deployed by the United Kingdom after 9/11. These are delineated in outline here and analysed in depth in Part III. But it also calls into question, at least as regards the United Kingdom, those commentators' assertion that counter-terrorism prior to 9/11 was more heavily criminal law and process-oriented,[2] instead revealing through this book the United Kingdom's long history of dealing with various manifestations of terrorism at home and in empire to have been heavily dependent on deployment of executive measures. This chapter begins almost at the end of the time period under study. It now considers the terms and implications of a statement made by Prime Minister Blair and subsequent

---

[1] Jessberger and Gaeta (2006): 891.
[2] Ibid: 893.

statements on both threat and response by other key players responsible for security.

The Prime Minister's statement was made not long after the 7 July 2005 terrorist attacks on London's transport network, which have entered the lexicon simply as 7/7. His message was that the 'rules of the game' were changing. The purpose of considering it here and indeed of the book as a whole is to show graphically the link with the past of executive measures deployed as a central part of the United Kingdom's counter-terrorism strategy after 9/11 and 7/7. The book emphasizes that, in terms of the security measures themselves, the rules of the game have not changed. Rather it is a case of more of the same medicine to treat a very similar problem of armed threats to the State and its inhabitants from non-State or State-sponsored actors. It is suggested here that the only 'rule of the game' that clearly has changed is the traditional one that United Kingdom courts faced with the exercise of executive powers in the 'security' sphere in reality (whatever sometimes bold rhetoric) give the executive a free hand and legitimate whatever action the executive considers necessary to deal with the threat. The hypothesis advanced here is that in this era of the Human Rights Act 1998 (HRA), United Kingdom courts have started to apply an enhanced level of scrutiny in an area they once characterized as too sensitive for judicial involvement and in which they exercised undue restraint in the face of the marked impact of the powers on the rights and freedoms of individuals. The book also endeavours to place in context recent claims by key actors that the United Kingdom currently faces its greatest threat since the Second World War.

After 7/7: 'The Rules of the Game are Changing' But in Which Ways?

At his monthly Press Conference on 5 August 2005, the Prime Minister set out certain measures proposed by the Government to strengthen its counter-terrorism powers and responses. Some of the measures involved the creation of new statutory criminal offences (encouraging terrorism) or extending the scope of others (proscribed organizations and offences of membership and financial, political and material support for such groups). Many, however, were located firmly in the sorts of executive measures examined in this book. They concerned exclusion and deportation from the United Kingdom on public good and security grounds under immigration law. This involved extending the range of behaviours that would bring individual non-citizens within their scope. It was a change in administrative practice which tended, in Government announcements and its counter-terrorist strategy document, misleadingly to be presented as a change in the law itself.[3] In addition, through deprivation of citizenship and the 'right of abode' – both conferring absolute freedom from exclusion or removal under immigration law – the proposed measures sought to increase the range of 'undesirable'

---

[3]   Cm 6888 (2006): para. 7.

individuals holding dual nationality who could be amenable to those powers of exclusion and deportation. Furthermore, the statement envisaged more use of control orders. These were introduced in the Prevention of Terrorism Act 2005 (PTA 2005) after the detention scheme in the Anti-terrorism Crime and Security Act 2001 (ATCSA) had in December 2004 been declared incompatible with Convention Rights by the House of Lords using the HRA,[4] one of the Labour Government's 'flagship' constitutional reforms. The HRA is the closest legal instrument in the United Kingdom to the Bills of Rights embodied in most other constitutions, and is examined further later in this chapter.

Control orders enable a range of restrictions to be imposed on the movement and activities of terrorist suspects, including, at the most extreme, house arrest or detention without trial. The Prime Minister made clear that he thought that attitudes and perceptions about the threat faced were changing. He criticized those in Parliament and the Courts he saw as having obstructed action the Government thought necessary. Revealing an inaccurate grasp of the constitutional position under the HRA and the date of enactment of crucial anti-terrorist legislation, he said:

> The action I am talking about has in the past been controversial, each tightening of the law has met fierce opposition, regularly we have a defeat in parliament or in the courts. The anti-terrorism legislation of course passed in 2002 after September 11th was declared partially invalid, the successor legislation hotly contested. But for obvious reasons, the mood now is different, people do not talk of scare-mongering, and to be fair the Conservative leadership has responded with a genuine desire to work together for the good of the country, as have the Liberal Democrats. .... we are today signalling a new approach to deportation orders. Let no-one be in any doubt, the rules of the game are changing. ... the circumstances of our national security have self-evidently changed.

In the question and answer session, he made a number of notable responses on this theme of change:

> whether measures are there administratively or legislatively, I think most people recognise that the climate in which these measures are being taken is somewhat different today. ... what has changed in the past four weeks since the attacks on 7th July, is that people now understand that when we warn of the terrorist threat this is not scare–mongering, it's real ... we've got to get the law in proper shape. If we can do that it will obviously be sensible for Parliament to begin this process as soon as possible. ... I've been constantly saying we need to take these measures. I mean I know that people want to gloss over what happened in the months leading up to the election, but I do remind you that we were being fiercely opposed in the measures we had taken and the actual legislation that we had was being struck down. Anyway, you can go back over this many times but I think you have a different situation now ... all over Europe there is this gearing up and I think it's right to do so, but I think to be frank if I had come forward

---

[4] *A and Others* v *Secretary of State for the Home Department* [2004] UKHL 56.

with these measures 3 or 4 months ago, I think it would have been a little bit more difficult.

As regards, the specific context of deportation and human rights, he noted the obstacle posed by Art. 3 of the European Convention of Human Rights (ECHR) which prohibits torture, inhuman or degrading treatment or punishment. The ECHR, examined further later in this chapter, is an international obligation of the United Kingdom and has been incorporated into United Kingdom law from October 2000. As interpreted in *Chahal* v *United Kingdom,* a landmark decision of the European Court of Human Rights in the context of a national security deportation, Art. 3 ECHR precludes removing a person to a country where there are substantial grounds for believing that if returned there he or she would face a real risk of such maltreatment even where the person was a threat to national security. The Prime Minister noted that this had precluded the deportation of suspects in a number of cases. He made clear that this preclusion had to change.

Taking these important comments in the light of subsequent clarifications and other statements by key security actors, one can tease out several levels of meaning on this theme 'the rules of the game are changing'. This tests how far any can be said to be true of the range of measures deployed after 9/11 and 7/7 examined in Part III this book, when set against the broader historical context presented in Part II and the standards set by the ECHR and its incorporation in the HRA.

Clearly the Government will do all it can to deport foreign national/non-British citizen terrorist suspects, either consistently with *Chahal* or by changing the law to permit balancing the risk to the individual of maltreatment against the risk he or she poses to the national security of the United Kingdom. This is examined in more depth in Part III. But one can note here that it might be done in national law by amending the HRA to restrict the approach United Kingdom courts can take on the matter. Attempting to secure its change at ECHR level is more difficult, but could be done by persuading the Court of Human Rights in another case to revise its interpretation of Art. 3 ECHR or securing a textual change to the terms of Art. 3 itself through the conclusion by States Party of an amending Protocol. Neither outcome is likely at ECHR level. But in any event the processes envisaged are themselves puzzling in a number of ways. First of all, in that success at either or both levels might seem futile given the self-same prohibition in other international agreements such as UNCAT or the ICCPR. Neither embodies with respect to the United Kingdom a right of individual petition and may thus, politically, be seen as more remote and less threatening to preferred policy options. Secondly, the criticism it implies of the judiciary and the HRA may also strike an observer as strange given that the empowerment of the judges through that landmark constitutional reform was something effected by this very same Government. It raises in stark form, the matter of the proper role of the judiciary in the face of executive powers enabling serious interference with fundamental rights of individuals, a theme which runs through this book.

The statement ('the circumstances of our national security have self-evidently changed') also suggests that the nature of the threat is different and is greater than in the past. Both propositions are tenable but equally debatable. The theme has been taken up both by the Home Secretary and the Metropolitan Police Commissioner. In a speech to Demos on 9 August 2006, Home Secretary Reid stated: 'We are probably in the most sustained period of severe threat since the end of the Second World War'.[5] A report for the Joseph Rowntree Reform Trust quotes the Home Secretary as later likening the current 'war on terror' to that war against Nazi Germany and as claiming the threat now to be worse than the Cold War. Sir Ian Blair, the Metropolitan Police Commissioner, told BBC Radio Four listeners just before Christmas 2006 that the level of threat was both unparalleled and growing, and, as regards civilians, one would have to go back to the Second World War or the Cold War to find a comparable level. It was more dangerous than that posed by the Irish Republican Army (IRA) because that organization:

> with very few exceptions, did not want to carry out mass atrocities, they didn't want to die, they gave warnings and they were heavily penetrated by the intelligence services. None of those apply with al Qaida and its affiliates.[6]

In November 2006, Dame Eliza Manningham-Buller, Director General of the Security Service, revealed that the security services were aware of 30 serious plots by Islamic extremists, and as many as 200 British-based 'networks' involved with terrorism. The security services also knew of 1,600 people who were actively engaged in, or facilitating, terrorist plots, either in Britain or abroad.[7] This is of grave concern, but does raise the question: if that is the level of threat, why are there in contrast so few charges and convictions and why, despite the width of the powers and the low level of proof required, are so few caught up in executive measures of detention, deportation and control orders?

Several commentators have expressed concern about governmental use of the politics of fear as a lever to obtain new powers or extend the range of existing ones.[8] Lack of an historical perspective or the deployment of a distorted one is damaging. Claims that the threat is unparalleled, greater than that of the IRA or even the Cold War, do nothing to allay public fear. They prevent the realization that it can successfully be contained using the same methods as have in the past contained IRA and other terrorism. Moreover, arguably such hyperbole is redolent of the Iraq and weapons of mass destruction debacle itself so corrosive of trust in government. These concerns are shared by this author who has elsewhere deprecated the portrayal by governments of both political persuasions of opponents

---

[5] < http://press.homeoffice.gov.uk/Speeches/sp-hs-DEMOS-090806?version=1.

[6] As reported in *The Guardian*, 23 December 2006.

[7] Speech delivered at Queen Mary College London on 9 November 2006, <http://www.mi5.gov.uk/output/Page568.html.>.

[8] Rowntree Report (2006); Feldman (2006).

of certain enhancements of counter-terrorist powers as somehow 'soft on terrorism' when, in reality, the difference is one of considering the best means to contain terrorism.[9] The characterization of this as a 'war on terrorism' can equally be deplored as lending a false status to terrorists. It fosters a climate of fear that may actually assist them.[10] It can be contrasted with approaches to terrorism, examined in Part II, connected with the Irish and Northern Ireland questions and with the withdrawal from colonial empire, where government was all too keen to avoid characterizing them as war for fear of according insurgents the status of prisoners of war under international conventions or (as regards Malaya) because of concerns with respect to the insurance market. It has rightly been suggested that this rhetoric of war is 'misleading and disproportionate' and 'has encouraged an overreaction in which human rights and the rule of law are among the more obvious casualties'; it is language encouraging an increase in executive powers.[11] It is therefore to be welcomed that United Kingdom officialdom now refrains from using the phrase. It remains the lingua franca of policy statements by the United States.

Despite these concerns, one thing needs to be made clear at the outset of this book. It is not suggested here that every statement of Government on the threat and the means to combat it is highly suspect. Its current counter-terrorism strategy (examined in depth in chapter 6) has been described even by those expressing these concerns as 'balanced and sensible' but one 'prejudiced and masked by the deluge of anti-terrorism legislation, ministerial rhetoric and some high-profile police activity.' That there is a significant threat, likely to be long-term, to persons and property in the United Kingdom is clear and not disputed in this book. On current ECHR jurisprudence it is accepted here that it amounts to a 'public emergency threatening the life of the nation' enabling derogation from some ECHR rights. That characterization of the position prior to 7/7 has been contested by one eminent Law Lord (and the terms and tone of his speech suggest that his view might not change despite 7/7) and several others expressed some scepticism.[12]

The view that the threat is the greatest since the Second World War is clearly contestable. It will rightly raise eyebrows among those who lived through or were victims of the IRA's bombing campaign in Northern Ireland and on mainland Great Britain from 1969 to 1999. Many will remember the carnage caused by bombs in Bishopsgate and Docklands in London; those in Brighton (targeting the Conservative Prime Minister, Mrs Thatcher and her governmental team); those that devastated the Manchester shopping centre; and the Birmingham pub bombings in 1974, that decade's equivalent of 7/7.[13] In the early 1990s the whole public transport system appeared thrown into chaos by bombs and hoaxes. The Irish National Liberation Army, a violent Republican terror group, even managed in

[9] Bonner (1985): 19; (2006): 629.
[10] Rowntree Report (2006): 11, 13.
[11] Rowntree Report (2006): 13; Richardson (2006): 215.
[12] See especially Lord Hoffman in *A and Others*.
[13] Mullin (1987): chap. 1.

1979 to assassinate the Conservative Northern Ireland spokesman, Airey Neave, with a car bomb in the Palace of Westminster. The threat from Al Quaeda is not qualitatively different.[14] Those who lived through the nuclear threat during the Cold War may also question the Home Secretary's statements. There are certainly some differences in the mode of delivery of death and destruction. The phenomenon of the suicide bomber poses problems in terms of lack of prior warning and in that those willing to sacrifice their lives will not be deterred by harsh laws or penalties.[15] But the phenomenon is historically by no means unprecedented or confined to Islamist or other religious terrorism.[16] The prospect of death on the scaffold (particularly gruesome for those guilty of treason)[17] or before a firing squad did not deter previous generations of those willing to use death and destruction to further their political cause. There are also parallels with those who undertake hunger strike to death for that end or those operatives who if captured choose to use their cyanide pill or to shoot or blow themselves up to avoid capture.[18] Richardson argues that there is nothing 'fundamentally different about suicide terrorism' and that willingness to face certain death for a cause 'is entirely consistent with the behaviour of soldiers throughout the ages',[19] the obvious example being Japanese *kamikaze* airmen in World War II. Similarities can also be seen between modern manifestations of terrorism and the impact and response at the time of attacks on the London Underground and prominent public buildings and bridges by violent Irish nationalists during the 'dynamite war' in the 1880s.[20] The fear then as now was of use of new weapons that advances in technology can afford (then dynamite and gelignite and the development of crude time fuses enabling readier escape by the bomber; Semtex during the 1980s; a 'dirty bomb' in the immediate future). The response was the enactment of the Explosives Substances Act 1883. There is also a parallel with respect to the unsuccessful attempts by the Fenians (a Irish nationalist group using political violence) in 1867 to free comrades in prison (the Clerkenwell explosion) using an excessive quantity of gunpowder in a beer cask placed against the outer wall of the prison.[21] There were six fatalities from a blast heard more than 40 miles away. Over a hundred were injured. More than 400 houses were damaged; many were destroyed. Thousands poured from the houses onto the streets in fear as fire spread through

---

[14] Feldman (2006): 369.

[15] Phillips (2006): 1.

[16] Richardson (2006): chap. 5.

[17] On the deaths of Guy Fawkes and the other Gunpowder Plotters, see Fraser (1996): chap. XV; on those of the Manchester and Clerkenwell Fenians, see Quinlivan and Rose (1982): chaps. 5 and 9.

[18] Short (1979): 232 gives the example of Dillon, a key Clan na Gael dynamiter prepared to do this.

[19] Richardson (2006): 135, 136.

[20] Short (1979): chaps. 4–8; Quinault (2005).

[21] The claim that 548 pounds was used is unlikely to be true: Quinlivan and Rose (1982): 84. Short (1979): 9 suggests 200 pounds.

overcrowded slums. The response was to cancel all police and army leave and to enrol 166,000 special constables to help with the emergency.[22]

It has, of course, proved very difficult, without sufficient officers from the relevant communities, to penetrate Islamist terrorist groups. Perhaps it did prove easier to penetrate Irish Republican groups in the past. In addition, there are also problems about resolving the threat through negotiations, as was a feature of withdrawal from empire and the Irish questions. But attempts at conflict resolution in the Middle East and governmental approach to the Arab and Muslim world surely have a role to play in reducing the radicalization which brings recruits to terrorism in a similar way to the 'hearts and minds' and 'constitutional' dimensions of the earlier threats with which this book deals. In short, while not in any way asserting that every statement by governmental and security spokespersons is questionable and suspect, the suggestion made here is that it is not possible properly to appraise statements on and the efficacy or propriety of current strategies to manage the current threat from Islamist terrorism without setting both in the historical context afforded in Part II of this book and the human rights context examined there and as an important aspect of appraising current measures in Part III.[23]

Before embarking on a detailed examination of use of executive powers in those diverse and challenging contexts, it may be helpful to set the scene (particularly for non-legal readers) in a number of ways. First of all, clarity of analysis demands identification of the nature of the United Kingdom's constitutional and legal orders as well as definition of some central concepts: national security; terrorism; and 'executive measures'. Secondly, consideration needs to be given, in the context of the United Kingdom's 'unwritten' constitutional arrangements, to the sources of legal power for the executive measures examined in this book. This stresses their concentration of power within the executive branch of government. It briefly considers modalities deployed to try to limit the risk of restraining action or interference by of other branches of government or agencies of accountability. The key word there is 'limit'. So it notes provision of administrative means of challenge for those affected by the powers. Accountability to and scrutiny by other branches of government or other agencies of accountability has, moreover, never been wholly excluded. Accordingly, the chapter then goes on to examine the matter of the means used by, and the proper roles of, the national and international judiciary in securing legal accountability for actions taken and, in the post-1945 period, respect for human rights. It considers the broader question of political accountability. This chapter then ponders a key question: why respond to threats to national security through executive measures rather than through the sanctioning role of the criminal process? Finally, it touches on the need to deal with the underlying causes of a national security or terrorist

---

[22] Richardson (2006): 40–41. See further Quinlivan and Rose (1982): chap. 6.

[23] For criticism of Mr Blair's lack of historical context and a tendency in Government to exaggerate the terrorist threat, see Jenkins (2006).

threat, sometimes expressed as the need to win 'hearts and minds' or the political and constitutional dimensions of the problem.

The United Kingdom and its Legal and Constitutional Orders

The United Kingdom consists of mainland Great Britain (England, Wales and Scotland) and of Northern Ireland (the six counties of the north-eastern corner of the island of Ireland). Until 1922, the whole island of Ireland formed part of the United Kingdom, but the remaining 26 counties now form the Republic of Ireland. Like New Zealand and to some extent Israel, unlike most States in the world, the United Kingdom's legal and constitutional orders are characterized by lack of an overriding, 'written', higher law constitution forming the supreme law of the country with which all other laws must conform. In contrast, the United Kingdom constitution is 'unwritten' and non-codified. The rules on the central matters with which constitutions are concerned are found in a variety of sources: statute (Act of Parliament), subordinate legislation, common law, conventions (binding but non-legal rules of constitutional behaviour), law and custom of Parliament, and the opinions of constitutional writers. In this legal and constitutional order, it is traditionally held, since the Glorious Revolution of 1688, that Parliament is sovereign. Legally speaking, it can make or unmake any law whatsoever (statute is supreme in the hierarchy of legal norms). No court has power to invalidate an Act of Parliament. That clear picture has become more clouded given United Kingdom membership of the European Union (EU) (formerly European Communities (EC)). But, EC law aside, its legal and constitutional order lacks an overriding Bill of Rights limiting the power of a parliament dominated by the executive: this is in a context in which only relatively recently have its courts unequivocally accepted the supremacy of EC law over statute and all other national laws (so long as the European Communities Act 1972 remains in force and the United Kingdom remains a member of the EU).[24] The Bill of Rights 1688 was essentially concerned with the relationship between Crown and Parliament, subordinating monarchical to Parliamentary power. As regards colonies, in many the Governor, sometimes assisted by an Executive Council, was the sole law-maker, his powers limited by the need to have approval for laws from the Government in London. In others, laws were made by a Legislative Council, but the Governor, on advice from London, could withhold assent. For Governors, getting London's approval for the proclamation of a State of Emergency gave them more freedom in that there was then no legal requirement to have London's approval for the emergency laws made pursuant to it. Constitutional practice, however, required consultation on key matters. As with government in the United Kingdom, governmental authorities in its colonies were not limited by any Bill of Rights.

---

[24] *R v Transport Secretary, ex parte Factortame Ltd* [1990] 2 AC 85.

In such a system (whether in the United Kingdom or, with due adaptation for legal terminology as regards legislation, a colony), human rights values found legal expression in common law presumptions and principles of legislative intent (what Keir and Lawson called an 'implied Bill of Rights')[25] when undertaking one of the courts' central tasks, that of the interpretation and application of Acts of Parliament (statutes) to disputes brought before them. From 1953, they also found legal expression in a multilateral international treaty created by the Council of Europe. This treaty, the ECHR, is central to the matters considered in this book. The ECHR obliges a State party to it to accord to everyone within its jurisdiction the protection of the rights and freedoms set out it. The rights and freedoms protected are essentially 'first generation' civil, political and legal rights: the right to life; freedom from torture, inhuman and degrading treatment and punishment; freedom from slavery and servitude; the right to liberty and security of person (freedom from arbitrary arrest and detention); the right to a fair trial; freedom from retroactive criminal law or punishment; the right to respect for private and family life, home and correspondence; freedom of thought, conscience and religion; freedom of expression; freedom of association and assembly; the right to marry and found a family; the right to an effective remedy for violation of any of these rights and freedoms; and freedom from discrimination with respect to their enjoyment. Later Protocols (additions to the obligations under the ECHR) protect the right to property and peaceful enjoyment of one's possessions, outlaw capital punishment, and protect freedom of movement. This last – Protocol Four – has never been ratified by the United Kingdom.

Some of the ECHR rights and freedoms are absolute (freedom from torture, inhuman or degrading treatment or punishment).[26] Most permit specific exceptions. Thus the right to life in Art. 2 expressly endorses the death penalty or the use, where absolutely necessary, of lethal force to suppress a rebellion. The right to liberty and security of person is not infringed by imprisonment after conviction or by arrest on reasonable suspicion of having committed an offence with a view to bringing the person within the criminal process of charge and trial.[27] Rights to respect for home and private life,[28] to freedom of thought, conscience and religion, to freedom of expression and to association and assembly are all qualified rights. They can each be limited by law so far as is necessary in a democratic society to protect a range of community interests (public order, the rights and freedoms of others and, in some cases, national security or territorial integrity).[29] Moreover, Art 15 ECHR enables derogation from most of the obligations in the ECHR to the extent strictly required by the exigencies of war or other public emergency threatening the life of the nation, so long as the measures are consistent with other

---

[25] Keir and Lawson (1979): 15–22.

[26] Art. 3.

[27] Art. 5.

[28] Art. 8.

[29] See para. (2) to each of Articles 8–11.

international obligations of the State derogating. No derogation, however, is permitted from Art. 3 (freedom from torture, inhuman or degrading treatment or punishment), Art. 7 (freedom from retroactive criminal law or punishment) or, save in respect of deaths resulting from lawful acts of war, the right to life.[30] The prime context of operation of Art. 15 has been in respect of internment (detention) without trial.

In 1976, the United Kingdom ratified a similar set of obligations in the United Nations' (UN) International Covenant on Civil and Political Rights (ICCPR). It has also ratified the UN Convention Against Torture (UNCAT). But these obligations, while relevant to examination of the use of executive measures considered in this book, in one sense lack the practical immediacy of those under the ECHR. ECHR obligations are more immediate because of the sophisticated enforcement machinery provided by it and accepted by the United Kingdom. Those under the ICCPR and UNCAT are with respect to the United Kingdom as yet of a reporting nature only. Under the ECHR, in contrast, until 1997 another State party to it or an individual affected by action by a State party could complain to the European Commission of Human Rights about a violation of the ECHR by a State party. The Commission had a filter role on the admissibility of the application. As regards those found admissible, it had a dual role: investigating the complaint; and seeking a friendly settlement of the matter on a basis consonant with the protection of the human rights in the ECHR. If no settlement was possible, it had to draw up a report giving its opinion on the merits of the case (was there a breach of the ECHR or not?). That report was transmitted to a political body, the Committee of Ministers of the Council of Europe. The matter might go for decision, if the States concerned accepted its jurisdiction, to a judicial body, the European Court of Human Rights, whose judgments States Party had agreed to abide by and whose execution would be supervised by the Committee of Ministers. Otherwise, the matter would be decided by that Committee, whose decisions were again binding on States party to the ECHR. The main sanction was one of publicity, but a recalcitrant State could be expelled from the Council of Europe. Surprisingly, despite the existence there of a number of emergencies, the United Kingdom extended the protection of the ECHR to its colonies, without any real consideration of whether the law there, or indeed in the United Kingdom itself, conformed to it. As will be seen in chapters 3, 4 and 5, this was to bring problems with respect to the use of executive measures. But the practical impact of the ECHR on the United Kingdom and its colonies was somewhat blunted since not until 1966 did the United Kingdom recognize the right of individual complaint to the Commission. Nor did it before then recognize the jurisdiction of the European Court of Human Rights. Since 1997, however, the Commission has gone. All States must accept individual petition and the jurisdiction of the Court as sole decision-maker on ECHR compliance. The Committee of Ministers has no decision-making function on that matter. Its role is merely to supervise the execution of the judgments of the Court.

---

[30] Art. 15(2).

Until 2000, however, the ECHR only had a limited role in terms of being used in legal challenges to executive action within a United Kingdom court. Essentially, its role was as a tool for interpreting ambiguous statutory provisions. If such a provision was capable of several meanings, a court should accord it the meaning consonant with the ECHR. If no such meaning could be found, the statute prevailed even though violative of ECHR obligations; an Act of Parliament reigned supreme as far as the courts were concerned.[31] On 2 October 2000, however, the Human Rights Act 1998 (HRA) entered into force, incorporating most of the ECHR rights and freedoms as directly enforceable parts of United Kingdom law. This subtly drafted measure aims to 'bring rights home', to allow United Kingdom courts to do what until then could only be done by the European Court of Human Rights.[32] The HRA provides a greater degree of protection of human rights within the United Kingdom's legal and constitutional order while preserving in full the key legal constitutional principle of the sovereignty of Parliament. United Kingdom courts have enhanced powers of interpretation of statutes to achieve compatibility with the ECHR. But, even where a provision in an Act of Parliament is found by the court to be incompatible with ECHR rights, the court cannot invalidate or (in United States' terms) 'strike down' the Act of Parliament. The powers the HRA afford the courts are outlined in more detail in this chapter in the section on legal accountability. Their application to post 9/11 executive measures is analysed in Part III.

Key Concepts

National Security

The concept of 'national security' is somewhat amorphous. Whatever the terms of a particular definition proffered, the things included are likely in themselves to prove elusive (for example, 'defence of the realm', 'terrorism') and to leave much to the judgment of the decision-maker in the executive or in the court applying them to particular contexts or activities. But the popular conception of a national security threat (the invader; the threat of aerial bombardment or nuclear attack; the spy; the saboteur; the terrorist) is not far off the mark.

There is in the United Kingdom no single statutory or case law definition. Stone suggested that the concept embraced the defence of the realm, the prosecution of war, the armament and disposition of the armed forces, nuclear weapons, and the activities of the security and intelligence services, presumably including those of the 'listening centre' at GCHQ.[33] Leigh and Lustgarten sought in their seminal work to provide a 'democratic conception of national security'.

---

[31] *Brind v Secretary of State for the Home Department* [1991] 1 A.C. 696.

[32] Cm 3782 (1997): chap. 1.

[33] Stone (1990).

Recognizing the potential for abuse (and their identification of past abuses), they sought as a basis for justifying the taking of extraordinary measures to ascertain an 'irreducible minimum', a central 'core of validity'. They considered that:

> Certain activities – notably political violence and covert attempts to influence a nation's political processes – *are* incompatible with both the institutions and ideals of a democratic state and cannot be tolerated. All states are entitled to protect their territory from invasions or attempts to detach portions of it by insurrection. In addition efforts to gain access to certain narrow and specific categories of information ought to be prevented to protect any nation's immediate or longer-term defence needs. Therefore these matters deserve to be regarded as ones whose 'security', in the sense of safeguarding, requires protection. Beyond them all further encroachment of the claims of national security must be regarded as highly suspect in a strong democratic state.[34]

The definition thus covers 'terrorism'. There is a danger that a security and intelligence agency created to protect 'national security' is capable, because of the extraordinary powers it possesses, of destroying the freedoms enjoyed by the inhabitants of a democratic polity or even its democracy itself. The agency might become an independent power centre not controlled by its constitutionally accountable political masters. It might pursue legitimate ends by unlawful or undesirable means. On its own volition or that of those in government, it might deploy the powers to target organizations such as the Campaign For Nuclear Disarmament (CND) or opposition parties espousing similar views for no greater reason than that their activities aroused opposition to government policies asserted by government to be the sole means of protecting national security, or to target trades unions and trades union leaders engaged in certain 'political' industrial disputes.[35] In part this might come about because of an inclusion of 'subversion' within an agency's remit; 'without that mandate and the use made of it by security services, it is very unlikely that their work and their position within government would even have entered public consciousness'.[36] But there is a danger in equating 'national security' with the terms of a security agency's remit in that, since the end of the Cold War, the agency concerned or its political masters need a new task, so that the skills of its personnel can be directed to deal, for example, with crime, albeit serious organized crime. The fact that dealing with terrorism requires cooperation on a global scale between states and with international organizations has in recent years seen a broadening of the term in that a threat to one nation's security can be regarded as one threatening that of the United Kingdom. Thus in *Rehman*,[37] the House of Lords were concerned with a decision to deport on national security grounds a foreign national resident in the United Kingdom because he was thought to be concerned in fund-raising and recruiting for

---

[34] Leigh and Lustgarten (1994): 35 and, more generally, chap. 1.
[35] Leigh and Lustgarten (1994): 363–4.
[36] Leigh and Lustgarten (1994): 375–6.
[37] [2002] 1 All ER 122.

organizations involved in terrorism in Kashmir. Their Lordships in rejecting Rehman's appeal took a wide view of what risk to 'national security' entails. The risk need not be the result of a direct threat to the United Kingdom. It is not limited to action by an individual targeted at the United Kingdom, its system of government or its people. It embraces activities directed against the overthrow or destabilization of a foreign government if that foreign government is likely to take reprisals against the United Kingdom that affect the security of the United Kingdom or of its nationals. Given the current state of world affairs, action against a foreign state can indirectly affect the security of the United Kingdom. The means open to terrorists both in attacking another state and attacking international or global activity by the community of nations are capable of reflecting on the safety and well-being of the United Kingdom or its citizens. Factors to be taken into account in deciding whether there is a real possibility that the national security of the United Kingdom may immediately or subsequently, whether directly or indirectly, be put at risk by the actions of others include the sophistication of terrorist weaponry, the rapidity of movement of persons and goods, and the speed of modern communications. The interests of the state needing protection include its military defence, its democracy, and its legal and constitutional systems. The reciprocal co–operation between the United Kingdom and other states in combating international terrorism can promote its national security; such co-operation may itself foster such security 'by, inter alia, the United Kingdom taking action against supporters within the United Kingdom of terrorism directed against other states'.[38]

Terrorism: Violence as Political Communication[39]

'Terrorism' is a concept for which there are almost as many definitions as commentators.[40] Definition is not rendered easier by the highly politicized context in which this pejorative term (one tends to apply it to one's enemies or opponents) is discussed.[41] Discussion is tainted by the conception that one man's terrorist is another's freedom fighter. This adage, however, confuses ends and means; the end may or may not be a justifiable one, but the concept of terrorism focuses on the means to attain the end rather than the end itself.[42]

Acts of terrorism are readily also characterizable in national and international legal orders as criminal. Terrorism consists of (or terrorists commit) violent acts against persons and/or property constituting homicide (murder or manslaughter), serious offences against the person, criminal damage, firearms offences or ones of

---

[38] [2002] 1 All ER 122, at paras 15–17 (Lord Slynn, with whose views the others concurred).

[39] Schmid and de Graaf (1982).

[40] Schmid (1984) considers over 100 definitions. See also Schmid and Jongman (1988).

[41] Hoffman (1999): 31.

[42] Richardson (2006): 26.

causing explosions. Unlike the criminal law, where motive is immaterial to liability, to constitute 'terrorism' the motive behind the act becomes crucial. The core of the concept is the deployment of violence for political ends (understanding that term widely) with the aim of sending a message to persons who may or may not be directly injured by the act of violence in question. Thus, for the RAND research project on the subject, it was important to focus on the quality of the act rather than the identity of its perpetrator or the nature of the cause in respect of which the act was committed. Hence, 'terrorism' was 'a crime in the classic sense … , albeit for political motives'. It was distinguishable from the actions of soldiers in armed conflict or war in terms of its 'deliberate targeting of non-combatants or hostages'. 'Terrorism' also contained a psychological component, being

> … aimed at the people watching. The identities of the actual targets or victims of the attack were often secondary or irrelevant to the terrorists' objective of spreading fear and alarm and gaining concessions. The separation between the actual victim of the violence and the target of the intended psychological effect was the hallmark of terrorism. It was by no means a perfect definition and it certainly did not end any debates, but it offered some useful distinctions between terrorism and ordinary crime, other forms of armed conflict, or the acts of psychotic individuals.[43]

Wardlaw, a criminologist, proffers the following 'politically neutral' definition, in part as an insightful amalgam of the best elements of others:

> The use, or threat of use, of violence by an individual or group, whether acting for or in opposition to established authority, when such action is designed to create extreme anxiety and/or fear-inducing effects in a target group larger than the immediate victims with the purpose of coercing that group into acceding to the political demands of the perpetrators.[44]

This catches as terrorism acts or threats of violence by individuals, groups or States. It covers pro-State and anti-State terror. It would rank as terrorism acts perpetrated or threatened against political leaders and members of the security forces whether police or military, whereas others would seen such acts against such persons as acts against 'combatants' and therefore better analysed, not as 'terrorism', but as political assassination or acts of warfare. An Israeli philosopher, Primoratz captures this well. For him, 'terrorism' is

> … the deliberate use of violence, or threat of its use, against innocent people, with the aim of intimidating them, or other people, into a course of action they otherwise would not take.[45]

---

[43] RAND (1999): 9.
[44] Wardlaw (1989): 16.
[45] Primoratz (1995): 23–4.

He elaborates on two key points about this 'politically neutral' definition:

> Terrorism has a certain structure, It has two targets, the primary and the secondary. The latter target is directly hit, but the objective is to get at the former, to intimidate the person or persons who are the primary target into doing things they otherwise would not do. Sometimes the same person or group of persons is both the primary and secondary target; but ordinarily the two targets are different (groups of) people. The secondary target, which is hit directly, is innocent people. Thus terrorism is distinguished both from war in general, and guerilla war in particular, in which the innocent (non-combatants, civilians) are not deliberately attacked, and from political assassination, whose victims – political officials and police officers – are responsible for certain policies and their enforcement. This, of course, does not mean that an army cannot engage in terrorism; many armies have done so. Nor does it mean that political assassination does not often intimidate the government or the public, or is not often meant to do so.[46]

He saw his definition as capable of embracing both state and non-state terrorism, revolutionary and counter-revolutionary terrorism, terrorism of the left and of the right. Including States within the definition of terrorism is not without its critics. Richardson rightly comments that States take action (bombing of civilian targets in war, or collective punishment of communities from which terrorists spring or in which they hide) which is the moral equivalent of terrorist acts.[47] But for her, terrorism is *par excellence* the action of sub-state groups:

> If we want to contain terrorism we must first understand it. Therefore if we want to have any analytical clarity in understanding the behaviour of terrorist groups we must understand them as sub-state actors rather than states. We have generations of work conducted by political scientists, historians and international lawyers to help us to understand the behaviour of states. If we want to understand terrorists we must see them operating as sub-state clandestine groups.[48]

Academic definition, of course, is undertaken with a view to delineating a phenomenon for discussion and analysis. The task demands precision to differentiate it from related but distinct phenomena. The task of the politician or law-maker, whether national or international, is to identify a target in respect of which action can be taken. On the level of drawing up an international convention to commit states to certain actions (for example, extradition or prosecution) this may mean going only for that degree of coverage which will achieve consensus among politically different sovereign actors. Thus the European Convention for the Suppression of Terrorism focuses on terrorism as the commission of certain listed specific crimes. In contrast, governments and national law-makers framing anti-

---

[46] Primoratz (1995): 23–4.
[47] Richardson (2006): 21.
[48] Richardson (2006): 22.

terrorist legislation are apt to go for an overbroad definition of the phenomenon. Typically they seek to accord the executive and the security forces greater powers to deal with a perceived threat to the security or stability of the State in order to protect the public from death, serious injury or destruction of property. On a 'better safe than sorry' principle, rather than go for a definition that might leave legitimate targets of the powers untouched, they are more likely to proffer a wider definition that will hit all legitimate targets even though it might possibly catch some unintended targets. The definition would be accompanied by justificatory statements in the consultation and enactment process that the powers are not intended to catch those targets and will not be deployed to do so. That would be reflected in guidance to prosecutors and enforcers. Thus, when a definition of terrorism was first brought into legislation in the United Kingdom in Northern Ireland in 1973, that legislation defined it very broadly as 'the use of violence for political ends and includes any use of violence for purposes of putting the public or a section of the public in fear'.[49] When specific anti-terrorism legislation was in 1974 thought necessary to protect Great Britain from political violence connected with Northern Ireland, that definition was carried into that legislation[50] and the successive Prevention of Terrorism (Temporary Provisions) Acts which operated until 2000. Sometimes the powers conferred were limited to terrorism connected with Northern Ireland affairs, sometimes stated more broadly. That the latter were not meant to be used in connection with national terrorism unconnected with Northern Ireland affairs was conveyed in Home Office guidance in circulars sent to police forces. From 1984, its powers of arrest and time-limited extended detention without charge, intended also to cover international as well as Northern Ireland terrorism, specifically provided that they were not to apply to acts solely connected with the affairs of the United Kingdom or any part of it other than Northern Ireland.[51] In marked contrast, the definition in the replacement legislation to govern counter-terrorism powers for the twenty-first century – the Terrorism Act 2000 (TA 2000) – is much broader and capable of applying coercive powers linked to it to a range of situations one would not normally describe as 'terrorism'. This arises largely because it has expanded the concept beyond a central notion of the use or threat of violence. It has done so in order to cover 'cyber-terrorism', that is, serious disruption to computer systems designed to advance a political, religious or ideological cause.[52] So extending it is criticized by Richardson:

> If the act does not involve violence or the threat of violence it is not terrorism. The term 'cyber-terrorism' is not a useful one. The English lexicon is broad enough to provide a term for sabotage of our IT facilities without reverting to the language of terrorism. Those who hack into our computers for fun or profit are of an entirely different ilk than

---

[49] NIEPA 1973, s. 28.

[50] Bonner (2006).

[51] PTA 1984, s. 12. See Bonner (1985): 170–171.

[52] HL Debs, Vol. 614, col. 160 (Lord Bach, 20 June 2000).

those who are prepared to blow up our buildings and our buses. Labelling such hackers cyber-terrorists may elevate their importance but serves only to confuse. The fear of cyber-terrorism is, moreover overblown.[53]

Under section 1 of the TA 2000 'terrorism' means the use or threat of certain action designed to influence the government or to intimidate the public or a section of the public, where made for the purpose of advancing a political, religious or ideological cause. Action involving the use of firearms or explosives is terrorism, whether or not designed so to influence or intimidate. But in all cases, the action in question can only rank as terrorism if it involves serious violence against a person or serious damage to property; or endangers the life of someone other than the perpetrator; or creates a serious risk to the health or safety of the public or a section of the public, or is designed seriously to interfere with or seriously to disrupt an electronic system. The definition covers action in the United Kingdom or elsewhere, persons or property wherever situated, the public of the United Kingdom or any other country, and the government of the United Kingdom, or one of its constituent parts, or indeed the government of any other country.

The definition is so broad as possibly to legitimate action taken against public protest (demonstrations or processions), picketing as part of a political protest or industrial action or even the withdrawal of labour itself (for example, strike 'action' by key workers in the emergency or health services).[54] It comes close to embracing 'subversion'. Government assured Parliament that the powers were not intended to be deployed in any of these ways. Such assurances are welcome, but suffer from two defects. First of all they do not bind subsequent governments as is graphically shown in the history of those given with respect to the widely drawn 'spying and sabotage' offence in section 1 of the Official Secrets Act 1911, another piece of legislation taking the 'blunderbuss' or 'scatter-gun' approach to ensure appropriate targets are not missed at the risk also of hitting unsuitable targets.[55] Secondly, many of the powers are not exercised at governmental level at all but by individual police officers (often low-ranking) in the United Kingdom's multiplicity of police forces, who have to decide whether they can legitimately be used in a particular context and, if so, whether doing so in the particular case is a proportionate interference with applicable rights and liberties.[56] The width of the definition inevitably creates uncertainty of application. This is magnified when in emergency situations law-makers, on the 'better safe than sorry' principle, have drawn up omnibus formulations for powers to as to catch those who threaten the constitutional or political status quo whether as outspoken opposition politicians, church leaders, trades union agitators, security threats as spies or saboteurs, or

---

[53] Richardson (2006): 20.
[54] But compare Walker (2002): 26–7.
[55] Thompson (1963).
[56] Feldman (2006): 377.

those encouraging or perpetrating political violence. Examples abound in the contexts examined in Part II. The definition is under review by Lord Carlile.

Executive Measures: Nature, Legal Bases and Modes of Challenge

This book focuses on the use of executive measures as part of an overall governmental strategy to contain threats to national security and terrorism. The term 'executive measures' is here taken to mean a product of the empowerment through law of the executive branch of government to take action affecting the rights of legal individuals, whether people or corporations, without any need for prior judicial approval of that action. Thus, conferring by law on a policeman or a soldier a power to arrest a terrorist suspect without warrant (that is, without the order of a court) is an executive measure. So is a power given in immigration law to a Secretary of State (in practice the Home Secretary) to refuse entry to the country to a non-citizen on security grounds or, if the person is already in the country, to deport or eject him or her from it on such grounds. This book focuses on both of these, but also embraces the ability of the executive to intern or detain persons indefinitely without trial as national security threats or as terrorists, and executive power to subject them to a lesser range of restrictions on their freedom of movement and activities or even to exile them from one part of the national territory.

All of these powers historically have formed a major part of governmental action to protect the country from threats to its security and its people from the consequences of terrorism. They have been deployed to deal with the 'enemy within' (enemy aliens and sympathizers, spies and saboteurs) in both World Wars (chapter 2); as part of the strategy to deal with ethno-nationalist political violence connected with Irish and later Northern Ireland affairs (chapter 3); and, more pervasively, as part of immigration laws to deal with threats to security in the broad sense thought to be posed by foreign nationals in, or seeking to enter, the country (chapter 4). Such powers were major components in the creation, extension and maintenance of colonial empire and in resisting ethno–nationalist insurrection which played a major role in encouraging British withdrawal from colonial empire (chapter 5).

In varying degrees, each of the executive measures treated in this book impacts significantly on the fundamental rights and freedoms of individuals, whether as recognized at common law or under the ECHR and HRA: that is, liberty and security of person (freedom from arbitrary arrest and detention and its dangers of torture or other maltreatment); fair trial and due process; respect for private and family life, home and correspondence; freedom of religion or conscience, expression, assembly and association; rights of residence and freedom of movement (the right to choose one's residence, the ability to enter and remain in a State). Internment, viewed as preventative by governments and punitive by those subjected to it, most obviously has the same direct impact as imprisonment after criminal conviction, with the added impact (not usually felt by the convicted prisoner) of no legitimate expectations about a likely release date ascertainable in accordance with predetermined and relatively transparent rules (see chapters 2, 3 and 8). The 'house arrest' enabled should derogating control orders be deployed, is internment by another name, albeit in what may be pleasanter surroundings. But, as will be seen in chapter 3, exclusion of a terrorist suspect from Great Britain to Northern Ireland in the period of operation of such powers (1974–98) could transfer individuals from a secure to a hostile environment, tainted with the finding of 'terrorism', move them from employment to unemployment, from good housing to bad, and place them at risk of death or serious bodily harm from paramilitaries on the other side of the sectarian divide, acting as 'pro-State terrorists' or even 'proxy terrorists' for the security forces.[57] The same could well be true of refusal of entry or deportation on security grounds (especially ones conferring a stigmatizing badge of involvement in terrorism) to the State of which the excludee/deportee is a national or some other willing receptor State, even where there is no real risk of death, torture or other inhuman or degrading treatment or punishment. It may be tempting to dismiss the lesser range of restrictions imposable under control orders as minor inconveniences (especially when contrasted with the danger they are there to prevent), as mere restrictions on movement, not, legally speaking, one of the fundamental human rights binding the United Kingdom. Closer examination in chapter 8 of those actually imposed, however, reveals very significant degrees of interference with rights to respect for home, correspondence, private and family life, with freedom of thought, conscience and religion, and with associated and intertwined freedoms of expression, assembly and association, central to a liberal democracy, and central to the individual as a social animal. Those impacts run through all the situations examined in this book

Initially eschewed (apart from the immigration control option) and thus given much reduced significance in the creation of permanent legislation (TA 2000) to counter-terrorism at the start of the twenty-first century, after 9/11 and 7/7 the same range of executive measures examined in earlier periods again became a central feature of the State's legal armoury in what has misleadingly been called the 'war on terror'. These powers are examined in depth in Part III. The most draconian of the legal responses in ATCSA was its regime of detention without trial of foreign national international terrorist suspects with links to Al Qaeda, unable to be prosecuted or to be deported for a legal or practical reason. It successor – the regime of control orders in the PTA 2005 – enables a spectrum of restrictions from mere reporting to the police or the immigration service, at one end, to indefinite detention without trial, at the other. All of these measures draw on experience in dealing with earlier threats to the security and well-being of the State and its people examined in Part II. Overall, the degree of correspondence between present powers and those deployed in the past is striking both as regards

---

[57] See chapter 2; *R v Secretary of State for the Home Department, ex parte McQuillen* [1995] 4 All ER 400, at 422. On 'pro-State terrorists and 'proxy' terrorists, see Bruce (1992): chaps 8, 11.

the terms and coverage of the legislation and of means of redress. There are, however, two significant differences of note. First of all, as a result of human rights challenge using the ECHR in the European Court of Human Rights at Strasbourg, each of the modern regimes affords a more sophisticated mode of legal challenge to their deployment of powers significantly affecting the rights of individuals. Those modes consist, firstly, of appeal to the Special Immigration Appeals Commission (SIAC) in the case of security decisions under immigration and citizenship law and in that of appeal against certification as an international terrorist suspect and detention under ATCSA. They consist, secondly, as regards control orders under the PTA 2005, of the Home Secretary generally having to seek prior approval to make one from the Administrative Court (part of the High Court) and a right of appeal to that court in respect of the situations in which the Home Secretary is enabled to act without prior court approval. This may suggest as a second point of distinction from the past that control orders are not executive measures at all. That would not, however, be an accurate depiction of the position. They are better characterized as hybrid powers and require treatment in a book on executive measures, given the limited power of the High Court to refuse the Home Secretary's initial application for either type of order. In contrast, especially with derogating control orders (yet to be used) the powers of the Administrative Court with respect to confirming the order become properly classifiable as judicial. But even there the nature of the processes involved (see chapter 8) are such as to accord the executive a very strong hand in securing from the court its desired outcome. In short, a key theme here is one of increased judicial involvement. It is to be noted, however, that this is not the result of the actions of a benevolent executive, but a position attained only after successful human rights litigation in the European Court of Human Rights and in securing in December 2004 the determination of the House of Lords (the United Kingdom's highest court) that ATCSA detention was incompatible with the ECHR. Before that, the governmental position was consistent. Decisions on these types of power were the province of the executive alone and were not susceptible to judicial decision. For example, in 1919, when discussing with representatives of the British Board of Deputies the matter of a right of challenge to deportation decisions, the Home Secretary, Edward Shortt stated:

> If you set up a Court of Appeal, that Court of Appeal must exercise its functions with regard to the evidence that is brought before it; and in many cases which our Secret Service tells you of, if the evidence were brought before an open Court, the method by which we had obtained the information would be disclosed to the very people who ought not to know it. There are very many real difficulties in the way, when you are dealing with matters in times of national danger, very great difficulties in the way of trials in open Court. Many a time, if you have to have a hearing in open Court, you are bound to

let a man go; because if once you had your trial, you would disclose sufficient for those who have no business to know it, the method by which you obtain your information.[58]

In most situations there was only a right to make representations to the Secretary of State with or without an ability to have those considered by a body of advisers. In 1975, Lord Gardiner, having examined the workings of the internment Commissioner system in Northern Ireland – one of the few instances of a quasi–judicial challenge body able to bind the executive – recommended its abandonment in favour of a return to the traditional advisory system:

> The most cogent criticism was that the procedures are unsatisfactory, or even farcical, if considered as judicial. The adversarial method of trial is reduced to impotence by the needs of security. The use of screens and voice scramblers [to protect witnesses], the overwhelming amount of hearsay evidence and the in camera sessions are totally alien to ordinary trial procedures. The quasi-judicial procedures are a veneer to an enquiry which, to be effective, inevitably has no relationship to common law procedures. ... the adversarial quasi–judicial procedures are unsatisfactory for testing the reliability of evidence from paid informers and accomplices of terrorists. The most effective testing of such evidence can only with safety be conducted in a situation of utmost confidentiality.[59]

Indeed, it will be seen in subsequent chapters that law-makers have tried when framing powers to limit the possibility of challenge in court by a judiciary which for the vast bulk of the period under study embraced extreme restraint rather than activism in the face of 'security' powers. They did so not so much through direct ouster clauses but rather by conferring widely drawn, subjectively worded discretion.[60]

The executive measures considered in the book concentrate considerable power in the Executive. Sometimes, as with refusal of entry and deportation on national security grounds, this is done through permanent legislation. But so often the concentration has been effected through temporary or 'emergency' regimes typical of 'state of emergency' or 'state of siege' in other constitutional and legal orders. Indeed, chapter 4 shows that the current immigration law security powers have their roots in wartime restrictions. The legal base for the powers is principally statutory: Acts of Parliament or subordinate legislation made under rule-making powers conferred by a parent Act. But there remains alongside (sometimes expressly retained by statute to fill any gaps the details of the statutory regime may have left) a relevant remnant of prerogative power (common law powers unique to the Crown), for example, the power to intern enemy aliens in wartime.[61] In

---

[58] HO 45/11069/375480 107, The National Archives (TNA).

[59] Gardiner (1975): paras 152–4.

[60] But see the 1818 Bengal example in Hussain (2003): 6–7. On its effects in later nineteenth-century coercion legislation in Ireland see Simpson (1996b): 639.

[61] Chapter 4; Bonner (1985): 8–10.

addition, there is the power of the Crown to resort to martial law, either as part of a wider common law principle of necessity or an aspect of prerogative power.[62] Last deployed in Great Britain three times in the eighteenth century,[63] it was a feature of suppressing insurrection in the Empire in the nineteenth century,[64] and was deployed during the Boer War in South Africa (1899–1901) and twice in the 'troubles' in parts of Ireland (1916–22).[65] 'Martial law' refers to the exceptional non–statutory powers that the common law permits to governmental authorities in situations of war or armed rebellion.[66]

Legal Accountability

The United Kingdom has long been a state committed to respect for the Rule of Law. Historically, it was what distinguished its polity from both continental European and Oriental despotism, a hallmark of legitimacy in colonies without representative government.[67] There is consensus that the Rule of Law means more than a pure principle of legality (that the executive must show positive legal power to interfere with the legally protected rights of the individual) although that is important in making the law applicable to all, including Government. But commentators are not at one on what else is included.[68] It is here taken to embody a number of further precepts. The law itself must be 'accessible and so far as possible intelligible, clear and predictable'.[69] Discretionary powers are not unlimited but should generally be narrowly defined and their exercise capable of reasoned justification. The law should neither be arbitrary nor discriminatory and should comply with obligations under the ECHR and other international human rights' instruments. Laws must be interpreted by an independent judiciary. The Rule of Law is something that can be cited as a positive benefit for those countries which formed part of the United Kingdom's colonial empire[70] and something reflected in its extension to colonies of protection under the ECHR (see chapter 5).

The extent to which its security and counter-terrorist laws and policies matched up to standards set by the Rule of Law – other than in respect of a mere principle of legality – can, however, legitimately be questioned. A sense of 'fair play' and due process forming part of that ideal, has meant that governments have shown concern

---

[62] Campbell (1994): 123–47; Hussain (2003): chap. 4.

[63] Simpson (1994): 3.

[64] Kostal (2005); 8–13; (2000) 21–7.

[65] Townshend (2006): 187–8, 192–4, 270–271, 303–5; Campbell (1994): 123–47.

[66] Campbell (1994): 123–4.

[67] Hussain (2003): 3–4.

[68] Jowell (2004); Hussain (2003): 8–16.

[69] Bingham (2006): 6.

[70] Ferguson (2004): xxiii–xxiv; James (1998): xiv.

to adhere to the strict forms of the law[71] and, as noted above, to create in respect of most of the executive security powers examined in this book, administrative review machinery enabling their subjects to make representations on the adverse decision made in respect of them. But the width of discretion often conferred (for example, the Governor may deport any person from Cyprus) and the vagueness of some of the provisions hardly match the precepts of the Rule of Law; for example, take section 2(4) of the Northern Ireland (Civil Authorities) Special Powers Act 1922:

> If any person does any act of such a nature as to be calculated to be prejudicial to the preservation of the peace or the maintenance of order in Northern Ireland and not specifically provided for in the regulations, he shall be deemed to be guilty of an offence against the regulations.

As Hussain has commented,

> if a rule of law was the settled theoretical standard of colonial politics, the institutional practices of the colonial state constantly fell short of such a standard. When much was said and done, British India was a regime of conquest, not incapable of creating certain levels of political legitimacy, but consistently dependent upon the discretionary authority of its executive and the force of its army.[72]

There is always a tension between the rule of law and the desire, in times of emergency or threat to national security, to give almost *carte blanche* to the executive (effective rule by sovereign decree) following the maxim *salus populi suprema lex esto* (the safety of the people is the highest law).[73]

The United Kingdom and its colonial constitutional orders have always lacked a Bill of Rights, superior in status to all other laws. Its courts had, however, developed and adapted over centuries a range of methods whereby they could review the legality of executive action or inaction. Most famously, the writ of habeas corpus, originally designed to get people into detention,[74] developed into a remedy for getting them out of it by subjecting its legality to judicial scrutiny.[75] Hence can be understood the use by the authorities in the eighteenth and nineteenth centuries of Habeas Corpus Suspension Acts to immunize executive detention, for example, in cases of treason.[76] In addition what one now calls an application for judicial review, to test the legality of administrative action or the decision of inferior courts could be made by seeking one or more of a number of prerogative writs or orders adapted by the High Court to that end: certiorari (in modern parlance, a quashing order); prohibition (a prohibiting order); or mandamus (a

---

[71] Kostal (2005): 460–488; (2000): 21–7.

[72] Hussain (2003): 6.

[73] Hussain (2003): 6–8.

[74] Baker (2002): 146.

[75] On its use in colonial India, see Hussain (2003): chap. 3.

[76] Sharpe (1976): 91–3; Simpson (1994): 3.

compelling order). In addition, the same end could be achieved by bringing 'private' law proceedings (for most of the period in separate proceedings from those for the prerogative orders) for a declaration that action or inaction was unlawful or for an injunction (a prohibitive or compelling order). One can identify a range of grounds on which, construing the statutory provisions relied on as justifying the action in order to ascertain Parliament's intention as to the scope of the legal authority it confers on the decision-maker, the action could be found unlawful by the court. These were judicially summarized in 1984 as illegality; procedural impropriety; and irrationality (manifest unreasonableness). With executive measures, one is in most circumstances concerned with the exercise of discretionary power. Ostensibly the courts are not concerned with the merits of the choice but rather with limits on the range of permissible choice and with principles of good administration applicable to the making of the decision. Thus, in normal circumstances, they may insist that the discretion be not fettered by predetermined rigid rules of policy; that it be applied only for a proper purpose; that its exercise is not dependent on irrelevant considerations or the ignoring of relevant ones; that its exercise is not so unreasonable as would cause one to doubt that any such power was remitted to the decision-maker; that the decision-maker exercised it in good faith; and that those affected by it were given a right to be heard. The scope of permissible review is determined in part by the words of the statute. But these are interpreted against a background of presumptions of interpretation (for example, that Parliament does not intend to contravene international obligations such as the ECHR),[77] constitutional principles and common law values – something like an implied Bill of Rights – as well as the rarely expressed societal and political attitudes with which judges are imbued. Commentators on administrative law also stress the importance of context, that the judicial approach to scrutiny of one area of governmental activity cannot always be assumed automatically to apply to another, although there is more of a trend towards universality. Much may depend on judicial attitudes to the suitability for judicial control of the subject area concerned and to the respective worth of the particular interests advanced for protection by the protagonists before them; and on the identity and status of the decision-maker. The area of executive measures to contain terrorism and protect national security, so often deployed in times of 'emergency' or 'serious threat' has long been a policy or value-laden area of law in which it can be difficult to predict the outcome of cases.

The task, as regards primary legislation, is merely one of interpretation. Only where there is a conflict with EC law can a court set aside an admitted statute.[78] Otherwise there is no power to invalidate it. Where the executive measure concerned is found in subordinate legislation, however, the court can invalidate it if the measure exceeds the rule-making power conferred by the parent act, traditionally expressed as *ultra vires* (beyond the powers) or if the measure

---

[77] *Brind* v *Secretary of State for the Home Department* [1991] 1 A.C. 696.

[78] *R* v *Transport Secretary, ex parte Factortame Ltd* [1990] 2 A.C. 85.

breaches a Convention Right protected by the HRA and that breach is not dictated by the parent Act.

The HRA has enhanced the court's powers of interpretation of legislation, whenever enacted or created. Taking due account of ECHR case law, courts are duty bound to give a provision alleged to be incompatible with Convention Rights an interpretation which removes the incompatibility, unless it is plainly impossible to do so.[79] If no compatible interpretation can be found, the court cannot invalidate an Act of Parliament. It can merely make a declaration of the provision's incompatibility with Convention Rights. That declaration has no legal effect. It is not binding on the parties to the case. It does not deprive the impugned provision of force or effect (for example, it will not force the executive to release the person from detention or prevent his imprisonment for the offence in the provision).[80] Rather it is a declaration with effects in the political sphere, the culmination in a case which has in effect been a judicial dialogue with the law-makers (the Executive/Legislature partnership). It is for them to decide whether the declaration should be acted on (there is no legal obligation to do so) by repealing or amending the impugned provision either through primary legislation, or, using a 'fast–track' procedure authorized by the HRA, subordinate legislation (a remedial order). To date, all declarations not successfully challenged on appeal, have been acted on, even in the counter-terrorism, security field. Should the lawmakers not act on one, the individual concerned can take his complaint to the European Court of Human Rights for its decision on whether the ECHR has been breached.

The HRA has also extended the grounds for judicial review. To be lawful, the actions of a public authority must be in conformity with Convention Rights.[81] As regards an exercise of discretionary power impinging on a non-absolute Convention Right, this subjects their exercise to the test of proportionality, as does a conflict with rights under EC law. This allows for a greater level of judicial review. Traditionally, review for unreasonableness was concerned with setting the parameters of choice (within the permitted area there might be a range of choices, none of which would be unreasonable and the decision-maker could prefer one rather than another). Under proportionality review, in contrast, if say there were two choices, the one adopted must not be disproportionate (achieving its legitimate objective by interfering with a Convention Right to a greater degree than was necessary to achieve that objective in a democratic society).[82]

The traditional role of the courts in these fields, however, has been that of deference to executive knowledge and expertise; to bow down and to appear at times more executive-minded than the executive when the red flag of national security or emergency was waved. Despite ringing rhetoric, they did not, during most of the period covered in this book, use the powers available to them with

---

[79] HRA, ss. 2, 3.
[80] HRA, s. 4.
[81] HRA, s. 6.
[82] *R (Daly)* v *Home Secretary* [2001] 2 A.C. 532.

appreciable effect. Traditionally, judicial review in these security areas was attenuated.[83] That may reflect the precedental impact of 'hands off' decisions of the House of Lords in the extreme circumstances of wartime (*ex parte Zadig*; *Liversidge* v *Anderson*: see chapter 2). It may reflect cases from an age where judges who decided them had also been members of the executive. This was certainly true of Lord Reading CJ who formulated the 'presumption of executive innocence', one that assumes validity unless proved otherwise, with which judges traditionally approached executive powers and which becomes very hard to displace if the law permits the executive to deny the individual and the courts the evidentiary base on which the exercise of power is founded.[84] Sometimes characterized as 'deference', the approach might more accurately be described as one of acknowledging and acting upon relative institutional competence (the executive is better equipped to decide on certain matters – what 'security' requires – than are courts). At ECHR level, the European Court of Human Rights has invariably accorded States a wide 'margin of appreciation' on derogation questions under Art. 15 and with respect to limitations on other rights (for example, private life and freedom of expression and association) on national security grounds.[85] It has done so in respect of Art. 15 because in principle the national authorities, in direct and continuing contact with the pressing needs of the moment, are viewed as being in a better position than the international judge to assess the existence of the emergency and the measures necessary to deal with it.

The HRA era has brought some changes in that approach of United Kingdom courts with judicial action beginning to match rhetoric. The post-*Chahal* creation of SIAC, and the powers of a High Court deploying SIAC-type processes with respect to control orders under the PTA 2005, has been accompanied, under the alternative remedies rule, by the withdrawal from this particular stage of the application for judicial review. The involvement of the Court of Appeal and the House of Lords instead stems from statutory appeals on a point of law, that of the former under the specific provisions of these post-1997 schemes, that of the latter flowing from the standard generalized rights of appeal to their Lordships' House. The HRA era may have ushered in a more confident judiciary more willing to subject to much closer scrutiny use of executive measures interfering with important human rights – witness most markedly the approach of the House in *A and Others* and of other courts to control orders. In part this may reflect their perception of the mandate the other actors in the constitution have afforded them through the HRA. It may in part constitute 'aversive constitutionalism' in which a judiciary, engaging both judicially and extra-judicially with the 'legal blackhole' in American constitutionalism that was Guantanamo, inevitably reflects 'on their own behaviour in similar cases'.[86] It could be a reaction to the dominance of the

---

[83] McEldowney (2005): 768, 770, 774, 780–781.

[84] Simpson (1994): 29–30.

[85] Marks (1995); Goss and Ní Aoláin (2001): 625; Kavanaugh (2006).

[86] Poole (2005): 550.

executive in an unbalanced constitution, as well as reflecting more general scepticism, after Iraq and the weapons of mass destruction debacle, of governmental claims with respect to 'security'. It also builds on a recent common law judicial revivalism – associated with a number of senior judges and manifested both in decisions and thoughtful and provocative extra-judicial papers – which began before the enactment of the HRA.[87] It is also founded firmly on the general revival of judicial review from 1964.[88] It may well also be that the judges are learning from history, whether of the United Kingdom or elsewhere.[89]

But that enhanced degree of scrutiny has come under attack from both Government and Opposition in ways that call into question the role and viability of the HRA. Governmental attacks have been described as 'misguided and constitutionally illiterate'.[90] They are mistaken and ignore the vital role the judicial branch of government has in preserving fundamental rights and liberties and the nature of our democratic society in the face of draconian and populist measures enacted by governments, faced with real enough threats, which descend to the rhetoric of panic and knee-jerk legislative measures. It is for the executive to propose and Parliament to enact measures to protect the security and safety of those in the United Kingdom. It is for an independent judiciary to decide whether such measures are incompatible with cherished rights.[91]

Political Accountability

The Executive, under the United Kingdom's constitutional arrangements and electoral system, will in most circumstances have a working majority in the House of Commons (the elected chamber in a bicameral Parliament). The Executive is very much in the driving seat over decisions to formulate new counter-terrorist or security powers and secure their enactment by Parliament, over decisions to invoke existing powers, in planning possible responses to particular contingencies which may involve the use of such powers, and in operating or directing the operation of these powers when in force. The Cabinet and its committees have a significant role in respect of the first three decisions, aided (if not dominated) by advice from civil servants and other civilian officials or advisers, the police, the armed forces and the security and intelligence services. Cabinet, its committees and individual Ministers can play an important policy-making and supervisory role with respect to the fourth decision-making function. Day-to-day operation may be in the hands of the permanent executive: civil servants, the military and the police. But the executive measures on which this book focuses have tended to require in individual cases a

---

[87] Poole (2005): 546–8.
[88] Wade and Forsyth (2004): 15–18.
[89] Poole (2005): 543.
[90] Rowntree (2006): 66.
[91] Cohen (2007): 108–114; Jowell (2003): 599.

personal decision at some point from a Secretary of State (so often the Home Secretary), the Governor or Chief Secretary in a colony. The decision-making processes are so often collegiate and hierarchical: the police or security service asking senior civil servants to put before the Home Secretary a request that an individual be detained, deported or made subject to a control order. This can produce mechanisms which may limit the potential for an abuse or overuse of powers. For example, Lord Carlile's reviews of ATCSA detention orders suggested that the Home Office acted as something of a brake on demands for detention orders, just as reviews of the prevention of terrorism legislation considered had happened with respect to exclusion orders.

The political Executive (Prime Minister, Cabinet and other Ministers) is, of course, constitutionally accountable to Parliament, particularly its elected Chamber, in that it (or an individual Minister) will fall if it (or he/she) loses the confidence of the House of Commons. Naturally, given that a Government has a working majority in the House of Commons, political loyalty to Party renders either unlikely. But the relationship at least makes the Government and individual ministers account to Parliament for what it (they) have done, opening it (them) to scrutiny by the electorate through the prism of reporting by the media, the 'Fourth Estate' of the realm. Parliament's role is not to govern, not to carry out or direct the carrying out of policies, but instead to scrutinize, influence and legitimize the Government and its actions. It provides a degree of critical oversight and endeavours to ensure that executive measures (generally taken under powers operating under terms enacted by Parliament in Acts or under rule-making powers conferred by its primary legislation) are used appropriately. In short, it strives in a number of ways and through a variety of mechanisms to maintain the political responsibility to it of Government and ministers. Its political composition and the imbalance of financial and research resources between the Executive, on the one hand, and Parliament, members of Parliament and peers, on the other hand, mean that there are well-known limitations on the efficacy of exercise of those functions. Legislative proposals to respond to a crisis may receive scant time for debate. Wide powers (for example, deportation of undesirable foreign nationals as conducive to the public good or their detention as terrorists) may well be granted because they appeared, in principle and especially at the time, to be a good idea, may remain on the statute book permanently or well after the crisis which spawned them has passed. The Official Secrets Act 1911 and the security powers in immigration law are an example of the former; the Prevention of Violence (Temporary Provisions) Act 1939, one of the latter. Since 1997, however, and the coming into force of the HRA in October 2000, the Government has let specialist select committees (for example, the House of Commons Home Affairs Committee and the Joint House of Lords/House of Commons Committee on Human Rights) have an early sight of proposed counter-terrorism legislation. The reports of those committees have made a valuable contribution to the shaping of the terms of the powers (enabling increased review by judicial bodies) and the inclusion of other safeguards such as annual review by an expert reviewer whose report will be presented to Parliament in time for the debate on continuance in force of the more controversial powers, or such as 'sunset' clauses. Those committees have supplemented the annual reviews and review by a committee of Privy Councillors of ATCSA with continued monitoring of their own of both ATCSA and its successor legislation, the PTA 2005. Those reports have also helped elucidate matters for the judiciary in challenges brought before them.[92] They also supplement and inform more traditional parliamentary methods of calling government to account: questions to ministers, emergency and adjournment debates, supply debates and debates on the Address (the Queen's Speech outlining the Government's proposals for the new session of Parliament). Such scrutiny can further be blunted because of the constitutional practice of not generally exploring security matters in any depth on the floor of either House. But, over the years, numerous questions, many eliciting only written answers, have been posed concerning counter-terrorism powers and the security situation in general.[93] Such questions and the role of backbench Opposition MPs have been seen by commentators as of particular importance in the context of colonial emergencies (for example, Kenya[94] and Cyprus[95]) in ensuring that the Colonial Office itself retained some oversight of the Governor, although that was tempered by the need to leave key elements of decision-making to the man on the spot and avoid his resignation. In those contexts of lack of oversight by representative institutions in the colony itself, channels of communication to MPs by concerned groups there and pressure groups in the United Kingdom such as the Movement for Colonial Freedom were very valuable.[96] A parliamentary speech by Conservative right-winger Enoch Powell after the Hola Camp incident impacted heavily on the Government's willingness to hold on to Kenya.[97]

Accountability has also been afforded in enquiry into a matter by a Royal Commission (for example, that into the use of martial law by Governor Eyre in mid-nineteenth century Jamaica), by a Tribunal of Inquiry (for example, those into the deaths of civilians shot by paratroopers in Londonderry, Northern Ireland, in 1972). Reports from NGOs and other pressure groups can be important in disputing the findings of such a tribunal (for example that of the Widgery Inquiry into Bloody Sunday) or in informing its considerations or those of a review body, a Select Committee or a Royal Commission. Reports from and campaigns by concerned individuals can also have an informative and pressurizing role, as with that of Emily Hobhouse over conditions in internment camps during the Boer War, confirmed in the Fawcett Commission;[98] or of Eileen Fletcher, Victor Shuter and

---

[92] Hiebert (2005).

[93] Bonner (1985): 37–8.

[94] Elkins (2005) 97–9; Anderson (2005): 308–9.

[95] Simpson (2004): 895; Foley (1964): 48, 96–7, 137–8.

[96] Anderson (2005): 322–3.

[97] Elkins (2005): 350–353; Anderson (2005): 327.

[98] Roberts (2000): 802–7; Pakenham (1979): chap. 39.

Captain Ernest Law with respect to maltreatment of suspects and detention camp conditions in Kenya.[99]

Executive Measures and their Relationship to the Criminal Process

The executive measures examined in this book represent a 'security' approach to terrorism and national security threats. Such an approach involves departing from the presumption of innocence or being too concerned about the nature of or standards of evidence. It does not require proof, even on a balance of probabilities, of any criminal act, but rather of something vaguer: a threat to national security or to public order or of involvement in terrorism. The approach typically removes the right of the person subjected to the measure to know and be able to challenge the full details of the case against him. As President Nyerere of Tanzania put it with respect to internment without trial:

> You are imprisoning a man when he has not broken any written law, when you cannot be sure beyond reasonable doubt that he has done so. You are restricting his liberty, and making him suffer materially and spiritually, for what you think he intends to do, or is trying to do, or for what you believe he has done. Few things are more dangerous to the freedom of a society than that.[100]

The statement is readily adaptable to lesser restrictions on movement or residence, or in control orders, to exclusion and to deportation. Such executive measures have operated against a backdrop of responses in terms of criminal prosecution, sometimes a 'pure' criminal prosecution' approach, but, more typically, a 'modified criminal prosecution' approach. In the period and contexts covered by this book, it is also apparent that there has been some resort to an 'extra-legal' or 'extra-constitutional' approach, involving the use of lethal force in circumstances not permitted by law by State personnel or proxy agents ('State' or 'pro-State' terror). One example would be Bloody Sunday (1920) when the Army fired on a Dublin football crowd in retaliation for the IRA murder of British Intelligence personnel that morning.[101] Another would be the Amritsar Massacre (1919).[102] Yet another would be the murder by Scots Guards of 26 Chinese at Batang Kali in Malaya.[103] And more recently one could point in Northern Ireland to reports of RUC collusion in the murder of a solicitor, Patrick Finucane,[104] and RUC Special

---

[99] Anderson (2005): 323–4.
[100] Cited in Franck (1968): 231.
[101] Dolan (2006).
[102] Hussein (2003): chap. 4.
[103] Bayly and Harper (2007): 445–57.
[104] Stevens (2005): chaps 17, 18.

Branch protection of Loyalist informants who had carried out murders to maintain cover within their paramilitary organization.[105]

A 'pure criminal prosecution' approach involves using against terrorist or national security suspects the same criminal process as for 'ordinary' serious crime. It proceeds on the presumption that someone is innocent unless proven guilty beyond reasonable doubt according to protective evidentiary rules in a fair criminal trial, generally by judge and jury. Its underlying principle is that it is better that nine guilty persons go free than that one innocent person is convicted. That approach was, for example, deployed against Irish nationalist suspects in respect of murder charges prior to the enactment of the Prevention of Terrorism (Temporary Provisions) Act 1974; also in the cases of the perpetrators of the Clerkenwell explosion in 1867,[106] of many of the dynamite bombings in the 1880s and those charged (and so often wrongfully convicted) with one of the variety of bombings in the campaign on the mainland, culminating with the Birmingham pub bombings of November 1974.[107]

More typically, however, resort in terrorism and national security cases has been to a 'modified criminal prosecution' approach. By this is meant a criminal process modified in one or more of a number of ways to enable more arrests or more convictions, in short to make easier the task of the police and prosecuting authorities. Thus the pre-trial criminal process has in some circumstances been modified to ground arrest merely on honest rather than, as is the norm in the ordinary criminal process, reasonable suspicion.[108] Or, while requiring reasonable suspicion, that suspicion need not be linked to a specific criminal offence, but something more amorphous: 'concerned in the commission, instigation or preparation of acts of terrorism'.[109] The investigative period of detention after arrest and prior to charge or release might itself be extended beyond the now four-day maximum for other serious crime, permitting detention without charge up to seven days,[110] 14 days or the current 28 days applicable in terrorism cases.[111] Sometimes the period might be set simply by the police (as in the 72-hour power applied in Northern Ireland in NIEPA 1973) or the period beyond 48 hours might only be obtainable with the approval of the Home Secretary[112] or, latterly, a judge of particular rank.[113] Specific and broader criminal offences might be created to make conviction easier, perhaps coupled with a transfer of the burden of proof to

---

[105]   Police Ombudsman (2007).

[106]   Quinlivan and Rose (1982); Short (1979).

[107]   Mullin (1987); Kee (1989).

[108]   NIEPA 1973, s. 10.

[109]   PTA 1984, s.12; TA 2000, ss. 40, 41.

[110]   PTA 1984, s. 12.

[111]   TA 2000, s. 41 and Sch. 8, as amended respectively by the Criminal Justice Act 2003 and the Terrorism Act 2006.

[112]   PTA 1984, s. 12.

[113]   TA 2000, s. 41, Sch. 8.

the defence on certain issues, something of more limited effect in the HRA era since the courts tend to read these as transferring only an evidential burden on those matters, leaving the prosecution with the overall burden of proof beyond reasonable doubt.[114] One example in the context of national security would be the widely drawn spying and sabotage offence in section 1 of the Official Secrets Act 1911 (for example, entering a prohibited place for a purpose prejudicial to the safety or interests of the State). Another would be the 'catch all', 'blunderbuss' offence in its now-repealed section 2 of unauthorized disclosure of official information (said to embody in its voluminous wording more than 2000 differently formulated charges). The legislation also went beyond criminalizing attempts to commit those principal offences by embracing 'acts preparatory' to their commission.[115] In addition, the 1911 Act eased the burden on prosecutors with respect to section 1:

> On a prosecution under this section, it shall not be necessary to show that the accused person was guilty of any particular act tending to show a purpose prejudicial to the safety or interests of the State, and, notwithstanding that no such act is proved against him, he may be convicted if, from the circumstances of the case, or his conduct, or his known character as proved, it appears that his purpose was a purpose prejudicial to the safety or interests of the State; and if any sketch, plan, model, article, note, document, or information relating to or used in any prohibited place within the meaning of this Act, or anything in such a place or any secret official code word or pass word, is made, obtained, collected, recorded, published, or communicated by any person other than a person acting under lawful authority, it shall be deemed to have been made, obtained, collected, recorded, published or communicated for a purpose prejudicial to the safety or interests of the State unless the contrary is proved.[116]

Other evidentiary rules, aimed at ensuring the reliability of evidence as well as protecting the suspect, might be modified, for example, to enable the readier admission at criminal trial of inculpatory statements made by the suspect during a period of extended investigative detention authorized by law.[117] There might be some limitation on the right of the accused to know the identity of those giving evidence against them and to be able to challenge them. A variety of methods might be deployed to deal with the problem of witness intimidation, for example, by protecting witnesses at trial from identification, permitting them to give evidence anonymously, hidden from view of the accused and his/her lawyers, perhaps with their voices modulated by a scrambling device.[118] The other

---

[114] TA 2000, s. 12; *Attorney General's Reference No. 4 of 2002* [2004] UKHL 43.

[115] OSA 1920, s. 7.

[116] OSA 1911, s. 1(2).

[117] NIEPA 1973, s. 6; contrast Greer (1973) with Greer (1980).

[118] *R* v *Davis*; *R* v *Ellis* [2006] 1 WLR 3130; *R (Al-Fawwaz)* v. *Governor of Brixton Prison and Another* [2002] 1 A.C. 556; *R* v *X* (1989) 91 Cr App Rep 36; Youth Justice and Criminal Evidence Act 1999, ss. 16–33.

alternative (full witness protection programme with a new identity and life elsewhere) is grossly invasive of the witness's private and family life. The police are normally entitled under rules on public interest immunity to protect their sources of information from identification and disclosure. There can be departure from the normal expectation that criminal trials are heard in public. Official Secrets Act cases can be heard, in whole or in part, behind closed doors with press and the public excluded if this is necessary because publication of any evidence to be given or of any statement to be made in the course of the proceedings would be prejudicial to the national safety. Sentencing must however take place in open court.[119] Jury trial might be dispensed with, as in Northern Ireland and the Republic of Ireland, where juror intimidation is seen as a major problem or, in a divided community, where a risk of perverse acquittals is thought possible. Trial by judge alone, or by a judge assisted by assessors, was a common feature in the Empire. More recently, Home Secretary Blunkett considered lowering the standard of proof in terrorist trials to the civil standard of balance of probabilities and, in order to protect security matters, the court hearing certain evidence in the absence of the accused and their regular legal team in much the same way as in SIAC national security proceedings.

Government has traditionally given primacy to the criminal process as the most desirable way to remove national security or terrorist threats from circulation in the community. The public will more readily accept as warranted the imposition of serious punishment where the offender has been proved guilty beyond reasonable doubt of a specific and serious criminal offence according to just evidentiary rules and fair trial procedures. A modified criminal prosecution approach has been used more extensively in some contexts than others. It was not the principal mode of dealing with the enemy within in the wartime United Kingdom, but became the prime mode deployed in Northern Ireland after 1975.[120]

Not every threat can be dealt with adequately even by a criminal process modified to try to cope with security demands. As Simpson rightly states, when times are normal, the principal mechanism employed by the State against those who threaten its national security, the public peace and public order, is that of the criminal law – which may well have draconian elements – backed up by coercive police powers and the criminal trial process and its range of punitive sanctions.[121] But 'regular criminal law, with its requirement of trial, proof of guilt [beyond reasonable doubt], and presumption of innocence, does not operate effectively in conditions of insurrection'[122] or a well-organized campaign of terrorism; legally acceptable evidence may be hard to come by, witnesses may be intimidated or there may be a level of community support for the terrorists or insurgents such that witnesses are not forthcoming. An effective counter-terrorism or counter-

---

[119]   OSA 1920, s. 8(4)
[120]   Bonner (1985): 100; Walsh (1982); Boyle, Hadden and Hillyard (1980): 5.
[121]   Simpson, (2004): 54.
[122]   Simpson, (2004): 55.

insurgency strategy is intelligence-led, and is increasingly the realm of a State's security and intelligence services, as well as of its police. That strategy involves human intelligence sources and a variety of covert surveillance techniques. It thrives on protecting those sources from disclosure and keeping methods of surveillance under wraps to avoid educating the targets in avoidance strategies. The interest in protecting methods of surveillance has meant that United Kingdom legislation precludes the admissibility in court of communications intercept evidence.[123] Government, to date, has preferred to retain that preclusion, in the face of widespread support for its modification. The position is, however, once again under review.

The traditional paradigm of the criminal law and the criminal trial process, and arguably public acceptance of the legitimacy of it inflicting severe punishment, may be thought to involve two aspects. First, on the rule of law principle requiring that laws should be a clear guide to prohibited conduct, it requires properly framed criminal offences: clear and precise, not vague and overbroad; prospective not retrospective in effect;[124] and penalizing behaviour of a type likely to attract general condemnation.[125] It then mandates that the decision on guilt or innocence be reached by a fair and impartial tribunal, generally sitting in public, to a standard of proof beyond reasonable doubt, in a fair and transparent process, embodying 'equality of arms' in which the accused and their legal team know and can challenge the evidence against them.[126] This poses problems for sensitive intelligence-based evidence in the United Kingdom, since, while the court can exclude press and public in the interests of security and the rights of others, notions of fair trial and 'equality of arms' preclude excluding both the accused and their defence team and trying the case on material not made known to them. Generally even unused prosecution evidence must be disclosed to the defence.[127] But exceptions are made

> ... for 'sensitive material', including that dealing with national security, 'identifying a member of the Security Services who would be of no further use to those services once his identity became known'; disclosing the identity of an informer who or whose family would be put in danger or disclosing some unusual form of surveillance or method of detecting crime.[128]

---

[123] Regulation of Investigatory Powers Act 2000, s. 17.

[124] In compliance with non-derogable Art. 7 ECHR.

[125] Compare the 'procedural justice approach' to the 'rule of law' in Mathews (1988): chap. 2; and his criticism in chap. 6 of 'Security Crimes' in apartheid South Africa.

[126] See Art. 6 ECHR; Art 14 ICCPR. For a critique of this perspective see McBarnet, (1981).

[127] Leigh and Lustgarten (1994): 312.

[128] Ibid.

The system endeavours to protect the identity of informers, since the public interest in security and the prevention and detection of crime are at stake.[129] But if the identity of the informer goes to the issue of guilt or innocence, that identity will have to be revealed. Similarly, while, as has been seen, steps may be taken to guard the identity of a witness, disclosure of identity would be required if central to the issue of guilt or innocence. Public interest immunity certificates may afford a degree of protection to some other sensitive material (for example, official documents). However, the courts (possibly – exceptionally – in the absence of the defence) have the final say on whether the public interest against disclosure is outweighed on the basis that the ends of justice can only be met by the production of evidence vital to the issue being tried.[130] The authorities must first make a decision whether or not to proceed with a prosecution at all and, if proceeding, to decide whether to abandon the attempt should conviction mean sacrificing the source. Given all this, it is perhaps unsurprising that another strategy to protect sensitive evidence is often used: avoiding criminal trial and deploying against the suspect a range of other security options.

The executive measures examined in this book are part of those options, constituting an alternative to or a supplement of the 'pure' or 'modified' criminal process. They come into play as an alternative where resort to that process is thought unproductive and so not tried, or where it is tried but fails (acquittal or dismissal because of no case to answer or because the prosecution decides not to proceed rather than disclose the identity of a witness or informant). Despite its failure, the fact of prosecution and of the trial judge leaving the case for the jury can properly form part of the assessment of someone's involvement in terrorism or their threat to national security.[131] The measures can, however, also supplement a successful outcome of the criminal process as where the accused is convicted but still thought a danger/undesirable when sentence is served and so, for example, is transferred to detention without trial or detention for deportation rather than being released into the community.

Executive Measures: the Hearts and Minds and Constitutional Dimensions

This admixture of either type of criminal prosecution approach and the 'security' approach exemplified by the executive measures on which this book focuses, has not operated in a vacuum. A central theme running through is that terrorism cannot be contained by security policies alone. Efforts must be made to remove

---

[129] *R* v *Hardy* (1794) 24 St Tr 199; *R* v *Watson* (1817) 32 St Tr 102; *Marks* v *Beyfus* (1890) 25 QBD 494; *R* v *Hennessey* (1978) 68 Cr App R 419; *R* v *O'Brien* (1974) 59 Cr App R 222; *R* v *Agar* (1989) 90 Cr App R 318.

[130] Leigh and Lustgarten (1994): 312–319.

[131] SIAC Appeal SC/36/2005, judgment 24 August, *Y* v *Secretary of State for the Home Department*, para. 72.

underlying causes, to reduce the 'water' of grievance-generated community support enabling the terrorist 'fish' to swim. Accordingly, each of the contexts examined – other than perhaps the two World Wars – has had its constitutional, political or 'hearts and minds' dimension, particularly obvious and striking in the responses to the Irish and latterly Northern Ireland questions and in the emergencies that marked the withdrawal from colonial empire. Those broader aspects of those responses operated alongside and often in tension with the security powers the main subject of this book. They involved – whatever the initial public responses of non-negotiation – talking to and reaching an accommodation with those previously condemned by Government as terrorists, rebels, malign elements, or subversive or seditious agitators. Ireland, Northern Ireland, Cyprus and Kenya are, of course, the prime examples in this book. This constitutional, political or 'hearts and minds' dimension is not wholly absent from the so-called post 9/11 'war on terror', but the nature of the threat has been perceived to make that dimension much more problematic than when dealing with irredentist or nationalist terrorism. Constitutional and political solutions are not so readily apparent; the causes which serve to feed the threat are among the most intractable, their resolution not readily lying in the hands of States facing the threat; the demands of the 'opposition' or 'enemy' are more diffuse or simply seen by the threatened as areas which are simply 'non-negotiable'. Nonetheless, commentators from diverse professional backgrounds have stressed the 'foreign policy' dimension as important in reducing the radicalization that produces recruits for terrorism or groups on whom terrorists can rely for at least passive support (those who may give 'sympathy and silence'[132]). In a recent speech, Dame Eliza Manningham-Buller, Director General of the Security Service (MI5), spoke of what motivates young men and women to carry out terrorist attacks in the United Kingdom and the need to be able to understand that, in order to counter it,

Al Qaida has developed an ideology which claims that Islam is under attack, and needs to be defended. This is a powerful narrative that weaves together conflicts from across the globe, presenting the West's response to varied and complex issues, from long-standing disputes such as Israel/Palestine and Kashmir to more recent events as evidence of an across-the-board determination to undermine and humiliate Islam worldwide. Afghanistan, the Balkans, Chechnya, Iraq, Israel/Palestine, Kashmir and Lebanon are regularly cited by those who advocate terrorist violence as illustrating what they allege is Western hostility to Islam. The video wills of British suicide bombers make it clear that they are motivated by perceived worldwide and long-standing injustices against Muslims; an extreme and minority interpretation of Islam promoted by some preachers and people of influence; and their interpretation as anti-Muslim of UK foreign policy, in particular the UK's involvement in Iraq and Afghanistan. Killing oneself and others in

---

[132] Rowntree (2006): 16.

response is an attractive option for some citizens of this country and others around the world.[133]

The authors of a recent report for the Joseph Rowntree Reform Trust were convinced that

> ...the government should review its foreign policy in the light of British interests at home and abroad. We say so not out of a knee-jerk anti-Americanism but from a profound conviction that the Prime Minister's close and publicly unquestioning stance alongside the United States is damaging to British influence in the world at large and in Europe; that it feeds extremism and violence at home and abroad; and that it casts severe doubt on this country's commitment to democracy and human rights which must be the cornerstone of our struggle against extremism.[134]

Aspects of this dimension are not absent from government thinking, save (publicly at least) in respect of Iraq, as is clear from Prime Minister Blair's desire to move forward on the Israel–Palestine conflict, although practice, as with respect to the Israeli bombing of Lebanon in 2006, does not always mesh well with rhetoric. There is also a need to engage with, rather than lecture, the Muslim communities.[135]

The Central Message and Structure of This Book

This chapter has sought to lay a basis in terms of concepts, themes and perspectives for this book's detailed examination of the use of executive measures to assist in containing terrorism and to protect national security in a range of contexts both historical (Part II: 1905–9/11) and current (Part III: after 9/11). This book endeavours to show graphically the link with the past of current executive measures deployed as a central part of the United Kingdom's counter-terrorism strategy after 9/11 and 7/7. Its central argument is that as regards the executive measures themselves, the 'rules of the game' have not changed. It is very much a case of 'old wine in new bottles'. The only 'rule of the game' that has changed is the traditional one that United Kingdom courts faced with the exercise of executive powers in the 'security' sphere in reality (whatever sometimes bold rhetoric) give the executive a free hand and legitimate whatever action the executive consider necessary to deal with the threat. The book further suggests that in this era of the HRA, United Kingdom courts have embraced a welcome degree of interventionism protective of human rights in an area they once characterized as too sensitive for judicial involvement and in which they exercised undue restraint in the face of the

---

[133] Speech delivered at Queen Mary College London on 9 November 2006, found at <http://www.mi5.gov.uk/output/Page568.html.>.
[134] Rowntree (2006): 12.
[135] Rowntree (2006): chap. 2.

marked impact of the powers on the rights and freedoms of individuals. The book also endeavours to place in context recent claims by key actors that the current terrorist threat is unparalleled or that it constitutes the greatest threat faced by the country since the Second World War, ultimately leaving readers to form their own judgments on this from the material presented. Executive measures of detention without trial were a feature of the Revolutionary and Napoleonic Wars (1793–1815) and in seeking in the nineteenth century to manage recurrent political violence connected with the Irish question. It is, however, the response to the 'enemy within' during the two World Wars that has done so much to shape the executive measures deployed by government as a means of containing terrorism and protecting national security. Part II thus begins with that response to the 'enemy within' during those wars (chapter 2). Chapter 3 considers the deployment of such measures to deal with political violence connected with the Irish and, latterly, the Northern Ireland questions. Dealing with undesirable 'aliens' through powers that have their roots in wartime restrictions forms the subject matter of chapter 4. The fifth chapter explores their use in managing withdrawal from colonial empire in the period after 1945, focusing on the 'emergencies' in Malaya, Cyprus and Kenya as in different ways illustrative of that process as a whole. Part II looks to the use of such measures since the 'watershed' of 9/11. Chapter 6 affords an essential overview of the Government's counter–terrorism strategy and the place of executive measures within it. The use and criticisms of those executive measures are examined in chapter 7. Chapter 8 considers the modes of legal challenge afforded, while chapter 9 appraises the outcome or likely outcome of a range of challenges to the measures and their use, particularly on human rights grounds. Finally, chapter 10 strives to draw together and reflect on some of the themes and issues emerging from the analysis in Parts II and III and the base laid in this chapter.

PART II

Before 9/11: United Kingdom and Empire 1905–2001

Chapter 2

Dealing with the 'Enemy at Home' during the Two World Wars

Introduction

The threat of invasion by another State is the gravest threat to a country's national security. It raises spectres of the occupation of the country by foreign forces, the death, imprisonment or enforced exile of its leaders, the imprisonment of members of its armed forces or their removal to the other state as forced labourers, and the alteration of its system of government and its cherished liberties, the more so if the would-be invader is a totalitarian state or a persecutor of other religions. The experiences of the Nazi occupation of most of Western Europe, and fear of the spread of Soviet Communist totalitarianism were key factors in the establishment of the Council of Europe in 1949 and its human rights instrument, the European Convention on Human Rights (ECHR), embodying a right of derogation without which States would have been unlikely, given their recent experiences, to have signed up to this novel protective instrument and its enforcement machinery.[1]

This country, of course, has not been invaded since the Norman Conquest in 1066 or, on one view of the 'Glorious Revolution', since that Revolution's 1688 transfer of the Crown from the Roman Catholic Stuart monarch, James II, to his Dutch, Protestant son-in-law, William of Orange, and his wife, James's daughter, Queen Mary.[2] It has, however, been under severe threat of invasion several times. Protestant, Elizabethan England was threatened by Catholic Spain and its Armada in 1588; Great Britain was in danger of invasion from Revolutionary France and its Emperor Napoleon at the end of the eighteenth and beginning of the nineteenth centuries; the United Kingdom feared invasion by Kaiser Wilhelm's Germany in the First World War; and invasion by Hitler's Nazi Germany in the Second World War was in 1940 a very real threat. The post-1945 Cold War threatened Soviet invasion and possible nuclear attack.

While the intensity and nature of each of those threats differed, one common theme has been the taking by the Government of the day of exceptional measures to deal with those perceived as the 'enemy within', whether nationals of the threatening State or British subjects thought to be sympathetic to the foreign power. Thus, the Elizabethan government several times interned without trial

---

[1] Simpson (2004): viii, chap. 4, 874–5.
[2] Harris (2006): 3–6.

Jesuits, priests and other English Catholics when Spanish invasion loomed.[3] The Revolutionary and Napoleonic Wars with France (1793–1815), and the fear of the spread of French revolutionary ideas to the lower classes, saw the Government impose statutory restrictions on immigration by aliens. It also resorted to a form of internment (detention) without trial. The Habeas Corpus Act was suspended several times, removing the central remedy for securing release from unlawful detention. As Thompson recorded, few were detained without trial; government wanted to use suspension to make louder the bark but not sharpen the bite of treason laws.[4] In the decade before the First World War, spy scare stories and fear of German invasion secured the enactment of a draconian Official Secrets Act 1911.[5] The War itself saw the State concentrate immense power in the Executive and deal with the 'enemy within', in part through criminal prosecution, but more often through detention without trial and powers of deportation.[6] The security elements of the modern immigration system have their origins in the aliens restriction legislation of 1914.[7] The Second World War followed much the same pattern in terms of responses to supposed 'Fifth Columnists'.[8] The Cold War saw threats met by criminal prosecutions, national security deportations and the expulsion of diplomats thought to be spies. But plans were in place for the introduction of internment.[9]

Another common theme as regards invasion threats has been the accompanying danger from elements in another country within these islands, particularly Ireland, with nationalists very much seeing Britain's difficulty as Ireland's opportunity; witness rebellions in 1798 and 1916 and, during the Second World War, the IRA seeking and obtaining a degree of Nazi support for its irredentist campaign. James II won Catholic support in Ireland to try to regain his throne, besieged Londonderry (contributing to the 'siege' mentality gripping Ulster Protestants which bedevilled attempts to deal with the Irish and Northern Ireland questions) but was roundly defeated at the Battle of the Boyne in 1690. And twice in the 1715 and 1745 Jacobite rebellions, the Highland Scots supported the Stuart 'Pretender' against the Hanoverian monarchs of the fledgling Great Britain. In 1745 Bonnie Prince Charlie's army 'invaded' as far south as Derby, and London saw itself threatened before the Scots withdrew to Scotland and defeat at Culloden in 1746.[10]

---

[3] Hogge (2005): 278.

[4] Thompson (1982):159–61; Sharpe (1989): 94–5.

[5] Andrew (1985), chap. 2.

[6] Simpson (1994).

[7] See chapter 4.

[8] Simpson (1994): 105–8.

[9] KV/4/425 TNA (Policy re the Setting Up of Detention and Internment Camps in the UK for the Detention of British Subjects and the Internment of Aliens in the Event of Emergency 1948–1954).

[10] See Williams (1960):156–64, 251–8; Prebble (1967).

This chapter focuses squarely on the use by Government in both World Wars of powers of detention without trial (internment) and restrictions on residence and movement within the country as modes of dealing with those perceived as the 'enemy within'. Modalities of deportation and expulsion of aliens as another way of dealing with the threat, mentioned above, are instead dealt with in chapter 4 on undesirable 'aliens', as better befits an examination of the beginnings of the United Kingdom's modern, statutory immigration system. While in historical terms, a case can be made for regarding the two Wars as a single conflict, this chapter divides consideration as between the First and Second World Wars, given the rather different legal bases for the similar powers used and as the best structure to appreciate Government learning with respect to its plans for 1939 from mistakes made in 1914–18. Each section looks first at internment of aliens and then at internment of security threats/sympathizers, many of whom were British subjects and thus irremovable by deportation powers and not possible to intern under prerogative powers. There then follows consideration of the means open to those deprived of their liberty, without being proven guilty of any criminal offence, both in terms of the administrative schemes of challenge (representations to advisory bodies) and challenge in the ordinary courts using habeas corpus applications and applications for judicial review to try to secure release and invalidate the decision depriving them of liberty. It will be seen that extensive powers were available to Government both under the prerogative and under skeleton, 'parent' Acts of Parliament equipping Government with immense power to make further rules subject to a very much reduced parliamentary control. Traditional rights of recourse to the courts were not removed, but the courts, led by the House of Lords, despite often ringing rhetoric, failed to protect personal liberty, leaving the Government to get on with things very much free of judicial restraint. Both periods represent the low ebb of judicial review and, arguably, an abdication of the judicial function, which happily no longer extends into judicial review generally and does not form part of judicial scrutiny of the Executive in the security sphere in the HRA era.

The First World War

The United Kingdom went to war with Germany and its ally, the Austro-Hungarian Empire, on 4 August 1914, in part because of German aggression towards and invasion of neutral Belgium in its attempt to execute the Schlieffen plan and knock France out of the war before the Russian armed forces (Russia was the ally of France and the United Kingdom) could mass on Germany's eastern border. The precise causes of and catalysts for this cataclysm, in Europe a war of attrition and blockade, have been minutely analysed elsewhere.[11] So too the carnage in terms of almost one million United Kingdom and Commonwealth soldiers, sailors and

---

[11] Strachan (2003), chaps 1 and 2; Stephenson (2004): chap. 1.

airmen killed and some one and a half million wounded on the Western Front, the Gallipoli Peninsula, the Middle East and East Africa.[12] While the causes are beyond the scope of this book, both the carnage and the sacrifices (a degree of casualties from airborne bombing, rationing, etc.) borne on the Home Front in this four-year war (1914–1918) have much more bearing in the sense that they may help explain the demands for, and the acceptance as warranted of, the draconian and illiberal powers here examined by the public, parliamentarians and judges.[13] As Simpson noted, while the most draconian power of internment without trial of persons (including British subjects) of 'hostile origins or associations', had critics, particularly with respect to its use against Irish nationalists after the Easter Rising of 1916,[14] the power 'was not under any real political threat during the period of hostilities, and remarkably few individual detainees attracted any public comment'.[15] Writing in April 1918, Scrutton LJ noted the impact on the legal profession in terms of casualties, that judges, 'fighting by their sons' with offspring fighting and dying in the front line, were experiencing, particularly on circuit, the impact of war on manpower and food supplies, and were assisting the war effort in terms of chairing inquiries and internment advisory panels.[16] Going to war, and the bitterness and hatred towards Germans and those allied with them, the 'Germanophobia' which fed the climate of acceptance of and, indeed, demand for, draconian powers,[17] was in part due to what in hindsight can now be seen as a series of misapprehensions on both sides as to the other's intentions in what was characterized from 1903 onwards as 'as state of mutual fear' as both engaged in a naval arms race. The United Kingdom feared that the purpose of the growing German navy was the invasion of the United Kingdom. Germany feared that, like the Danish navy destroyed at Copenhagen by Admiral Nelson in 1800 during the Napoleonic wars, the British navy would destroy the German fleet when peacefully at anchor.[18] Germany also feared encirclement by the United Kingdom, France and Russia. In the United Kingdom, the climate was fuelled by a wave of invasion and German spy stories both in fiction and what would now be called the 'tabloid' press (then the 'yellow' press).[19] Once war broke out, further fuel was added to the fire with reports of atrocities by German troops in Belgium,[20] heavy British losses on the Western Front and German deployment of poison gas as a weapon of war. The Governmental reaction to the pre-war spy fever was an investigation in March 1909 by a subcommittee of the Committee for Imperial Defence. In July 1909, it

---

[12] Taylor (1973): 165–6; Clarke (1996): 80–82.

[13] Ewing and Gearty (2000): 36.

[14] See chapter 3.

[15] Simpson (1994). 24.

[16] Scrutton (1918): 117–119.

[17] On it as part of more general xenophobia, see Winder (2005): 258–73.

[18] French (1978): 355. On the 'Copenhagen' factor, see Steinberg (1966): 23.

[19] French (1978): 355–8; Andrew (1985): chap. 2.

[20] French (1979): 369.

made a number of crucial recommendations relevant to this book.[21] The first, to strengthen 'the whole apparatus' of the country's intelligence system by the establishment of a regular secret service, was quickly acted on.[22] It would operate abroad and at home. Abroad, 'it would act as a shield for naval and military attachés as they bought and collected information from foreigners willing to sell it'.[23] At home, it worked alongside the Special Branch of the Metropolitan Police, no longer tied to the Irish question, to tackle spies and saboteurs.[24] The police had the necessary coercive powers of arrest, search and seizure not possessed by the new secret service. The second recommendation, a systematic set of controls on monitoring and limiting the freedom of movement of aliens, had, in terms of legislation, to await the outbreak of war, and the administrative establishment of an unofficial register of aliens kept secret, given traditionally liberal attitudes towards political asylum.[25] That legislation is considered in chapter 4. The third recommendation was for what would now be called 'target-hardening', requiring action to be taken to defend vulnerable installations, land and buildings against sabotage. The fourth recommended up-to-date legislation with respect to spies and saboteurs. The product, enhancing the powers of the police, the scope of the criminal law and easing the task of the prosecution, was the over-inclusive Official Secrets Act 1911, rushed through Parliament during the Agadir crisis when war between France and Germany was feared.[26] The subcommittee also considered the special powers that would be needed if war broke out. The military favoured enactment of a specific and detailed statutory code. The result was a trio of Defence of the Realm Acts in 1914 (DORA),[27] empowering a raft of delegated legislation, but as late as June 1914 there was preference for relying, despite attendant uncertainties, on the prerogative and martial law.[28] DORA, and associated regulations, dealt with many and most things, including restrictions on movement and internment of those of hostile origins and associations. The

---

[21] French (1978): 358–64.

[22] French (1978): 362–4; Andrew (1985): chap. 2.

[23] French (1978): 362.

[24] Ibid; Ewing and Gearty (2000): 37

[25] French (1978): 359–60.

[26] French (1978): 360–61; Ewing and Gearty (2000): 39–43.

[27] Defence of the Realm Act 1914 (8 August 1914); Defence of the Realm (No. 2) Act 1914 (28 August 1914); Defence of the Realm (Consolidation) Act 1914 (27 November 1914).

[28] Simpson (1994): 6. For a more detailed account of those debates, see Rubin (1994), chap. 1. Prerogative powers are common law powers unique to the Crown, whether exercised by the monarch in person or by members of the central government political executive (ministers) or the permanent executive (civil servants). For contemporary argument that everything done under DORA and its regulations could have been done under the prerogative, see Tudsbery (1916): 384, and contrast the more restricted view of its scope, drawing on World War I cases, in St Clair Mackenzie (1918): 152.

internment of enemy aliens, however, which began on the outbreak of war, was founded on the prerogative, and will be examined first.

Internment and Restrictions on Residence and Movement of Enemy Aliens

Prerogative powers of internment were supplemented by restrictions on movement and residence found in the Orders in Council made pursuant to the Aliens Restriction Act 1914, 'emergency' legislation, explicitly supplementing prerogative powers in this field, 'which essentially gave the Secretary of State a free hand to regulate aliens as he saw fit' for the duration of the war, and passed through Parliament on 4 August 1914, before DORA was introduced.[29] Both internment and restriction of enemy aliens were, of course, aided by the creation in secret in 1910 of the unofficial register of aliens referred to earlier. By July 1913, the register covered 28,830 aliens out of a census estimated alien population of just under a quarter of a million (167,762 being male).[30] Of those on the register 11,100 were German or Austrian, [31] but the estimated resident male population indicated some 32,400 Germans and 9,400 Austro-Hungarians.[32] In 1914 there was an estimated population of some 70,000 enemy aliens over the age of 14.[33] By the outbreak of war some 30,000 aliens and others regarded as potential dangers were on the register, with standardized letters on each index card denoting degrees of friendliness (for example, 'AA': Absolutely Anglicized, undoubtedly friendly) or hostility (for example, BB: 'Bad Boche', undoubtedly hostile).[34] Further 'Special Intelligence Black list' letters might be added (for example, 'G': 'Guarded, suspected, or under special surveillance or not yet classified; 'K': Kaiser's man, enemy officer or official or ex-officer or ex-official).[35] Under the Aliens restriction legislation, enemy aliens had to register with the police and could not live in 'prohibited areas' (close to ports, docks or military installations) without permission from the police.[36]

   The internment and restriction powers were aimed at spies, other enemy agents or saboteurs. But, initially at least, the preferred policy appears to have been prosecution where possible, whether before courts martial or the ordinary courts. On 4 August 1914, 22 supposed spies were arrested, but only one brought to trial. During the war 35 spies were caught and 22 convicted. Fourteen were executed,

---

[29] Bevan (1986): 72–3; *R v Knockaloe Camp Commandant* (1918) 87 LJKB 43.

[30] Andrew (1985): 174; Simpson (1994): 12.

[30] Simpson (1994): 12; Committee of Imperial Defence: Report of Subcommittee on Treatment of Aliens in Time of War (1913), CAB16/25 TNA, App. 5.

[31] Simpson (1994): 11.

[32] CAB16/25 TNA, App. 5.

[33] Andrew (1985): 174. See also Kochan (1983): 1.

[34] Kochan (1983): 12.

[35] Details of the classification system come from Andrew (1985): 175–6.

[36] Andrew (1985): 181.

the last in April 1916.[37] The last espionage trial of the war was in August 1917.[38] It seems clear that internment and restriction were not merely preventative but embraced cases where there was insufficient evidence to use the criminal prosecution route to removal from the community. The General Staff at the outbreak of war had wanted internment of all Germans, but even the smaller numbers interned caused logistical problems of where to put them in a country hosting Belgian refugees in Alexandra Palace and preparing to receive German prisoners of war, such that some 3,000 internees were released over the winter of 1914–15.[39] Following the sinking by a German submarine of the Cunard passenger liner *Lusitania* off the south of Ireland on 7 May 1915,[40] the Government six days later reluctantly decided on the general internment of all enemy aliens, in part for their own safety given the high level of anti-alien feeling:[41]

> Henceforth the government adopted (though it did not always enforce) the principle that all enemy aliens should be interned unless they could prove themselves harmless. Ultimately at least 32,000 (mostly men of military age) were interned, at least 20,000 (mostly women, children and non-combatant men) repatriated, and the remainder subjected to numerous restrictions.[42]

'More notable' alien businessmen with the right connections escaped internment.[43] The Royal Family and other prominent families 'anglicized' their Germanic surnames.[44] Just over a hundred internees died of typhus in the 500 or so internment camps[45] which were established in a bewildering variety of places: two in the Isle of Man (some 23,000 – about half of the then Manx population); in Olympia; in a former factory (Stratford) and a disused wagon works (Lancaster); and on prison ships moored off towns such as Ryde and Gosport.[46] Resentment at conditions spilled over into violence at the Douglas camp on the Isle of Man.[47] Winder records that 9,000 appealed unsuccessfully against their internment, but

---

[37] Simpson (1994): 12. Andrew (1985): 177 indicates that 21 of the 22 were real spies, arrested immediately war broke out.

[38] Andrew (1985): 188.

[39] Winder (2005): 265–6.

[40] Ibid. On the sinking (on which Winder mistakes the direction of travel) and its propaganda value for the allies, see Preston (2003).

[41] Simpson (1994): 13; Andrew (1985): 181.

[42] Andrew (1985): 181–2. Stent (1980): 18 gives a precise figure of 32,274 German and Austrian civilian internees by the end of 1915.

[43] Winder (2005): 271–3.

[44] Ibid. 'Saxe-Coburg-Gotha' to 'Windsor' and 'Battenberg', more literally, to 'Mountbatten'.

[45] Holmes (1988): 96.

[46] Winder (2005): 269–73.

[47] Holmes (1988): 96.

7,150 won freedom by appealing to the advisory committees.[48] There were no appeal rights in respect of restrictions on movement and residence within the country, although advisory committees dealt with deportation of aliens. By the time peace was signed, '24,450 were still in the camps'.[49] By mid-November 1919, 28,744 aliens, mainly German, had been repatriated, many voluntarily, some compulsorily.[50]

Internment of, and Imposition of Restrictions on, Security Threats or Sympathizers

Detention without charge or trial of British subjects, whether they had acquired their citizenship by birth, descent or voluntary act like naturalization, could not be effected under the prerogative, and the Aliens restriction legislation was inapplicable. Under the Defence of the Realm Regulations (DORR) made under DORA, however, very wide powers were entrusted 'to the Executive to act on suspicion on matters affecting the interests of the state'.[51] From their inception, DORR 14 enabled the imposition of controls prohibiting a person 'from residing in or entering any locality' when he or she 'was suspected of acting, or of having acted, or of being about to act in a manner prejudicial to the public safety or the defence of the Realm'.

There were no provisions for any hearing or appeal. The subject of the order was required to leave an area within the time specified in the order. Over the period of the War, 612 people were removed or excluded from areas under its provisions.[52] In many ways, it is a forerunner of prohibition and exclusion orders to protect Great Britain under the Prevention of Violence (Temporary Provisions) Act 1939 and of similar powers operable from 1974 to exclude British citizens from one part of the United Kingdom (Great Britain or Northern Ireland but not both simultaneously) under successive Prevention of Terrorism (Temporary Provisions) Acts.[53] There are also clear affinities with powers under the Civil Authorities (Special Powers) Act operating in Northern Ireland from 1922 to 1972.[54] Analogies can also be drawn with current powers to restrict movement, residence and liberty imposable by control orders under the modern Prevention of Terrorism Act 2005 (PTA 2005).[55] A closer analogy for the PTA 2005 powers, however, is afforded by the provisions of regulation 14B operable from June 1915. Moreover the more modern powers differ in arrangements for challenge.

---

[48] Winder (2005): 270.

[49] Holmes (1988): 96.

[50] Ibid.

[51] *Ronnefeldt* v *Phillips* (1918) 35 TLR 46, at p. 47.

[52] Ewing and Gearty (2000): 54–5.

[53] See chapter 3.

[54] See chapter 3.

[55] See chapters 6 and 7.

The more draconian powers granted the Home Secretary[56] under DORR 14B were specifically stated to supplement rather than restrict or detract from the powers under DORR 14 and prerogative powers to intern enemy aliens, examined above. The powers were presented, disingenuously, to Parliament as a mere extension of control over enemy aliens, to deal with those who to all intents and purposes were enemy aliens rather than genuine British subjects, thus suggesting that the targets were British subjects of German or Austro-Hungarian descent. They had been introduced because the Government believed 'that the Germans were trying to establish a new corps of agents recruited from residents of German descent' against whom there might not be enough evidence to convict at a criminal trial by court martial.[57] But the regulations covered a wider range of people, whether British subjects or 'friendly' aliens. Regulation 14B provided:

> Where on the recommendation of a competent naval or military authority or of one of the advisory committees hereinafter mentioned it appears to the Secretary of State that for securing the public safety or the defence of the realm it is expedient in view of the hostile origin or associations of any person that he shall be subjected to such obligations and restrictions as are hereinafter mentioned, the Secretary of State may by order require that person forthwith, or from time to time, either to remain in, or to proceed to and reside in, such place as may be specified in the order, and to comply with such directions as to reporting to the police, restriction of movement, and otherwise as may be specified in the order, or to be interned in such place as may be specified in the order.

There was no definition of the terms 'hostile origins' or 'hostile associations'. Matters were left to be decided on a case-by-case basis.[58] The latter phrase seems to have been used to detain British-born subjects suspected of espionage or subversion.[59] As is seen in chapter 3, the main use (initially abuse) of the regulation was with respect to events in Ireland. Otherwise, it was used 'with restraint'.[60] The numbers of 'non-Irish affairs' cases pale in significance when contrasted with the number of enemy aliens interned or deported. Simpson estimates that the peak was reached in June 1917 with 125 detainees, of whom 73 were British subjects, and the final releases did not take place until November 1919.[61] In all, probably some 160 orders were made in the course of the War.[62]

Although a few were held in Brixton, Pentonville and Reading prisons, most 14B detainees were held in the Islington 'Camp' (an old Poor Law Institution).[63] Apart from the 'Irish' cases, the names of detainees were not published in the

---

[56] In Scotland the Secretary of State for Scotland.
[57] Simpson (1994): 13.
[58] Simpson (1994): 19–20.
[59] Simpson (1994): 16–17.
[60] Simpson (1994): 17.
[61] Ibid.
[62] Ibid.
[63] Simpson (1994): 16.

press, so that 'as in the most odious of tyrannies, the executive could make people disappear'.[64] Unless the Home Secretary relaxed the regime, internees were to be subject to the same restrictions and to be dealt with in the same manner as prisoners of war. Failure to comply with any provisions of the order constituted a criminal offence under the regulations. Internees were afforded a right to make representations to an advisory committee appointed to advise the Home Secretary on the internment and deportation of aliens.

Administrative Challenge

Representations against detention under the prerogative and under regulation 14B could be made to an advisory panel, inaptly described as one 'of a judicial character',[65] appointed to assist the Home Secretary in the operation of these powers. The England and Wales panel was chaired by a High Court judge or a judge above that level. Fairly junior judges were selected (Sir John Sankey, who presided as the senior judge, and Sir Robert Younger). Of the other six members, two were women and the other four were MPs, among them Stanley Baldwin, later to be Prime Minister. The separate Scottish panel was chaired by Lord Dewar who sat with two other members.[66] The advice of the panels for release was invariably accepted.[67] In 14B cases they did not sit in panels. They operated in private, hearings followed the mode of interrogations, detainees had access to legal advice, but lawyers, while they might serve as witnesses, could not act as advocates. Detainees were provided, so far as security allowed, with a written statement of the case against them, the details of which would vary from case to case, with only some giving full details of alleged misconduct. Here as elsewhere in the use of such executive measures, a paramount concern was to protect the confidentiality of security evidence. Simpson characterises the committees as conforming 'to the popular vision of Star Chamber',[68] the prerogative court of the Tudor and Stuart monarchs. A real problem for the researcher here lies in the lack of records, which have almost totally been destroyed. Those remaining in HO144 at the National Archives deal principally with the Irish cases, although there is a classified list of internees and some material on censorship of correspondence. But it remains the case that

> The veil of secrecy imposed by the Civil Service makes it impossible to tell whether those detained ought to have been, or whether the advisory committee operated

---

[64] Simpson (1994): 19.

[65] Simpson (1994): 16.

[66] Simpson (1994): 15–16.

[67] Simpson (1994): 20.

[68] Simpson (1994): 21.

respectably. The executive never accounted publicly for its actions then and, with the destruction of records, it never will.[69]

Challenging Restriction and Detention in the Courts

A number of court challenges were mounted to the use of DORR 14 (restriction on residence and movement) and the validity and use of DORR 14B (internment) using prerogative remedies of judicial review (certiorari) to seek to quash the decisions or orders of habeas corpus to test the legality of the detention and procure release. All were unsuccessful and show judges, other than a single dissentient, eager to support the validity of executive action and, unwilling to use the tools at their disposal, deploying an inappropriately attenuated judicial review:

> the judicial attitude exhibited ... was very much one of deference to the executive, permitting almost absolute freedom of decision making, sacrificing the presumption that wide powers ought to be narrowly construed in favour of the traditional liberties of the subject, and proceeding on the basis that those liberties had to be sacrificed for a greater good, the survival of the nation in an acute crisis – *salus populi suprema lex.*[70]

Analysis of reported decisions reveals two challenges to the use of regulation 14. *R* v *Denison*[71] concerned the German-born Hermann Nagele, an exporter of human hair (turnover £35,000 per annum) based in Boston, Lincolnshire, who was married to an Englishwoman and had three children all born in Boston. On 19 March 1916, in an order under regulation 14 dated 29 February, Nagele was ordered by the competent military authority (CMA) not to reside in Number 9 area of Northern Command, which covered Boston, but instead to reside in one of four other specified areas. He had to report his new place of residence and not to move from it without permission. The CMA stated no grounds for his suspicion about Nagele contending that it was his decision alone. The Divisional Court held that it was up to Nagele to show that the regulation had been misused. It rejected the argument that the CMA's suspicion had to be 'reasonable', thus accepting that the legislature had handed to a single person without appeal a power of this kind. No such term appeared in the regulation itself and the better interpretation merely required it to be an honest one, leaving it to the applicant to establish bad faith, an impossibility when no grounds for suspicion were stated. It rejected the argument – unsurprisingly given the terms of regulation 14B which was expressly stated not to restrict powers under regulation 14 – that removal could only be effected under regulation 14B, to which there attached a right of appeal. The disparity in appeal rights was a matter for the executive and not for the courts. Nagele had to bear the costs of the case. This 'hands off' or 'leave the authorities to it' approach was also

---

[69] Simpson (1994): 17.

[70] Bonner (1985): 55.

[71] (1916–17) 32 TLR 528 (Lord Reading CJ, Scrutton and Avory JJ).

deployed in *Ronnefeldt* v *Phillips*, both in the High Court[72] and in the Court of Appeal.[73] The applicant, Ronnefeldt, sought a declaration that the restriction order was *ultra vires* (beyond the powers conferred by) regulation 14 and void, as well as an injunction to prevent the authorities stopping him from returning to his home and coal-exporting business in Penarth near Cardiff. The CMA ordered Ronnefeldt to leave the area of the Severn Garrison (which included his home and business) within four days, being of the opinion that this was necessary for naval and military purposes. The basis for this, as set out in the law report, appears very weak, and Ronnefeldt was unable to gain disclosure of a police report because of Crown privilege (public interest immunity). Rumours were circulating in the Cardiff and Penarth area. One was that Ronnefeldt's father had at a dinner stated support for German action in sinking the *Lusitania*. Another claimed that Ronnefeldt had elsewhere stated that the Kaiser's head would soon be on this country's coinage. Ronnefeldt on oath denied both of these accusations. The CMA stated that he disbelieved the one concerning the father but was inclined to believe the other rumour and that, in any event, he had acted honestly. Recognizing the little ground for the suspicion, Darling J decided nonetheless that the order was valid. It did not need to be in any particular form. It was up to the applicant to establish that the CMA had not acted honestly. There was here no evidence of dishonesty. His decision was upheld by the Court of Appeal. Bankes LJ recognized the hardship to which the order subjected this businessman but, applying *R* v *Denison*, stressed that

> … these were not ordinary times. In a time of grave national peril it was necessary that the competent military authorities should be clothed with wide powers to act, and to act on suspicion. Honest mistakes might easily be made, and if they were honestly made the consequences must be borne as one of the consequences of a lamentable war.[74]

Warrington LJ went further. So long as an honest suspicion existed, the CMA need not be the one who held it. Even if the rumours were untrue, Warrington LJ thought that there was a strong suspicion that Ronnefeldt's sympathies might be translated into acts prejudicial to the public safety, so that there was enough evidence to say here that there was a real suspicion honestly held. It is hard to see that from the material disclosed in the law reports, so perhaps the learned judge may have thought that there must be enough basis in the undisclosed police report, otherwise the CMA would not have acted as he did. If so, once again, it is hard to see how any challenger could mount a successful attack on such a case, and his approach is redolent of 'the executive must be trusted'. Scrutton LJ noted that the legislature has entrusted the power to the CMA rather than to a judge. The CMA's honest suspicion sufficed here to validate his action.

---

[72] (1917–18) 34 TLR 556 (Darling J).

[73] (1918–19) 35 TLR 46 (Bankes, Warrington and Scrutton LJJ).

[74] (1918–19) 35 TLR 46, at 46.

The same approach was adopted in what appears to have been the only challenge to the use, as distinct from the validity, of DORR 14B. The case concerned a habeas corpus application by Miss Hilda Howsin, detained on the basis of 'hostile associations'. She was said to be a friend of someone who fled from England in 1909 and had become a German agent in Berlin. This may have been Virendranath Chattopadya, a British subject said to be an Indian revolutionary seeking the independence of India. Both the Divisional Court and the Court of Appeal refused her application.[75] Both abdicated any supervisory role; 'so long as there was any evidence upon which the Secretary of State had acted the court would not intervene'.[76]

In two other cases, however, the applicants for habeas corpus simply contended that regulation 14B was not valid law as it was not within the powers to legislate given by the parent Act, DORA. Neither application was successful, although one went all the way to the House of Lords in a case in which rule of law values – as opposed to the narrower and bare principle of legality embodied in it – found expression only in a dissenting opinion. The first case, *In re D*, remains unreported. The second, *R v Halliday, ex parte Zadig*,[77] brought by a naturalized British subject interned on grounds both of hostile origins and hostile associations – has been said to constitute 'a sort of watershed between the world of Victorian liberalism and the world of the vigilant state'.[78] Thereafter, with rare exceptions before the HRA era, the interests of good government have prevailed over British liberty in judicial decisions involving the use of executive measures in the national security context.[79] Plainly, the parent Act, DORA, made no mention of powers to make regulations authorizing internment. The issue was whether a Parliamentary intention to enable such regulations could be inferred from the more generally worded power in section 1 to issue regulations 'for securing the public safety and the defence of the realm'. The majority of the House of Lords, and the eight lower court judges involved in the earlier stages of the litigation, upheld DORR 14B (internment) as falling within that general power, thereby giving the statute a literal, virtually unlimited interpretation. In this time of 'supreme national danger' Lord Chancellor Finlay found no problem in deducing a Parliamentary intention to confer near absolute powers on the executive, trusting that they would be exercised reasonably.[80] The presumption that penal statutes should be construed narrowly had no application to a measure such as internment which he viewed as preventive not punitive.[81] It was immaterial that the Legislature, as in past wars, had not taken

---

[75] The Court of Appeal decision is reported in (1916–17) 33 TLR 527. That of the Divisional Court is unreported.

[76] Simpson (1994): 25.

[77] [1917] A.C. 260.

[78] Simpson (1994): 25.

[79] Ibid.

[80] [1917] A.C. 206, at 268–9.

[81] [1917] A.C. 206, at 270.

the path of suspending the remedy of habeas corpus; instead 'it had selected another way of achieving the same purpose, probably milder as well as more effectual than those adopted in previous wars'.[82] Lord Dunedin, concurring, saw the position as a necessary consequence of parliamentary sovereignty: the absolute power of Parliament untrammelled by any judicially enforceable written constitution. The theoretical danger of abuse in such a system was in practical terms non-existent, since, if the power were abused by interning all Catholics or all Jews, Parliament would swiftly repeal DORA. The remedy lay in the political rather than the legal arena. He continued:

> That preventive measures in the shape of internment of persons likely to assist the enemy may be necessary under the circumstances of a war like the present is really an obvious consideration. Parliament has in my judgment, in order to secure this and kindred objects, risked the chance of abuse which will always be theoretically present when absolute powers in general terms are delegated to an executive body; and has thought the restriction of the powers to the period of the duration of the war to be a sufficient safeguard.[83]

Lord Atkinson, also concurring, held that the statute contemplated preventive action into which internment fell. He rejected the view that a statute clear in its terms should be interpreted differently merely because liberty was at stake. Moreover,

> however precious the personal liberty of the subject may be, there is something for which it may well be, to some extent, sacrificed by legal enactment, namely national success in the war, or escape from national plunder or enslavement. It is not contended in this case that the personal liberty of the subject can be invaded arbitrarily at the mere whim of the Executive. What is contended is that the Executive has been empowered during the war, for paramount objects of State, to invade by legislative enactment that liberty in certain states of fact.[84]

The remedy of habeas corpus and other remedies for testing the legality of executive action had not been removed. The circumstances in which such action was legal had instead been extended through a valid law-making process. The fourth Law Lord in the majority, Lord Wrenbury, considered that on proper construction DORA contemplated prevention of certain acts (for example, communicating with the enemy) not always achievable by the threat of criminal prosecution and trial. Subject to the limitation that action be taken honestly, there was 'no other limit upon the acts that the regulations may authorise to achieve the defined object'.[85]

---

[82] Ibid.
[83] [1917] A.C. 260, at 271.
[84] [1917] A.C. 260, at 271–2.
[85] [1917] A.C. 260, at 307.

The sole dissentient, Lord Shaw, gave the most extensive judgment (the only one engaging in traditional legal analysis of principles and case precedents) on what he regarded as a grave issue in a case in 'the first class of importance'.[86] In a matter 'so fundamentally affecting the rights of subjects', the absence of a clear reference in DORA to internment or to persons of hostile origins or associations was fatal.[87] Parliament could not be taken by implication to have approved such a far–reaching 'subversion of our liberties'.[88] His Lordship was

> ...clearly of opinion that, although bearing to be a regulation, this is, in truth and essentially, not a regulation at all, and that it was *ultra vires* of His Majesty in Council to issue under the guise of a regulation an authorisation for the apprehension, seizure and internment without trial of any of the lieges [British subjects]. In my view Parliament never sanctioned, either in intention or by reason of the statutory words employed in the Defence of the Realm Acts, such a violent exercise of arbitrary power. It follows that the order or fiat of the Secretary of State [the internment order] is also *ultra vires*.[89]

It was vital that judges approach construction of statutory language in a spirit of 'independent scrutiny' rather than one approaching any action of the Government in a 'spirit of compliance'.[90] The majority interpretation of DORA would allow deprivation of life as well as liberty on executive fiat, just like Star Chamber or the Committee of Public Safety during the French Revolution, something 'poison to the commonwealth',[91] enabling Executive attack on 'the inmost citadel of our liberties' and detention or worse on the basis of one's supposed beliefs or thoughts.[92] Furthermore, had DORA adopted plainer and more definite language than it did, then absent express authorization of regulations enabling internment, he would still have come to the same conclusion.[93] His construction was not unreasonable but accorded with accepted canons of interpretation. Rather it was the majority view (the same as the judgment of the Courts below) which was wrong and 'fraught with great legal and constitutional danger'.[94]

His ringing rhetoric was of no avail. Zadig lost his appeal with costs and DORR 14B was valid. Allen, considering the judicial role, put things conservatively when writing of the case:

> It was not doubted – nor indeed can it be doubted by sensible persons – that if the law allows room for a Court to 'lean', in time of national danger it will instinctively and

---

[86] [1917] A.C. 260, at 276.
[87] [1917] A.C. 260, at 278.
[88] Ibid.
[89] [1917] A.C. 260, at 277.
[90] [1917] A.C. 260, at 287.
[91] [1917] A.C. 260, at 291.
[92] [1917] A.C. 260, at 293.
[93] [1917] A.C. 260, at 303.
[94] [1917] A.C. 260, at 305.

properly lean toward public security. The important thing is that it should not lean until it topples over.[95]

It is difficult not to agree with Lowry that in *Halliday* the 'toppling point' was passed and the decision and approach represented 'an abdication of the judicial function',[96] something equally applicable to the approaches to the use of regulations 14, 14B and the arrest and detention powers in DORR 55. This view is strengthened when one considers that regulations purporting to authorize the requisition of property were found *ultra vires*, not to be embraced by the same words which the House of Lords had founded on to hold internment regulations valid. In addition, in another requisition case, the House of Lords held that prerogative power to take property in wartime, if it existed at all, had been put into abeyance by statutory schemes. This greater protection of property than personal liberty may say something about judicial priorities or 'politics' on rights and liberties,[97] but it may also be relevant that these cases were decided after the Armistice, when the relief that war was over made for cooler approaches.

The Second World War

The Second World War was very much a consequence of the First. Its origins and the rise of the Nazi regime to power by constitutional means are well-documented elsewhere. Attempts to appease Hitler's expansionist aims by sacrificing Austria and Czechoslovakia failed and the United Kingdom, allied with France, on 3 September 1939 went again to war over the German invasion of Poland. The quietude of a 'phoney war' was shattered in May 1940 with the German invasions and occupations of Norway and Denmark, Belgium, the Netherlands, and of France which surrendered in June 1940. German success through its Blitzkrieg method of attack was also attributed to the existence in the countries concerned of a 'Fifth Column' of enemy aliens and German sympathizers and agents preparing the ground and assisting the invasion. Italy then entered the war on the German side (the Axis powers). The United Kingdom was then in great danger of invasion by Germany, something thwarted by the RAF, which prevented the German Luftwaffe from gaining command of the air sufficient to protect the invasion fleet. The danger of invasion and occupation, as distinct from that from aerial bombing, only fully passed after Germany invaded the Soviet Union and the United States entered the war after the Japanese attack on Pearl Harbor in December 1941, forming with the United Kingdom, the Soviet Union, China and the Free French, the Allied Powers in the global conflict.

---

[95] Allen (1965): 45.
[96] Lowry (1977): 53, 58.
[97] Griffith (1977): 80.

Detailed inter-War planning laid the basis for the passage on 24 August 1939 of the first parent Act, the Emergency Powers (Defence) Act 1939 (EPDA 1939) and the Defence Regulations (DR), made by Order in Council, were thus able to be brought in on 25 August and 1 September and be in place at the outbreak of war. The Act specifically enabled regulations on internment[98] and provided that the powers were to supplement rather than detract from prerogative powers.[99] Despite that, and despite the extensive restrictive powers in the Aliens restriction legislation, the Government deliberately chose to intern enemy aliens under prerogative powers, considering that this was the best way to limit what must surely have been little risk, given the First World War experience, of intrusive judicial review. Another parent Act was enacted in 1940: the Emergency Powers (Defence) Act 1940 (EPDA 1940), but it was EPDA 1939 which governed detention and restriction of those 'threats' who were not enemy aliens.

Internment and Restrictions on Residence and Movement of Enemy Aliens

Some active members of the Nazi Party had already been deported in April 1939. Others were allowed to leave at the outbreak of war. Although the Home Office opposed mass internment of enemy aliens on the First World War model, nonetheless in that month accommodation was earmarked for some 18,000 detainees. From the outset, enemy aliens were categorized to distinguish the most dangerous from the harmless. The task of grading was carried out by a plethora of local Enemy Alien tribunals in different parts of the country. These were chaired by a judge or lawyer. The decision was his alone but he was assisted by a secretary and someone from the voluntary aid agencies with whom refugees were registered. Class 'A' aliens (the most dangerous) were to be interned: these were aliens about whose loyalty the tribunals had doubts and who might be a security risk. Class 'B' aliens were those about whose loyalty the tribunals were not absolutely certain and who should therefore be subject to some supervision. Until May 1940 they faced restrictions on movement and residence and possession of certain equipment such as cameras, maps, field glasses, arms, etc. Class 'C' aliens remained subject only to their usual peacetime restrictions. Tribunals were to distinguish within this class between those who were 'refugees from Nazi oppression' and non-refugees.[100] Some refugees were, however, noted as such but categorized as Class 'B'; tribunal decisions exhibited wide variation so that 'the fate of many refugees was determined more by where they lived and at what point their hearing took place than by the evidence offered'.[101] While changes in Home Office instructions were made they did not result in reconsideration of cases already heard.[102] The Nazi-

---

[98] EPDA 1939, s. 1(1)(a).

[99] EPDA 1939, s. 9.

[100] Stent (1980): 35–6.

[101] Stent (1980): 37, 63–4.

[102] Stent (1980): 37

Soviet pact proved problematic for communists and socialists whose loyalty would otherwise not have been in doubt.[103]

Home Office pressure on MI5 reduced its demands in terms of requests for internment, so that even after four months of war only 554 enemy aliens had been interned out of an estimated German and Austrian population of 60,000 to 75,000, many of them Jewish refugees who had fled Nazi persecution. By March 1940, some 2,000 were held. A policy of mass internment was only implemented after 10 May 1940, when Churchill took over as Prime Minister .The policy came in part as a response to sustained media pressure, later in part to growing anti-alien feeling after the invasion of the Low Countries, and ultimately to pressure from the military establishment.[104] Initially, all male enemy aliens in a defined but ever expanding 'coastal zone' were interned. Days later males aged 16–60 in Category B were targeted.[105] Then came Class' B' women aged 16–60, with other Class B women subject to special restrictions.[106] Throughout June the policy moved steadily towards one of 'collar the lot', including Class 'C'.[107] To a degree this was envisaged for their protection as bombing intensified public feelings. It was a 'safety-first' policy: intern all and over time release those thought reliable. With 70,000 enemy aliens in the country after Italy had entered the war, internment of all was not administratively possible, but the execution and administration of the process proved highly distressing, especially as many detained were refugees from Nazi persecution. There was undoubtedly a degree of anti-Semitism in the process. The numbers detained soared to 28,000 by October. Many were detained in camps (essentially fenced-off seaside boarding house accommodation) on the Isle of Man.[108] Some lived in Butlins', Dixons' or Warners' holiday camps, in horseboxes on a variety of racecourses, or at the Oratory school in Chelsea.[109] Conditions varied with inevitable problems when Nazis and refugees, many Jewish, were mixed together. Surprisingly, the most dangerous category had the best conditions. Some internees were transported on the *Dunera* and suffered ill-treatment on the way to Australia.[110] Others were sent to Canada. More than 700 Germans and Italians died when the *Arandora Star* was torpedoed on its transatlantic journey.[111] Some were repatriated to Germany in exchange for Britons interned there.[112] Most internees were men. Only some 4,000 women were interned, none from Class 'C'.

---

[103] Stent (1980): 38. For a fictionalized representation influenced by internees' accounts, see Baddiel (2005).

[104] Stent (1980): chaps 3–5.

[105] Stent (1980): 55.

[106] Stent (1980): 62.

[107] Stent (1980): chap. 5.

[108] See Chappel (1984), *passim*.

[109] Stent, (1980): 83–92; Kochan (1983): xii, 6–7; Lafitte (1988): 139 (original edition 1940).

[110] Patkin (1979).

[111] Lafitte (1988): 123–43.

[112] Stent (1980): 94.

But most of the women would have spent at least some time detained in HMP Holloway with common criminals, but treated as remand prisoners. Artistic, cultural and educational endeavours eased the lot of many detainees, whether male or female. Most were depressed. Some committed suicide. As with the Belmarsh detainees after 9/11,[113] dealing with their predicament was worse for them than for convicted criminals in having no release date to work towards. Added to that was the injustice as refugees from Nazi persecution of being thought pro-Nazi, when experience in countries occupied by the Nazis showed their helpers to have been pro-Fascist nationals of the countries concerned, suggesting that here too the 'enemy within' lay in such groups and others previously supportive of Hitler. This 'dreadful business' of mass internment fortunately did not last long: in defined stages, with categories for release ever widening, 'the policy was soon reversed in response to pressure from both inside and outside the governmental machine'.[114] It had certainly not 'played well' in the United States.

Internment of and Restrictions on Security Threats or Sympathizers

While mass internment of enemy aliens, many anti-Nazi and Jewish, was certainly a panicked overreaction, the authorities did not ignore other potential 'Fifth Columnists'. The seminal study relied on here is that of Simpson.[115] Internment in most cases was effected under DR 18B.[116] Initially this enabled internment where the Home Secretary was satisfied that it was necessary to do so with a view to preventing its subject acting in any manner prejudicial to the public safety or the defence of the realm. It was replaced on 23 November 1939 to read:

> If the Secretary of State has reasonable cause to believe any person to be of hostile origin or associations or to have been recently concerned in acts prejudicial to the public safety or the defence of the realm or in the preparation or instigation of such acts and that by reason thereof it is necessary to exercise control over him, he may make an order against that person directing that he be detained.

The scheme also enabled the imposition of lesser restrictions than internment by suspending the detention order subject to conditions:

> (a) prohibiting or restricting the possession or use by that person of any specified articles; (b) imposing upon him such restrictions as may be specified in the direction in respect of his employment or business, in respect of the place of his residence, and in respect of his association or communication with other persons; (c) requiring him to

---

[113] See chapters 7 and 9.

[114] Simpson (1994): 163.

[115] Simpson (1994): *passim*, but especially chapters 9, 12–14.

[116] Almost 1000 non-enemy alien 'threats' were detained under Art. 12(5A) of the Aliens Order (on which see chapter 4) or DR 20A. Appeal lay to a different advisory committee which heard some 500 appeals: Simpson (1994): 258.

notify his movements in such manner, at such times, and to such authority or person as may be so specified; (d) prohibiting him from travelling except in accordance with permission given to him by such authority or person as may be so specified, as the Secretary of State thinks fit; and the Secretary of State may revoke any such direction if he is satisfied that the person against whom the order was made has failed to observe any condition so imposed, or that the operation of the order can no longer remain suspended without detriment to the public safety or the defence of the realm.

From 22 May 1940 further provision was made to enable internment or lesser restrictions to be imposed on members of particular groups or organizations.

(1A.) If the Secretary of State has reasonable cause to believe any person to have been or to be a member of, or to have been or to be active in the furtherance of the objects of, any such organization as is hereinafter mentioned, and that it is necessary to exercise control over him, he may make an order against that person directing that he be detained. The organizations hereinbefore referred to are any organization as respects which the Secretary of State is satisfied that either (a) the organization is subject to foreign influence or control, or (b) the persons in control of the organization have or have had associations with persons concerned in the government of, or sympathies with the system of government of, any Power with which His Majesty is at war, and in either case that there is danger of the utilization of the organization for purposes prejudicial to the public safety, the defence of the realm, the maintenance of public order, the efficient prosecution of any war in which His Majesty may be engaged, or the maintenance of supplies or services essential to the life of the community.

Despite its width, its sole target was the British Union (BU), a fascist organization. Almost all of its active membership was detained including its leader, Oswald Mosley and his wife, Diana. There were real fears that he might stage some sort of coup or otherwise come to power and make peace with Germany, operating as some sort of puppet.

In the course of the War in Europe, some 1,847 orders were executed under DR 18B. Almost all detainees were British subjects. The peak was reached in August 1940 with 1,428 detained and gradually declined over the period until April 1945 when only 11 remained in detention. As the danger of invasion passed, Churchill – himself an interned war correspondent in South Africa during the Boer War – became increasingly sceptical about its value and often prodded his Home Secretary over the detention of notables like the Mosleys.[117] Less than 500 were in detention at the end of 1942. Indeed, when Herbert Morrison took over as Home Secretary from Sir John Anderson in October 1940 'he was principally responsible for releasing, or delaying the release, of his fellow citizens, rather than detaining them'.[118] The best estimate is that about a third of orders were against the BU under 18B(1A), just over half were as regards persons of 'hostile origins or

---

[117] Churchill (2000): App. F.
[118] Simpson (1994): 260.

associations' and only some 10 per cent in respect of 'acts prejudicial'. Orders were made sometimes where criminal charges could have been brought but the penalty was thought insufficient for the conduct or danger, or public proceedings might prove unduly embarrassing. Others were made because the evidence available would not suffice to meet the criminal standard of proof or could not for security reasons be produced in adversarial proceedings so as to be made known to the accused and his lawyers. Not all orders were 'individual'. Some were 'omnibus' orders enabling the detention of hundreds of individuals named in the Schedule. The legality of 'omnibus' orders was never ruled on by the courts and seems not to have troubled the Advisory Committee. In 1940, when most of the detentions were initiated, it was very much a process of 'lock up first' in response to unchecked material from MI5 or the police and 'worry about it later',[119] leaving the detailed investigation of cases to be done by the Advisory Committee should the individual appeal or on review in the Home Office should he or she initiate court proceedings. Sometimes such individuals were released subject to conditions, including that of foregoing legal proceedings where the Home Office preferred a court not to rule on an issue and set an awkward precedent.

Administrative Challenge

Appeals by interned enemy aliens were heard from the outset by a central advisory committee.[120] Initially those not interned but restricted had no appeal against wrongful classification. One was only granted to one of 12 regional committees in February 1940. They operated slowly, and their rationale may as much have been one of enhancing the numbers interned as freeing Class 'B' aliens from undue restriction.[121]

Those detained or restricted under DR 18B had a right to make objections to one of several advisory committees appointed by the Home Secretary[122] and representations to the Home Secretary.[123] A meeting of an advisory committee was presided over by a lawyer chairman nominated by the Home Secretary. The chairman had to inform the objector of the grounds on which the order had been made against them and to furnish them with such particulars as were in the opinion of the chairman sufficient to enable them to present their case.[124]

The panels, eventually four in number, were chaired by Sir Norman Birkett KC (later Birkett J), and expanded to include four deputy chairmen and a larger secretarial staff. Eventually a separate Committee chaired by Sir Percy Lorraine dealt with the Anglo-Italians. The Scottish Committee was chaired initially by

---

[119] Simpson (1994): 258.
[120] Stent (1980): 40.
[121] Ibid.
[122] DR 18B(3).
[123] DR 18B(4).
[124] DR 18B(5).

Lord Alness and later by Lord Jamieson. It dealt with much smaller numbers. Delay was a significant problem, a consequence of numbers (which gave the lie to this being a personal decision of the Home Secretary), an overworked Home Office, the practice of the Advisory Committee (AC) submitting its draft reports for comment to MI5 (a practice soon discontinued), and delays in the Home Office over whether to accept the committee's advice. A detainee could have more than one appeal, but this was not widely known and did not result in vexatious appeals which might have swamped the committees.

Proceedings before the AC were less by way of hearings than interrogations. Detainees could have legal advice (sessions with a lawyer usually in the presence of prison or camp staff) but lawyers could not appear as advocates before the AC. Detainees were not apprised for security reasons of the full case against them. Nor would they be told the outcome. Formally speaking the recommendation of the AC was not binding. Anderson, as Home Secretary, who had always opposed mass internment, invariably accepted AC advice as to release. His successor, Morrison, did not in a significant number of cases (for example, 3 in November 1940, 18 in December 1940, and 55 in January 1941) and would also sometimes release when the AC had recommended detention. One complaint about the system was that 'one side', MI5, had two bites of the cherry, one before the Act and one with the Home Office/Home Secretary considering what to do with the AC report. The involvement of MI5 and its view – hard pressed with the Home Secretary – that the AC should not deal with the necessity for detaining someone who came within the regulation came close to tarnishing the AC's independence. This was especially so in 18B(1A) cases since, membership of the BU being clear, necessity for detention or control was the central issue, so following that approach would have left the AC as a mere rubber stamp. Fortunately, whatever its other defects, the AC did not fully adopt that approach.

Court Challenge

The courts ruled on a number of key matters in applications for habeas corpus or other judicial review remedies and in actions for damages for false imprisonment. Their record is mixed. In a number of cases they ordered release where the wrong 'head' of DR 18B had been used but those released were then usually re-detained under the correct head.[125] Arguments that undue delay in bringing someone before the AC rendered detention unlawful were not successful, but the Lord Chief Justice involved raised the matter with the Home Secretary (they had been Cabinet colleagues at one time) and procured some improvements. There was some division over whether 'reasonable cause' in DR 18B(1) gave the courts a power to challenge the Home Secretary's view in his sworn affidavit, but the House of Lords in *Liversidge* v *Anderson*[126] (action for false imprisonment) and *Greene* v

---

[125] Simpson (1994): 318–332.
[126] [1942] AC 206.

Secretary of State for Home Affairs[127] (habeas corpus application) held that this apparently 'objective' standard imparted, in the particular context under consideration, a purely 'subjective' standard. It meant 'if the Secretary of State honestly thinks he has reasonable cause to believe', so that unless the applicant could prove 'bad faith' on the part of the Home Secretary the detention order must stand. Moreover, the production of the order without providing the reasons which supported the decision to make it, constituted a complete answer to any such action or application. The courts could not go behind the Home Secretary's affidavit (one which he was not required to make) of honest belief on the basis of reports from trusted subordinates, thus rendering proof of 'bad faith' impossible. Lord Atkin entered a solitary if inappropriately over-celebrated dissent in *Liversidge*. An objective standard was intended. This was the plain and natural meaning of the words used; other Defence regulations were phrased subjectively indicating that DR18B imparted a different test; and, as noted earlier, an earlier version of it had been framed subjectively thus indicating the importance of the change to 'reasonable cause'. His interpretation was in tune with accepted notions of the cherished liberty of the subject. The majority preferred (they had choices) to see little significance in differences in wording between regulations, arguing that they were drafted at different times by different draftsmen and that too much stress should not be put on mere phraseology since regulations did not receive the same degree of consideration in their framing or scrutiny as did statutes. Moreover, a difference in meaning did exist: 'reasonable cause' admonished the Home Secretary to consider the matter with greater care than one in which 'satisfied' governed the task. In any event, Lord Atkin's approach even if adopted by the majority would have afforded little practical help to detainees since, as he made clear in his speech in *Greene*, the Home Secretary's affidavit was sufficient in law to justify the detention to Lord Atkin's satisfaction and the Home Secretary could not be compelled to produce the evidence behind the affidavit.[128] In 'an absurd and disgraceful ruling', 'in defiance of all common sense', the High Court in another case upheld the 18B detention of a gangland criminal whom the police were finding impossible to catch using the criminal process.[129] The same alignment of courts and executive – arguably an abdication of the judicial function – is thus as apparent in the Second World War as in the First.

[127] [1942] AC 284.
[128] Bonner (1985) 57–8. Cf. Simpson (1994): 363.
[129] Simpson (1994): 313–315.

Chapter 3

Political Violence and the Irish Question

Introduction

With Ireland and the United Kingdom working together as European Union partners and to provide stability so that Northern Ireland continues to enjoy its longest period of comparative peace since 1945, it is easy to forget the problems produced by the troubled relationship between these two islands on the western edge of Europe. Those problems had persisted since the 'systematic colonization' of Ireland undertaken under the later Tudor and early Stuart monarchs by means of 'plantation' of colonists to provide stability to a land England had occupied in part much earlier.[1] Unlike other colonies, however, Ireland became an integral part of the United Kingdom, losing its own Parliament in 1800 after an abortive rebellion in 1798. The territory now comprised by Ireland (initially the Irish Free State) only ceased to be so in 1922 after a War of Independence managed to separate part of the Irish national territory. It was successful where earlier attempts to gain independence by violent means or gain more autonomy by constitutional means (Home Rule) had failed. But that separation did not 'solve' the Irish question. The presence in the north-eastern corner of Ireland of a majority of Unionists – some descendants of the 'planted' and mainly of Protestant religion – saw the island partitioned with six of the nine counties of Ulster remaining, as now, an integral part of the United Kingdom, but with a sizeable 'nationalist' minority, almost exclusively Roman Catholic in religion. Until recently, the Irish Government maintained a constitutional claim to Northern Ireland, and a number of nationalist groups worked within constitutional politics for Irish unity. It also produced violent irredentist nationalism in various manifestations of the paramilitary Irish Republican Army (IRA), illegal in both countries, which waged armed campaigns to try to achieve Irish unity and in times of sectarian crisis to protect the nationalist minority in Northern Ireland. These armed campaigns were resisted by United Kingdom security forces (police and army) and a variety of 'Loyalist' paramilitary groups, prepared to use violence to preserve a Protestant hegemony and Northern Ireland's place as part of the United Kingdom. The IRA and other violent nationalist groups operated invariably as 'anti-State' terrorists. For the most part, 'Loyalist' paramilitaries acted as 'pro-State' terrorists or even as 'proxy' terrorists for the State itself.[2] But they were not averse to armed resistance to the Crown to

---

[1] Ferguson (2004): 55–7.
[2] Bruce (1992): chaps 8, 11.

which they were supposedly loyal, or the deployment of industrial action paralysing the Province, if Government action was perceived to threaten the status of Ulster as part of the United Kingdom or involved the Irish Government too much in decision-making on the governance of Northern Ireland.[3] The success to date of the Belfast 'Good Friday' Agreement of 1998 has seen the Provisional IRA (PIRA), the main nationalist paramilitary group, disarm and its political 'wing', Sinn Fein, take part in the government of Northern Ireland, leaving only fringe republican terrorist groups perpetrating a very low level of violence.[4] 'Loyalist' paramilitaries have similarly withdrawn from political violence. The extent to which both sides engage in other criminality remains in dispute. Despite the electorate in the Province being polarized into sectarian camps represented mainly by Sinn Fein (nationalist) and the Democratic Unionist Party (unionist), May 2007 brought an historic establishment of a power-sharing devolved government with a DUP First Minister and a Sinn Fein Deputy. 'Emergency' anti-terrorist legislation (a permanent feature of Northern Ireland since 1922) remains fully to be dismantled. Moreover, while the focus in the United Kingdom's anti–terrorist legislation has increasingly moved from 'Irish' to 'international' terrorism since the 1980s, the Terrorism Act 2000 built on earlier measures to deal with the extension (in most of the phases) of the IRA campaign to mainland Great Britain. And its post-9/11 response draws heavily on earlier measures to suppress political violence connected with Irish (and later Northern Irish) affairs since 1798 as well as on measures from the two World Wars examined in chapter 2.

One can identify a number of recurrent but not invariable features of that political violence and those suppressive measures. 'England's difficulty', when facing invasion from other States (France in the Revolutionary/Napoleonic wars, the Kaiser's Germany in the First World War and Nazi Germany in the Second), has often been seen as violent Irish nationalism's 'opportunity'. Hence support from the would-be invader formed part of rebellions in 1798,[5] in 1916 and again in 1939–45, although the degree of support other than in 1798 was marginal. Financial and material support in terms of arms from the Irish diaspora, particularly in North America, has been a prominent feature from the Fenian dynamite war of the nineteenth century onwards.[6] More recently, the IRA received support from Libya.[7]

Violent Irish nationalism has not confined its campaigns to Ireland, but has tended (other than in 1956–62) to extend them to Great Britain, and, in the case of PIRA which emerged as the dominant group in the 1970s, to British targets on the European mainland. Whether in Ireland or Great Britain, a prime suppressive mechanism has been widened criminal law and modified criminal processes,

---

[3]   Nelson (1984); Fisk (1975).

[4]   McKittrick and McVea (2001); Cox (2006).

[5]   Pakenham (1969).

[6]   Short (1979), 1–6.

[7]   English (2003), 222, 249–50.

including in Ireland and Northern Ireland, the use of criminal courts sitting without a jury in serious criminal cases. But also prominent has been supplementing or providing an alternative to that criminal process by means of executive measures of internment without trial, of restrictions on residence and movement, of protecting Great Britain through orders prohibiting entry to or expelling persons (including British citizens) from Great Britain, and of deporting Irish citizens to the Republic of Ireland. In security terms, such powers have been seen to work best when that country was taking action against violent nationalism both through its modified criminal process (a juryless Special Criminal Court) and through internment without trial.[8]

Unsurprisingly, such measures (each affording their own administrative challenge mechanisms) have come before the courts. The same judicial deference is seen here as that pervading challenges to such powers in wartime (chapter 2), in dealing with undesirable 'aliens' (chapter 4) or in combating emergencies as part of the withdrawal from colonial empire (chapters 5 to 8). Individuals might win technical victories, rendered pyrrhic by a further application of the powers avoiding the technical error or with the defect removed by retrospective legislation. Major parts of the violent campaign to achieve Irish unity have occurred since the coming into operation of the ECHR. Challenges to anti-terrorist powers have provided some of the major cases before the Commission and the Court of Human Rights. They establish that there is an element of European judicial supervision of such executive measures restricting liberty, free movement and other rights, but that the ECHR bodies will accord a wide margin of appreciation to the State deploying them.

Seeking constitutional structures to reconcile communities with opposing political aspirations on the governance of Ireland has also been a prominent feature of the period, an attempt to win 'hearts and minds' and lessen support for paramilitary groups. Significantly, both in 1922 and 1995-to-date this has involved Government dealing directly with representatives of those previously condemned as terrorists, just as in Cyprus and Kenya.

The chapter divides treatment into four different phases of the campaign for Irish unity in the twentieth century, phases in which the exact line between those involved in political activity and those in the use of violent means has sometimes been uncertain. Each considers the executive measures used, the challenge mechanisms afforded and the response of national courts and, where appropriate, the ECHR organs. Those phases are: Home Rule to partition (1900-23); the 1939–45 campaign; the 1956–62 Border campaign; and from Civil Rights to urban terrorism/guerrilla war to lasting peace (1969–2007).

---

[8] OASA Review (2002), chap. 4.

Home Rule to Partition (1900–23)

The intricacies of the Home Rule question have cogently been analysed by others.[9] Prime Minister Gladstone's desire from the 1870s on to end the 'Irish' question by according Ireland 'Home Rule' (a degree of self-government with a devolved legislature) split his own Liberal party. The existence in Parliament of a sizeable number of Irish nationalist MPs (the Irish Party) ensured the recurrence of the issue, Unionist opposition its longevity. Measures to achieve it passed the Commons but were rejected by the Unionist majority in the second chamber, the House of Lords. Moreover, the issue was hardly a vote-winner with the electorate in Great Britain.[10] In Ireland itself, Unionists and Nationalists formed bands of armed 'volunteers' with Unionists determined to resist Home (Rome) Rule by force of arms, supported in their endeavour by the Conservative and Unionist Party and some Liberal 'unionists'. It became clear to the Liberal Government, however, that the Army might not be willing to deploy to coerce Ulster. Its Government of Ireland Act 1914 passed into law without the assent of the Lords whose powers had been reduced by the Parliament Act 1911 to two years' delay. It transferred certain powers to a devolved Irish parliament. The onset of the First World War saw it consigned to cold storage for the duration of the war, expected to be over by Christmas 1914. It was overtaken by events. Nationalist opposition to conscription in Ireland might ultimately have produced the same result, but the Easter Rising in 1916 by some of the Irish Volunteers, which lacked any substantial public support, in effect secured its ends of mobilizing nationalist public opinion against the Government because of the harshness of the Government's response to what had been an unpopular rebellion. The Government overreaction succeeded where the rebels' military attempt inevitably had failed. The execution of 15 of the Rising's leaders after court martial trials under DORA and the internment of the rank and file of the rebels produced a swing in majority public opinion away from the constitutionalism of the Irish Party towards Sinn Fein by 1918. In striving for a political solution, Government failed to recognize the non-existence in Ireland of moderate ground. It was unwilling or unable to coerce 'loyal' Ulster, many of whose 'volunteers' had died for 'king and country' on the Western Front. Partition was the only workable solution in the circumstances existing at the time. The Government of Ireland Act 1920 devolving legislative powers to two Parliaments, one for Northern Ireland and another in Dublin for the remainder, also established a Council of Ireland to which those Parliaments might transfer powers. It was the culmination of Government attempts to find a reconciliatory constitutional compromise to an apparently insoluble political problem. For most of Ireland, these steps proved meaningless. Sinn Fein had in effect established its own Government, legislature (Dail Eireann) and some courts, and sought admission at

---

[9] Walsh (2002) gives a good, short account.
[10] Townshend (1988), 174–5.

the Versailles peace conference to the League of Nations.[11] Since 1919, there had been an ongoing guerrilla war in Ireland between the IRA seeking an independent Irish republic and British Government forces aiming to restore law and order and a return to constitutionalism.

It was an escalating war of IRA attacks on policemen and police posts; a war of movement, of 'flying columns' and in rural and urban areas 'hit and run' roadside ambushes of Crown forces; of intelligence and counter-intelligence as Michael Collins succeeded in penetrating the heart of the Dublin Detective Branch intelligence operation; of the killing of informers and of the assassination of key British intelligence officers. It was a war in which 'rebel' forces were met by a range of Crown forces: the regular army and a militarized police force, the Royal Irish Constabulary (RIC), whose strength was augmented by the recruitment of former soldiers (the Black and Tans and an Auxiliary force). The war was one in which those forces with some government approval met terror with terror, with savage reprisals against people and property.[12] It was a conflict in which 'rebel' forces fought with substantial support from Irish public opinion and as if they were the army of an established State.[13] Indeed the British Government declined publicly to call it a 'war' to avoid enhancing Irish claims for belligerent status. The Sinn Fein Provisional Government and the IRA received substantial political, financial and material support from the Irish diaspora in the United States, including, late in the conflict, Thompson sub-machine guns. It was a conflict in which the British Government found little support in Irish public opinion, save in Ulster, and its deliberate reprisal policy steadily alienated British public opinion. The atmosphere is said to be vividly conveyed in Ken Loach's 2006 film *The Wind that Shakes the Barley*. The conflict is analysed in a more scholarly manner in a number of works, on which the treatment here has drawn.[14] Nor was the conflict confined to Ireland. IRA units also perpetrated attacks in major centres of population in Great Britain, hitting docks and public utilities.[15] In the Unionist heartland, the conflict was more markedly sectarian, with major public order clashes between Catholic 'nationalists' and Protestant 'loyalists', and Loyalist 'pogroms' of Catholics, a degree of ethnic cleansing. Government mobilized the remnants of the Ulster Volunteer Force, eventually accommodating it in a Special Constabulary (the A, B and C Specials). The A and C soon disappeared, but the B Specials played a significant role in producing the breakdown of order in Northern Ireland in 1969. While the Government was not prepared to coerce Ulster into a united Ireland, leading Liberals sought to persuade them to leave the United Kingdom. As at April 1921, in Ireland 276 policemen and 99 soldiers had been killed, and 456 and 216 respectively wounded. There had been almost 10,000 raids

---

[11] Costello (2003): 39–46

[12] Hayes-McCoy (1966): 55–66.

[13] Mitchell (2002): 70–86.

[14] Hart (2005a and b); Costello (2003); Kautt (1999); Townshend (1983): chaps 5–8.

[15] Hart (2005a): chap. 6.

for arms, more than 500 police barracks destroyed and 246 damaged. Sinn Fein claimed that British reprisals had seen 2000 private homes put to the torch.[16] In Great Britain, Hart estimates that in the period October 1920 to the truce in July 1921, there were almost 400 cases of arson or sabotage, 25 robberies and 17 shootings. Most operations were in London, Liverpool, Manchester, Tyneside and Scotland. One policeman, five IRA men and four civilians were killed, with respectively nine, seven and eight wounded.[17]

The conflict settled, like the PIRA campaign in the last three decades of the same century, into a stalemate which desperately needed a political solution. A 'truce' was agreed. The Government then negotiated, as in the 1990s and as in the withdrawal from colonial empire (see chapter 5) with those it had previously condemned as criminals.[18] The majority faction in the Dail accepted the resultant Anglo-Irish Treaty 1921[19] giving effective self government to the 26 counties of the Irish Free State and a Boundary Commission to consider the Border between the North and South of Ireland. The Northern Ireland Parliament had the right to opt out and soon did so, and set about constructing a 'statelet' in which unionists (mainly Protestants) would always hold power, protected against coercion into a united Ireland by a security regime modelled on DORA and the DORR. The Border Commission produced nothing of note.[20] In the Irish Free State, the pro-treaty Provisional government (with support from the United Kingdom) won a civil war with the anti-Treaty irregulars.[21] From 1925, Partition was a reality which produced peace for a time but within which lay the seeds of future conflict as the militant wing of Irish nationalism several times by force of arms sought to achieve its goal of Irish unity and the true 'Republic' (the other three phases analysed in this chapter).[22] For this book, the more important question is how Government dealt through law with this political violence in the period 1916–23 in Ireland itself and in Great Britain. The question, interesting in itself, is the more important because in the methods chosen then and subsequently to deal with outbreaks of irredentist violent Irish nationalism, can be found the essence of much of the modern anti-terrorist response in terms of executive measures.

DORA Restriction of Movement and Internment

DORA internment came in two phases: immediately after the Easter Rising; and as part of the response to the so-called 'German plot' in May 1918.

---

[16] Costello (2003): 124–5.
[17] Hart (2005a): 165–7.
[18] Pakenham (1966): 107–115; Townshend (1988): 191.
[19] Costello (2003): 382–7.
[20] Donohue (2001), chap. 1..
[21] Townshend (1983): 372–3.
[22] Townshend (1983): 322–3.

The Easter Rising of 1916 saw the invocation of martial law under which a curfew was put into effect and it was proclaimed that those carrying arms risked being shot without warning. But action against the rebels was in fact effected under DORA and the DORR which operated throughout the United Kingdom. The only specifically 'Irish' change was to remove the right to jury trial (inserted into DORA in 1915), thus authorizing even the capital trial of civilians by courts martial under DORA rather than the military tribunals usually a feature of martial law. Martial law and its renewal were short-lived and there as a symbolic rather than legally important deterrent. Ample powers existed in the raft of wartime statutory measures.[23]

Initially, almost 3500 were arrested; orders were that all Sinn Feiners who had supported the movement were to be arrested even though they had taken no part in the Rising.[24] Very soon afterwards, 1,424 men and 73 women were released. A few (159 men and one woman) were tried by courts martial. Only eleven were acquitted. Ninety, including De Valera and Countess Markiewicz, were sentenced to death. Only 15 were executed. The others received various periods of imprisonment. The Countess was saved because of her gender, De Valera (some thought) because of his supposed United States' citizenship, although there is no direct evidence for this.[25] Those suspects against whom there was insufficient evidence of guilt to put before a court martial were interned. Internment covered 1,836 men and five women, and saw their removal for security reasons, some to mainland prisons (Aylesbury for the women, Stafford, Usk, Lincoln, Lewes, Dartmoor and Reading prisons for the men) but the majority of the men to the two Frongoch camps in Wales (replacing German prisoners of war there). Initial detention was on the basis of custody pending charge or trial under DORA. Internment and removal, however, were effected by a misuse of DORR 14B. It was suggested that a new retrospective regulation specifically framed to cover participation in the Rising would be advisable to ensure the legality of action. Government, however, decided to proceed under 14B. That enabled detention or restriction in respect of persons of 'hostile associations'. These

> ... could only have been associations with each other, not with foreign enemies. So the regulation was stretched and used for this entirely new purpose, for in no conceivable sense were the Irish detainees in effect enemy aliens, covered by Simon's explanation of the purpose of the regulation in June of the previous year.[26]

A planned legal challenge never materialized, the internees being released before it ever came to court.[27] The advisory committee that considered detentions must not

---

[23] Townshend (1983): 310.

[24] Townshend (1983): 307–8.

[25] Ward (1969): 117–119.

[26] Simpson (1994): 19.

[27] Campbell (1994): 102 n. 442.

have been troubled by it.[28] As with internment in Northern Ireland 1971–75, the action was counterproductive in that the camps in particular became something of a 'Sinn Fein University' within which the 'rebels' maintained a degree of their command structure, and which enhanced cohesion among otherwise regionally disparate groups.[29] Most were released relatively quickly, there being only some 550 still interned in mid-August 1916. An amnesty was granted for the remainder in June 1917.

In April 1918, faced with an initially highly successful German offensive on the Western Front, applying conscription to Ireland again became an issue. The government also wished to cripple Sinn Fein. DORR 14B was thought inaptly worded to catch Sinn Feiners not connected with discussions with Germany. The ability to exile Sinn Fein leaders to Great Britain using DORR 14 was thought inappropriate as leaving them essentially free there. Accordingly, but only in Ireland, 14B was amended so as to allow detention or restriction where someone was 'suspected of acting, having acted or of being about to act in a manner prejudicial to public safety or the defence of the Realm'. In May 1918, 73 activists in Sinn Fein and the Irish Volunteers were arrested supposedly on the basis of involvement in aiding Germany and interned in England. This was an odd way of doing things since such (if true) would have justified detention under the unamended 14B ('hostile associations'), but this 'German plot' was presumably highlighted to try to reduce Sinn Fein support. Most were released in March 1919. A 'fresh counter-insurgency drive' early in 1920 saw increasing arrests and detentions so that by May over 250 'rebel leaders' were interned in England. Detention increased thereafter at a slower rate.[30] Relatively few were held under 14B in Ireland and those on hunger strike in Dublin were released.

Restoration of Order in Ireland Act 1920: Restriction of Movement and Internment

The official ending of the war with Germany saw the demise of DORA and the DORR. From 31 August 1920 the Restoration of Order in Ireland Act 1920 (ROIA) enabled the effective continuance of 14B in terms of threats to 'the restoration or maintenance of order in Ireland' rather than 'public safety or the defence of the Realm'. The powers could also be exercised by the relevant Secretary of State in Great Britain. Mass internment began after the assassination by Collins' IRA 'Squad' of British intelligence officers on Bloody Sunday (21 November 1920).[31] Essentially the Chief Secretary rubber-stamped recommendations by Divisional Commanders. By July 1921 4,554 orders had been made. Some were interned in England, others at camps near Dublin and Belfast. Internment now operated alongside a more draconian regime of military justice

---

[28] Simpson (1994): 19.

[29] Costello (2003): 23–4; McGuffin (1973), 27–8.

[30] Campbell (1994): 104–5.

[31] Hart (2005b): 241–2.

under ROIA and, in certain areas, martial law powers. None of this seems to have impacted significantly on IRA activity in Ireland.[32] Hart estimates that in 1920–21 in Great Britain, well over 200 people were arrested, charged, convicted or interned on IRA-related suspicion.[33] Internees in Ireland were released on conclusion of the Treaty. Action, including internment, continued to be taken in Great Britain under ROIA into 1923 against Irish individuals opposed to the Treaty, in effect being disguised extradition to aid the Government side in the fledgling Free State's civil war.[34]

Northern Ireland 1922–23: Restriction of Movement and Internment under the Civil Authorities (Special Powers) Act 1922 (SPA)

In response to high levels of violence in Northern Ireland between December 1921 and the end of May 1922, the new Northern Ireland Parliament in 1922 enacted the SPA. Political violence in that period produced 236 deaths and 346 persons suffering injuries.[35] There was a spate of sectarian assassinations attributed to the Ulster Protestant Association (UPA).[36] The SPA enabled the Northern Ireland Government to take action and make regulations (SPAR) 'for preserving the peace and maintaining order in Northern Ireland',[37] essentially giving the Executive the same powers as under DORA and ROIA. SPAR 23 (corresponding to DORR 55), gave the police and army extensive powers of arrest without warrant on suspicion of past, present or future prejudicial activity, possession of certain items or an offence against the Regulations, and enabled detention.[38] SPAR 23A (restriction on residence and expulsion from an area) and 23B (restrictions and indefinite internment) conferred powers to deal in one or more of those ways with those 'suspected of acting or having acted or being about to act in a manner prejudicial to the preservation of peace and the maintenance of order in Northern Ireland' corresponding to those in DORR 14 and 14B, discussed above and, with respect to other wartime use, in chapter 2. Restriction orders were used independently from internment or detention.[39] In 1922, persons arrested were split by the police into one of two categories. The first was made up of the organizers and perpetrators of serious crimes and those with the potential to be so. The second category were less important 'rebels' who if admitting membership or opposition to the Crown or the

---

[32] Campbell (1994): 107–8, 111.

[33] Hart (2005a): 168.

[34] Ibid.; Simpson (1994): 30–31.

[35] Donohue (2001): 16.

[36] Campbell (1994): 300.

[37] SPA, s. 1. Campbell (1994): App. 3 shows graphically SPA and SPAR derivation from DORA, ROIA and their regulations.

[38] Initially, from April 1922, 'reasonable grounds' had been required. From 6 July 1922 'suspicion' sufficed (Campbell (1994): 291).

[39] Donohue (2001): 45.

Northern Ireland Government could be released, after fingerprinting and photographing, if they agreed to leave or be deported from Northern Ireland. Apparently most of the Loyalists interned did so, emigrating to Canada and Australia. Other internees were 'exiled' to England or the Irish Free State for two years.[40] Screening for deportation was eventually carried out by a court. Internment orders were made at the behest of the police. By May 1923, 575 people were interned and some 700 in all in the period 1922–24. Less than 20 were loyalists (mainly UPA members),[41] the vast remainder republican/nationalist. They were held in prison (men in Belfast and Londonderry, women in Armagh Female Prison) and on a prison ship, initially in Belfast Lough and later in Larne harbour. Eventually the Larne workhouse and the Malone Reformatory were also used. Their cases were kept under review in response to a changing security situation. Many would later be released on terms or subject to a SPAR 23A or 23B restriction order which imposed 'limits on the geographical area in which the ex-internee could reside or enter, established bail, detailed requirements for reporting place of residence and regularly registering at specific times and dates at the nearest RUC station', and required its subject to carry an identity card and to report an intention to be out between the hours of 11 at night and 5 in the morning.[42] The parallel is striking with the post-9/11 creation and demise of detention without trial and the restrictions embodied in non–derogating control orders under the PTA 2005.[43] Additionally, SPAR 23A orders were used to exclude suspects coming to the North from Great Britain or the Irish Free State or, if allowing entry, to restrict their operation to a small area and monitor them there.[44] The SPA was enacted on the basis of necessity and was seen by the Northern Ireland Government as highly effective in restoring order:

> Republican elements in the midst of the province, aided by sympathetic anti-Treatyists in the South, sought to overturn the constitutional structure of the State. Within months of its enactment, violence plummeted. Rather than repeal the legislation, though, the perceived effectiveness quickly became part of the defence for its continued use.[45]

The Act, as amended, was rendered permanent in 1933. It may be, however, that factors other than the SPA powers also had a role in the decline of violence, not least the bitter civil war in the Free State fully occupying militant nationalists who might otherwise have taken action against the North. Moreover, 'the partisan

---

[40] Campbell (1994): 300.

[41] Ibid.

[42] Donohue (2001): 53.

[43] See chapter 7.

[44] Donohue (2001): 54.

[45] Ibid.: 39.

manner' in which the SPA powers were used 'was the stuff of which future conflicts were made'.[46]

Administrative Challenge

The measures allowed representations against internment or restriction under DORR 14B and its progeny (but not under DORR 14 and its successors) to be made to the authorities for consideration by an advisory committee (AC). Such committees operated in the different jurisdictions in essentially the same manner as those governing alien and 14B internment in Great Britain (see chapter 2), but with rather mixed take-up and effect. There was typically an element of judicial or qualified lawyer involvement as chair and in each case their advice was in no way binding on the authorities. That chaired by Sankey released 69 per cent of those interned in England and Wales after the Rising.[47] That in Ireland after 1918 (initially a judge and two MPs, later entirely judicial in composition) was scarcely used. The advice of the AC under the SPA in Northern Ireland to release was not invariably accepted.[48] Initial use was limited, but in all 488 of the 732 interned resorted to the Committee.[49] Neither Campbell nor Donohue indicate the success rate. Simpson notes the AC in England in 1923 dealing with a number of appeals in respect of the disguised extradition of Irish suspects under the ROIA but indicates nothing on the outcome. Lack of records precludes further analysis.

The Responses Tested in the Courts

Within Ireland, prior to the creation of the Irish Free State, the main questions before the courts were ones relating to courts martial under DORA and ROIA and ones regarding the legal nature and effects of martial law (prerogative or common law necessity). One case produced an Army/judiciary crisis. The cases indicated some room for judicial control.[50] Within Northern Ireland, a challenge might have been mounted to the *vires* of the SPA (the competence of the Northern Ireland Parliament to enact it). The SPA and SPAR provisions essentially drew on DORA and ROIA, provisions arguably for the 'defence of the realm', a matter not within the Northern Ireland Parliament's competence. Moreover, as was argued in *R (O'Hanlon) v Governor of Belfast Prison*,[51] internment under the SPA was equivalent to the suspension of habeas corpus and thus contrary to the terms of the

---

[46] Campbell (1994): 308.

[47] Townshend (2006): 318–319.

[48] Campbell (1994): 299. He cites and expands on the Kafkaesque case of James Mayne (301–7).

[49] Donohue (2001): 50.

[50] Campbell (1994): 136–44.

[51] [1922] 56 ILTR 170.

1920 Act.[52] The court failed to distinguish the position of the Northern Ireland Parliament (subordinate and limited by its constituent Act) from that of the Westminster Parliament (sovereign).[53] Following *R* v *Halliday, ex parte Zadig*[54] (the House of Lords' decision upholding the validity of internment regulations under DORA), the court, ignoring the issue that had been argued, simply found that the SPR were not *ultra vires*. Moreover, ignoring dicta in *ex parte Zadig*, it denied that a court had anything to do with the matter of evidence against the detainee, only with whether he was legally held. *O'Hanlon* thus affords another instance of 'judicial abdication ... marking continuity with the British and Irish emergency law decisions of the previous years'.[55] So too do two of the three cases brought in England.[56] In *R* v *Governor of Wormwood Scrubs Prison*,[57] Foy, a Dublin shop assistant, was held in that London prison under a DORR 14B internment order made five days before the signing of the peace treaty with Germany. Nonetheless, the court held that, legally speaking, the war that supported DORA and the DORR had not yet been brought to an end. Moreover, it was no part of the role of the court to judge whether military necessity had come to an end; whether the emergency still subsisted was a matter for the executive alone to determine. In *ex parte Brady*,[58] the applicant, a member of a Sinn Fein organization, was detained under an ROIR 14B order with a view to returning him to Ireland, then still under full United Kingdom jurisdiction. The Court of Appeal, with one dissent,[59] upheld the lower court's view that the ROIA applied outside Ireland so that detention in England could be regarded as linked to the restoration of order in Ireland.[60] He was removed and interned in Ballykinder.[61] Arrests and detentions in Great Britain continued under ROIA even after the establishment of the Irish Free State in 1922, as part of British Government attempts to aid its Government in its civil war with those nationalists not accepting the Anglo-Irish Treaty. The detentions under ROIR 14B were coupled with administrative instructions identifying Ireland as the place of detention. O'Brien, a Sinn Fein organizer and suspected Irish extremist, challenged his detention. He was unsuccessful in the Divisional Court. But the Court of Appeal upheld his challenge; ROIR 14B had impliedly been repealed by the establishment of the Irish Free State. In addition, the court rejected the view that the Home Secretary could order persons to be detained outside the United

---

[52] Palley (1972): 401.

[53] Campbell (1994): 335.

[54] [1917] AC 000; see chap. 3.

[55] Campbell (1994): 337.

[56] Simpson (1994): 29.

[57] [1920] 2 KB 305, at 310–11 (Earl of Reading CJ).

[58] (1921) 37 TLR 854 and 975.

[59] Scrutton LJ.

[60] *R* v *Inspector of Cannon Row Police Station, ex parte Brady* (1921) 37 TLR 854 and 975.

[61] Simpson (1994): 31 (n. 106).

Kingdom since he had no effective control over what happened to them there. Governmental attempts to challenge the decision in the House of Lords failed.[62] In a reversal of the normal course, O'Brien was immediately re-arrested, brought into the criminal process, later convicted of seditious conspiracy, and jailed until 1924.[63]

The 1939–45 Campaign

The authorities in Northern Ireland, concerned at the bombing of a number of customs posts, introduced internment of nationalist suspects on 22 December 1938. The number of internees steadily increased and, after the outbreak of war with Germany, more were interned because of an announced IRA campaign of sabotage against military installations and war industries. By Mid-October 1942 400 men and a few women were interned without trial. Internment was for the most part in Belfast and Londonderry prisons, but, for a while, in deplorable conditions on an old merchant ship. Release was not authorized until near the end of the War, even though the IRA campaign had petered out by the end of 1942.[64] An advisory committee was again established. There seem to have been no reported court challenges. Security in Northern Ireland and Great Britain was assisted by the Irish Government's internment of IRA suspects in 1940. Neutral Ireland was concerned at the impact the IRA connection with Nazi Germany connection might have.

The IRA campaign also directed significant violent attacks on mainland Great Britain throughout 1939. The IRA declaration of 'war' came in January. The campaign was effectively over by the end of the year. In great part, it was countered through successful use of the criminal process (66 convictions by July, and large quantities of explosives and *materiel* for explosives seized by police).[65] But it also produced a significant legislative reply in the Prevention of Violence (Temporary Provisions) Act 1939 (PVA) with the introduction, as temporary emergency provisions, of a range of executive measures: prohibition orders; expulsion orders; and registration orders.[66] It was on this Act that was based the central governmental response to the PIRA campaign in Great Britain from 1972: the Prevention of Terrorism (Temporary Provisions) Acts 1974–89, the first of which was enacted after the 1970s equivalent of 7/7, the Birmingham pub bombings of 21 November 1974.[67]

---

[62] *R* v *Secretary of State for Home Affairs, ex parte O'Brien* [1923] 2 KB 361; [1923] AC 603.

[63] Simpson (1994): 33.

[64] Donohue (2001): 55–6.

[65] Donohue (2001): 214.

[66] On the creation of the PVA, see Lomas (1980) and Donohue (2001): 208–216.

[67] Bonner (2006): 602–7.

The PVA – itself clearly owing much to SPAR 23A and 23B, examined earlier – made the Irish in Great Britain once more a 'suspect community' because of the violent activities of the IRA, seen by the Government as a 'fascist organization'. The PVA proclaimed itself designed 'to prevent the commission in Great Britain of further acts of violence designed to influence public opinion or Government policy with respect to Irish affairs; and to confer on the Secretary of State extraordinary powers in that behalf', supplementing those under the 'ordinary' law.[68] It was enacted in two days in response to the terms and execution of the IRA 'S' Plan (a photograph of which was in the Home Secretary's hand during his speech on the Second Reading of the Bill). By July 1939 there had been 127 terrorist incidents in Great Britain, just under half in London, the remainder elsewhere, and the Government painted a picture of links with foreign organizations and threats to essential services, transport networks and the fire brigades. Further explosions occurred at the same time as the Parliamentary debates on the Bill. The worst incident in a campaign that had largely targeted property not people came after the 29 July enactment of the PVA. This was a bungled bombing in August in Coventry in which five people died. The bomb-makers, although not the 'planter' of the bomb, were convicted and executed. In the words of an historian internee in the 1970s,

> the campaign was a short-lived disaster which nonetheless cost the lives of seven innocent English civilians, wounded over 100 and resulted in the execution of Barnes and McCormack (Richards) on 7 February 1940, to say nothing of lengthy jail sentences, up to 20 years, for over 100 Irish prisoners (23 men and women got 20 years penal servitude, 34 got 10–20 years, 25 got 5–10, and 14 received less than 5 years).[69]

The PVA enhanced the arrest powers of the police and enabled a longer period of detention without charge than afforded under 'ordinary' law.[70] It also increased their powers of search under a magistrates' or in emergencies a police superintendent's warrant.[71] As British subjects, IRA suspects from Ireland and Northern Ireland were not aliens and thus not subject to exclusion or deportation under the Aliens restriction legislation.[72] But the effect of the PVA was to establish an analogous regime of 'internal exile' to protect Great Britain from its neighbours across the Irish Sea, one of which was ostensibly part of the same United Kingdom. This regime caught those non-resident in Great Britain and those resident there but for less than 20 years.[73] Those not in Great Britain could be

---

[68] Long Title and s. 1(1).

[69] McGuffin (1973): 36.

[70] s. 4.

[71] s. 4(3), (4).

[72] See chapter 4.

[73] See ss. 1(2), (4) for exemptions. Anyone resident in Great Britain throughout his or her life was also exempt.

prohibited from entering it (prohibition order).[74] Those in Great Britain could be expelled from it (expulsion order).[75] An expulsion order could be made where the Home Secretary was reasonably satisfied that the person concerned was engaged in the preparation or instigation of acts of violence designed to influence public opinion or Government policy with respect to Irish affairs, or was knowingly harbouring such a person. A prohibition order could be made where he was so satisfied that the person was or might try to enter Great Britain with a view to becoming so engaged. As a lesser measure, the Home Secretary could order registration with and regular reporting to the police (registration order).[76] Breach of any of the orders was an offence punishable with up to two years' imprisonment.[77]

Those to be expelled were already on a Home Office list. By the end of May 1940, 167 orders had been made, 148 in the first two months of the operation of the PVA (113 expulsion orders, 10 prohibition orders and 25 registration orders).[78] In all, 190 expulsion orders were made, 71 prohibition orders, and 29 registration orders. The PVA was not repealed until 1973. It had ceased to be an active part of the statute book in 1953, and its discontinuance was earlier resisted on the basis that it contributed to the lack of violence connected with Irish affairs. As at 1952, 112 expulsion and 60 prohibition orders remained in force.[79]

Government had considered (and kept the provisions in reserve in case introducing them as amendments would help secure the passage of the Bill) deploying a fuller 'immigration-type' control of port controls, visas and passports to regulate movement between Great Britain and the island of Ireland. It also contemplated 'restriction orders', comparable to those under SPAR 23 and analogous to those now deployed against terrorist suspects under the PTA 2005. Also considered and rejected was internment, although the Government realized it might have to be deployed should one of the destination entities refuse entry to suspects expelled from Great Britain. This never occurred. Indeed the existence of internment in both destination entities contributed to the perceived success in security terms of the PVA. Moreover, the outbreak of war with Nazi Germany brought its own wide-ranging powers of internment and restriction of movement, into which some IRA suspects were swept.[80]

Parliamentary attempts to inject a system of judicial review failed, on the traditional grounds that Government saw these as 'executive' acts. It did accord a right to make representations to the Home Secretary and (unless he thought them frivolous) to have them referred for consideration by one or more advisers.[81] There

---

[74] s. 1(4).
[75] s. 1(2).
[76] s. 1(3).
[77] s. 3(1), (3).
[78] Donohue (2001): 215.
[79] Donohue (2001): 216.
[80] McGuffin (1973): 37.
[81] s. 1(6).

is no reported instance of court challenge and appear to be no files on the use or effectiveness of the adviser process.

'Operation Harvest': the Border Campaign 1956–62

This saw the IRA largely based in the Republic, from where its 'flying columns' mounted attacks on police posts in the Border area and aimed to set up 'liberated areas' in Northern Ireland near the Border. Violence in the Republic itself was sparse, the IRA having taken a decision in 1949 not to use violence against Government forces in the Republic but direct its operations against Northern Ireland and the British 'enemy'.[82] Nor was there a sustained campaign in Great Britain, activity there being confined in the years preceding the launching of the Border campaign to raids on Army depots to try to get arms. Those arrested were dealt with through the criminal process.[83] As in the IRA's 'wartime' campaign, Northern Ireland and the Republic again dealt with the threat to them by means of internment, the former under the SPA, the latter under its Offences Against the State Acts 1939–40. Under the SPA, resort could be had to the standard Advisory Committee. There appear to have been no court challenges. In the Republic, resort to internment was challenged in its courts and upheld. This does not directly concern us. What is highly relevant, however, is the further resort by one internee, Gerard Lawless, to the European Commission of Human Rights with the case eventually going to the Court of Human Rights which, in its first ruling on the right of derogation in Art. 15 ECHR, set out the parameters of legitimate State action and of review of derogation by the ECHR organs.

In *Lawless* v *Ireland*,[84] the Court held that, despite material suggesting Lawless's involvement in IRA armed activity, Art. 17 ECHR (abuse of rights) did not deprive him of his fundamental rights under Art. 5.[85] Detention without trial could not be supported under any of the 'heads' of permissible restriction on liberty and security of person in Art. 5. The phrase in Art. 5(1)(b) 'in order to secure the fulfilment of any obligation prescribed by law' did not embrace detention 'for the prevention of offences against public peace and public order or against the security of the State but for securing the execution of specific obligations imposed by law.'[86] Nor had Lawless been detained 'for non-compliance with the order of a court', the other limb of para. (1)(b).[87] Internment without trial was not supported by the provisions of Art. 5(1)(c) which has to be

---

[82] O'Higgins (1962): 249; Coogan (1988): chap. 12.

[83] Bishop and Mallie (1988): 38–9.

[84] (1961) 1 EHRR 15.

[85] Para. 7.

[86] Para. 9 (opinion of the Commission; the Government did not pursue this justification before the Court).

[87] Para. 12.

read with Art. 5(3) and thus contemplates arrest and detention for the purposes of bringing the suspect into the criminal process of charge and criminal trial.[88] Internment could thus only be justified under the right of derogation in Art. 15 ECHR. The Court defined 'public emergency threatening the life of the nation' as

> ...an exceptional situation of crisis or emergency which affects the whole population and constitutes a threat to the organised life of the community of which the State is composed.[89]

The Court held that the Irish Government had reasonably deduced the existence of such an emergency from three factors in combination: the existence in the Republic of the illegal and unconstitutional IRA using violence to attain its purposes; the IRA using the territory of the Republic to launch attacks over the Border thus seriously jeopardizing the Republic's relationship with the United Kingdom; and a steady and alarming increase in terrorist activities from Autumn 1956 to mid-1957.[90] The imminent danger to the nation was shown by a murderous ambush in Northern Ireland early in July in the period leading up to the commencement of the Loyalist marching season, a season which 'for historical reasons is particularly critical for the preservation of public peace and order'.[91] Internment was a measure strictly required by the exigencies of that situation (what we would now call the 'necessity' and 'proportionality' issues). Lesser measures such as criminal prosecution even in juryless courts were rendered ineffective because of intimidation of witnesses. Sealing the Border to prevent attacks across it would have been a disproportionate restriction on the rights of a wider range of people. The scheme was also subject to adequate safeguards in that a detention commission to which internees could appeal had binding powers as regards release. In addition, release on a solemn oath to renounce IRA activity was also granted. Accordingly, there was no violation of the ECHR.

The Irish government had argued that the Convention organs could not review its decisions unless the Government had acted in bad faith and abused its powers contrary to Art. 18 ECHR. The Court firmly rejected this view.[92] It is for the Court to decide the matter of compliance with the ECHR. But the terminology of its reasoning ('reasonably deduced') makes clear and subsequent cases on Art. 15 ECHR have confirmed, that this 'European supervision' is qualified by the concept of the 'margin of appreciation', according the State in this context a wide leeway in decision-making.[93]

---

[88] Paras 13–15.

[89] Para. 28.

[90] Ibid.

[91] Para. 29.

[92] Para. 22.

[93] Ovey and White (2006): 442.

The campaign – in which there were more than 500 incidents 'and much awful violence inflicted and suffered'[94]– was largely confined to rural areas. It petered out in 1962 into isolated incidents of sniping.[95] In part its failure was due to internment of IRA suspects in both parts of Ireland. Overall, 256 men and one woman were interned in Northern Ireland under SPAR 12 (the replacement for the former 23B).[96] Some 130 were interned in the Republic, but all had been released by mid-March 1959.[97] Perhaps more important, the nationalist population on neither side of the Border had shown any support for it.[98]

Civil Rights to Urban Terrorism/Guerrilla War to Lasting Peace (1969–2007)?

The recent history of the 'Northern Ireland' question is more well–known. Suffice it to say here, that in 1968–69 a valid and peaceful campaign for Civil Rights for Catholics in Northern Ireland met with a violent response from extreme 'loyalists, many of whom were 'off duty' police personnel, who saw in it yet another IRA campaign to change the status of Ulster. It also met opposition from reactionary elements in Northern Ireland government committed to maintaining a gerrymandered Protestant hegemony in local government and a permanent Protestant majority in the Northern Ireland Parliament. This was only overcome by sustained pressure on moderate members in the Northern Ireland Government from the United Kingdom Government as violence ensued. Communal conflict brought British troops to Northern Ireland and saw the emergence of a new nationalist armed force, the Provisional IRA, as well as the 'Official' IRA. Both wings engaged in attacks on army and police. Demonstrations for Civil Rights transmuted into urban and rural guerrilla warfare. Levels of violence against person and property were extremely high. Both IRA 'wings' spread a campaign of violence to Great Britain. Violence in the Province was a 'complex of insurgent guerrilla warfare, sectarian killings and attacks, inter and intra-factional conflicts among paramilitaries in both communities, knee-cappings, punishment shootings and other modes of enforcing discipline, and activity of more traditional criminal provenance (for example, protection rackets).[99] The Government of Northern Ireland and, after the introduction of Direct Rule in 1972, the United Kingdom Government, sought to counter the violence with a security response (most graphically various modalities of internment), coupled with attempts to reconcile divided communities with constitutional schemes of power-sharing with an 'Irish'

---

[94] English (2003):76.

[95] Donohue (2001): 57.

[96] Donohue (2001): 56–7.

[97] Coogan (1988): 404. Lawless was released in December 1957.

[98] English (2003): 76.

[99] Bonner (1985): 96.

dimension, to supplement attempts to win hearts and minds through reforms meeting most of the Civil Rights grievances. From the ending of internment in December 1975, counter-terrorist powers were cast in terms of reliance on a heavily modified criminal process, police primacy (the police rather than the Army taking the lead in law enforcement) and a never wholly achieved 'Ulsterization' (growing reliance on Northern Ireland forces inevitably predominantly Protestant, recruited in Ulster, rather than regular British Army units). The modified criminal process enabled arrest and extended detention without charge, relaxed the rules on admission of confessions, and afforded trial by judge alone of terrorist ('scheduled') offences in so-called 'Diplock' courts. These trials were heavily reliant on confession evidence. As that evidence declined in the wake of greater controls over interrogations, the authorities made use of accomplice ('supergrass') evidence on a large scale. Like his counterparts in Great Britain, the Northern Ireland Secretary had power under the PTAs to exclude terrorist suspects from Northern Ireland, but this was rarely used. The powers to exclude from the United Kingdom as a whole were exercised by the Home Secretary, as were powers to keep undesirable aliens out of the country (used to prohibit the entry of some fundraisers from the United States) or to deport them.[100]

The conflict settled into a stalemate requiring, as in 1921, political moves to break the deadlock. Movement on the part of both Government and Sinn Fein/IRA saw Government talking to 'terrorists'. Movement by Unionists into 'all party' talks produced the Belfast Agreement of 1998 (rejected by the Democratic Unionist Party (DUP)) and a new round of power–sharing devolved Government, since suspended. Monitored IRA decommissioning and developments after the St Andrews' Agreement (13 October 2006) have brought in May 2007 the return of a devolved Northern Ireland Administration and Assembly, with former extremes in polarized Northern Ireland politics – the DUP and Sinn Fein – sitting together in Government, hopefully to turn Northern Ireland's longest period of peace since 1945 into a lasting one.

Northern Ireland: Internment Without Trial 1971–75

The SPA regime (1971–72) Powers of detention and internment were once again invoked by the Northern Ireland Government and implemented in 'Operation Demetrius' early on the morning of 9 August 1971. It was ostensibly resorted to (so Government informed the European Court of Human Rights) because of the inability of the criminal process to restore peace and order. This in part flowed from widespread intimidation of the population such that it was difficult to find witnesses willing to testify in open court and that jury trial was rendered problematic through perverse acquittals. In addition, the land frontier with the Republic enabled ready escape to a 'safe haven'. Government records now available in the National Archives show that it was brought in, with reluctant

---

[100] See chapter 4.

United Kingdom Government approval, against military advice on its necessity, to shore up the Unionist Prime Minister of Northern Ireland, Brian Faulkner, against attacks from his right wing.[101] It was also done as a last attempt to stave off direct rule.[102] Resort to the powers, as we have seen, was perceived as having defeated the last IRA campaign. But it was successful then in security terms because of its parallel deployment in the Republic. In addition that campaign did not have the support of a significant sector of the nationalist community on either side of the Border. Neither of these factors was present in 1971. It was made crystal clear by the British Ambassador to Ireland and by the Irish Premier, Jack Lynch, that internment in Ireland was no longer a political possibility, unless there was an IRA outrage in the South, something the IRA leadership was striving to avoid.[103] Within Northern Ireland, the nationalist community was no longer cowed or quiescent and repeal of the SPA which authorized detention and internment had long been one of the items on the Civil Rights agenda of demands for reform.[104] Resort to internment, although eventually being seen as useful by the Army in its counter-terrorist campaign,[105] proved disastrous. Far from violence falling in its wake, it escalated. For example, bombings jumped from 78 in July to 131 in August and 196 in September.[106] The number of deaths, 30 prior to August, soared to 174 by the end of the year.[107] The invocation of the powers, their muddled and discriminatory execution (only nationalists were initially swept up), and the increasingly well-documented ill-treatment of many of those detained, set the seal on the estrangement of the Catholic (nationalist) community from the Stormont regime. This manifested itself in peaceful demonstrations on both sides of the

---

[101]   See CAB 134/3012 TNA (the Official Committee on Northern Ireland thought on 15 March 1971 that it would not help the military position). The Army Operational instructions 3/71 for 'Operation Demetrius' found in WO 296/71 TNA refer explicitly to the operation as 'reassurance of the majority community' in a context in which 'the political nerve of the [Northern Ireland Government] is limited and that of its supporters even more so' (para. 1(b)(3)). In PREM 15/478 TNA a note of a Downing Street Meeting on 5 August 1971 with the Northern Ireland Prime Minister records Prime Minster Heath refusing to allow a statement that internment had been undertaken on the advice of the security forces. Only one indicating that it had been introduced taking account of the views of the security forces, could be issued. See also CAB 128/49/40 TNA (Cabinet Conclusions, Confidential Annex, 22 July 1971) and CJ 4/56 TNA (telegram 5 August 1971 from United Kingdom Government representative in Belfast to Permanent Secretary at Home Office).

[102]   FCO 33/1465 (note of meeting of Ministers and the Northern Ireland PM, 5 August 1971).

[103]   See CAB 134/3012 (Paper NIO (71) 8); CAB 128/48 (CM 197146th Conclusions Min 3); CAB 128/49/45 (Minute 3 and Confidential Annex); CAB 128/49/46 (Minute 3 and Confidential Annex); PREM 15/478 (Ambassador telegram 30 July 1971) (all TNA).

[104]   Boyle, Hadden and Hillyard (1975): 56–7.

[105]   CJ 4/57 TNA (briefing for Prime Minister 20 September 1971, para. 8).

[106]   Donohue (2001): 62.

[107]   Donohue (2001): 118.

Border. Within Northern Ireland it saw severe public disorder in which both Catholics and Protestants were in some areas driven from their homes by the 'opposing' community; and there was a civil disobedience campaign with refusal to pay rent or rates or fill in government forms. The withdrawal of moderate nationalist politicians from the Northern Ireland Parliament was paralleled by 'token' hunger strikes by nationalist MPS outside Downing Street and by riots and hunger strikes in the main internment camp, Long Kesh. The treatment of internees was raised by nationalist representatives with the UN Secretary General. The Irish Government established 'refugee' camps along its side of the Border to deal with Catholics displaced by the severe disorder. Internment and accompanying ill-treatment saw the Irish Government lodging with the European Commission on Human Rights a petition alleging breach of Articles 3 (freedom from torture), 5 (liberty and security of person) and 14 (discrimination) ECHR. Estrangement from the regime and violence further intensified in the wake of the shooting dead by soldiers of the Parachute Regiment of 13 unarmed demonstrators at an illegal demonstration in Derry on 30 January 1972 ('Bloody Sunday') and the Irish Government added to its petition a complaint under Art 2 ECHR (right to life).

Direct rule from Westminster was introduced in March 1972. Thereafter the Government sought ways to deal with the security problem other than through internment, and at the same time tried to find a constitutional compromise to reconcile two communities with radically different agendas on the status of Northern Ireland. The Government undertook its own review of the SPA and of internment orders made. In addition, the Diplock Commission was set up to find ways other than by internment whereby terrorists could be brought to justice. It recommended major changes to the criminal process. It was critical of the implementation of internment since August 1971 as founded on poor intelligence.[108] Nonetheless it thought some form of executive detention without trial on a limited basis would continue to be necessary to deal with

> ...dangerous terrorists against whom it will not be possible to obtain convictions by any form of criminal trial which we regard as appropriate to a court of law ... so long as these remain at liberty to operate in Northern Ireland, it will not be possible to find witnesses prepared to testify against them in the criminal courts ... the only hope of restoring the efficiency of criminal courts of law in Northern Ireland to deal with terrorist crimes is by using an extra-judicial process to deprive [terrorists] of their ability to operate in Northern Ireland, the only way of dong this is to put them in detention by an executive act and to keep them confined, until they can be released without danger to the public safety and to the administration of criminal justice.[109]

There is evidence that successive United Kingdom Governments used internees as political 'hostages', tailoring detentions or releases according to which community

---

[108] Diplock (1972): para. 32.
[109] Diplock (1972): para. 27 (chap. 4).

it needed at the time politically to assuage in seeking its reconciliatory constitutional settlement.[110]

> Internment and detention was never administered simply as a regime of preventive restraint, though this was one of its objects. It served as a good that could be given to the SDLP [the constitutional nationalist party] or to the Loyalists for their support or during Mr Rees' phased releases, a good to be withheld until the P.I.R.A. declared and kept its ceasefire.[111]

It also operated differentially between Republican and loyalist 'terrorist' suspects, with Loyalists interned only belatedly and their numbers never reaching a tenth of their Republican counterparts.[112] Some, including the Irish government in its ECHR application, saw this as clear discrimination. In part it reflected lack of police intelligence on Loyalist groups. An element of pro-Loyalist bias may have existed in the predominantly Protestant police force. There was no real political pressure from either side of the sectarian divide to intern Loyalists.[113] It might also have been a result of the Army policing nationalist areas with its 'military security' approach leading to internment, while the police in loyalist areas operated more of a 'criminal prosecution' approach.[114] There was growing recognition that internment (which could only ever be effective in the very short term) was in fact the best recruiting sergeant PIRA had.[115] It was gradually phased out by the Labour Government from October 1974, ending completely (although remaining on the statute book until the late 1990s) in December 1975.

The initial legal base for arrest, detention and internment was the SPA and SPAR, regulations 10, 11 and 12, which replaced in much the same terms the powers used in 1922–23 (then SPAR 23, 23A and 23B), themselves derived from the DORR and the ROIR. The system envisaged arrest for purposes of interrogation under SPAR 10 by police or army for up to 48 hours, then arrest (for up to 72 hours) and/or a detention order under SPAR 11 in practice for up to 28 days, followed in suitable cases by an internment order (internment without trial for an indefinite period) under SPAR 12. The provisions permitted detention followed by internment of persons suspected of acting, having acted or being about to act in a manner prejudicial to the preservation of peace or the maintenance of order. Arrest under SPAR 10 was for the purpose of ascertaining if the person ought to be detained under a SPAR 11 detention order. Detention orders under SPAR 11 and internment orders under SPAR 12 (which could also impose lesser

---

[110]   Spjut (1986): 731–5; McGuffin (1973): 136.

[111]   Spjut (1986): 738 (an article based on then published records and his interview with Viscount Whitelaw and Mr Rees, each former Northern Ireland Secretaries of State operating internment).

[112]   Donohue (2001): 62–3; Spjut (1986): 735.

[113]   Spjut (1986): 736–8.

[114]   Boyle, Hadden and Hillyard (1975): 75, chap. 4.

[115]   SACHR (1976–77): para. 22.

restrictions) were made by the Civil Authority, that is, the Minister of Home Affairs for Northern Ireland (in this case a post held also by Prime Minister Faulkner) on the recommendation of a senior police officer. The decision was said to be a personal one for the Minister.[116] 'Operation Demetrius' saw 342 persons arrested, although 116 were released within two days. The trawl was said to have taken in 50 officers and 107 volunteers from PIRA and, from the 'Official' IRA, 33 officers and 37 volunteers.[117] But it also took in some from the Northern Ireland Civil Rights Association and People's Democracy, neither connected with the IRA.[118] By the end of August 260 detention orders had been made and 18 persons released. In September 72 detention orders were made and 22 released, while in October the figures were 101 and 7. At the end of October 377 people were held without trial (96 under detention orders and 281 under internment orders).[119] Under SPAR 12 796 orders were made, all before the introduction of direct rule. All were to be reviewed by the Northern Ireland Secretary of State with a view to release of those in the 'low risk' security category (said to be 25 per cent of internees).[120] Nearly 170 orders were still in force on 7 November 1972 when SPAR 12 was revoked by the Detention of Terrorists Order (DTO), a regime later embodied in the Northern Ireland (Emergency Provisions) Act 1973 (NIEPA).[121]

The Detention of Terrorists Order and NIEPA The DTO sought to present internment without trial with a better face, by renaming it 'detention'. Existing detention and internment orders were converted into 'interim custody orders' (ICOs). The DTO authorized the Northern Ireland Secretary of State to make an ICO in respect of a terrorist suspect where necessary for the protection of the public.[122] An ICO was based on a number of intelligence 'traces' (for example, material from an informer plus other more circumstantial 'traces'). The initiative could come from the police, the Army via the police or direct from the Army.[123] An ICO enabled detention for 28 days unless, as invariably happened, the detainee's case was referred by the Chief Constable for decision to a Commissioner. Detention continued (generally for a six-month period) pending the Commissioner's determination. If authorized by him detention would continue indefinitely, subject to appeal to the Appeal Tribunal. NIEPA re-enacted, in

---

[116] *Ireland* v *United Kingdom* (1979–80) 2 EHRR 25, paras. 82–4; CAB 133/409, Doc NIPMV (71), TNA, Record of a Discussion with the Prime Minster of Northern Ireland at 10 Downing Street, 7 October 1971.
[117] CJ 4/56 TNA (telegram No. 35, 14 August 1971).
[118] CJ 4/57 TNA (brief for Prime Minister 20 September 1971).
[119] Donohue (2001): 62.
[120] CJ 4/169 TNA (notes of meetings at Stormont Castle, 4 April 1972 and at Home Office, 11 February 1972).
[121] (1979–80) 2 EHRR 25, para. 84. Para. 83 refers only to 120.
[122] DTO, art. 3.
[123] Boyle, Hadden and Hillyard (1975): 62–6.

substance, the powers contained in the DTO, retaining its definition of terrorism ('the use of violence for political ends'). Powers to make ICOs and detention orders, and the review thereof by a commissioner and the appeal tribunal, continued as before apart from some changes to the time at which information was supplied to detainees and the installation of a mandatory periodic review procedure. From 21 August 1975, the Northern Ireland (Emergency Provisions) Amendment Act 1975 reverted to the principle of detention by order of the Secretary of State, rather than of a commissioner, such order to be preceded by a report from a legally qualified Adviser. It was only ever used to effect the release of detainees.

According to material filed with the European Court of Human Rights, in the period November 1972 to 1 February 1973 there were 166 ICOs (under the DTO). The Commissioner converted 128 ICOs to detention orders and 94 persons were released. On 5 December 1975, the Northern Ireland Secretary of State ordered the release from emergency powers' detention of the remaining 75 detainees under the emergency legislation. Some remained in custody on criminal charges or serving sentences of imprisonment because of criminal conviction.[124]

Administrative challenge to internment and detention The SPA system deployed the standard mechanism of the Advisory Committee. Those under DTO and NIEPA were more sophisticated (as befitted a scheme trying to change public perception of the process from internment under executive diktat to one of necessary preventive 'deprivation of liberty resulting from an extra-judicial process').[125] They embodied review of the Northern Ireland Secretary of State's ICO by a quasi-judicial process of Commissioner and Appeal Tribunal. The system under the 1975 Amendment Act reverted, on the recommendation of the Gardiner Committee, to the advisory body mechanism, but was never operated to order detention.

The Advisory Committee under SPAR was composed of a judge and two laymen.[126] The European Court of Human Rights summarized its nature and processes:

> Every order had to provide for the consideration by an advisory committee of representations made by the individual. In fact it reviewed the position of all internees whether they made representations or not. The committee ... could recommend, but not order, release. The individual had no right in law to appear or be legally represented before the committee, to test the grounds for internment, to examine witnesses against him or to call his own witnesses. In fact, he was allowed to appear and be interviewed and every effort was made to trace witnesses he proposed. The committee required the security forces to produce the information in their possession but statements of evidence against the internee so obtained remained anonymous, apparently to avoid retaliation.

---

[124] (1979–80) 2 EHRR 25, paras 89, 91.

[125] Donohue (2001): 132.

[126] Judge Brown, Mr Berkeley and Mr Dalton: see CAB 133/409 TNA.

According to the [European] Commission [of Human Rights], the committee probably relied on evidence not admissible in a court of law.[127]

By 30 March 1972, the committee had reviewed 588 of the 796 cases but 451 internees refused to appear. The AC recommended release in 69 cases. The practice was to accept the AC recommendation, so long as the internee gave an undertaking as to future good behaviour. Six refused and were not released. In September 1971, the United Kingdom Government rejected the Irish Premier's suggestion of making the AC's decisions binding,[128] but the stance changed after Direct Rule.

The DTO and NIEPA allowed release to be ordered, either by the quasi-judicial commissioner, after a process involving quite sophisticated adversary techniques involving the provision for the detainee of State-financed legal representation, or by the Appeal Tribunal (to which the detainee had an automatic right of appeal) empowered to review a commissioner's decision to detain. The Secretary of State could release detainees with or without conditions and recall to detention an individual conditionally released by him. Under the DTO he could also at any time ask a commissioner to review a detention order; in which event release was obligatory unless the commissioner considered continued detention necessary for public protection. NIEPA required in addition a first review by a commissioner of detention orders after one year and thereafter every six months.

Both commissioners and Appeal Tribunal members were appointed by the Northern Ireland Secretary of State. They had to have experience of judicial office or at least 10 years' experience as a barrister, advocate or solicitor. Some commissioners were judges or former judges of various types (for example, a circuit judge from England, a judge (Sheriff) from Scotland, and one from Nigeria). The Appeal Tribunal was chaired by a former English Court of Appeal judge, and, as well as reviewing the decision made by the commissioner, could also consider new material which had come to light since. Detainees had to be furnished with details of the case against them, insofar as consonant with security, in good time before the commissioner's hearing (three days under DTO, seven under NIEPA). Proceedings were in private and, to protect security and sources from reprisals, operated in terms of dealing with some 'sensitive' material in sessions from which detainees and their lawyers were excluded. This can be seen as a forerunner of the 'open' and 'closed' session processes deployed in national security immigration, citizenship and detention cases by the Special Immigration Appeals Commission (SIAC) and by the High Court in control order proceedings

---

[127] (1979–80) 2 EHRR 25, para. 87. See also McGuffin (1973): chap. 13. His claim on p. 133 that the AC's advice was invariably ignored and that 90 per cent of internees refused to have anything to do with it is contradicted by the statistics accepted by the European Court of Human Rights and by Boyle, Hadden and Hillyard (1975): 58.

[128] PREM 15/480 TNA (record of discussion with Irish Premier at Chequers, 27 September 1971, p. 13).

under the PTA 2005. The key difference, however, is the lack in commissioner proceedings of any Special Advocate. Any probing of the material on the individual's behalf had to be done, if at all, by the commissioner unaided, and doubts have been expressed as to whether this was undertaken.[129] They were by no means, however, 'rubber-stamps'.[130] Donohue encapsulates the commissioner process thus:

> The DTO required that the commissioner hear evidence to determine whether the interim custody order should be sustained. This hearing substantially departed from the ordinary judicial process – the session was to be held in private, with normal rules of evidence waived. On the basis of both public and private information – unavailable to either the detained individual or his solicitor – the commissioner could issue an indefinite detention order.[131]

In addition, it appears that the identity of sources would not even be disclosed to the commissioner.[132] Detainees had to be informed, as far as possible, of matters dealt with in their absence for security reasons but had no right to test evidence given at that time. Indeed, there was no legal right to cross-examination at any time in the proceedings, but in practice it was allowed in respect of 'open' session witnesses.[133]

Despite obvious flaws in 'fair hearing' terms (comparable to those considered in chapter 9 in respect of SIAC and High Court control order proceedings), the DTO and NIEPA processes could have positive outcomes for the detainee. In the period November 1972 to 5 September 1973: the commissioners reviewed 579 cases. These involved 296 ICOs made under the DTO or NIEPA, and 165 former internments and 118 former detentions under SPAR. The commissioners made 453 detention orders and ordered release in the remaining 126 cases. The Appeal Tribunal was seised of 44 appeals in the period November 1972 to 3 October 1973. Thirty four had been heard and 25 releases directed.[134] Lord Gardiner, however, concluded that, well-intentioned as the DTO and NIEPA arrangements were, the procedures were unsatisfactory if considered as judicial since security needs reduced adversarial trial to impotence. Heavy reliance on hearsay evidence, the use of screens and voice scramblers to protect the identity of witnesses and 'closed' sessions were totally at odds with common law adversarial procedures. Their apparent similarity to such processes had brought into disrepute the ordinary processes of the administration of justice in Northern Ireland.[135]

---

[129] Boyle, Hadden and Hillyard (1975): 67–9.
[130] Boyle, Hadden and Hillyard (1975): 70.
[131] Donohue (2001): 133.
[132] Ibid., citing Lord Diplock, HL Debs, Vol. 337, col. 442 (7 December 1972).
[133] (1979–80) 2 EHRR 25, para. 87.
[134] (1979–80) 2 EHRR 25, para. 89.
[135] Gardiner (1975): paras 152–4.

National court challenges to internment and detention These focused only on the SPA regime. *Re McElduff* held that arrest under SPAR was invalid where insufficient reasons were given, as there where the arrestor merely stated that the arrest was effected under the SPA and he was not required to supply further information.[136] In a scenario reminiscent of that in *ex parte Budd (No.1)* during the Second World War,[137] invalidity on this ground merely produced re-arrest as McElduff left the court, with more extensive reasons being given. An unsuccessful earlier attempt had been made to seek habeas corpus from the High Court in London so as to obviate re-arrest (the SPA not applying outside Northern Ireland).[138]

As regards internment, however, the standard deferential approach of the wartime cases and of the 1922 SPA challenge in *O'Hanlon*, was again prominent. In *Kelly* v *Faulkner*, Kelly was an internee arrested even though he was not on the arresting officer's list (the officers had come to arrest his brother who was not in the house).[139] The court accepted as bona fide the officer's statement that Kelly was arrested because the officer had recalled other information linking Kelly with the IRA.[140] Kelly challenged the order on the bases of no evidence and lack of good faith on the part of the Minister for Home Affairs. Gibson J (murdered with his wife by the IRA in the late 1980s) cited the House of Lords in *Liversidge* v *Anderson*, the low point of judicial review during the Second Word War. He then stated, deploying the standard presumption in favour of the legality of executive action in this sphere:

> It is not open to the court to inquire into the reasonableness of the belief or decision of a Minister of the Crown when making such an order. Whether it is expedient to make an order is a political decision into which the courts will not enquire and if a Minister says he suspects any person of any activity then failing evidence either of bad faith or that the conclusion could not reasonably be related to the circumstances of the case, the sufficiency of the statement must be taken as concluded. Here the plaintiff in his statement of claim denied the various elements requisite to the making of a valid order, no evidence has been led to support these averments. In the absence, therefore, of evidence specifically raising an issue of bad faith, or that the state of mind of the Minister which induced the order depended upon the application of incompetent standards or the admission of irrelevant consideration the averments on its face or

---

[136] [1972] NILR 1, 14–5.

[137] Noted in *R* v *Home Secretary, ex parte Budd* [1942] 2 KB 14, 22–3.

[138] *Re Keenan* [1972] NILR 118n (Ackner J); [1971] 3 WLR 844 (Court of Appeal).

[139] [1973] NILR 31.

[140] Army instructions for 'Operation Demetrius' (now in WO 296/71 TNA) made clear that if the military arresting party was unable to identify suspects, all males of 18 and above at the selected address were to be arrested, leaving the RUC Special Branch to sort the matter out later and release those inappropriately detained. In addition, those reacting violently and any suspected subversive extremists encountered in the operation should also be arrested (Instruction 3/71, paras 3(3) and co-ordinating instruction (m) pp. 7–8).

otherwise requisite for its efficacy are to be taken as established without any further evidence.

This would enable review in cases where the challenger was manifestly not the person named in the order. It could in principle also encompass cases of politico-religious discrimination or the use of internment to silence critics of internment who were not themselves security threats. But without the material on which the Secretary of State had acted, material of which the court would not compel production, how in the real world could the challenger meet the necessary standard of proof of these defects?

Re McElduff showed judicial keenness that the executive comply with non-substantive limits. In *ex parte Mackay*, the court further held that an internee was entitled to be told the information on which the order was based, but immediately qualified that by also holding that the Secretary of State could withhold such of the information disclosure of which would in his opinion endanger the security forces or public safety.[141]

Challenging internment and detention under the ECHR The European Court of Human Rights' decision in *Ireland* v *United Kingdom*[142] is most famous for its rejection of the Commission's opinion that 'interrogation in depth' of 14 SPA detainees constituted torture. The Court instead characterized it as 'inhuman and degrading treatment', nonetheless a breach by the United Kingdom of the non-derogable Art. 3 ECHR. Like the Commission, however, the Court also held that internment and detention without trial under the SPA, DTO and NIEPA did not breach Art. 5 ECHR, the incompatibility being saved by Art. 15 ECHR: measures strictly required by the exigencies of a public emergency threatening the life of the nation. The Irish Government did not contest that such an emergency existed. Given the low level of violence accepted in *Lawless* as the base for such an emergency, any such challenge would have failed. Moreover, Ireland was hardly likely to want to push the Court into developing a more restrictive principle on 'public emergency' which would hinder any Irish Government which wished in the future to invoke internment under the terms of the Offences Against the State Acts (OASA). The Court, applying the margin of appreciation qualifying its European supervision, and the *Lawless* definition, found 'perfectly clear' the existence of such an emergency in Northern Ireland.[143] It stated that

> It falls in the first place to each Contracting State, with its responsibility for 'the life of [its] nation', to determine whether that life is threatened by a 'public emergency'and, if so, how far it is necessary to go in attempting to overcome the emergency. By reason of

---

[141] (1972) 23 NILQ 331. *Cf. R* v *Secretary of State for Home Affairs, ex parte Hosenball* [1977] 1 WLR 766, at 781, 783 (Lord Denning MR), discussed in chapter 4.

[142] (1979–80) 2 EHRR 25.

[143] (1979–80) 2 EHRR 25, para. 205.

their direct and continuous contact with the pressing needs of the moment, the national authorities are in principle in a better position than the international judge to decide both on the presence of such an emergency and on the nature and scope of derogations necessary to avert it. In this matter, Article 15 (1) leaves those authorities a wide margin of appreciation.[144]

Internment, as such, could be said to be required by the exigencies of that situation, the Court, in limited reasoning, accepting that it had here a limited role:

> It is certainly not the Court's function to substitute for the British Government's assessment any other assessment of what might be the most prudent or most expedient policy to combat terrorism. The Court must do no more than review the lawfulness, under the Convention, of the measures adopted by that Government from 9 August 1971 onwards. For this purpose the Court must arrive at its decision in the light, not of a purely retrospective examination of the efficacy of those measures, but of the conditions and circumstances reigning when they were originally taken and subsequently applied. Adopting, as it must, this approach, the Court accepts that the limits of the margin of appreciation left to the Contracting States by Article 15 (1) were not overstepped by the United Kingdom when it formed the opinion that extrajudicial deprivation of liberty was necessary from August 1971 to March 1975.[145]

Where the Court can most validly be criticized is on the matter of safeguards. In *Lawless*, it seemed crucial to the outcome of the case that the Detention Commission had a power of binding decision on detention; it could order release. The AC under the SPA did not. Here the Court accorded too much weight to the margin of appreciation and failed to set down meaningful human rights standards for States to follow. It simply declared that

> An overall examination of the legislation and practice at issue reveals that they evolved in the direction of increasing respect for individual liberty. The incorporation right from the start of more satisfactory judicial, or at least administrative, guarantees would certainly have been desirable, especially as regulations 10 to 12 dated back to 1956–1957 and were made under an Act of 1922, but it would be unrealistic to isolate the first from the later phases. When a State is struggling against a public emergency threatening the life of the nation, it would be rendered defenceless if it were required to accomplish everything at once, to furnish from the outset each of its chosen means of action with each of the safeguards reconcilable with the priority requirements for the proper functioning of the authorities and for restoring peace within the community. The interpretation of Article 15 must leave a place for progressive adaptations.

This seems to say that the United Kingdom needed to take very little notice of what had happened in *Lawless*. The stance indicates, however, a judicial reluctance to become too involved in the 'national security' sphere and seems comparable to the

---

[144] (1979–80) 2 EHRR 25, para. 207.
[145] (1979–80) 2 EHRR 25, para. 214.

deferential approach adopted by the national courts. A degree of judicial caution was inevitable at that stage of the ECHR development in relation to action by a generally-conforming Government faced with the most serious public order threat seen in Europe since the ECHR's conception. On the safeguards issue, however, the Court was so over-cautious as to abdicate its function. Fortunately, just as the Court has indicated with respect to Art. 3 ECHR that standards have become stricter with time,[146] so it seems inconceivable that it would now hold that a mere power of recommendation for release would suffice as a sufficient safeguard.

The Court, bearing in mind the margin of appreciation, also rejected claims of politico-religious discrimination contrary to Art. 14. The Government was entitled to target the main threat (IRA) first and, when considering internment of Loyalists, to deploy a criminal prosecution approach where possible, something easier to do with police able to operate in Loyalist areas.[147]

Protecting Great Britain from Terrorist Violence: Exclusion Orders under the Prevention of Terrorism Legislation: 1974–98

The Powers and their use The Prevention of Terrorism (Temporary Provisions) Act 1974 (PTA 1974) was enacted within 180 hours of that decade's equivalent of 7/7: the Birmingham pub bombings of 21 November 1974 when two bombs in city centre pubs killed 21 and injured 162, many severely.[148] The horror and tragedy of that night presented, in the then Labour Government Home Secretary's words, 'a different order of casualties from anything we previously had known'.[149] The legislation was the product of careful Home Office contingency plans much discussed during the previous Conservative Administration and very much built on the PVA 1939. Indeed the title of that Administration's draft Bill, adapted by the Labour Home Secretary and his officials, used the same short title, other than the year. The PTA 1974 was replaced by another of the same name and purport in 1976. In 1984, the legislation was re-enacted but extended in some respects also to international terrorism, a pattern repeated on re-enactment with additions in 1989. Three of the central features of that initial Act and subsequent legislation have been carried through into the Terrorism Act 2000 (TA 2000), the initial blueprint for a 'modified criminal prosecution' approach to problems posed by international terrorism: arrest and extended detention without charge; travel controls at ports and airports for international and domestic journeys by air or sea; and proscription of terrorist organizations, then confined to the IRA, now extending to a much wider variety of groups.[150] Proscription in 1974 was principally then for show, but since 1989 has been much more a mode of bringing groups within a wide range of

---

[146] *Selmouni* v *France* (2000) 29 EHRR 403, para. 101.

[147] (1979–80) 2 EHRR 25, paras 229–31.

[148] Mullin (1987): chap. 1.

[149] Jenkins (1991): 393.

[150] TA 2000, Sch. 2, as amended.

offences dealing with political, financial and material support for terrorism, and far-reaching investigative and asset seizing powers to cripple that financial and material support. The main feature of the PTA 1974 relevant for this chapter, however, is its rolling up into one order (an exclusion order) what had been found in two forms of order in the PVA 1939: prohibition and expulsion orders.

The exclusion order power could be exercised so as to prevent acts of terrorism, wherever committed, designed to influence public opinion or Government policy with respect to Northern Ireland affairs. As the Home Secretary's memorandum informed the Cabinet considering the Bill only days after the bombings, it was designed to

> ... enable preventive action to be taken against people who appear to the Secretary of State to be involved with terrorism (i.e. concerned in the commission, preparation or instigation of acts of terrorism) but against whom it is not possible to bring charges under the present law. Orders can be made both to prevent plotters from coming here and to expel them when found here, but it is not expected that they will be made in large numbers.[151]

As will be seen, the latter prediction proved incorrect.

The aim was clearly to protect Great Britain from violent fallout from Northern Ireland, to protect the rest of the United Kingdom 'body' from 'gangrene in one limb'.[152] Thus, the PTA 1974 enabled the Home Secretary to exclude a person from being in or entering Great Britain (to cover British citizen terrorist suspects connected with Northern Ireland) or the United Kingdom (principally to cover Irish citizens). A comparable power for the Northern Ireland Secretary to exclude someone from Northern Ireland only came in 1976, and it is on the scheme as thus extended that treatment here focuses. No order could be made excluding a British citizen from the United Kingdom. Nor could such a citizen be excluded from Great Britain and from Northern Ireland at the same time. British citizens resident in the part of the United Kingdom (Great Britain or Northern Ireland, as the case may be) from which it was proposed to exclude them throughout their lives or a 20-year period (reduced to five years from 1984) could not be excluded. As regards British citizens, exclusion was 'an executive power to condemn a citizen ... to what has been known in other parts of the world as internal exile or banishment'.[153]There was no exemption from exclusion for Irish citizens of long–standing residence in the United Kingdom or either part of it. But that was exactly the point; the power to exclude from the United Kingdom was to enable action against Irish citizen terrorist suspects falling (because of residence) within exemption from deportation under the immigration legislation. The powers were deliberately phrased in the

---

[151] CAB 129/180/14, TNA, para. 5, p. 2.

[152] Jenkins (1991): 396.

[153] *R* v *Secretary of State for the Home Department, ex parte McQillan* [1995] 4 All ER 400 (Sedley J).

broad, subjective language likely to attract only limited judicial review and attempts to inject proper appeal procedures invariably failed. Each scheme only afforded an opportunity to make representations to the Home Secretary and a right to have them referred to an adviser with whom the excludee could have a personal interview. An exclusion order could be made where the Secretary of State was satisfied that its subject was concerned in the commission, preparation or instigation of acts of terrorism or was or might attempt to enter the relevant territory (United Kingdom, Great Britain or Northern Ireland as the case may be) with a view to being so concerned.

Until their withdrawal from force in 1998, the powers were used quite extensively, almost exclusively by the Home Secretary, to return Republican terrorist suspects to Northern Ireland or the Republic. Around 400 orders were made overall, about an eighth returning persons to the Republic. The Northern Ireland Secretary made less than 40 orders, a few to keep out of Northern Ireland 'Loyalist' sympathizers from Scotland suspected of involvement in arms supply to Loyalist paramilitaries, the remainder to exclude persons from the United Kingdom. The peak of use of exclusion orders was in the 1970s and early 1980s. Orders originally were for an indefinite period. From 1984 a welcome reform gave them a three-year life but they could be (and often were) renewed. Exclusion to Northern Ireland in particular could be said to have an impact on an excludee and his family, markedly akin to that of imprisonment or internment, with greater impact on those of long-standing residence (but falling short of 20 years) in Great Britain. It could involve loss of employment; marked problems of accommodation; separation from friends and loved ones or, at least heightened pressures on family life; and transfer to a potentially hostile, if not lethal environment, marked with the stigma of 'involvement in terrorism'.[154] This last point was made graphically clear in the case of McQuillan who experienced three assassination attempts, one by a violent breakaway faction from the paramilitary group to which his legal political party (IRSP) was linked, two from Loyalist paramilitaries acting in their role as 'pro-state' (although not 'proxy') terrorists.[155] Moving to the Irish Republic would not necessarily improve things (both 'hostile' groups operated there) and settlement elsewhere was rendered less viable given that the order tainted him as a terrorist suspect.

The less drastic option of 'residence' orders was rejected by the contingency planners; they had been little used under the PVA 1939. The option of internment in Great Britain was considered by the Conservatives administration in 1973 but rejected as inappropriate.

Administrative challenge The usual right of recourse to an advisory system was afforded, in this case, as in 1939, to a single adviser. It was never taken up on a large scale. Initially one had to remain detained pending exclusion to gain an

---

[154]   Bonner (1985): 199.
[155]   [1995] 4 All ER 400.

interview with the adviser. From 1984 arrangements were made for it to be conducted after a consensual removal. This may have been a step to ensure that detention pending exclusion was less likely to be challenged under the ECHR as a deprivation of liberty not justified by Art. 5 ECHR. The adviser was not a simple 'rubber-stamp'. A one third success rate on a small take-up was noted.

Exclusion orders in the courts A number of cases were brought unsuccessfully in English courts, three bringing in the added dimension of rights of free movement under European Community law.[156] Challenges under the ECHR in respect of family life (Art. 8 ECHR) invariably were ruled inadmissible by the European Commission of Human Rights.[157] Despite concerns expressed by advisers in the Foreign Office, no challenges were made under Art. 3 or 5 ECHR.[158] The English court cases, as regards national law, all held that the Home Secretary's order merely reciting the statutory powers and that the excluded fell within them was effectively unchallengeable since national security interests precluded getting at the material supporting the making of the order. In *McQuillan*, however, Sedley did so reluctantly because constrained by established case authority binding on him. Otherwise he might have distinguished between 'high' national security matters (unreviewable) and matters here claimed as national security but which he regarded as more comparable to standard public interest immunity claims in respect of protection of police informants.[159] The extent to which orders might contravene EC law as regards substance (were restrictions protected by EC law exemptions – public order, public security?) remained unresolved. The Court of Appeal in *Adams* referred them to the ECJ but withdrew the reference when the exclusion orders against the leaders of Sinn Fein were revoked by the Home Secretary as part of ongoing 'peace' talks'. The questions referred in *Gallagher* were procedural ones connected with the review process. The ECJ ruling indicated the need for rights of appeal to an independent authority to enable proper examination of the circumstances of the case. It may be that the adviser process would now fall short. But exclusion as a power was dropped from March 1998.

---

[156] *R* v *Secretary of State for the Home Office, ex parte Stitt* (1987) *The Times* 3 February 1987; *R* v *Secretary of State for the Home Department, ex parte O'Neill* (13 February 1993, unreported); *R* v *Secretary of State for the Home Department, ex parte Adams* [1995] All ER (EC) 177; *R* v *Secretary of State for the Home Department, ex parte Gallagher* (1994) *The Times*, 16 February; *R* v *Secretary of State for the Home Department, ex parte McQillan* [1995] 4 All ER 400.

[157] Walker (1992): 96–7.

[158] Bonner (2006): 620–621.

[159] [1995] 4 All ER 400.

Chapter 4

Undesirable 'Aliens': Immigration Control and Deportation

Introduction and Overview

This chapter examines the security controls exercised through immigration law on undesirable 'aliens' (foreigners, non-citizens) in terms of refusing admission to the United Kingdom, restrictions on them if admitted, and the deportation of those who, in security terms, prove themselves 'undesirable', either as suspected spies for a foreign power, saboteurs, subversive agitators or terrorists. Internment of enemy aliens and sympathizers in wartime has been examined in chapter 2. In this chapter, it is shown that detention for purposes of deportation can, in some situations, effectively become detention without trial where for practical reasons the State cannot secure the deportation of a suspect 'alien' to a State that will receive him, as was the case in the Gulf War 1991 with the detention pending deportation from the United Kingdom of persons thought connected to the Palestinian Liberation Organization (PLO) allied with Saddam's Iraq. The chapter examines the position in immigration law up to 9/11. Use of these powers, however, is a central feature of the Government's post-9/11 counter-terrorist strategy the interlocking elements of which are examined in chapter 6 and the use of immigration powers in chapters 7 and 9. A number of themes and issues can usefully be highlighted here.

Despite the potential of prerogative powers, the legal regimes deployed since the Revolutionary and Napoleonic Wars (1793–1815) to deal with undesirable aliens have been statutory. They have all sought to distinguish between 'desirable' aliens (those benefiting the economy and the life of the country, those seeking asylum or refuge from persecution) and those who are 'undesirable' (criminal elements, terrorists or other threats to public peace and national security). War and the threat of invasion are seen to have been very important in the development of legal restrictions on their admission, restriction and deportation. Apart from such periods of severe threat, until 1905 something of an attitude of *laissez-faire* prevailed as regards the movement of aliens. The Victorian period is regarded as one in which a liberal and democratic United Kingdom gave refuge to the political opponents of 'despotic' regimes elsewhere.[1] The First World War, with its dramatic extension of restrictions on aliens, enemy and otherwise, changed all

---

[1] Stevens (2004): 23–31; Thornberry (1963): 415.

that.[2] Although meant to last only for the duration of that War, the Aliens restriction legislation was continued effectively to become a permanent feature of the legal landscape. Empire and its concept of a common status of British subject meant that this regime did not apply; British subjects were not in law aliens. After the Second World War, with the gradual disintegration of that Empire and faced with increasing migration to the United Kingdom from countries of the new Commonwealth (mainly persons of colour), the politics of race and immigration intermingled. The 1960s saw the extension (with some modification) of the 'alien' immigration regime to those British subjects without a personal, parental or grandparental connection to the United Kingdom itself (as distinct from its extant and former colonies). Some of its security elements extended from 1973 to Irish citizens, although gaps in it had to be closed with executive measures on exclusion in successive Prevention of Terrorism (Temporary Provisions) Acts (PTAs). And, in turn, the immigration regime itself was limited in its application to citizens of fellow member States by EC (later EU) law, setting stricter limits on the security powers of the State than were applicable generally. Essentially, statute has throughout given the Home Secretary very wide powers (characterizable in some respects as 'statutory prerogative' with all that implies about the nature and width of discretion) to deal with undesirable 'aliens'. He or she now has security powers to prevent their entry to the United Kingdom. Powers to require registration with and regular reporting to the police enable a degree of control once here. Very wide powers – unchanged in terms but extended as regards whom and what behaviours they cover post-9/11 – enable their deportation on 'public good' grounds, the 'national security' designation within that essentially operating to withdraw their cases from the standard immigration appeals' regime. While numerically the use of these powers has been small their exercise has typically proved controversial.

The area until 1969 was characterized by a lack of appeal rights. Most of the period since 1973 has administrative challenge in the security area governed by an advisory committee (as it was in principle for a short period in the inter-war years). Legal challenges were mounted by way of judicial review or habeas corpus applications. They were pervaded by the standard deferential or 'hands off' approach both as regards substantive and procedural issues. The regime may have been statutory. The shallowness of review parallels that traditionally shown to the exercise of prerogative power prior to *GCHQ* and, after it, to that accorded the non-justiciable 'security' sphere. Litigation at Strasbourg under the ECHR saw, in *Chahal* v *United Kingdom*,[3] the European Court of Human Rights preclude removal to another State where there was a real risk of serious maltreatment there of the person to be removed and set limits on the time someone could be detained pending deportation. That preclusion and those limits shaped the United Kingdom response to suspected terrorists after 9/11 – detention without trial of foreign national terrorist suspects under the Anti-terrorism, Crime and Security Act 2001

---

[2] Ewing and Gearty (2000): 36–7.
[3] (1997) 23 EHRR 413.

(ATCSA) examined in chapter 7. The Court also condemned both modes of challenging an adverse decision, necessitating (given its apparent 'steer') the creation in 1997 of appeals to the Special Immigration Appeals Commission (SIAC) for national security immigration and citizenship matters and to deal with ATCSA detention, procedures central to the post-9/11 story and carried over into the High Court as regards control orders under the Prevention of Terrorism Act 2005 (PTA 2005).

This chapter first examines briefly the position prior to 1905. It next considers the Aliens Act 1905, the first attempt at permanent legislation on alien immigration and control. It then analyses in much more depth the statutory regimes of immigration control in the security sphere, operable 1914–73, the coming into force of a single statute, the Immigration Act 1971, largely assimilating controls over aliens and British subjects other than British citizens, which continues to govern the position today. The operation of that Act up to 9/11 forms the final section of this chapter. Each of the periods treated in detail considers the powers and their use, modes of administrative challenge, and the response of the courts to applications for review of these executive measures to deal with terrorism and other threats to national security.

The Position until 1905

Although prerogative power to refuse to admit and expel aliens has been assumed by the courts to exist,[4] uncertainties about it and its scope have meant that immigration control, in times of crisis or otherwise, has, since the Revolutionary Wars with France, rested more firmly on a statutory footing. Even though research for Prime Minister Pitt in the 1790s established that action against aliens in Elizabethan England threatened by the Spanish Armada in 1588 was founded on the prerogative, measures of alien control were throughout the Revolutionary and Napoleonic Wars (1793–1815) embodied in a variety of temporary Acts of Parliament in which can be discerned the origins of modern powers.[5] These Acts varied in the scope and degree of restrictions imposed but a number of central features (all only embodied in the more restrictive Acts) emerge in the attempt to distinguish between 'good' and 'bad' aliens: the requirement that vessels put into designated ports; the ship's master to give a return listing all alien passengers to the authorities (Customs and the Magistrates) (an early use of carriers as quasi-immigration police); powers in those authorities to forbid or license the admission of aliens; inability to leave the port of entry without a 'passport' from the magistracy and a requirement to renew it with each change of residence; those with whom aliens lodged to inform the local authorities (Overseers of the Poor) and provide a description of the alien; the requirement that to leave the country an alien

---

[4] *Att-Gen for Canada v Cain* [1906] AC 542; Thornberry (1963): 422–8.
[5] Bevan (1986): 58.

have a passport issued by the Home Secretary and a duty to use it within a reasonable time; a power to forbid an alien to reside in a particular area; the ability of the Home Secretary to order that a suspect alien be taken into custody; and the Crown's powers to order aliens to leave the realm and to effect their departure.[6] There was some concern to protect genuine refugees from Revolutionary France, but also concern about dangers of abuse of asylum.[7] With some ebb and flow, legislative restriction became more relaxed in the period 1815–48, and deportation was rarely used.[8] Political unrest on the Continent and in Ireland, coupled with the Chartist Riots in 1848, enabled the passage through Parliament in that year of legislation, supplementing the 1836 legislation on Alien Registration, enabling the Home Secretary to remove aliens (other than those resident in the country for the preceding three years or more) where he deemed it expedient 'for the preservation of the peace and tranquillity of the realm'. The alien was to be given a 'general summary of the matters alleged against him' and could appeal to the Privy Council prior to removal. No one was removed under it and the Act lapsed after two years.[9] The Aliens Registration Act 1836 stayed on the statute book until its repeal by the Aliens Act 1905 which re-introduced, after Victorian reluctance to have such a power or to restrict as opposed to register alien immigration, a limited ability to deport.[10]

Statutory Controls 1905–73

Aliens Act 1905

Concern across the political spectrum about alien, particularly Jewish, immigration was reflected in the reports of two Parliamentary Select Committees. and caused the establishment in 1901 of a Royal Commission on the subject. Previous attempts to legislate had been defeated by liberal elements in Parliament, but the recommendations in the Commission's Report in 1903 were in 1905 carried through into law at the second attempt. Significant concerns brought before the Commission were ones about indigence and health risks, overcrowding, lack of assimilation, and the undercutting of trade and wages. But they also concerned the presence among the alien population of 'criminals, anarchists, prostitutes and persons of bad character'.

The enactment of the Aliens Act 1905 (AA) 'was the watershed for aliens' entry. The liberal tradition of most of the nineteenth century was finally breached

---

[6] CAB 16/25 TNA, Committee of Imperial Defence. Report of the Subcommittee on the Treatment of Aliens in Time of War (1913), Appendix III.

[7] Stevens (2004): 21.

[8] Ibid.: 23.

[9] Bevan (1986): 65.

[10] Stevens (2004): 23–4.

and was never to return.'[11] It was, however, largely concerned with matters of admission and refusal of entry. 'Immigrant ships' had to dock at designated ports and their masters supply the authorities with returns on the numbers and types of alien passengers on board. Immigration officials were able to enter and inspect the ship. The targets were the destitute without and unlikely to obtain their own means of support; those in ill-health (physical or mental, the latter referred to as lunacy) 'likely to become a charge on the [poor] rates or otherwise a detriment to the public'; criminals convicted abroad of a non–political extraditable crime; and those previously excluded.[12] The Home Secretary's decision on 'immigrant ship' and 'extraditable' crime were stated to be 'final'. There were liberal elements in the legislation. Thus,

> … in the case of an immigrant who proves that he is seeking admission to this country solely to avoid prosecution or punishment on religious or political grounds or for an offence of a political character, or persecution, involving a danger of imprisonment or danger to life or limb, on account of religious belief, leave to land shall not be refused on the ground merely of want of means, or the probability of his becoming a charge on the rates.[13]

There were also Home Office attempts to ameliorate the rigidity of the regime with instructions to immigration inspectors to show leniency as regards those fleeing districts where religious or political persecution was known to occur, to allow entry in cases of hardship to women or children or to men in a critical state of health or to people who might be at serious risk if turned away, to give where possible the alien the benefit of the doubt. But relatively few were accepted as refugees: a peak of 505 in 1906 declining steadily to a mere five in 1910.[14] Moreover any alien refused entry had to be given grounds for the refusal and a notice of his right to appeal to an Immigration Board based at the port of entry. The Board hearings (generally within 24 hours of the refusal of entry) were open to the Press, the immigration inspector had to be present, and from 1910 the alien could obtain legal representation.[15] Each Board was composed of persons with 'magisterial, business or administrative experience'.[16] Each sat with a legally qualified clerk. Many of the panel members on which the Board drew were, like most immigrants, Jewish. Justice, if rough and ready, was speedy. Something like a third of appeals was successful. An exaggerated Home Office perception that the Boards were too lenient probably helps explain their abolition in 1919 and subsequent reluctance, until the late 1950s, to consider reinstating rights of appeal.[17]

---

[11] Bevan (1986): 70.

[12] AA, s. 1(3).

[13] AA, s. 1(2).

[14] Dummett and Nicol (1990): 150–151.

[15] Bevan (1986): 72.

[16] AA, s. 2.

[17] Dummett and Nicol (1990): 151; Stevens (2004): 41–2.

The Home Secretary's powers of expulsion of an alien in the country were limited and required a court recommendation. This could only be given (a) on conviction of a criminal offence (including prostitution), or (b) where the alien had been found wandering without ostensible means of support, or was living under unsanitary conditions the result of overcrowding, or had entered the country having been sentenced abroad for an extraditable crime.[18] Although not repealed on the onset of war in August 1914, the Act was essentially rendered otiose during it[19] with the massive extension of executive powers over aliens then embodied both in the Defence of the Realm Act 1914 (DORA) and the Defence of the Realm Regulations (DORR) (see chapter 2) and, more pertinently for this chapter, in the Aliens' restriction legislation, both primary and secondary.

Aliens Restriction Act 1914

Enacted on 5 August 1914, this 'essentially gave the Secretary of State a free hand to regulate aliens as he saw fit'.[20] Section 1 ('powers with respect of aliens in case of national emergency') provided him with powers supplementing existing statutory and prerogative powers.[21] It enabled 'His Majesty, at any time when a state of war exists between His Majesty and any foreign Power, or when it appears that an occasion of imminent danger or great emergency has arisen' to impose through Order in Council 'restrictions on aliens'. Specifically, an Order could make provision for the deportation of aliens from the United Kingdom; for requiring them to reside and remain within certain places or districts; conversely, for prohibiting them from residing in any areas specified in the Order, and for requiring aliens present in the United Kingdom to comply with provisions as to registration, change of abode, travelling or otherwise that might be made by the Order. Provision could relate to aliens in general or to any class or description of alien. The burden of proving that a person was not an alien lay on the person who sought to deny it. The Act 'confirmed the style of UK immigration *viz*, a skeletal statute supported by detailed rules drafted by the Secretary of State';[22] the details of restriction were set out not in the Act but in the Orders made under it. There was no explicit protection of refugees, but protection was extended during the war, as before, to Armenian refugees from Turkish persecution and, after invasion, to numerous Belgian refugees; the Government would not send a genuine refugee somewhere it was persuaded he or she would suffer persecution.[23] Neither Act nor Orders provided any rights of appeal. Indeed, the operation of the Immigration

---

[18] AA, s. 3(1)(a), (b).

[19] Stevens (2004): 43.

[20] Bevan (1986): 72.

[21] *R* v *Knockaloe Camp Commandant* (1918) LJKB 43.

[22] Bevan (1986): 73.

[23] Holmes (1988): 87–8; Dummett and Nicol (1990): 145, citing *R* v *Secretary of State for Home Affairs, ex parte Duke of Chateau Thierry* [1917] 1 KB 922.

Boards under the 1905 Act was suspended. There is a strong resemblance to the provisions of the Napoleonic era in this illiberal regime (designated ports, quasi-police duties imposed on carriers, requiring aliens to live in particular places).[24] Most significantly, the Orders considerably enhanced the powers of the Home Secretary in terms of expulsion. Art. 12 of the Aliens Restriction (Consolidation) Order 1914 and its successors enabled him to 'order the deportation of any alien [other than a prisoner of war or someone under 14], and any alien with respect to whom such an order is made shall forthwith leave and thereafter remain out of the United Kingdom'. It also conferred power to detain the alien pending deportation. There was no requirement of a court recommendation. Thus with war began the history of executive deportation on 'public good' grounds. So too did the requirement for a passport to travel abroad. All aliens, not just enemy ones, had to register with the authorities, making easier their future control. The 1914 Act was a decisive milestone in immigration law:

> It finally swept away the vestiges of the traditional laissez-faire approach which had generally prevailed during periods of peace, had flourished in the nineteenth century and was not wholly destroyed by the ill-conceived Aliens Act of 1905.[25]

The powers were used, for example, after the Russian Revolution to remove Litvinov, a leading Bolshevik *émigré* who had initially been granted diplomatic immunity for a period as a Soviet representative, to deport after conviction a number of other Bolshevik agents,[26] to secure the return to France of persons fleeing military service,[27] and to deport criminals unable to be prosecuted for lack of sufficient evidence.[28] They were also used in several cases to deport Chinese opium exporters since at the time their activities were not criminal, an omission from the criminal law soon rectified by a DORR offence (40B). Others were given time to leave and did so.[29]

---

[24] Bevan (1986): 73.

[25] Bird (1981) cited in Holmes (1988): 95.

[26] Andrew (1985): 236

[27] [1917] 1 KB 922 (Derais aka Duke of Chateau Thierry) and [1918] 1 KB 578 (Sacksteder).

[28] [1916] 2 KB 742.

[29] HO 45/24683 TNA. The deportation was said to have had a salutary effect on the Chinese community in Liverpool (its Chief Constable had recommended the deportation) and also in Glasgow and London whose police forces were informed of it.

Aliens Restriction (Amendment) Act 1919: the Permanence of the 'Temporary'

After the Armistice in November 1918, there were two political pressures for continuing the wartime regime of alien restriction: dealing with enemy aliens; and fear of subversion in terms of the spread of ideas associated with the Russian Revolution, especially as the United Kingdom was involved in the civil war there, aiding through overt and covert action 'White' Russians against the 'Red' Russians in power.[30]

The matter of continuance had been considered early in 1918 in a report by the Aliens Committee of the Ministry of Reconstruction's Reconstruction Committee. It considered that the matter of whether this country should throw open its doors after the war to former enemy aliens was a 'matter of national policy of the first importance', one on which Committee members did not feel entitled to offer an opinion. As regards the matter of aliens, generally, however, the Committee was bolder and recommended that there should be a more thorough control on admission and control when here than had been afforded under the Aliens Act 1905, which the Committee thought had not been suited to safeguard against the return undetected of undesirables ('the foreign prostitute or criminal') previously expelled. As regards admission,

> The substance of our suggestions is that no alien should be allowed to land unless he holds a passport or other document clearly establishing identity and is in a position to satisfy an aliens officer that he is not an undesirable, undesirables being defined (following in this the Aliens Act 1905) as persons who (a) have not the means of decent support, or (b) are lunatics, idiots, or diseased, or (c) are criminals, or (d) have been already expelled from the country. The admission of political refugees should be safeguarded, as at present, by the provision that they are not to be rejected solely for lack of means. In practice these requirements will mean that British subjects also, when returning to this country, will have to carry passports or other documents readily establishing their nationality, so as to facilitate their landing.[31]

The wartime restrictions (designated ports; examination of all aliens at the port) would have to be retained to avoid 'a serious invasion of undesirables' which 'would place an undue burden both on the police force and on the general resources' of the country undergoing reconstruction after the conflict.

As regards control after entry, the Committee recommended 'a general system for the registration of aliens' so that their movements could be monitored through a requirement to register 'their residence and other personal particulars with the police' and one of registration in hotels, boarding and lodging houses on the French model.

The committee also made proposals as regards expulsion or deportation, recognizing that the country's tradition of political asylum 'which in earlier periods

---

[30] Andrew (1985): chap. 6.
[31] CAB 1/26 TNA, *Report*, para. 18.

of our history has had considerable political importance' could only be maintained 'insofar as in modern conditions its maintenance is not inconsistent with the security of this country'. It was not 'fitting' that the United Kingdom 'should be made the headquarters of foreign criminals or undesirables'. The 1905 power to deport on recommendation of a court of law was too limited:

> It is not advisable that the possibility of removing aliens whose presence in this country is thoroughly undesirable should depend on their being convicted by a court; cases may occur (cases, for instance, of suspected espionage) where prompt action may be very desirable, but there is no prospect of securing a conviction. Further ... it will be desirable to give the Secretary of State power to expel a person whose certificate of naturalization has been revoked and who still possesses a foreign nationality. We propose, therefore, that the power of the Secretary of State to expel without a conviction should be continued in peacetime and that it should be exercised where the Secretary of State deems it conducive to the public good to make the order, but that, on the other hand, the Secretary of State should be precluded from making an order for deportation in these cases if the alien satisfied him that in the event of the order being carried into effect he may be subjected to prosecution or punishment in his own country on political or religious grounds.[32]

The Aliens Restriction (Amendment) Act 1919 enabled the continued operation of the powers in the 1914 Act on a permanent basis by removing from section one of that Act the restrictive words 'at any time when a state of war exists between His Majesty and any foreign powers, or when it appears that an occasion of imminent danger or great emergency has arisen', providing for the scheme so to operate for one year, but to be able to be renewed annually through the medium of the Expiring Laws Continuance Act, something done every year so that the scheme only disappeared when the Immigration Act 1971 came into force at the beginning of 1973. The Act and the Order in Council to which it gave breath formed 'a comprehensive code ... to deal with the entry, residence and expulsion of aliens, which took its inspiration from the Napoleonic legislation and the scheme of which [embodied in the Immigration Act 1971 regime] ultimately governed all entrants'.[33] Art. 12 of the Aliens Restriction Order 1919[34] implemented part of the Aliens Committee recommendation on deportation: it empowered the Home Secretary, if he deemed it conducive to the public good, to make a deportation order requiring an alien to leave and remain out of the country and could require such persons to return to the country of which they were subjects or citizens. He could also order detention pending deportation and that aliens be placed on ships leaving the United Kingdom. The ship's master could be required to take them and Art. 13 allowed the Home Secretary to apply aliens' own money to defray the costs of maintaining them until removed and the costs of the voyage. The recommended

---

[32] Ibid., para. 24.
[33] Bevan (1986): 73–4.
[34] S R & O 1919 No. 1077.

'refugee' restriction, however, found no expression in the legislative scheme. Art. 11 (again to a degree foreshadowing 'control orders' under the PTA 2005) empowered the Home Secretary to

> ... impose on any alien or class of aliens such restrictions (either in addition to or in substitution for the other restrictions imposed by this Order) as to residence, reporting to the police, registration, the use or possession of any machine, apparatus, arms and explosives, or other article, or otherwise, as he may deem to be necessary in the public interest, and any alien in relation to who any such order is made shall comply with the order.

Non-compliance was punishable with a fine and/or imprisonment.[35] Visa requirements (applicable to all countries other than Western Europe) saw the establishment abroad of Passport Offices. These, funded by consumer fees, both provided a front for intelligence operations by the growing Secret Service, one vehicle for preventing entry to undesirables on the intelligence 'blacklist' and, in conjunction with intelligence services in other countries, a mode of keeping track of the movement of international revolutionaries.[36]

The further provisions of the 1919 Act, by enhancing powers of internal control over aliens, reflected the grave concern at the spread of the Soviet communist revolution and of foreign and British agitators fomenting and exploiting growing industrial unrest at home. Thus it was made an offence for an alien to cause sedition or disaffection amongst the civilian population or the armed forces or to cause industrial unrest in any industry in which he had not been *bona fide* employed for two years.[37] A bar was placed on alien employment in the civil service,[38] on obtaining a pilotage certificate,[39] and restrictions put on service in the merchant marine.[40] Further restrictions were placed on former enemy aliens.[41] In 1920, a new Aliens Order was issued which formed the basis of control of alien immigration until 1953.[42] It retained the essential features of the 1919 Order, but made changes with respect to the power of deportation. Rather than rely purely on a broad discretionary power, Art. 12 now specifically provided for deportation upon recommendation of a court. It did so, firstly, in the case of scheduled offences, where a court on conviction or appeal from conviction recommended deportation instead of or in addition to another sentence. Secondly, it enabled deportation where, after proceedings taken within a year of their last entry to the United Kingdom, a magistrates' court certified that the alien had been found

---

[35] Art. 18.
[36] Andrew (1985): 240–2 ('Defence Black List' later 'Precautionary List'), 276.
[37] s. 3
[38] s. 6.
[39] s. 4.
[40] s. 5.
[41] ss. 9–12.
[42] SR&O 1920 No. 448 (as amended).

wandering without ostensible means of subsistence, or had made resort to parochial relief, or where they had been sentenced by a foreign court for an extradition crime. The more general power to deport arose as on the 1919 model if the Home Secretary deemed an alien's deportation 'conducive to the public good'.

A Home Office Circular just before the entry into force of the 1920 Order drew the attention of Chief Constables to the parallel of the Aliens Act 1905 and reminded them when prosecuting of the need to bring the issue of deportation to the attention of the court, so that the matter was not overlooked. It also gave an indication of when the broader power would be utilized.

> Orders will not, as a rule, be made under this power in any case in which allegations are made against an alien for which he could properly be tried, convicted and recommended for deportation, or in which a Court has either acquitted an alien or has declined in spite of a conviction to recommend deportation. In the absence of a recommendation by a court, deportation will, as a general rule, be confined to cases where the alien may properly be regarded as a serious menace to public order or public morals or (in the case of a recent arrival) as likely to become a charge on the rates. Any case of a former enemy alien entering the country without permission or failing to comply with the conditions on which he was admitted, will also be dealt with by deportation.[43]

A memorandum stressed that this power of deportation without recommendation was reserved for use only in very exceptional and infrequent cases. It would be used only after the most careful consideration.[44] Home Office files on deportation orders 1922–40 indicate its use to deport following conviction without a recommendation; for being in breach of a deportation order; for landing without leave or breaching conditions on entry and stay; for being the wife of a principal deportee; and for dealing with a range of other categories of undesirable. These embrace those involved in prostitution, in other criminal activity where prosecution was not undertaken, the destitute and lunatic, and those involved in, or in the arrangement of, bogus marriages for immigration purposes. The powers were used as part of recurrent campaigns to clean up Soho and other 'clublands' in conjunction with powers under the Order enabling closure of clubs, cafes and restaurants frequented or recently frequented by aliens where, in the opinion of the chief officer of police (when enabled by the Home Secretary to use these powers), those aliens were of criminal or disloyal associations or otherwise undesirable or where the premises were conducted in a disorderly or improper manner or one prejudicial to the public good.[45] They were also used to deal with the occasional spy, sometimes as a supplement to criminal conviction (and thus executed after service of sentence) or an alternative to the prosecution process. In the inter-war years one focus of the 'security' powers in immigration law was on the position and role of those in successive Soviet Trade Delegations. There was, for example,

---

[43] HO 45/11907 TNA (Circular 386026/23).

[44] Ibid. (File 386.026 referring to memo 432156/5).

[45] Art. 10.

concern over Nikolai Bukharin. Was he a Soviet scientist or a political propagandist or agitator? In 1922, instructions were that he was to be refused a visa. In 1931, however, much to the chagrin of the *Daily Mail* and a questioner in Parliament, he was granted a diplomatic visa to enable him as a professor to attend a scientific conference.[46] Security was sometimes thought better served by allowing suspects entry, subjecting them to Special Branch surveillance, and intercepting their messages when here. Prosecution where possible, even in secret trials, seems to have been the preferred policy. A Home Office paper early in the Second World War records that the 'conducive to the public good' power was rarely exercised in peacetime and gives as an example that of an alien with slight connection with the United Kingdom who was engaged in criminal activity but had either escaped conviction or, if convicted, a recommendation for deportation.[47] Its use in the security sphere proper seems, as in the more recent past, to have been even rarer.

That same paper clarifies inter-war use of the Art. 11 restriction power. It had been used almost exclusively in situations where it had proved impracticable to remove from the country an alien whose deportation had been recommended by a court. The aim of imposing restrictions was to induce the alien to make his or her own arrangements to leave. A typical restriction here was one of daily reporting to the police. If imposing restrictions did not have the desired effect, however, and the alien applied for a relaxation of the order,

> it was usual, if enquiry of the Police showed that no other useful purpose was likely to be served by keeping it in force, first to replace the original Order by a less stringent one and eventually to cancel the restrictions altogether. This practice was based on the view that a Restriction Order should not be used as a punitive measure against the individual concerned, but only in the public interest. For the same reason, Restriction Orders were not usually made against long-resident aliens.

As to use since the outbreak of war, the paper stressed the inaptness of such use to induce departure but the suitability of a Restriction Order where there were insufficient grounds for immigration detention, or where someone detained had been released. In either case restrictions such as regular reporting to the police, as to residence, occupation or employment, or even the imposition of ones of a type usually applied to enemy aliens under specific provisions of the amended Order could all be appropriate. Restrictions on occupation and employment should, however, only be imposed where justified in the interests of national security. Wartime amendment enabled detention under the Aliens Order on security and public order grounds.[48] In addition, of course, there were available the wartime

---

[46] HO 45/14449 TNA.
[47] HO 213/1837 TNA.
[48] Articles 5A and 12(5A).

powers of internment and restriction applicable to alien and British subject alike, analysed in chapter 2.

In the post 1945 period, security powers in immigration law were an important part of defence mechanisms in the Cold War. A new Aliens Order 1953 replaced the 1920 model.[49] As before, aliens could only land in the United Kingdom with leave of the immigration officials. Aliens refused leave to land could be detained and the carrier who brought them to the United Kingdom could be required by directions from immigration officers to remove them on the same or on another specified ship or aircraft bound for the country of which the aliens were nationals, the country from which they last embarked or a country which it was believed would admit them.[50] As regards deportation, the Order provided for deportation on the recommendation of a court on conviction of a scheduled offence.[51] More pertinently for present purposes, it also permitted deportation where the Home Secretary deemed it 'conducive to the public good'.[52] It also empowered the Home Secretary to specify the ship or aircraft which was to remove deportees from the country and to detain them pending removal.[53]

Deportation was rarely used on grounds other than conviction of a criminal offence or breach of conditions on entry or stay.[54] As in the inter–war years, the use of the power on security grounds was even rarer. In 1956 a Greek orthodox priest was deported as a suspected fund-raiser for the Cyprus guerrillas, EOKA.[55] The case of Dr Soblen in 1962 provided a cause célèbre of the use of the powers at the height of the Cold War, an illustration of the ends to which they could be put – in this instance a case of 'disguised extradition', reminiscent of the attempted use of the Restoration of Order in Ireland Act in 1923 to return IRA suspects to the government of the Irish Free State[56] and returning to France during the First World War persons who had fled military service obligations.[57]

Dr Soblen, a medical practitioner born in Lithuania, became a naturalized citizen of the United States in 1947, having moved there after 1941. In 1961, he was convicted in the State of New York of a number of 'espionage-related' offences and sentenced to life imprisonment with a recommendation that, due to his medical condition, he serve that sentence in a medical centre for federal prisoners in Missouri. He was released on bail pending appeals. When the Supreme Court rejected his attempt to seek a new trial, he flew to Israel, using his dead

---

[49] SI 1671/1953.

[50] Articles 1, 2 and 8.

[51] Art. 20(2)(a).

[52] Art. 20(2)(b).

[53] Art. 21.

[54] Wilson Committee (1967): paras 49–51.

[55] CAB 128/30 TNA, 38th meeting, minute 3, 29 May 1956.

[56] See chapter 2.

[57] *R* v *Secretary of State for Home Affairs, ex parte Duke of Chateau Thierry* [1917] 1 KB 922 and *ex parte Sacksteder* [1918] 1 KB 578, discussed later in this chapter.

brother's passport. On 1 July 1962, the Israeli Government forcibly expelled him on a specially chartered flight to Athens. There he was transferred, in the custody of US Marshals, onto an El Al flight bound for the United States via London. During it he managed to inflict severe knife wounds on himself making it necessary for him to be hospitalized in London. Two days later in hospital he was served with notice of refusal of permission to land in the United Kingdom and that he was to be removed from the country on the aircraft on which he had arrived. Legally speaking he was refused entry. When his lawyers obtained leave to apply for habeas corpus, he was ordered to be detained pending removal under Art. 8 of the Aliens Order 1953. The application for habeas corpus was refused on 18 July and that decision was upheld by the Court of Appeal on 21 July. Meanwhile, Dr Soblen had petitioned the Home Secretary and his lawyers on 23 July received a letter from the Government of Czechoslovakia (then a 'satellite' state in the Soviet bloc) stating that it was willing to take Dr Soblen when removed from the United Kingdom. Early in August, however, the Home Office gave directions to El Al that he was to be removed on one of its direct flights from London to the United States, his national state, which was willing to admit him. On 5 August the Israeli Government (responding to public pressure) indicated that El Al, its national carrier, would in no circumstances transport him to the United States but only to Israel. It was very clear from newspaper reports that the United States Government very much wanted him returned to the United States to serve his sentence for espionage. But spying offences (being obviously 'political') had never formed part of extradition arrangements, so his return by way of that legal process was impossible. Instead, given the Israeli attitude, on 11 August Dr Soblen was served with a deportation order under Art. 20 of the Aliens Order 1953 and it was indicated that he would be placed on an aircraft bound for the United States. Dr Soblen again sought habeas corpus, contending that the Home Secretary was abusing his discretion in specifying an aircraft bound for the United States. In the application he also sought disclosure of written communications between the United Kingdom and United States' governments in respect of his case. Disclosure was denied by Government and the courts on the basis of Crown Privilege (public interest immunity). His claim that the Home Secretary had misused his deportation power to achieve an object (extradition) otherwise impermissible in law was unsuccessful for reasons which will be examined later in this chapter. The day before his deportation, Dr Soblen committed suicide in prison.[58] Thornberry criticizes the inconsistent use of the power in the 1950s and 1960s. Cort, another United States citizen, not wishing to return to the United States, fearing both military service and the Macarthyist anti-communist witch-hunts, was denied political asylum but allowed time to find another country to go to. A Russian deserter was allowed to stay but a deserter fleeing Franco's Spain was not. Later in the 1960s, a degree of inconsistency was shown in respect of supporters of the Communist cause in South Vietnam during the course of the war there. Others

---

[58] See further: Thornberry (1963); O'Higgins (1964).

excluded or whose leave was curtailed were supporters of the illegal UDI regime in Southern Rhodesia (now Zimbabwe) and members of the Church of Scientology.[59] Thornberry identified the great defect of the United Kingdom deportation laws as

> ... placing in the hands of one man complete discretionary power. The consequences of their exercise upon their object are immense ... too immense not to be subject to judicial process.[60]

As will be seen, it was not subjected to such process until 1998, and only after an adverse decision of the European Court of Human Rights.

The example of Rudi Dutschke, a German student radical at the time of political unrest across Europe in the late 1960s, further illustrates the breadth and controversial nature of the 'conducive to the public good' power, whether to refuse entry, deport, or, in this case, refuse to vary or extend a limited leave to stay in the United Kingdom. Unlike *Soblen*, this focused squarely on the issue of liability to curtailment of stay etc., rather than the matter of destination when removed. Here the Home Secretary sought to remove Dutschke, a student who was said to have made political speeches in defiance of an undertaking that, if admitted to the United Kingdom, he would not engage in political activities. He lost his appeal to the Immigration Appeal Tribunal in the new system of appeals afforded by the Aliens (Appeals) Order 1970,[61] brought in as corresponding rights of appeal were granted by the Immigration Appeals Act 1969 to Commonwealth citizens (British subjects) to whom immigration control had been extended in two stages in 1962 and 1968.[62]

While such cases are inevitably controversial, putting in issue commitment to freedoms of speech, and association and to refuge from political persecution, their numbers are comparatively small. Several cases a year was Hepple's estimate.[63] As now, the bulk of deportations under this head related to breach of conditions on entry or abuse of the immigration process.

Extension of Powers to Commonwealth Citizens, 1962 and 1968

When significant numbers of immigrants of colour came to the United Kingdom in the years after the Second World War, the politics of 'race' and of 'immigration' became intermingled. The first immigration restrictions on Commonwealth citizens came in the Commonwealth Immigrants Act 1962, which 'broke the barrier of

---

[59] Evans (1983): 194 (n.22). On Scientologists see *Schmidt v Secretary of State for Home Affairs* [1969] 1 All ER 904.

[60] Thornberry (1963): 467–8.

[61] SI 1970/151.

[62] Hepple (1969).

[63] Hepple (1971): 513.

sentiment and attachment to the Commonwealth'.[64] In 1968, restrictions were extended, quite deliberately, to achieve the exclusion of United Kingdom and Colonies citizens of Indian subcontinent origin insecurely resident in East Africa, the former British colonies of Kenya and Uganda. The aim was primarily to prevent or manage entry. But the legislation opened up the prospect of deportation on recommendation of a court on conviction of a criminal offence. There was no 'conducive to the public good' deportation power. That came only with the amalgamation of controls in the Immigration Act 1971.

Administrative Challenge

A striking feature of the 'public good' and 'security' powers in immigration law up to 1969 is the lack of any machinery for administrative challenge such as we have become accustomed to finding with more draconian executive measures such as internment even during the exigencies of total war. The omission was deliberate and in part flows from what the Home Office perceived as the unhelpful approach of the Immigration Appeal Boards under the Aliens Act 1905. The Home Secretary, Edward Shortt, referred explicitly to this in a meeting in November 1919 with representatives of the Board of Deputies of British Jews when rejecting their proposals for an appeal to a judge in chambers prior to the making of a deportation order. The record of the meeting indicates graphically the 'new' approach to alien immigration and security issues and the attitude to rights of recourse other than informal representations to the Home Secretary.[65] On the 'new' world order he stated:

> Owing to the stern necessities of war, we have ... been obliged to adopt measures in wartime because of bad men which have inevitably told heavily upon those who were innocent, who did not deserve the hardships that were inflicted upon them. That is inevitable in warfare. ... the time has not yet come when we can go back entirely, at any rate, to pre-war conditions. ... With regard to deportation, there is ... in the world at present a very dangerous spirit abroad, a spirit which is being fostered by many men, generally fostered by them not in their own country. We and France and America, and every other country that is attempting to retain some form of civilized government, are bound to adopt methods of meeting the work and intrigues of men of that description. .... We are, therefore, bound to retain powers which will enable us to deal with a man who is too clever to bring himself within the meshes of the law, and who is yet doing very dangerous work; ... we are, therefore, bound to keep those powers. Equally with regard to immigration, we know perfectly well that there are men who are endeavouring to come into this Country [or] are sending their emissaries into this Country for the sole purpose of stirring up mischief; and we must take powers which will enable us to cope with those men; and just as in time of actual warfare we are bound to take abnormal powers, powers which I think every constitutionally minded man dislikes intensely, yet

---

[64] Bevan (1986): 77.
[65] HO 45/11069/375480 107, TNA.

we are bound to take them and bound to use them; and equally I am afraid the time has not yet come when it is possible to relinquish once and for all those abnormal and disagreeable powers.

As regards appeal, he continued:

We have adopted as largely as we can: I mean we have had, as you all know, advisory committees dealing with the question of repatriation of enemy aliens ... but unfortunately we are still bound to keep the powers which have been possessed for dealing with men sometimes without much notice, where it is essential that action should be taken at once. ... They are being used much more sparingly than they were; but we cannot relinquish them. If you set up a Court of Appeal, that Court of Appeal must exercise its functions with regard to the evidence that is brought before it; and in many cases which our Secret Service tells you of, if the evidence were brought before an open Court, the method by which we had obtained the information would be disclosed to the very people who ought not to know it. There are very many real difficulties in the way, when you are dealing with matters in times of national danger, very great difficulties in the way of trials in open Court. Many a time, if you have to have a hearing in open Court, you are bound to let a man go; because if once you had your trial, you would disclose sufficient for those who have no business to know it, the method by which you obtain your information.

As for recourse to a judge in chambers, he characterized this as 'quite hopeless'. He promised to keep the matter under review. After continued pressure from the Board of Deputies, Home Secretary Samuel set up under royal warrant a non-statutory body, the Aliens Deportation Advisory Committee, in 1932. This could examine 'public good' deportation orders other than illegal entry or breach of immigration conditions. 'Security' cases were not explicitly excluded by the terms of reference, but it appears to have examined none. It was chaired by Judge Leonard KC and its membership included one person of 'Labour' persuasion. It sat at the Home Office. It was able to take account of material whether or not admissible in a court of law.[66] It insisted that the Home Office bring forward its witnesses for cross-examination.[67] Legal representation was allowed. But its remit was narrow, its caseload small (33 cases in four years) and its life short. Its advice not to deport (14 cases) was invariably accepted, the Home Secretary feeling pressured to do so even where he might have preferred not to. As result of one such case and some other clashes, it fell into disuse after 1936. Automatic referral of cases ceased then. Cases of special difficulty could be referred, although none were, and it fell completely into abeyance on the outbreak of war in 1939.[68] It dealt with cases of those involved in prostitution or possession of drugs, indecent

---

[66] HO 45/14909 TNA.
[67] Dummett and Nicol (1990): 210.
[68] Wilson Committee (1967): paras 50–55, 131, App. III.

exposure, a fraudster and swindler, and those generally undesirable.[69] There appears to have been one case of attempted bribery of immigration officials or police officers. The Metropolitan Police accepted the Board as preferable to 'a full dress trial between distinguished lawyers'.[70]

In 1956, the United Kingdom ratified the European Convention on Establishment. This necessitated establishing a mode of appeal to an independent body in deportation cases involving nationals of States party to it. The Home Secretary allowed those who had been resident for more than two years recourse to the Chief Metropolitan Magistrate in fulfilment, and extended it to nationals of other countries too. But it had no remit in security cases. The Chief Magistrate considered 68 cases over the period until 1966 (118 persons were eligible to make representations). The Home Office accepted all of his 18 recommendations for revocation of the deportation order.[71]

From 1970–73, the appeals system set out in the Immigration Appeals Act 1969 (Commonwealth citizens) and the Aliens (Appeals Order) 1970 operated.[72] In general, appeal lay to an adjudicator and then to the Immigration Appeal Tribunal. Under that system, however, appeals in 'security' cases went direct to a special five-member panel of the Immigration Appeal Tribunal. Its decision was merely advisory. It operated in the Dutschke case where the Conservative Home Secretary refused on security and political grounds to vary the leave of a radical leader of the student movement in Germany who had been granted admission for medical treatment by his Labour predecessor on Dutschke's undertaking to refrain from political activities. Dutschke wished to continue as a research student at Cambridge University, something for which he was academically well qualified. This 'Star Chamber in the Strand' heard evidence in 'open' and 'closed' sessions, and considered itself bound by the Home Secretary's certification that certain material could not be disclosed to Dutschke and his legal team. In closed session (in the absence of Dutschke and his legal team) it heard evidence from the former Labour Home Secretary and the security service. It upheld the refusal to vary or extend his leave. The 'closed' session material showed that, contrary to his undertaking, he had engaged in political activity. While not as yet a security risk, he could well be one in the longer term. The proceedings were characterized by several commentators as a bad day for administrative justice in Britain and as damaging the country's reputation for tolerance and that of the Home Office for consistency and fairness.[73]

---

[69] HO 45/14909 TNA.

[70] Dummett and Nicol (1990): 211.

[71] Wilson Committee (1967): App VII, Table 6.

[72] Dummett and Nicol (1990): 207 suggest that it was on a non-statutory basis.

[73] Hepple (1971): 513.

Challenges in the Courts

The lack of administrative challenge to 'security' deportations inevitably meant that some facing deportation instead had recourse to the courts. None appear to have been successful. From the First World War onwards, in immigration cases generally judges 'practised noticeably greater restraint than they have in public law generally'.[74] The degree of restraint was even greater in 'public good' cases, most markedly in 'national security' cases. By 1925 'the High Court' which heard applications for habeas corpus or for judicial review 'had abdicated any power of review except on proof of perversity, and the Home Secretary's decision was effectively final'.[75] Nor were the courts keen to accord procedural protection, whether to someone refused admission or to someone to be deported from what may have been a secure home in the United Kingdom. Although there were indications as the century went on that the latter might in principle enjoy a greater level of procedural protection (on a legitimate expectation basis) than the would-be entrant (the person seeking a privilege), the demands of 'security' silenced those of procedural fairness. The narrowness of review and the deferential attitude adopted may owe something to the 'prerogative' background of alien control,[76] and the initial wartime context in which cases first arose for consideration.

In *ex parte Sarno*,[77] the Home Secretary sought to deport Sarno as undesirable being someone assisting in keeping a brothel. The court rejected the argument that Art. 12 of the Aliens Order was outside the ample powers conferred by the 1914 Act to deal with aliens. It did not accept that the Home Secretary had misused his discretion in this case, but, at first glance, seemed to accept that it could interfere if he clearly had. Although Sarno's activities were not necessarily criminal, the suspicions about his character in this regard set out in the Home Office affidavit sufficed to justify the order. Lord Reading CJ thought that the wartime context might justify such executive action in circumstances which would not be warranted in peacetime, wartime manpower exigencies making it harder to bring criminals to justice.[78] The Divisional Court did not accept that Sarno was a political refugee from Russia, but Low J, concerned at the argument that the court had no power at all to interfere to protect the liberty of an alien subject to a deportation order, left open the question whether the court could interfere 'if there were a deliberate attempt by the exercise of the powers conferred by the statute and the regulations to enforce the return of a real, genuine political refugee to his country of origin'.[79] In *ex parte Duke of Chateau Thierry*,[80] however, the Court of Appeal was faced

---

[74] Legomsky (1987): 5.
[75] Dummett and Nicol (1990): 152.
[76] Legomsky (1987): 96.
[77] [1916] 2 KB 742.
[78] [1916] 2 KB 742, at 750.
[79] [1916] 2 KB 742, at 752.
[80] [1917] 1 KB 922.

with a deportation order seeking to return the 'Duke' (an alias) on a ship to France where he was wanted for military service. The Court of Appeal was not satisfied that he was a political refugee or that he was medically unfit for service. It seemed to hold that the only issue the court could deal with was the narrow jurisdictional matter of whether the deportee was an alien. Otherwise, the matter of his deportation was one for unreviewable executive decision.[81] The Court held that there was no legal power to order deportation to a particular country, but that such could indirectly be achieved by the Home Secretary's exercise of the power to specify the ship on which the deportee was to be detained and removed. In *ex parte Sacksteder*,[82] another case of return to France with respect to military service obligations there, the Court of Appeal followed this. It also held that deportation to be valid had to be a personal decision of the Home Secretary, as it was in this case. Where an order for detention pending deportation was valid on its face, a Court could only go behind it if it was 'practically a sham, if the purpose behind it [was] such as to show that the order [was] not a genuine or bona fide order'. But here the motive of directing departure on a ship to France to secure return for those purposes was not such as to invalidate the order.

The matter of the powers of the courts in terms of substantive challenge with respect to a deportation order was returned to more than 40 years later in a 'disguised extradition' case, *ex parte Soblen*, the facts of which cause célèbre have already been outlined. In his first challenge, it was held that (despite his *de facto* 'entry' to a London hospital) he had no legal leave to enter the United Kingdom. [83] The second challenge concerned not whether he could be deported under the 'conducive to the public good' head but rather the destination to which he could validly be sent.[84] It was understood that the Home Secretary would direct that he be placed on a non-stop flight to the United States which wanted him back to serve his life sentence for 'espionage', a crime not covered by extradition arrangements. Soblen wanted to go to Czechoslovakia, a Soviet 'satellite' country willing to take him.

Arguments about the *vires* of the deportation power were quickly brushed aside, given the breadth of the 1919 Act and its clear application beyond wartime or emergency.[85] Nor could it be said that ability to use the powers of removal on refusal of leave to land precluded use of the deportation power; the powers were complementary and cumulative, not mutually exclusive.[86] The Court indicated that it could go behind the order if there were evidence that it was a sham or was made

---

[81] [1917] 1 KB 922, at 930 (Swinfen Eady LJ), 933 (Pickford LJ), 936 (Bankes LJ).
[82] [1918] 1 KB 578, at 586–7 (Pickford LJ), 589 (Warrington LJ), 591–2 (Scrutton LJ).
[83] [1963] 1 QB 829.
[84] [1963] 2 QB 243.
[85] [1963] 2 QB 243, at 297 (Lord Denning MR), 305 (Donovan LJ), 316 (Pearson LJ).
[86] [1963] 2 QB 243, at 297–8 (Lord Denning MR), 305 (Donovan LJ), 316 (Pearson LJ).

in bad faith or 'for any unlawful or ulterior purpose'.[87] Its finding here that none of these defects was shown, places the statements as mere rhetoric. As the Court recognised, the protection afforded by Crown Privilege (Public Interest Immunity) to the communications between the two Governments made Soblen's task more difficult, as it does in any situation where the challenger is denied the full reasons for and material in support of an adverse decision. But all three judges held that the Home Secretary's true purpose was to give effect to the refusal of leave to land which Soblen's actions to bring about his hospitalization had thwarted. They found no evidence of sham or ulterior purpose. The fact that Soblen was wanted in the United States did not mean that the Home Secretary could not regard it as conducive to the public good that he be removed from the United Kingdom. They were concerned that precluding the removal of an alien wanted as a criminal by the only State that could be compelled to take him placed the criminal in a better position than less heinous individuals. But, with respect, this was not the situation here. The object of protecting the country by removing him from it could in this case be achieved by removing him to another country. For Lord Denning MR bypassing the restrictions on extradition set out in the legislation governing that process would have been an ulterior purpose, but he was not prepared to accept that such had been proved to be the Home Secretary's purpose in this case. In contrast, his two colleagues took the view that the 'public good' could embrace helping an ally, as here, by not enabling the deportee to escape its justice,[88] suggesting that deportation to achieve an extradition effect is not in fact an ulterior purpose at all.[89] It seems abundantly clear that the courts have been unwilling to set meaningful substantive limits on the 'conducive to the public good' power. The record is, however, no more encouraging with regard to procedural issues, other than the requirement that the decision actually be taken by the Home Secretary.

Ex parte Venicoff dealt with the 1919 Order, and confirmed that the inclusion of the phrase 'conducive to the public good' in the deportation power did not alter its effect from the 1914 regime to which no such qualification attached.[90] This was another case of a deportee regarded as undesirable being suspected of exploiting women for prostitution. The Divisional Court rejected the argument that the deportee had a common law right to be heard before a deportation order was made or before it was put into effect. In rejecting it, the court put forward arguments (contact before an order was made might defeat its object by enabling the person to abscond to avoid the order) which only dealt with the first-claimed opportunity to be heard. They could not be a basis for rejecting the opportunity for representations after the person was detained pursuant to the order. Yet in *Soblen*, the blanket exclusion was upheld. The revision of the Aliens Orders after *Venicoff* (the 1920

---

[87] [1963] 2 QB 243, at 302, 305 (Lord Denning MR), 307–8 (Donovan LJ), 312, 315 (Pearson LJ).

[88] [1963] 2 QB 243, at 310 (Donovan LJ).

[89] Legomsky (1987): 98; Thornberry (1963): 462.

[90] [1920] 3 KB 72.

and 1953 Orders) without according any right to representations was regarded as indicating a legislative intention that the usual rules of procedural fairness should not apply. Only Lord Denning MR was willing in some (unspecified) circumstances to afford such a right. He saw it as immaterial here because of the Home Secretary's willingness to hear and consider any representations. But, in any event, as Pearson LJ said (using it as a reason for not departing from the blanket exclusion) there would have to be exceptions for emergencies or for security reasons or for obstructive conduct on the part of the alien. As *Hosenball*, a case to be discussed later shows, the exception for 'security' would be wide indeed, its width essentially a matter left by the courts to the Home Secretary.

Control under the Immigration Act 1971

The Powers and their Use

The Immigration Act 1971 and the associated Immigration Rules stipulating how immigration discretion is to be exercised became operational on 1 January 1973. For more than 30 years they have formed a single immigration code for all those who lack the right of abode, whether aliens, Irish citizens, citizens of independent Commonwealth countries or persons deriving their United Kingdom and Colonies citizenship from connection with an existing colony or dependency. The right of abode (complete freedom from immigration control other than in respect of proving status) was confined initially in the main to United Kingdom and Colonies citizens with a direct personal, parental or grandparental connection with the United Kingdom itself. Since 1983 it has been limited to British citizens. In addition, it was granted to citizens of an independent Commonwealth country with a parent born in the United Kingdom. Irish citizens benefited from a Common Travel Area of free movement and from exemptions from deportation for longer-standing residents. Commonwealth citizens settled in the United Kingdom at the entry into force of the scheme were also protected, as were their wives and children.

　　Those without the right of abode require leave to enter. After entry they remain liable to deportation even if time limits on their stay have been removed after several years' residence. As regards security, several powers are of note: refusal of entry; refusal to extend or vary leave to remain; and deportation. Admission to the United Kingdom can be refused by immigration officials where, from information available to them, it seems right to do so because exclusion from the United Kingdom is conducive to the public good; for example, because in the light of the character, conduct or associations of the person seeking leave to enter it is undesirable to give him or her leave to enter. Admission must be refused where the Home Secretary personally directs that a person's exclusion is conducive to the public good. If a person has been allowed admission, an application for further leave can be refused on the basis of the undesirability of permitting them to remain in the light of their character, conduct or associations or the fact that they represent a threat to national security. A person is liable to deportation if the Home Secretary deems the deportation to be conducive to the public good.[91] So are non–British citizen members of the principal deportee's family.[92] A deportation order requires its subject to leave, and prohibits him or her from entering, the country. It invalidates any leave to enter or remain.[93]

Home Office statistics suggest that around 100 people a year are on average deported under the public good power.[94] Apparently about three quarters are based on breach of immigration conditions, principally overstaying, or abuse of the immigration process (for example, bogus marriages). A number of others represent deportation for criminal conviction where no court recommendation for deportation was made. Others may reflect cases where criminality was unable to be proven. The powers of exclusion or deportation have rarely been used on security grounds. Bevan estimated an average of one per year, but the numbers inevitably fluctuate, so that the eight orders in the ten years to 1985 represent two in 1977 (Agee and Hosenball) and six in 1984. The numbers rose dramatically in 1991 with many made against Iraqis or PLO sympathizers during the Gulf War, most of which did not result in removal. The powers do, however, effectively confer very considerable freedom to use them as the Home Secretary sees fit, and in ways curtailing not only the civil liberties of those the direct subject of the decision, but also of those in the United Kingdom who are thereby denied the ability to associate with the persons excluded, removed or deported.[95] The Home Secretary stated in the debates on the Act that while it was not the practice to deport people because of their political views, it was justifiable to exclude or deport those of extremist opinions who would make speeches highly offensive to sections of the public or whose presence in the country would cause widespread offence.[96] Hence refusal of admission since 1973 has covered a wide range of 'undesirables': leading Ku Klux Klan members, other racist speakers,[97] directors who purport to wish to make offensive films about the sex life of Christ, American fund-raisers for the IRA, or (until 1980) members of the Church of Scientology, apparently on the basis that its activities 'were thought injurious to the mental health and stability of its

---

[91] Immigration Act 1971, s. 3(5)(b).

[92] Immigration Act 1971, s. 3(5)(c).

[93] Immigration Act 1971, s. 3(5)(c).

[94] See Home Office (1991), (2001), (2004).

[95] Evans (1983): 162.

[96] Evans (1983): 272–3.

[97] *Farrakhan* v *Secretary of State for the Home Department* [2002] QB 1391. Louis Farrakhan, spiritual leader of the Nation of Islam, which has adherents in the United Kingdom, has been banned from entering since 1986 on the ground that his anti-Semitic speeches would threaten public order.

adherents'.[98] Similar exclusions have been applied to refuse admission to the spiritual leader of another 'cult', the Moonies.[99]

There have been a number of prominent deportation decisions. One was that of Caprino, an Italian Marxist trade unionist, whose deportation order was withdrawn in the face of press criticism. The most famous case of the 1970s was that of two American journalists Agee and Hosenball. They had published material exposing CIA activities and were deported on the basis that they had in the United Kingdom obtained material which both threatened national security and put at risk the lives of Government employees. Others involved were charged with Official Secrets Act offences.

In 1991 under UN auspices, the United Kingdom and the United State combined militarily to eject Saddam Hussein's Iraqi forces from Kuwait in the Gulf War. In the United Kingdom, the targets for immigration action were Iraqis (particularly those connected with the military) and persons linked with the PLO which was supporting Saddam Hussein and which it was thought might undertake attacks on targets in the United Kingdom.

Iraqis were subject to a variety of restrictions (for example, freezing of bank accounts). Those connected to the military were interned by the Ministry of Defence under prerogative powers and the Geneva Conventions in a prisoner of war camp near Stonehenge. But restrictions came principally through immigration law.[100] More Iraqis than would be usual were required to register with the police. The Immigration Rules were amended to prevent the admission of new Iraqi students. A transit visa concession was withdrawn.[101] In January 1991, after the outbreak of hostilities in the Gulf, immigration facilities for Iraqi nationals who wanted to come to the United Kingdom or extend their stay there were effectively suspended.[102]

Ceasefire arrangements in the Gulf enabled the Home Secretary to lift all these extra restrictions on Iraqi nationals from 12 April 1991, so that from then on applications would be subject to the normal Immigration Rules and requirements.[103] The most controversial decisions were in respect of deportation of those thought to be a national security risk. This resulted in the effective detention without trial of those unable to be deported because of lack of flights or lack of travel capability to landlocked Iraq.

The Iraqi community in the United Kingdom was between 5,000 and 10,000 strong. From September 1990 to January 1991, deportation decisions were taken, on security grounds connected with the Gulf conflict, against 176 individuals, 164 of whom were Iraqis, the others connected with the PLO. Many were students,

---

[98] Evans (1983): 273.
[99] *Sun Myung Moon* v *Secretary of State for the Home Department* [2005] Imm AR 624.
[100] Grant (1991): 305; Home Office News Release (21 September 1990).
[101] Home Office News Release (21 September 1990).
[102] Home Office News Release, 12 April 1991.
[103] Home Office News Release, 12 April 1991.

some businessmen,[104] two employees of a software company,[105] and one (Cheblak) a writer, journalist and officer of the Arab League, previously a lecturer in public law.[106] Eighty individuals left the country 'voluntarily'. The Home Office described them as 'Ba'athist thugs',[107] an appellation that may be inaccurate in the light of criticisms of intelligence material in respect of those detained or interned. Thirty-five individuals (students and academics sponsored by the Iraqi Army) were interned under prerogative powers as prisoners of war. The remainder (predominantly postgraduate students on Iraqi Government scholarships and said to be subject to Iraqi Embassy discipline) were detained in prison under detention powers ancillary to deportation powers in immigration law. In all, some 200 of the estimated 1,000 Iraqi students in the UK were affected by detention and internment.[108]

In the 1990s a prime focus of the powers was on individuals in the United Kingdom, subject to immigration control, thought to be involved in providing political, financial and other material support for nationalist terrorist groups or causes in their countries of origin. Thus Chahal was thought to be aiding terrorism connected with the cause of Sikh separatism in India. Similarly Rehman, a Pakistani national practising as a minister of religion (Islam) in England, was thought by the Home Secretary to have connections (as a recruiter, fund-raiser and sponsor of trainees) with an Islamic terrorist organization involved in the Kashmir conflict.[109] The Newton Committee, when reviewing ATCSA detention, noted in 2003 that 'there have been no successful deportations on national security grounds since 1997'.[110] Rehman, whose appeal was rejected by the House of Lords, was not removed because by the end of the legal process he was no longer seen as a national security threat.[111]

Administrative Challenge and Review by the Courts: from Adviser System to SIAC[112]

Where someone's deportation was considered conducive to the public good on grounds of national security, they had no right of appeal within the statutory

---

[104] Carvel (1991a).

[105] *R v Home Secretary, ex parte B*, Law Report, *The Guardian*, 30 January 1991; Law Report, *The Independent*, 29 January 1991.

[106] *R v Secretary of State for the Home Department, ex parte Cheblak*, [1991] 2 All ER 319; Leigh (1991): 331.

[107] Grant (1991): 305.

[108] Grant (1991): 305.

[109] [2002] 1 All ER 122, at para. 1 (Lord Slynn)

[110] Newton Committee (2003): para. 197 (n.99).

[111] CAC 7th (2004–05b): Ev. 52.

[112] There would appear to have been no legal challenges by those detained by the Ministry of Defence as prisoners of war under the prerogative and Third Geneva Convention.

immigration appeals system, apart from one against destination.[113] They could seek redress in the High Court by way of a habeas corpus application or an application for judicial review. In addition, they could resort to a non-statutory advisory panel of three Advisers, appointed by the Home Secretary to review deportation (and thus detention) and advise him/her accordingly. Indeed, the net result of applications to the courts during the Gulf War effectively produced the answer that the detainee's first and appropriate port of call should be that non-statutory mechanism,[114] with the courts willing to review the decisions of the advisory panel where, for example, 'it could be shown to have acted unfairly within its terms of reference',[115] 'taking account of the fact that its procedures must necessarily be tailored to the unique nature of the subject matter within its remit.'[116] Otherwise, the court could only invalidate the Home Secretary's decision on narrow grounds of irrationality (abuse of discretion),[117] something impossible to prove when the courts would not compel the Secretary of State to disclose more of the case against the individual than he/she (the Home Secretary) was prepared, on grounds of security, to disclose. The common law rules of procedural fairness or natural justice were trumped by the demands of national security.[118] The Court here followed the earlier Court of Appeal decision in *R v Secretary of State for the Home Department, ex parte Hosenball.*[119] There Lord Denning MR said that

> When the national security is at stake even the rules of natural justice may have to be modified to meet the position. ... Save to the extent that the Home Secretary thinks safe. Great is the public interest in the freedom of the individual and the doing of justice to him, nevertheless in the last resort it must take second place to the security of the country itself.[120]

Geoffrey Lane LJ put it starkly:

---

[113]   Immigration Act 1971, s. 15(3).

[114]   *R v Secretary of State for the Home Department, ex p Cheblak,* [1991] 2 All ER 319, per Lord Donaldson MR, at 335.

[115]   Ibid.

[116]   *Cheblak* [1991] 2 All ER 319, per Lord Donaldson MR, at 330.

[117]   *Cheblak* [1991] 2 All ER 319, per Lord Donaldson MR, at 335. This involves the impossible task of establishing that the Home Secretary acted in bad faith (not believing what he claimed) or in a way so arbitrary, absurd or unjust that no reasonable Secretary of State could ever act.

[118]   *Cheblak* [1991] 2 All ER 319, per Lord Donaldson MR, at 331–332, 335, per Beldam LJ, at 339, per Nolan LJ at 342–343. See also *Council of Civil Service Unions v Minister for the Civil Service* [1984] 3 All ER 935 (the essential non-justiciability of national security once the court is satisfied by 'evidence' – usually the affidavit from the Secretary of State or the Permanent Secretary to the Home Office – that national security is properly an issue).

[119]   [1977] 1 WLR 766.

[120]   [1977] 1 WLR 766, at 779, 782.

The alien certainly has inadequate information upon which to prepare or direct his defence to the various charges which are made against him, and the only way that could be remedied would be to disclose information to him which might probably have an adverse effect on the national security. The choice is regrettably clear: the alien must suffer, if suffering there be.[121]

The deportee/detainee was not entitled to the reasons grounding those given in the standard notice served on deportees/detainees.[122] A notice of intention to deport was little more than a recitation of the statutory criteria and some rights of challenge.[123] The ground for deportation was thus 'conducive to the public good' and the reason for it 'national security'. In addition those who indicated a wish to make representations to the panel received a further letter amplifying this reason. For Palestinians like Mr and Mrs B[124] or those with a Palestinian connection like Cheblak,[125] it read:

The Iraqi Government has openly threatened to take terrorist action against unspecified western targets if hostilities break out in the Gulf. In the light of this your known links with an organization which we believe could take such action in support of the Iraqi regime make your presence in the United Kingdom an unacceptable security risk.[126]

Iraqis received a similar amplificatory letter referring to the individual's 'links and activities in connection with the Iraqi regime'.[127] As regards detainees under immigration legislation, the warrant for detention was little more than a recitation of the statutory basis.[128] Correspondence with lawyers and legal proceedings sometimes elicited a little more. Thus Mr B was said to be the nephew of Mr T, a notorious terrorist. Mr B claimed to have had no contact with his uncle since boyhood and to deplore his activities. When his solicitors asked the Home Office whether Mr B's links were based on more than the relationship with Mr T, they were merely told 'yes'.[129] The letter to Mr Cheblak as to others, did not specify the name of the organization in question and 'no information was given to enable the individual to know what "links", "activities" or "organization" the Home Office had in mind.'[130] Similarly in *Hosenball*, the sole material of substance in the notice

---

[121] [1977] 1 WLR 766, at 784.
[122] *Cheblak* [1991] 2 All ER 319; *R v Home Secretary, ex p. B*, Law Report, *The Guardian*, 30 January 1991.
[123] Cited in *Cheblak* [1991] 2 All ER 319, at p. 324.
[124] *R v Home Secretary, ex parte B*, Law Report, *The Guardian*, January 30, 1991.
[125] *R v Secretary of State for the Home Department, ex parte Cheblak*, [1991] 2 All ER 319.
[126] *Cheblak* [1991] 2 All ER 319, at p. 325.
[127] Grant (1991): 305.
[128] *Cheblak* [1991] 2 All ER 319, at p. 325.
[129] *R v Home Secretary, ex parte B*, Law Report, *The Guardian*, 30 January 30 1991.
[130] Grant (1991): 305.

was that the Home Secretary had considered information that while resident in the United Kingdom Hosenball 'in consort with others sought to obtain for publication information harmful to the security of the United Kingdom and that this information has included information prejudicial to the safety of servants of the Crown'.[131]

Recourse to the advisory panel procured release for some in the Gulf War, though this could be more a result of the weakness of the intelligence against the individuals rather than a vindication of a much criticized review scheme.[132] The *Times* condemned the advisory panel process as a charade.[133] The leading immigration law text thought it 'quite unsatisfactory'.[134] It was based on a procedure for rooting out communists, spies and security threats from the civil service.[135] The Home Secretary outlined the procedures to the House of Commons in 1971:

> All these proceedings start with a personal decision by the Home Secretary on national security grounds. The person concerned is notified of the decision and he will be given by the Home Office only such particulars of allegations as will not entail disclosure of sources of evidence. At the same time the person will be notified that he can make representations to the three advisors and will be given time to decide whether or not to do so. The advisors will then take account of any representations made by the person concerned. They will allow him to appear before them, if he wishes. He will not be entitled to legal representation, but he may be assisted by a friend to such extent as the advisors sanction. As well as speaking for himself, he may arrange for a third party to speak on his behalf. Neither the sources of evidence nor evidence that might lead to the disclosure of sources can be revealed to the person concerned, but the advisors will ensure that the person is able to make his point effectively and the procedure will give him the best possible opportunity to make the points he wishes to bring to their notice. ... Since the evidence against a person necessarily has to be received in his absence, the advisors in assessing the case will bear in mind that it has not been tested by cross-examination and that the person has not had the opportunity to rebut it. ... On receiving the advice of the advisors the Secretary of State will reconsider his original decision, but the advice given to him will not be revealed.[136]

In *Cheblak*, Lord Donaldson took a sanguine view of them seeing in their 'independent quasi-judicial scrutiny' elements of the inquisitorial approach adopted by courts elsewhere in Europe.[137] The Court of Appeal also made much of the Home Secretary's constitutional responsibility to Parliament for his decisions

---

[131]   [1977] 1 WLR 766, at 771–2.
[132]   Grant (1991): 305.
[133]   Ibid.
[134]   Macdonald and Blake (1991): 382.
[135]   Ibid.: 383.
[136]   HC Debs (5th series), Vol. 819, col. 376 (15 June 1971).
[137]   *Cheblak* [1991] 2 All ER 319, at p. 332.

and any failure to heed the advice of the panel.[138] Leigh was much more critical of a process involving oral hearings with the detainee of 45 minutes on average. In words which foreshadow an approach to 'national security' which Sedley J would have liked to adopt in the exclusion order case, *ex parte McQuillen*, examined in chapter 3, Leigh argued:

> To claim that they are the best that can be devised consistent with the requirements of national security demonstrates both over-subservience to that concept and a lack of imagination. [W]hile security *policy* is, quite properly, an issue reserved for the executive, arguably this does not justify the refusal to allow intelligence information in individual cases to be tested by cross-examination. Issues of accuracy, potential bias or self-interest of informers and alternative interpretations of the facts could all be dealt with without calling into question the policy underlying the decision contested. The real issue here ... is confidentiality. The challenge is to devise legal procedures which preserve executive responsibility and protect confidentiality, but also allow rigorous testing of the case on the appellant's behalf.[139]

He drew attention to a Canadian approach, a version of which was adapted for use by the United Kingdom after the decision of the European Court of Human Rights in *Chahal*.

The United Kingdom's dualist legal order limited the role of the ECHR. As it was then only an international legal obligation, national courts could not use its provisions to require the Home Secretary to exercise an unambiguous statutory discretion, apparently conferring unlimited power, in a manner consonant with ECHR obligations.[140] The *Soering* principle, later applied in *Chahal* with crucial shaping effect for the United Kingdom response post-9/11, relevant to the matter of a deportee's destination, was not considered in the High Court challenge by B because no decision on destination had at that stage been taken. It was not then established that detention for deportation could only be valid so long as deportation, diligently pursued, was a feasible prospect. This came only after Mr Chahal's human rights challenge at Strasbourg. As will be seen in chapter 6, this, when coupled with the incorporation of the ECHR into United Kingdom law through the HRA, dramatically changed the legal and constitutional landscape in which the United Kingdom Government had to operate in deciding how to respond to 9/11 as part of the 'war' on terrorism.

Chahal, resident in the United Kingdom, was thought to threaten its national security as someone involved in aiding Sikh terrorism in India. The Home Secretary was minded to deport him to that country. In the English courts, the Home Secretary won; he could deport because he had properly balanced the degree of threat to national security against the degree of danger to Chahal if returned to

---

[138] *Cheblak* [1991] 2 All ER 319, at p. 330.
[139] Leigh (1991): 337.
[140] *R* v *Secretary of State for the Home Department, ex parte Brind* [1991] 1 A.C. 696.

India.[141] Chahal's challenge in Strasbourg was successful.[142] This seminal case establishes a number of key points. Firstly, deportation is not possible where there are substantial grounds for believing that if returned the person faces a real risk of treatment contrary to Art. 3 ECHR (freedom from torture, inhuman or degrading treatment or punishment),[143] even where the person is a national security threat. This preclusion is absolute. It contains no 'national security' exception. It does not envisage balancing the degree of risk posed to national security against the degree of risk of harm to the putative deportee.[144] Chahal was at risk from State officials, but subsequent ECHR case law establishes that the preclusion can also operate where the risk of adverse treatment contrary to Art. 3 comes from non-State actors.[145] The second point established in the case was that the safeguards advanced by the Government as meeting 'fair hearing' standards were inadequate. Neither judicial review by the High Court nor the adviser system satisfied Art. 5(4) ECHR which requires that the legality of detention (a deprivation of liberty and security of person) must be determined by a 'court'. The High Court is such a body, but judicial review obtainable in it did not satisfy the provision; it was not incisive enough and could not look at the substance of the decision.[146] The Advisory Panel saw all the evidence grounding the Home Secretary's decision, but since its advice was not binding on him, it could not rank as a 'court'.[147] For much the same reasons neither body afforded the 'effective remedy' required by Art. 13 ECHR.[148] Finally, *Chahal* decides that although Art. 5 ECHR permits detention for deportation, that could only support detention for purposes of deportation where there was a reasonable prospect of deportation being pursued with due diligence.[149] Thus, where deportation is precluded because of Art. 3 ECHR, Art. 5(1)(f) cannot be used to support detention.

The governmental response was to release Chahal from detention. It also had enacted by Parliament a more sophisticated review process to cover national security deportations.[150] Under it, as will more fully be examined in chapter 8, the deportee has a full right of appeal to SIAC, a three-person security-cleared tribunal, chaired by a High Court judge. Its decisions are binding on the Home Secretary. It hears evidence and intelligence material by means of 'open' and 'closed' sessions. The latter – 'closed' sessions – are the ones in which SIAC reviews material which

---

[141] *R v Secretary of State for the Home Department, ex parte Chahal* [1995] 1 All ER 658.

[142] *Chahal* v *United Kingdom* (1997) 23 EHRR 413.

[143] (1997) 23 EHRR 413, paras 73–74.

[144] (1997) 23 EHRR 413, paras 75–80.

[145] *HLR* v *France* (1997) 26 EHRR 29.

[146] (1997) 23 EHRR 413, paras 119–121, 127, 130–133.

[147] (1997) 23 EHRR 413, paras 130–133.

[148] (1997) 23 EHRR 413, paras 153–155.

[149] (1997) 23 EHRR 413, paras 112–117.

[150] Special Immigration Appeals Commission Act 1997.

has not to be disclosed to the deportee or to his/her lawyer for security reasons. They are excluded from those sessions. However, during them SIAC is aided by a Special Advocate, a security-cleared experienced public law barrister, acting as counsel to SIAC, who plays 'devil's advocate' with the evidence/intelligence material, probing it in a way not possible before the Home Secretary.[151]

The ostensibly full appellate jurisdiction for SIAC was effectively narrowed to one more at the judicial review end of the spectrum by the decision of the House of Lords in *Rehman*. Their Lordships also gave a very wide meaning to 'national security'. Rehman was thought by the Home Secretary to have connections (as a recruiter, fund-raiser and sponsor of trainees) with an Islamic terrorist organization involved in the Kashmir conflict. He certified that Rehman's deportation would be conducive to the public good in the interests of national security.[152] SIAC allowed Rehman's appeal. It had to do so where it considered that the decision appealed against was not in accordance with the law (including any applicable immigration rules) or where it considered that the Home Secretary's discretion should have been exercised differently.[153] Here his decision was held not to accord with the law or the applicable Immigration Rule.[154] For SIAC, conduct could only threaten the United Kingdom's national security if it were targeted at the United Kingdom, its system of government or its citizens, or, if targeted against another State, if that State would take reprisals affecting the security of the United Kingdom or its citizens. Moreover, the Home Secretary needed to prove to a 'high civil balance of probabilities' the particular acts which were said to constitute that threat. This he had failed to do. The Court of Appeal allowed his appeal from SIAC, and that Court's decision to do so was upheld by the House of Lords when Rehman appealed to them. Both the Court of Appeal and the House of Lords held that SIAC had deployed too narrow a definition of 'national security' and had required an inappropriate standard of proof. The real test was whether, looking at the entirety of the case and taking account of the Home Secretary's policy on the importance to national security of international co-operation in the fight against terrorism, the individual could be said to be a danger to national security. In short it was a matter of impugning the exercise of discretion on a matter of judgment and policy by a senior and responsible member of the executive with 'the advantage of a wide range of advice from people with day-to-day involvement in security matters which the commission, despite its specialist membership, cannot match'.[155] The effect of *Rehman*, in requiring so much deference to be shown to the opinion of the Secretary of State (the more so after 9/11),[156] reduces SIAC's ostensibly full

---

[151] See chapter 8.
[152] [2002] 1 All ER 122, at para. 1 (Lord Slynn).
[153] Special Immigration Appeals Commission Act 1997, s. 4.
[154] [2002] 1 All ER 122, at paras 2–5 (Lord Slynn); Immigration Rule 364.
[155] [2002] 1 All ER 12, at para. 57 (Lord Hoffman); see also paras 23–6 (Lord Slynn).
[156] [2002] 1 All ER 122, at para. 29 (Lord Steyn) and most graphically at para. 62 (Lord Hoffman).

powers in the 'national security' field of immigration law essentially to applying to his/her decision the principles of judicial review, including compliance with the HRA.[157]

As seen in chapter 1, their Lordships also took a wide view of what risk to 'national security' entails. The reciprocal co-operation between the United Kingdom and other states in combating international terrorism can promote its national security; such co–operation may itself foster such security 'by, *inter alia*, the United Kingdom taking action against supporters within the United Kingdom of terrorism directed against other states'.[158]

But even with its powers thus reduced, SIAC affords a better forum than the courts applying judicial review on these issues. Unlike them, it can exercise those powers having seen all the security evidence. While the suspects and their lawyers will necessarily be excluded during consideration of sensitive security material, the scheme envisages that searching scrutiny of that evidence will be undertaken by SIAC with the benefit of security-cleared counsel probing and testing that evidence essentially in the interests of the appellant. SIAC can also take on board claims under the HRA.

The period since 1973 has seen immigration 'public good' powers subject to EC law limits on their application to citizens of member States. Restrictions on those exercising EC rights of free movement have to be justified on narrowly construed grounds of public policy, public health or public security, and the focus is very centrally on the personal conduct of the individual concerned. In *Van Duyn* in 1974, their use was upheld with respect to members of the Church of Scientology.[159] Concern, however, that the European Court of Justice would progressively tighten those limits (as indeed it has done emphasizing that the individual needs to pose a genuine and sufficiently serious threat to a public policy concern affecting a fundamental interest of society) has seen the Government keen to avoid the issue being raised and sometimes, faced with the threat of scrutiny by that Court, to prefer to revoke 'public good' orders or analogous ones under the terrorism legislation rather than risk an adverse ruling.[160]

---

[157] [2002] 1 All ER 122, at paras 17, 26 (Lord Slynn), 49–54 (Lord Hoffman) (listing no factual basis/no evidence, and irrationality [*Wednesbury* 'unreasonableness] as grounds).

[158] [2002] 1 All ER 122, at paras 15–17 (Lord Slynn, with whose views the others concurred).

[159] [1975] Ch 358.

[160] On EC law requirements see Barnard (2004): chap. 14. See revocations in the case of Galvin, an American fund-raiser for the IRA who had taken Irish citizenship and the exclusion orders against leading members of Sinn Fein (see *ex parte Adams* discussed in chapter 3).

Chapter 5

Withdrawal from Empire: the Malayan, Cyprus and Kenyan Emergencies

Introduction: Executive Measures and the Rise and Fall of Empire

In 1905, the British Empire covered in terms of population and geographical area a quarter of the globe. It also dominated almost all the world's oceans.[1] The United Kingdom had Dominions and colonies in North America, the Caribbean, the Far East (Malaya, Singapore and parts of Borneo, Hong Kong), East, West and southern Africa, and the Antipodes, with Gibraltar and Cyprus at either end of the Mediterranean and effective domination of Egypt and the Suez Canal. The jewel in the Imperial Crown was India (the Indian subcontinent as a whole, what is now Pakistan, India and Bangladesh). Its ultimate victory in the recent Boer War had seen more of what is now South Africa added and it had pushed northwards into Rhodesia (now Zimbabwe). Its economic power had given it a further 'informal empire', with dominance in Latin America and the Middle East.[2] More possessions and entities subject to control were to be added after victory in the First World War: former German colonies in East Africa and League of Nations mandates in Iraq, Jordan and Palestine. In the 1930s it was the largest empire in world history.[3] Part of England's first colony, Ireland, gained effective independence in 1922. That expansion had often been achieved by military force and was maintained in part by the deployment against disturbances and insurgencies of the types of executive measures examined in this book. Thus, martial law was used frequently in the colonies throughout the nineteenth century.[4] For example, it was deployed along with statutory regimes in 1857 brutally to suppress the Indian Mutiny.[5] It was invoked in 1848–51 by Governor Byng against the Kandyan insurgency in Ceylon[6] and by Governor Eyre in 1865 to suppress a rebellion in Jamaica.[7] During the Boer War, Sir Henry Campbell-Bannerman, the leader of the Liberal Opposition, complained of Government use of 'methods of barbarism' in respect of interning

---

[1] Ferguson (2004): xi.
[2] On 'informal empire' (dominance through economic power and 'free trade') see James (1998), Ferguson (2004): 244–7; Butler (2002): xii–xiii.
[3] Butler (2002): xi.
[4] Hussain (2003): 108.
[5] David (2000).
[6] Kostal (2000).
[7] Kostal (2005): chap. 1.

under martial law women and children behind barbed wire in what contemporaries called 'concentration camps'.[8] Then, as now, there was an anti-war movement, even if the dominant mood was one of jingoism.[9] Some 22,000 women and children died of malnutrition and disease, not as a 'deliberate and settled policy' of 'extermination', as Lloyd George charged,[10] but rather as a result of well-documented incompetence and neglect.[11] The executive measures used in Ireland have been examined in chapter 3. In the 1930s and 1940s, Indian nationalists, including Gandhi and India's post-independence leaders, were detained without trial.[12] Iraqi tribesmen were bombed from the air in the 1920s. And a prime weapon in the colonial armoury against 'troublemakers' was to exile them to another part of the Empire, as happened to an Egyptian nationalist ruler in the nineteenth century,[13] and, in the twentieth, to some Indian nationalists (exiled to what is now Burma),[14] to the Kabaka of Buganda in 1953 and to two Cypriot Greek Orthodox bishops (and eight others) in 1931.[15]

The period 1947 to 1997, ending with the return of Hong Kong to China saw this Empire dismantled quite rapidly in response to nationalism and in part to anti-colonial armed struggle in the changed world after the Allied victory in the Second World War. Japanese victories had shattered the myth of the invincibility of the 'white' powers. The Japanese devolution of governmental tasks to local administrations had given the lie to European arguments that Asian peoples were incapable of governing themselves.[16] Soldiers from different parts of the Empire had fought together and become aware of longer-standing Indian nationalism.[17] The Atlantic Charter (the statement of the Allied war aims in 1941) and the UN Charter put the self-determination of peoples firmly on the international agenda.[18] Soldiers returning after the War to countries that were colonies considered that they had fought fascism for the independence of nations and saw as hypocritical the maintenance of colonial power.[19] The War had given Asian nationalisms a youthful militaristic face.[20]

Some colonies achieved independence in the forties (India and Pakistan, Burma, Ceylon (now Sri Lanka)), a few more in the fifties (for example, Malaya, Ghana (formerly the Gold Coast)) but many more in the sixties (for example,

---

[8]   Pakenham (1979): 504, 508; Griggs (1997): 203.

[9]   Nash (1999):42–9.

[10] Roberts (2000): 806.

[11] Ibid,: 802–7; Pakenham (1979) chap. 39.

[12] Keay (2000): 498–9, 504; Simpson (1996b): 646–8.

[13] James (1998); 269–73; Ferguson (2004): 232–3.

[14] Keay (2000): 467.

[15] Simpson (2004): 881–4, 886.

[16] Hoffman (1999): 45–8.

[17] Elkins (2005): 23–4.

[18] Hoffman (1999): 45–8.

[19] Elkins (2005): 24.

[20] Bayly and Harper (2007): 16.

Cyprus, Nigeria, Kenya, Jamaica). Not all came to independence as a result of insurrection.[21] But the political, physical and economic cost of maintaining a colonial empire in the face of concurrent and geographically widespread armed insurgencies brought about a marked change in colonial policy by the end of the 1950s. In the early 1950s colonial empire was seen as valuable in both strategic and economic terms and as aiding Britain's position as a major world power.[22] Investing the material and personnel resources of a declining and overstretched economy in maintenance of it was seen as very much worthwhile. The governing policy was at best for moves over quite a long period towards internal self-government (with Britain retaining at the very least responsibility for defence and external relations) rather than independence. By 1957, after the Suez debacle of 1956, a review in part to examine the costs and benefits of empire showed that 'territorial empire was no longer seen as a sustainer of British great-powerdom'.[23] It was not a matter of wholesale retreat but more a question of how best to manage the process of colonial independence rather than mere internal self–government, with differing views taken about different areas.

> White-settlerdom was one of the key factors in Whitehall's dealings with its variable-geometry, multi-speed territorial empire in Africa. In West Africa, where it was minimal, the initial strides down the road to eventual independence could be – and were – longer. … But in the long white-settler finger thrust northwards from South Africa, through the Rhodesias and into Kenya, entirely different political and economic calculations were in play.[24]

It was not, however, envisaged in 1957 as a mad rush for 'exit' from colonial empire. The decision to scramble out of Africa came only after the Macmillan Conservative Government's General Election victory in 1959 and the appointment of Ian MacLeod as Secretary of State for the Colonies. This presaged a 'deliberate speeding up of the move to independence' in Africa as the only way to avoid 'terrible bloodshed'.[25]

> The immediate causes of the end of the British Empire are to be found not only in the nationalist movements in Empire itself but also in lessons learned from the Algerian revolution and in the danger of Soviet intervention in the Congo. It seemed altogether more prudent to settle with African liberation movements in eastern and central Africa before war broke out between blacks and whites or before the Africans turned to the Russians for sponsorship.[26]

---

[21] Ferguson (2004): 295.

[22] Hennessey (2006): 28–41; Butler (2002): xii; Ferguson (2004): 357.

[23] Hennessey (2006): 475.

[24] Hennessey (2006): 301.

[25] Hennessey (2006): 601, quoting MacLeod.

[26] Louis (1999): 354.

Most of the former colonies, dependencies and protectorates are now part of the Commonwealth, the extent of which mirrors the former extent of empire.[27]

This chapter examines the use of executive measures to deal with insurgencies in the withdrawal from Empire in three of the colonial emergencies: Malaya, Cyprus and Kenya. All three are examined because they occurred in whole or in part in the new human rights era ushered in with the ratification by the United Kingdom of the European Convention on Human Rights (ECHR). They thus form a sharp contrast to earlier eras with much more limited international accountability. But, because ECHR norms were not part of national law either in the United Kingdom or the colonies, they also form a significant contrast to the HRA era in terms of the practical applicability of judicial oversight of the application of such norms. Malaya is examined because it saw what is generally accepted as a 'model' victory against a Communist insurgency by means of the application of lethal force in the low-intensity operations of a guerrilla war and the deployment of security measures of the type examined in this book, on the one hand, and policies (including an accelerated move towards independence) designed to win the 'hearts and minds' of the bulk of the population of Malaya, on the other. The 'benevolent' picture painted by public records and earlier accounts has, however, been somewhat tarnished by a 'darker' side presented in a recent study.[28] Cyprus is examined as an emergency in an anomalous European colony, thought vital to the United Kingdom's strategic interests, in relation to which the direct interest of another State party to the ECHR, Greece, gave real force to ECHR norms in the first inter-State case brought before the European Commission of Human Rights. Kenya is examined because to many contemporaries it represented a conflict between civilization and barbarism, part of the United Kingdom's 'civilizing' mission, while to others it showed the racist face of Empire as the United Kingdom suppressed the Mau Mau revolt with use of executive measures on a massive scale (mass detentions and internal exile or banishment in 'Britain's *gulag*')[29] and large-scale use of the death penalty in what two recent histories characterize as a 'dirty war'.[30]

The Malayan Emergency

The emergency in British Malaya lasted from mid–June 1948 until Malayan Independence at the end of August 1957. It continued until 1960 for the newly independent State within the (then British) Commonwealth, with its government aided in combating an ongoing but diminished Communist insurgency by British

---

[27] James (1998): 624.

[28] Bayly and Harper (2007).

[29] Elkins (2005).

[30] Anderson (2005); Elkins (2005).

expertise and loans. It was the longest emergency in British colonial history,[31] the most protracted twentieth-century conflict, outside Northern Ireland, faced by Britain.[32] During it, 10,710 people were killed: 1,851 members of the security forces, 2,461 civilians, and 6,398 communist 'terrorists'. Just over 2,500 members of the security forces and 1,383 civilians were wounded. A further 807 civilians were listed as missing. The population of Malaya was only about a tenth of that of the United Kingdom in that period. It is right to recall that

> The violence of the conflict was to be found not only in the casualty lists from the 'shooting war', but in the growing trauma of arrests and detentions, the removals and deportations which tore apart the lives of individuals, families, and whole communities. ... hundreds of thousands of people would be ensnared by this crisis. ... a forgotten story of a forgotten war.[33]

The Emergency cost some £700 million pounds sterling, £520 million spent by the British taxpayer. Even discounting £100 million for military and defence costs which would arguably have arisen anyway, the net total of some £600 million is quite staggering.[34]

The Federation of Malaya – a governmentally unwieldy combination of two British colonies or settlements,[35] and nine Malay States[36] each nominally ruled by a Sultan but under British protection ('a tactful euphemism for governing authority')[37] – came into being on 1 February 1948, after a failed attempt to provide a more centralized governmental system.[38] The governing instrument was the Federation of Malaya Agreement, embodied in United Kingdom Law as part of a prerogative Order in Council.[39] Its essence was that each of the States and settlements 'should retain their individuality under a strong central government'.[40] Singapore formed a separate British colony at the tip of the Malay Peninsula (what is now West Malaysia).

The population of the Federation was some 5.7 million and ethnically diverse with 2.8 million Malays forming just over 48 per cent of the population, 2.1 million Chinese (some 38 per cent), 660,000 Indians/Pakistanis (some 12 per cent), less than 100,000 British and other 'Europeans' (including Americans), and small

---

[31] Carruthers (1995): 72.

[32] Townshend (1986): 155.

[33] Bayly and Harper (2007): 456.

[34] Director of Operations (Malaya) (1957): paras 17–19.

[35] Penang (including Province Wellesley) and Mallacca.

[36] Johore, Pahang, Negri Sembilan, Selangor, Perak, Kedah, Perlis, Kelantan and Trengganu.

[37] Shennan (2004): 6.

[38] Malayan Union Order in Council 1946 S.R. & O. 1946 (No. 463).

[39] The Federation of Malaya Order in Council (SI 1948/108). This was later criticized in Director of Operations Malaya (1957): para. 45(a) as having hindered prompt action.

[40] Forster (1957): para. 2.5.

numbers of aboriginal peoples (*orang asli*).[41] Most of the population lived in rural rather than urban areas. Topographically, Malaya was bisected by central mountain ranges running north to south and, apart from the coast, composed mainly of dense jungle. The economy was dominated by rubber (supplying half the world's needs) and tin. Malaya was the sterling area's largest dollar earner. This made protection from attack of plantations and mines, and their managers and workers, an essential part of the counter-insurgency strategy. Malaya was economically and strategically important to the Empire and the United Kingdom's domestic recovery after the War[42] – virtually its lifeline.[43]

British influence in the peninsula and islands began with the establishment of trading settlements by the East India Company in the late eighteenth and early nineteenth centuries, with the Straits Settlements becoming a Crown colony under the Colonial Office in 1867. It took over the role from the India Office with the waning of the power of the Company after the Indian Mutiny.[44] The inter-war years (1920–40) were the pinnacle of Empire in Malaya. The Sultans were never mere puppets. Stability was maintained by mutual respect between these rulers and the British and further aided by bringing non-Europeans into government and opening the Civil Service to educated Malays. There were few indications of insurgent nationalism. Malay and Indian nationalism were not thought threatening. In contrast the British took seriously the threat from the Malayan Communist Party (MCP), dealing with it in 1931–32 by imprisonment and deportation.[45] World War Two, with its revelation of the weakness of British power, and the Allies' promise of 'self-determination' made in the Atlantic Charter late in 1941, enhanced nationalism in Malaya, as elsewhere in colonial empires.[46]

The British had been ejected from both Malaya and Singapore by the Japanese in 1942. After the defeat of Japan at the end of the Second World War, the British returned in 1945. There had, however, been a 'power vacuum'. There were very few British forces in the country and both they and the Malaya Peoples Anti-Japanese Army (MPAJA), primarily Chinese guerrillas, were outnumbered by the Japanese. The MPAJA began to take over in a number of areas and there was a danger of intercommunal strife, even anarchy, as revenge was taken on perceived collaborators.[47] Enough of a peace was maintained by the small force of British irregulars who had fought alongside the MPAJA, and eventually a British Military Administration ran Malaya until 1 April 1946. It was then intended that the nine Malay States and the two British settlements would merge into a unitary state, the Malayan Union. The plan 'alienated the Sultans and galvanized the Malay people

---

[41] Clutterbuck (1966): 19.

[42] Butler (2002): 81–5; Bayly and Harper (2007): 11.

[43] Sandhu (1964a): 144.

[44] Shennan (2004): 5.

[45] Ibid.: 148–9.

[46] Hoffman (1999): 45–8.

[47] Bayly and Harper (2007): 41.

in an unprecedented way', with leading Malays forming the United Malay National Organization (UNMO). The resulting process of consultation and compromise produced the Federation of Malaya Agreement on which the government of Malaya rested during the emergency.[48]

The Nature and Scope of the Emergency

The MCP also grew in strength as a result of the Japanese invasion, and was seriously underestimated by the British authorities in Malaya. Many of its members had fought in the MPAJA, alongside the British, against the Japanese. It had tried but failed, through labour disruption and subversion of young Chinese through Chinese schools, to subvert the government service and bring Malaya to its knees.[49] The decision of the MCP to launch an all-out insurgency to establish a Communist Republic in Malaya was taken late in May 1948 at a conference in a sophisticated camp in the jungle. Its undisputed leader, Chin Peng, a Malaya Chinese had visited China in 1945 and 1946 and had learned guerrilla warfare from the British when with the MPAJA. He was a disciple of Mao, but probably not his puppet.[50] The 1957 review of the emergency by the British Director of Operations saw the MCP campaign as 'part of a wider Soviet-inspired drive to obtain control of what is strategically and economically one of the most important areas in South-East Asia'.[51] The campaign of murder, sabotage and terrorism, which began on 16 June 1948 and was designed to paralyse the Government and develop into armed revolution, was in response to instructions issued at two Cominform conferences in India earlier in the year.[52] There was, however, no evidence of any appreciable financial backing from sources outside Malaya, with the MCP and its armed 'wing' relying for the most part on 'subscriptions' from willing sympathizers or extorted from others, often in the form of supplies in kind (for example, food).[53] Its weaponry came from a mixture of material hidden in dumps by the MPAJA during the Japanese occupation, or captured from the security forces or leaked or lost by them, or from Ordnance stores or arms dealers, from smuggling or from confiscation and robbery from the public.[54] The 'armed wing' in the jungle – later called the Malayan Races Liberation Army (MRLA) – was matched by a civilian wing (Min Yuen) in towns and on the jungle fringes of villages, among the Chinese 'squatters', from which the MRLA derived material support, some coerced, some willingly given especially when the MRLA rather than government forces appeared to be in the ascendancy.

---

[48] Clutterbuck (1966): 22–4.

[49] Barber (1971): 30–35; Clutterbuck (1966): 25–8.

[50] Barber (1971): 30–35.

[51] Director of Operations Malaya (1957): para. 7.

[52] Director of Operations Malaya (1957): para. 8; See also Forster (1957): para. 3.4.

[53] Director of Operations Malaya (1957): para. 16.

[54] Director of Operations Malaya (1957): paras 12, 13.

A state of emergency was declared on 17 June in response to a number of murderous attacks attributed to Communist 'bandits', initially in parts of the two States concerned, Perak and Johore, and nationwide the next day. The legal base was the British Military Administration (Essential Regulations) Ordinance. The base became the Emergency Regulations Ordinance 1948 from 7 July. This enabled a proclamation of emergency whenever it appeared to the High Commissioner in Council that an occasion of emergency or public danger had arisen. The issuing of such a proclamation brought into play his power to make any regulations whatsoever which he considered desirable in the public interest and to prescribe penalties, including the death penalty, which may be imposed for any offence against any such regulations and to provide for the trial, by such Courts as might be specified in such regulations, of persons guilty of such offences.[55] The regulations could not authorize punishment by death, fine or imprisonment without trial, but, without prejudice to the generality of this wide rule-making power, could deal amongst other specifics with arrest, detention, exclusion and deportation, with restriction of movement, and with control of aliens. A new code of regulations was issued under the Ordinance on 15 July.[56] Amended continually throughout the emergency, this legal code provided the basis for most of the Government's actions to deal with the emergency. But the powers supplemented rather than replaced those under other ordinances, such as the Banishment enactment or the Immigration Ordinance 1952.

The conflict was primarily rural and jungle-based rather than urban. Those in larger cities were largely unaware of the scale of the conflict.[57] The MRLA sought to attain its aims over the period through a variety of means and shifts in strategy. Between 1948 and 1950, it undertook a campaign of murder, sabotage and terrorism, hoping by it to paralyse the Government and develop the campaign into an armed revolution. From 1950–52, it shifted into guerrilla war designed to wear down Government will; to dominate targeted small towns and villages; and thereby to liberate areas in which they would establish their own civil administration and develop a regular army. From 1952–55, to avoid antagonizing the masses, it operated only against military targets in the countryside. As regards centres of urban population its tactics were ones of infiltration and subversion in all walks of life. From 1955 onwards, reliance on subversive methods became dominant and the jungle 'war' petered out.[58] Throughout, Government policy deployed the military in aid of the civil power rather than martial law sought by many European planters. The matter was more one of perception, of maintaining the appearance essential to maintaining governmental legitimacy of order being maintained by regular law being made by civil authorities, since the Emergency Regulations Ordinance gave virtually unlimited rule-making power, and the reality was more

[55] Emergency Regulations Ordinance 1948 (No. 10 of 1948), ss. 3, 4.

[56] Simpson (2004): 833.

[57] Barber (1971): 42–4.

[58] Forster (1957): para. 3.1.

akin to a legal regime of a type associated with martial law than the regular legal system.[59] The conflict ebbed and flow, but four distinct phases have been identified. From the declaration of a State of Emergency in June 1948 until October 1949, the 'Communist attempt to seize power by violence and revolution was held and the [communist terrorists] withdrew into the jungle to reorganise for a prolonged war'. The period from then until August 1951 saw violence reach its peak. The MRLA was encouraged by Communist successes elsewhere in Asia. There were serious weaknesses in civil and military measures. Sir Harold Briggs was appointed as Director of Operations, the better to coordinate these. His plan was a combination of security measures and ones of regulation and control of the population and resettlement of the Chinese squatters (what his successor labelled as 'winning hearts and minds'). It built on work done by his murdered High Commissioner, Sir Henry Gurney, and was one of the keys to final success.[60] The Security Forces also began to achieve greater success in eliminating members of the MRLA in jungle encounters. The next three-year phase saw 'the back of the revolt ... broken'. The dispersed Chinese squatter population was brought under control as the Briggs plan matured. The MRLA suffered increased eliminations, losing half its strength, and consequently became less aggressive. Casualties among civilians and the Security Forces were now only one seventh of their 1951 peak. A key feature in this period was the combination of the roles of High Commissioner and Director of Operations in Briggs's successor, General Templer, who had 'full power over all civil and military resources'. The final phase of direct British involvement was July 1954 to August 1957. The crisis had passed. The posts of High Commissioner and Director of Operations were accordingly once more separated and held by different individuals. Crucially, to prepare for independence, governmental powers were gradually handed over to Malayan political leaders in a conservative coalition combining Malays, Chinese and Indians. Indeed in December 1955, the Chief Minister held peace talks with and at the request of the leaders of the MCP. They were willing to abandon the conflict and come out of the jungle, but only if the MCP was recognized as a legitimate political party. The new Government held firm and refused this, fearing a return to subversion followed by further armed conflict.[61] In 1956 a date for independence was agreed and key governmental, military and security posts were subject to 'Malayanization'. The MRLA continued to decline in strength. So did encounters with the Security Forces, casualties and incidents.

The Communist insurgency was defeated by a combination of tough security measures/policies, enabling extensive intelligence-gathering, coupled with measures to win the hearts and minds of the vast bulk of the population. Particularly important here was the clear and stated policy of moving steadily towards self-government and eventual independence, something Churchill saw as

---

[59] Townshend (1986): 157–8, 164–5.

[60] Townshend (1986): 158–9.

[61] Barber (1971): 227–35; Clutterbuck (1966): 135–7.

vital in keeping a strategically important Malaya within the British sphere of influence in a South-East Asia threatened by communism.[62] The effective deployment of propaganda by the Government was also important in maintaining the confidence of the civilian population and weakening that of the MRLA and MCP. The strategy was to deal first with the MRLA and MCP in areas where they were weakest and, when those were cleared (declared 'White'), to lift there as many of the stringent emergency restrictions as possible, and then move on to tackle their areas of greater strength, thus spreading ever wider the number of 'White', largely 'emergency-free' areas. In 'selected' areas, a more limited range of regulatory restrictions was removed. The aim of the Briggs plan was to break the link between the MCP/MRLA and the main source of their support, the Chinese squatters. A key element in this was to give the Chinese section of Malaya's diverse population a real stake in a new Malaya.[63] This was achieved in part through new citizenship laws[64] and in part by providing Chinese representation on key bodies in the decision-making process (War Executive Councils at Federal, State or District level, detention advisory committees). It was achieved crucially through a policy of resettling the squatters (and some Chinese who were legitimate land-holders) with proper land tenure in fortified 'New Villages', protected by the police and members of the Home Guard so as to free up the military for direct operations against the communist guerrillas in the jungle.[65] These villages were condemned in MCP propaganda as 'concentration camps', surrounded as they were by barbed wire fences and floodlit security zones ('killing grounds').[66] The fences were later changed to chain-link. In a context of national registration (explored further below) enabling prompt identification of an individual, they could through these physical measures be protected from MCP infiltration and MRLA attack by Security forces including not only soldiers and Malay police, but a Chinese element in a 'Home Guard'. The villages were gradually improved in terms of physical structure, utilities and amenities, schools and medical facilities, with the assistance of qualified teams under resettlement officers. A new social insurance system was introduced throughout Malaya. While initially there was a degree of voluntarism in the resettlement process, compulsion and coercion (the threat of repatriation to China) were also deployed,[67] the legal base being an unclear mix of the amended Restricted Residence Enactment and the Emergency Regulations.[68] In two areas where terrorist pressure was such that the usual procedures for

---

[62] Barber (1971): 140; Townshend (1986): 155; Butler (2002): 87.

[63] Townshend (1986): 159–160.

[64] The Federation of Malay Agreement (Amendment) Ordinance 1952 (Federation of Malaya No. 23 of 1952).

[65] Federation of Malaya, Paper No. 33 (1952); Sandhu (1964a).

[66] For detailed rules and logistical and material problems see CO 1022/30 and CO 852/113 TNA.

[67] Sandhu (1964a); Bayly and Harper (2007): 448–9, 489–91, 526–7.

[68] Federation of Malaya, Paper No. 33 (1952): 4–5.

resettlement would have produced undue risk and delay, resettlement was effected under Emergency Regulation 17D by arresting and detaining under a collective order everyone in the area concerned and then releasing and resettling all those in respect of whom there were no grounds for making individual detention orders.[69] In all, some half a million people were settled or resettled (some 9 per cent of the Malayan population), mainly Chinese and as short a distance as possible from their former homes, at a cost of some 41 million Straits dollars.[70] A similar number were regrouped in towns and on rubber estates.[71] It was 'the largest planned population relocation in recorded history'.[72]

Material support in terms of food, money and weapons was denied the MCP/MRLA in general by restrictions on the sale and distribution of food[73] and specifically by random stop and search of vehicles and persons and by routine searches of individuals (often strip-searches) when entering and leaving the New Villages to go to their places of work ('Operation Starvation'). The latter at times came close to harassment with racial overtones.[74] Mines and rubber plantations, so vital to the economy, were protected by armed police and by a regulatory system of regrouping of the larger labour forces into defended residential areas with the cost of some being borne by the mining companies and plantation owners.[75] Other important factors in defeating the insurgency were the lack of significant support for the MRLA/MCP among the Malay and Indian population and the fact that the Chinese Government and its military forces were occupied fighting against UN Forces in the Korean War.

In terms of security measures, the gathering of vital intelligence was aided by the expansion and reform of the Police Special Branch and the deployment of Chinese officers trained in undercover techniques to enable infiltration of suspect groups. A vital policy was one of National Registration which, with the requirement to carry one's identification documents embodying photograph and fingerprint, made it easier to monitor the population and identify suspects through lack of any or proper documentation.[76] A variety of ways were used to increase the flow of information to the police and Security forces: (a) the use of infiltration agents; (b) the 'turning' of former terrorists through money and amnesty; (c) having suitable 'converted terrorists' serve in a Special Operations Volunteer Force

---

[69] Federation of Malaya, Paper No. 33 (1952): 5.

[70] Ibid.: 3. On difficulties with accurate figures see Simpson (2004): 833–4.

[71] Sandhu (1964b): 178–180.

[72] Bayly and Harper (2007): 490.

[73] Emergency (Restriction and Prohibition of Foodstuffs and Other Supplies) Regulations.

[74] Director of Operations Malaya (1958): Chap IV, 9–18. Bayly and Harper (2007): 526–7.

[75] Forster (1957): para. 5.2. The legal base was furnished by Emergency Regulations 17FA and 17FAA in 1950.

[76] Clutterbuck (1966): 37; Barber (1971): 70–71; Emergency (Registration Areas) Regulations 1948 (1948/2033).

to help in hunting down their former comrades;[77] (d) a greater flow of information from a village either willingly because 'hearts and minds' had been won by the 'carrot' or because of the application of curfews and other restrictions, the 'stick' of 'collective punishment' of a 'disloyal village' to 'encourage' recalcitrant villagers to co-operate; (e) the use of arrest and detention without trial of suspects, something which had a preventive element and one of removing communist cells from the community where, because of witness intimidation or sympathy with the cause, conviction in the criminal courts was not possible.[78] Reconnaissance by aircraft and by ground patrols, aided by Iban native jungle trackers from Borneo, enabled the identification of camps, arms dumps and trucks. The use of such trackers proved controversial alongside payment of bounty for each 'kill' and a stop was put on the practice of producing the head for proof of the kill.[79] The 'food denial' policy forced the MRLA/MCP to cultivate food in a jungle inhospitable in food terms. This, however, made them more vulnerable to identification by aerial reconnaissance, enabling both the destruction of the crops by chemical spraying from the air or their manual and chemical destruction by ground troops. It also increased the number of MRLA and Security forces contacts and confrontations, which the latter increasingly won. The end result of all this was better to enable the targeting of MRLA groups or MCP suspects. Sometimes this resulted in their physical elimination through lethal force in military clashes or ambushes. There is some indication of using agents to set up a suspect for physical elimination. This would now be called a 'shoot to kill' policy.[80] There was also the Batang Kali incident in which 25 Chinese men were shot by a unit of the Scots Guards (Malaya's My Lai), an incident said to be exceptional only in its scale.[81] The legality of the use of lethal force in Malaya was, however, complicated by the creation of areas in which 'shoot on sight' was permissible. Its use also highlights graphically that this was a guerrilla war, whatever the official reasons for avoiding those terms. In the jungle conflict 'shoot to kill' was the order of the day, with arrest reserved for the wounded.[82] There were, however, cases in which lethal force was wrongfully deployed against civilians or terrorists 'shot while escaping'.[83] But effective targeting also enabled capture and removal from circulation in the community of suspected terrorists through criminal prosecution and trial by judge alone or in capital cases judge plus lay assessors rather than by jury, whether for

---

[77] Emergency (Special Operations Volunteer Force) Regulations 1952 (see NatCO 1022/50 TNA).

[78] Clutterbuck (1966): 38–9; Director of Operations Malaya (1957): para. 64; Federation of Malaya, Paper No. 34 (1953): 2–3.

[79] CO 1022/57 TNA.

[80] Barber (1971): 70–71; Clutterbuck (1966): 37; Bayly and Harper (2007): 430–433.

[81] Bayly and Harper (2007): 445–6.

[82] Simpson (2004): 834.

[83] Townshend (1986): 165. See also Chinese Government complaints about persecution of Chinese in Malaya FC 1821/3 dated 8 January 1951 in DO 35/2920 TNA.

offences against the general law or ones under the Emergency Regulations, many of which carried the death penalty (for example, possession of firearms, extorting food or money for terrorists).[84] For terrorist offences 226 were hanged, a relatively low number (given the scale of the conflict and experience in Kenya) attributable to the killing rate in jungle ambushes where few prisoners were taken.[85] The rules on confessions in the Criminal Procedure Code were departed from to enable, as regards offences against the Emergency Regulations, the admissibility in court of confessions made to a police officer at any time during an investigation.[86] In July 1950, the Secretary of State for the Colonies reported to the Cabinet's Malaya Committee that the High Commissioner 'stated categorically that the executive [had] never failed to prosecute under the emergency regulations when sufficient evidence [had] been available'.[87] There had been 207 prosecutions for the (later capital) crime of carrying unauthorized arms contrary to Emergency Regulation 4. There had been 136 convictions, 12 of which were upset on appeal locally and one on appeal to the Judicial Committee of the Privy Council in London. Seventy eight had been hanged. Nine were given life imprisonment in the period before the offence became capital. In the remaining cases capital sentences were remitted. Offences under the other Emergency Regulations had seen 232 prosecutions resulting in 161 convictions. The statistics showed not leniency on the part of the courts but evidential difficulties in a due process system. Where prosecution was not possible because of witness reluctance, lack of other evidence or the need to take preventive measures against someone yet to commit an offence, the authorities had to resort to detention without trial, release subject to controls and restrictions, restricted residence orders, or to deportation or banishment. There were overlapping powers both in regular Ordinances of the Legislative Council and in the Emergency Regulations. The banishment powers included one to remove British subjects connected with another part of the Empire rather than Malaya either to that other part or in principle (but not in practice) to the United Kingdom.

Executive Measures: the Powers and their Use

Arrest and detention without trial Over the course of the Emergency, periodic amendment resulted in a set of overlapping regulations on detention without trial and release, subject to conditions, by suspending the detention order. The provisions are redolent of those deployed in the United Kingdom during the two World Wars. Regulation 17 itself (the initial and principal regulation) allowed the executive (the Chief Secretary) to order the detention of any person for up to one year (later increased to two years), subject to periodic review of the necessity for the detention. Such an order could at any time be cancelled by him or suspended

---

[84] Federation of Malaya Paper No. 59 (1953): para. 19.
[85] Simpson (2004): 833–4.
[86] Director of Operations, Malaya (1958): Part IV, p. 19.
[87] MAL.C. (50) 25 dated 14 July 1950, para. 11 in CAB 21/1681 TNA.

subject to conditions. Many were: of the 29,828 orders made by the end of February 1953, 11,083 had been cancelled conditionally or unconditionally, although there is no indication of how many fell within each category.[88] Regulation 24(1) enabled the police to arrest and detain for up to 28 days anyone against whom an executive detention order was pending. Later Regulation 17D enabled collective detention orders to be made against everyone in a particular village or area which was thought to have been aiding and abetting the terrorists or suppressing or failing to provide information to the responsible authorities of the activities or presence in their areas of terrorists. Just over 10,000 were held on this basis in some 20 operations. Regulation 17D also enabled selective detention orders on this basis and the conditional release under bond or orders of restricted residence to bring the persons concerned into the resettlement programme considered earlier. Some detainees were held in prison but the numbers in detention became such that most were held in camps converted, for example, from former quarantine stations, or ones which were purpose-built. A specific set of regulations governed detention centres as regards treatment and rights of detainees, on visitation, the limited work that could be required of detainees and dealing with disciplinary matters.[89] It is difficult to ascertain precise and accurate figures on the numbers of people detained. Barber suggests almost 30,000.[90] One official report states that some 34,000 detention orders were issued during the Emergency.[91] But another comparing the emergencies in Kenya and Malaya gives average figures per year (including dependants) totalling some 43,000 over the period to mid-1956.[92] The disparity (dependants) may perhaps be explicable because where other arrangements could not be made for children, female detainees could have them with them in the camp.[93] In addition those detained awaiting deportation consisted of the principal deportee whose conduct grounded deportation and his or her dependants. The available figures do not distinguish detainees by sex, but the bulk of detainees were said to be Chinese males.[94] A prime aim of the system, however, was not indefinite detention, but the division of detainees into those who might successfully be rehabilitated and resettled in Malaya, and those who should be removed permanently from Malaya through banishment or deportation.[95]

---

[88] Federation of Malaya, Paper 24 (1953): 6.

[89] Emergency (Detained Persons) Regulations 1948 (1948/2032).

[90] Barber (1971): 199.

[91] Director of Operations, Malaya (1957): 17.

[92] Forster (1957): para. 5.10.

[93] Foreign Office Telegram No. 66 Intel, 22 March 1951 on Treatment of Chinese in Malaya, para. 9 in DO 35/2920 TNA.

[94] Federation of Malaya, Paper No. 24 (1953): 11, 14, 17.

[95] See the Colonial Secretary's report to the Cabinet's Malaya Committee (MAL. C. (50) 25, 14 July 1950), paras 12–13 in CAB 21/1681, TNA, and paras 11–12 of his Memorandum to Cabinet CP (50) 125 dated 13 June 1950 in CP 129/40 TNA.

Exclusion, banishment and deportation Under the Immigration Ordinance 1952, the executive had power to ban on public security grounds persons from entering Malaya. Any order could be quashed by the Legislative Council. There was no right of appeal.[96] Removal from Malay by executive order could be effected in two ways: under the Banishment Enactment; or under Emergency Regulation 17C.

The Banishment Enactment, as amended in 1948, like many such in a variety of Colonies, ostensibly enabled the removal, after due enquiry, both of aliens and British subjects, whereas as regards the United Kingdom, while there were extensive powers with respect to aliens (see chapter 4) there then existed no power to deny entry to a British subject or to deport such a person. Hence, since 1934, Governors and High Commissioners had been exhorted not to remove to the United Kingdom British subjects unconnected with it.[97] In practice, citizens of the Federation of Malaya were not removed. The Enactment (apparently following the lines of the United Kingdom's Aliens Restrictions legislation after the First World War) enabled removal through a banishment or expulsion order in relation to criminal offences on recommendation of a convicting court. It also gave power to order banishment of any person where conducive to the good of the Federation. Alternatively the subject of an order could instead be required to enter into a bond with sureties for good behaviour, failure to provide which would result in removal. The person to be banished could also be detained pending giving effect to the removal order.[98] Similar powers had reportedly been used to good effect earlier in the century to deal with Chinese secret societies, organized crime, banditry, and Communist subversives.[99] For several years MCP operatives were still referred to as 'bandits'.[100] Use of the powers required a due quasi-judicial enquiry, without legal or other representation, publicity or appeal, by a Banishment Officer, although this later appears to have been restricted to British subjects rather than aliens. The Banishment Officer was to liaise closely with the Police where minded to recommend a course of action other than the banishment they sought.[101] The Banishment Enactment was principally used in respect of British subjects since they could not be removed under Emergency Regulation 17C.

Regulation 17C enabled the removal from Malaya by executive order of anyone subject to a Regulation 17 detention order other than British subjects or citizens of

---

[96] No. 10 1952, s. 9. For an example, see LN 157 in Federal Subsidiary Legislation 156, p. 176

[97] CO 1022/137 TNA.

[98] Banishment Ordinance 1948 (No. 5); Banishment (Malay States) (Amendment) Ordinance 1953 (No. 64); Banishment (Straits Settlements) (Amendment) Ordinance 1951 (No. 50).

[99] Barber (1971): 70, 94; Shennan (2004): 148–9.

[100] Carruthers (1995): 77. See, for example, CP (50) 125, para. 13 in CP 129/40 TNA.

[101] See paper on Deportation of British Subjects in Malaya (dated 26 March 1953) in CO 1022/37 TNA; and Memorandum from the Malayan Attorney-General on Banishment Enquiries dated 7 May 1954 (ref. AG/Sec 158/48) in CO 1030/276 TNA.

Malaya. The order could not take effect until the person had been afforded the opportunity to put his or her case to a Committee of Review (see below).

The main brake on removals was, however, logistical, at least in the early years of the Communist Government in China. Nonetheless large numbers were removed from Malaya under these powers.[102] Simpson suggests that between 14,000 and 26,000 Chinese squatters were removed.[103] Forster gives repatriation figures of 31,249 during the years 1948–1955: 29,287 Chinese, 1,786 Indians, 12 Ceylonese and 164 Indonesians.[104] The last Director of Operations (Malaya) records only 12,190 persons deported and some 2,717 repatriated at their own request. His figures probably only reflect Regulation 17C deportations.

Detention and rehabilitation The documents available in the National Archives paint a rather glowing picture of detention, stressing the vocational training and work available as a means to rehabilitate detainees pending their resettlement in one of the New Villages or return to their community.[105] Unlike Cyprus and Kenya, however, where detention conditions were controversial and there were a number of 'tip of the iceberg' scandals (particularly in the case of Kenya), there is little contradicting the picture in those documents apart from what seems to be dismissed as Chinese Government propaganda. But in the early years at least conditions in the camps were very far from acceptable and there were riots in some camps as late as 1955 in suppressing which the camp authorities lost control and detainees were killed.[106]

The bulk of the detainee population was male Chinese, and it was on these that the rehabilitation programme focused. The small number of Indian detainees and their composition in terms of age and committed Communist affiliation rendered impractical for resource reasons a rehabilitation regime for them. It was, however, hoped that some of those involved because of intimidation might safely be resettled on rubber plantations in other parts of the country. Others excluded from the rehabilitation programme were those under 18 for whom other arrangements were made in Approved Schools; those over 40 lacking literacy skills (those intimidated into involvement were instead often resettled in New Villages); and diehard Communists, attempts to rehabilitate whom would be delayed until easier subjects had successfully been rehabilitated. 'Students' were carefully selected after a character assessment formed by a specialist officer in the light of the person's case history, education, background and conduct whilst in detention.

Rehabilitation was thought particularly valuable for the generation that had grown up in the social and economic dislocation of the Japanese Occupation. The

---

[102] On the process and its difficulties, see Barber (1971): 70.

[103] Simpson (2004): 833.

[104] Forster (1957): para. 5.11.

[105] Federation of Malaya, Paper No. 24 (1953): 10–14, on which the account given here is based.

[106] Bayly and Harper (2007): 482–3.

programme aimed to restore its 'students' 'to freedom as loyal and law-abiding members of the population who are capable of earning an honest livelihood and are opposed to violence as a means to enforce political changes'. The programme was transparent and open to public scrutiny. It involved basic education provision, vocational training (teaching a variety of relevant trades), facilities for recreation, and generally unlimited visits and letter-writing facilities. The idea was to help develop respect and public spirit, to give a good example of communal living, to counter Communist propaganda, and to renew or strengthen family ties, to which end the programme attempted to rehabilitate family and relational groups at much the same time. No one was released into the community without suitable employment and community support, in the provision of which the Malayan Chinese Association played a key role. It was reported that of 1,280 'graduates' as at 1 March 1953 at one rehabilitation centre only eight again became supporters of the Communist terrorists. Of 92 released from another centre, none were known to have relapsed. Not all who embarked on the programme completed it successfully; 103 were returned to ordinary camps as unresponsive to rehabilitation.

Administrative Challenge Machinery for Exclusion, Detention, Banishment and Deportation

Those excluded under the Immigration Ordinance had no right of appeal. Detainees and deportees under Regulation 17C had a right of recourse to administrative challenge machinery. British subjects dealt with under the Banishment Enactment were the subject of the quasi-judicial Banishment Enquiry noted earlier. Aliens appear not to have been, and neither they nor British subjects appear to have had any right of appeal.

Detainees had to be told of their right to make objections.[107] Most exercised it. The initial mode of recourse was to one of a number of Advisory Committees modelled on the United Kingdom's Regulation 18B procedures during the Second World War (see chapter 2), which were established in major centres in Malaya. An administrative instruction required them to inform the detainee of the grounds for his detention, insofar as consistent with the need to withhold information 'which might endanger the life or safety of any person or reveal sources of information'. They had no power to compel the attendance of witnesses or to administer an oath or affirmation. The detainee, however, had the right to call witnesses in support of his objections and to be legally represented by an advocate. The committees had to keep a written record of proceedings. Their task was

> To direct themselves to ascertaining the character and general bearing of the detained person, to consider the evidence against him, to hear the detained person's defence and

---

[107] Emergency (Detention Orders) Rules 1948; Federation of Malaya, Paper No 24 (1953): 3–6, on which the account given here is largely based.

to form an opinion on the possible repercussions of the release of the detained person on the security of the country.[108]

Their recommendations in their written report to the High Commissioner were merely advisory, the decision on release remaining purely executive resting with the High Commissioner.

This system operated until March 1949. To avoid undue delay in deciding cases because of the volume of work for the Colonial Executive, a three-member Review Commission had been established to consider the Advisory Committees' recommendations.[109] From March 1949 the system was further decentralized. New Committees of Review replaced the Advisory Committees and could make binding executive decisions on detention or release. The Committees of Review were chaired by someone holding or who had held judicial office or office as a Government law officer. One member of what was usually a triumvirate had so far as possible to be of the same race as the detainee. The Committees of Review operated in much the same manner as the previous Committee, although in 1950 the administrative instruction about as full a disclosure as was consonant with security was made statutory. They could order continued detention or conditional or unconditional release. They could also recommend admission to the rehabilitation programme. In cases of doubt, they could refer a case for decision to the central Review Commission established under Emergency Regulation 17(4B). This, chaired as at 1 March 1953 by the acting Attorney General, had the same powers as other Committees of Review. By 1955, although detention could be for up to two years, the Committees were not usually willing, absent very strong evidence, to allow detention to continue beyond six months, something the military considered rather vitiated the value of the detention provisions.[110] In addition, a detainee could request the Chief Secretary in the executive branch of government periodically to reconsider his case. He could confirm or cancel the existing order of detention or make another to take effect when the extant one expired. There appears to have been an automatic review after 18 months.

Clutterbuck considered that the committee's proceedings were conducted as openly as security allowed.[111] Recourse to the Committee and/or the Chief Secretary procured release in just over a third of cases in the period June 1948 to 1 March 1953. Others were released when orders lapsed after two years and were not renewed.[112] There are, however, some disturbing statements which can be interpreted as casting some doubt on the independence of the Committee in a Memorandum from the Secretary of State for the Colonies to the Cabinet's Malaya

---

[108]   Federation of Malaya, Paper No 24 (1953): 4.

[109]   Memorandum of Secretary of State for the Colonies to the Cabinet's Malaya Committee, MAL.C (50) 24, dated 10 July 1950, in CAB 21/1681 TNA.

[110]   Director of Operations, Malaya (1957): 17 (para. 62).

[111]   Clutterbuck (1966): 39.

[112]   Federation of Malaya, Paper No 24 (1953): 6.

Committee.[113] It deals with instructions to the Committees from the Malayan Executive. Those instructions stressed the need to give

> ... the fullest weight to the need for retaining in detention any persons who might, if released, afford assistance of any kind to the terrorists. They were also advised that if, after considering a case any reasonable doubt remained, they should resolve the case in favour of continued detention rather than release. Early in 1950 there were indications that some Committees of Review were taking too lenient a view and that some detainees were being released against the advice of the police. A further instruction was therefore addressed to Committees of Review on the 31st March 1950 drawing attention to the dangers of ordering release in any doubtful case.

A further instruction told Chairmen to refer upwards to the Review Commission all cases where the Committee was minded to release conditionally or unconditionally but the police had objections. The Secretary of State noted the composition of the Review Commission. The Chairman, a British official, was the Registrar of the Supreme Court. His 'wingmen' were another British official, the Secretary for Chinese Affairs, and a Malay, the Chief State Minister (Mentri Besar) of Selangor. The Secretary of State commented:

> The composition of this body is such that there can be no danger that instructions issued to it by the Federation Government will not be fully implemented. The High Commissioner has in fact given me an assurance that there will be no danger henceforward of detainees being released where such releases would have untoward consequences.

There was thus no danger that the prospect of too easy release would deter the police from applying for detention orders.

From January 1953 an administrative scheme – operating in addition to the modes of challenge so far discussed – saw the need for detention periodically (about every nine months) reviewed within the executive, taking full account of the view of the relevant police and detention authorities, generally involving a further police interview of the detainee. These reviews were instituted because as the emergency went on and was successfully being combated, the changing security situation rendered it safer to release detainees.

The Role of the Courts

Recourse to the courts by excludees, detainees, deportees or those subjected to banishment finds no mention in the material surveyed in the National Archives. The Malayan Law Reports and the Malayan Law Journal for the period report two successful habeas corpus applications in respect of banishment. The first was by a

---

[113] CAB 21/1681, TNA.

natural-born British subject exempt from the process.[114] The second found a punctuation error in the provision and read the phrase 'if he deems it to be conducive to the public good' as one qualifying the power to banish on conviction by a competent court rather than, as intended, a separate head of power to banish.[115] This presumably was not thought problematic given powers under the ER and the banishment process becoming less important in the campaign against the MCP. No change was made until the Banishment Ordinance as a whole was replaced with another in 1959, after independence. Otherwise these reports are rather replete with cases from the criminal process connected with the ER. They deal with such matters as the meaning of 'consorts', the requisite of knowledge for possession of, or consorting with someone with, a firearm, the meaning of 'within doors' as regards branch of curfew rules, and a variety of matters evidential (admissibility of confessions, corroboration requirements). There were a number of appeals against sentence in death penalty cases, some going all the way to the Judicial Committee of the Privy Council, the final appeal court for the colonies, sitting in London.

The European Convention on Human Rights

The ECHR had been extended to Malaya as to other colonies despite the existence of the emergency and without any searching appraisal of which laws might not be compatible with it. The United Kingdom Government, however, entered a notice of derogation under the public emergency clause in Art. 15. The reasons given for derogation provided on 24 May 1954 in a notice of derogation covering five colonies in all were deliberately minimal: in respect of Malaya and Singapore it was 'owing to a conspiracy to overthrow the lawfully constituted government of these territories by force'.[116] No detail of the scale of the emergency or the text, nature and use of the emergency powers was provided. Nor was the Secretary-General of the Council of Europe kept informed of changes through further notices of derogation, even when the emergency in Singapore had ended.[117] The impact of the ECHR was, however, emasculated by not recognizing the right of individual petition. Nor, unlike the position with Cyprus, did any other State Party to the Convention have any direct political axe to grind such as to motivate an inter-State application. None seems to have shown any interest in interfering with the exercise of colonial power so far from Europe.

---

[114] *In Re Lim Penk Ko* [1952] 18 MLJ 26.
[115] *R v Ching Kee Huat* [1954] 20 MLJ 205.
[116] Simpson (2004): 878.
[117] Ibid.: 878–81.

The Cyprus Emergency

Introduction and Overview

Cyprus, an island in the eastern Mediterranean, lies at the junction of three continents (Europe, Asia and Africa) and has long formed a trading crossroads between Orient and Occident. Despite its small size (some 3,752 square miles, 141 miles long by a maximum of 59 miles wide), its location has made it of strategic importance for a variety of countries and groups over the ages: the Byzantines; the English/Norman Crusaders seeking to free the Holy Land from the Saracens; the Latin House of Lusignan; the Venetians; the Ottoman Turks; and the British Empire. In 1878 at the time of the Congress of Berlin, Turkey retained nominal sovereignty but ceded effective control to Britain to use as a military assembly point in the event of conflict with Russia. For some significant time, Turkey has seen Cyprus as important to its security. But the transfer also enabled British protection of the island's Christian population.[118] The mainly Greek population of the island, however, has seen itself as part of a wider Hellenic world recreated after Greek independence from Turkey in the first part of the nineteenth century. The island has never belonged to Greece. Britain annexed Cyprus in 1914 when Turkey came into the War on the side of Germany and Austro-Hungary. It was prepared to cede it to Greece during the First World War in return for Greece coming into the War on the side of the Allied Powers. Greece never did. In the Treaty of Lausanne, which put an end to the Graeco-Turkish War, Turkey renounced its sovereignty over Cyprus in favour of the United Kingdom. Various attempts to create constitutional arrangements which would involve Cypriots in decision-making failed, with the Greek Cypriot community largely in favour of *enosis* (union) with Greece. From 1931, 'Cyprus became a bizarre anomaly: a colony with some half-million inhabitants, located within Europe, lacking any central democratic institutions whatsoever'.[119] Matters came to a head from 1954 when an out-of-touch Cyprus colonial Government (too much of the senior civil service was British rather than Cypriot) badly underestimated Greek Cypriot feeling on enosis, attributing it to a few malcontents and churchmen rather than seeing it as one shared by the majority of the Greek Cypriot community.[120] With a degree of support (at least as regards violent sabotage) from Archbishop Makarios, the primate of the Orthodox Church in Cyprus, EOKA (National Organization of Cypriot Fighters), a Greek Cypriot paramilitary organization ('terrorist' or 'freedom fighters' depending on the perspective of the observer), commenced on 1 April 1955 its campaign of violence designed to bring Greek Cypriot demands for self-determination to the attention of the world community. The Cyprus

---

[118] Simpson (2004): 885.
[119] Simpson (2004): 886.
[120] Foley (1964): 20–21, 43.

Government's reaction to it produced the resignation of the two appointed Greek members of the Governor's Executive Council.[121]

In the mid–late 1950s, the period with which this section is concerned, the Cyprus population was some 520,000: 80 per cent Greek Cypriot (416,000), 18 per cent Turkish Cypriot (93,600) and 2 per cent other. Living patterns were such that Turkish Cypriot minority was spread out across the island and at no one point did it form a numerical majority. A formal State of Emergency in response to increasing EOKA violence was proclaimed on 26 November 1955 by Governor Harding under a 1939 United Kingdom Order in Council issued to ensure that Colonial authorities had a sufficiency of powers to deal with the exigencies of the Second World War.[122] It enabled the promulgation of two main sets of Emergency Regulations giving wide powers to the executive authorities: the Emergency Powers (Public Safety and Order) Regulations;[123] and the Emergency Powers (Collective Punishment) Regulations.[124] The Emergency formally came to an end on 24 December 1959 following the EOKA ceasefire. But either side of that formal period of emergency there existed a *de facto* emergency responded to by the terms of the ordinary law or by specially enacted time-limited laws that would be categorized as 'emergency' legislation. That *de facto* emergency began on 1 April 1955[125] and continued at least in terms of available laws until Cyprus independence in 1960.[126] During the period at issue, a peak of 40,000 British military forces plus a 400-strong Turkish militia and a mixed police force were confronted by some 300 EOKA guerillas, who were supported financially, materially and politically by a far greater number of Greek Cypriots. Casualty figures seem small in comparison with some other conflicts: 104 members of the British Forces were killed, 84 Turkish Cypriots died and 366 Greek Cypriots (200 of whom were killed by EOKA as informants or opponents of the EOKA cause). The campaign was initially directed against the police, the military and the administration, but also saw attacks in which the wives of British Service personnel were targeted and killed. In 1958 in particular, violence became inter-communal. Turkish Cypriots had in 1957 developed their own, violent paramilitary organization, TMT (Turkish Defence Organization). Although Grivas and his fighters had mountain hideouts, this was an urban guerilla conflict, more closely resembling that in Northern Ireland (see chapter 3) than those in Malaya or Kenya.[127]

---

[121]   Simpson (2004): 886.
[122]   Emergency Powers Orders in Council 1939 and 1952; Statute Laws of Cyprus ii, No. 730 (Proclamation).
[123]   Statute Laws of Cyprus ii, No. 731.
[124]   Statute Laws of Cyprus ii, No. 732.
[125]   Baker Review (1958): 16.
[126]   Emergency (Residual Powers) Law 1959 [Statute Laws of Cyprus, No. 39 of 1959]. This was a law for the continuance in force of certain powers after the cessation of a State of Public Emergency in the Colony, enacted 2 December 1959.
[127]   Simpson (2004): 891.

The United Kingdom's prime interest in remaining in control of Cyprus was strategic rather then economic. It reflected its removal from Palestine in 1948 and being compelled in July 1954 to close its military base at Suez in Egypt because of pressure from its Arab nationalist government under President Nasser. Its Middle East Combined Headquarters had consequently been moved to the island in December 1954. The politics of a Conservative party stung by the Suez withdrawal meant that the Eden Government could not contemplate retreat from Cyprus as well. As for military requirements, in mid-July 1955, a report to Cabinet from the Chiefs of Staff was yet again categorical:

> We are not competent to comment on the many complex political factors involved in the problem of Cyprus, but we are of the opinion that our military requirements within the Island can only be met if the control of its administration in matters of defence, external affairs and internal security remain in British hands.[128]

The exertion of influence in the Middle East, meeting the United Kingdom's treaty obligations, moving towards a Middle East Defence Force and defending the area in war, all required the stationing of military forces in that theatre. Militarily that required an area able to ensure security of tenure, reliable public utilities and the ability to come and go in complete freedom. Cyprus was the only territory in the Middle East satisfying those conditions. It was 'of outstanding importance not only to British military effort but to Middle East defence as a whole'.[129] Turkey, a key element in NATO's eastern defences against possible Soviet aggression, regarded Cyprus as 'the keystone of British military effort and prestige in the Middle East and as the focal point of [British] influence in the area'.[130] Charles Foley, the editor of the *Times of Cyprus* from 1955, records being told by the poet and author, Laurence Durrell, the Colonial Government's Information Officer, on arrival in Cyprus as a *Daily Express* correspondent, that despite Britain's commitment to the principle of self-determination, it was simply for these reasons 'not on' for Cyprus, the more so since the Turkish Cypriot minority (18 per cent of the Cyprus population) as well as Turkey as a NATO ally, were opposed to the Greek Cypriot demand for union (*enosis*) with Greece. While Greece was also an important NATO ally its Government was too unstable to allow the island to pass to it, even with guarantees for British strategic bases on the island; hence, a Colonial Office minister's apparent statement to Parliament in July 1954 that Cypriots would 'never' be ready to decide their own future or to become independent.[131]

British military and political needs thus clashed directly with the aspirations of a majority of Greek Cypriots for *enosis*, a demand increasingly politically popular

---

[128] GEN. 497/4, para. 19 of a Paper for the Ministerial Committee on Cyprus, dated 18 July 1955 in CAB 130/109 TNA.

[129] Ibid.: para. 3.

[130] Ibid.

[131] Foley (1964): 16–17.

within a Greece recovering from civil war and its defeat of communism. British needs meshed very well, however, with the desires of the Turkish Cypriot community for retention of the status quo which also suited the strategic needs of Turkey, the south-eastern coast of which is only some 43 miles north of Cyprus. Greek Cypriots were not, however, in total unity. Like mainland Greece, Greek Cypriots had their own strong left-wing element in AKEL (the Communist party). Politically it was less nationalistic. As in other colonial emergencies, the Government deployed a range of security measures to deal, not always successfully, with the insurgency and the violence. These measures are examined in the next section of this account. It also sought, unsuccessfully, to win the hearts and minds of the Greek Cypriot majority with a variety of social and constitutional measures to enable a degree of self-government while preserving British strategic interests in terms of control of bases on the island. Retention of the status quo, *enosis*, or a degree of self-government in a unitary or partitioned island were all possible outcomes. It is rather ironic that the eventual outcome – an independent Cyprus with a complicated and ultimately unsuccessful power-sharing constitution to reconcile divided communities scarred by inter-communal conflict – was not one favoured at the outset by any of the protagonists. It is also ironical, however, that the outcome – the retention in an independent Cyprus of two sovereign military bases – has given Britain since 1960 essentially what the Chiefs of Staff said were required in 1955. What then was achieved by the EOKA campaign and resistance to it? Writing in 1978, Crawshaw probably hits the mark.

> The EOKA rising, however, backed by an intensive political campaign, played a part in forcing the British to look at the Cyprus problem in a new light. The changing strategic needs brought about by the development of faster aircraft, the lapse of treaty obligations in the Middle East and by the aftermath of the Suez crisis would have forced them to do this sooner or later. At best it can be said that Grivas [the EOKA leader] helped to bring colonial rule to an end a few years earlier than the British intended. Against this achievement the EOKA campaign left in its wake a bitter division of loyalties between the Greek Cypriots and intensified the animosity of the Turks – both factors which have bedeviled the island's politics for more than a decade.[132]

The constitutional steps to win hearts and minds and bring a stalemated conflict to a close are examined after a more detailed consideration of the security and anti-terrorism measures adopted by the colonial government and the legal challenges to them both in Cyprus and internationally.

Nature and Use of Security/Anti-terrorist Powers

The broader legal and political context This section focuses principally on the deployment of three 'security' powers: detention without trial; restriction on

---

[132] Crawshaw (1978): 350–351.

residence and movement; and deportation, exile or banishment from Cyprus. These powers operated not in isolation but in interaction with each other and against a well-filled backdrop of criminal laws and other emergency powers. All of the powers operated against a United Kingdom political context in which Government policies and action, set as they were firmly against self-determination, came in for attack from a vocal opposition on both Labour and Liberal benches. The overwhelming political interest in the matter of Greece, a fellow State Party to the ECHR, also meant that human rights matters which formed part of that United Kingdom political and constitutional discourse, were brought before the competent organ of the ECHR, its Commission of Human Rights in that Convention's first inter-State case. Each of these discourses in their own way set limits on what could be done in a way that seems singularly absent in the Malaya Emergency examined earlier. In addition, the need to draw the protagonists, including the Greek Cypriots through Archbishop Makarios, the head of its autocephalous Greek Orthodox Church, into a political settlement of the problem heavily influenced what powers could be introduced and when and against whom they could be used. The prospect of withdrawal of some of the powers (mainly those unused or little used) was also used as a bargaining tool during negotiations.[133]

As regards the context of the wider criminal law and process, the authorities were not short of available criminal offences to deal with subversion, sedition and violence. The Criminal Code contained a variety of serious offences against the person. Murder attracted the death penalty. In many respects Cyprus's sedition law emulated that of the United Kingdom, which required proof of an intention to incite violence, but went wider in criminalizing an intention to bring about a change in the sovereignty of the colony. The Emergency Regulations created a number of further offences: interference with communications, unlawful drilling, unlawful wearing of uniforms, causing disaffection, looting and kindred offences. Harbouring an offender was criminal. The Regulations criminalized, subject to a mandatory death sentence, discharge of a firearm at any person, persons or places where people congregated; the throwing, igniting or depositing of any bomb, other explosive or incendiary device with intention to cause injury or death; and carrying or having in one's possession or control any firearm. The exaction of the death penalty was controversial, made martyrs of those executed and alienated Greek Cypriot opinion and opinion in Greece, anger being reflected in violent demonstrations. Indeed, Simpson likens their effect to those that took place in Ireland after the Easter Rising of 1916 (see chapter 3).[134] In response to the executions of Karaolis and Demetriou, EOKA killed two soldiers it held as prisoners.[135] Only nine people were executed, and seven of the cases involved a killing. A prime role of the mandatory death sentence was to impel those who might face it to give information when interrogated. Those who did were never

---

[133] Simpson (2004): 911.
[134] Simpson (2004): 921.
[135] Foley (1964): 54.

executed.[136] Otherwise pleas for clemency were seldom successful under Governor Harding.[137] The right to impose capital punishment was expressly recognized in the ECHR's right to life provision[138] and resort to it was common in Europe. At the time there were about 12 executions a year in the United Kingdom.[139] But it is ironic that in Cyprus the range of offences attracting the penalty increased while in the United Kingdom there was an ongoing debate on ending capital punishment for murder.[140] Almost as controversial was Regulation 75 which permitted an alternative sentence to fines or imprisonment. It allowed convicted males under 18 to be sentenced to be whipped, that is, given up to 12 strokes of a light rod, cane or birch. It was said to be justified to deal with EOKA's use of schoolchildren in rioting and in the painting of slogans. It was unusual in Europe. As at 9 July 1956 118 young people had been sentenced to it and 96 sentences had been carried out.[141] The Regulations enabled extensive control and censorship of publications, post and radio. They sanctioned control of ports and the movement of ships and aircraft. They enabled control of other transport, meetings and places (for example, closing premises and places of public entertainment) and of burials. There were wide powers of requisition of property. The Regulations forbade the ringing of bells, the flying of flags, and enabled control of lights and sounds. They conferred wide powers of stop and search and to enter and search premises. Swimming could be prohibited. Curfews could be imposed and were, not only to maintain order but by way of punishing a particular area or community. Although the Colonial Office was not altogether happy with them, the second code of Regulations enabled the imposition of collective punishment.[142] A District Commissioner (with the Governor's approval) could punish with a collective fine the inhabitants of an area where there had occurred in that area an offence prejudicial to internal security or public order or loss or damage of property had been caused. He could only do so, however, if they could be said to be 'responsible'. This was construed widely and would cover their failure to co-operate with the authorities in respect of the offence or their failure to have taken reasonable steps to prevent its commission. It could also be imposed where there had been a series of offences in the area if he believed that the inhabitants had been generally responsible for those offences. The imposition of a fine required an enquiry and the inhabitants being allowed to make representations.[143]

---

[136] Simpson (2004): 977.
[137] Simpson (2004): 920–921.
[138] Art. 2 ECHR.
[139] Simpson (2004): 920 (n. 197).
[140] Anderson (2005): 292.
[141] Simpson (2004): 943.
[142] Emergency Powers (Collective Punishment) Regulations, Statute Laws of Cyprus ii, No. 731.
[143] Simpson (2004): 909.

Detention without trial Two legal regimes operated, for most of the period concurrently, during the Emergency: the Detention of Persons Law 1955;[144] and (after the declaration of a State of Emergency on 26 November 1955) Regulation 6 of the Emergency Powers (Public Safety and Order) Regulations 1955.[145] The former was used against those connected with or assisting EOKA. Detention under the Regulations was instead targeted on the Communists (AKEL). Unlike Malaya, there was no power of collective detention.

The decision to proceed with the Detention of Persons Law was taken by the Cabinet in London on 12 July 1955.[146] The Governor, Sir Robert Armitage, had wanted for some time to be allowed to declare a State of Emergency and had on 28 June asked to be allowed to do so at any time after 1 July in order to restore morale and confidence, to be able to negotiate from a position of strength and to give the police and the military the powers they required to deal with a deteriorating situation. He wanted to be able to seize the 150–200 active, militant members and supporters of EOKA but not bishops or leading intellectuals.[147] The Secretary of State's reply the next day told him to make no such preparations as these 'might be a most serious setback to the prospects of successful discussions with the Greeks and the Turks' in the envisaged tripartite talks between those governments and the United Kingdom.[148] The Governor expressed concern that without secret planning for a detention operation lives would be put in jeopardy.[149] He then sought permission to proclaim an emergency from 8 July both to support the police and demonstrate that EOKA could not act with impunity.[150] The Secretary of State replied the same day that such a declaration would damage talks with the Greek Government. Instead he suggested the enactment of a specific, time-limited, detention law.[151] A 'very happy' Governor Armitage cabled back with the text of the draft law. He said that he had preferred to proceed in this way all along but had been advised that the Secretary of State would not approve that course of action.[152] On 7 July, Cabinet was advised that the Government had decided to proceed in this way rather than through by declaring a State of Emergency which would have been inexpedient on the eve of the forthcoming tripartite Conference, the details of which were considered by Cabinet at this same meeting. Cabinet was informed that it was now proposed to detain without trial only 50 members of EOKA, the terrorist organization plotting to use violence against the police and members of the

---

[144] Statute Laws of Cyprus i, No. 26 of 1955.

[145] Statute Laws of Cyprus ii, No. 731.

[146] CAB 128/29 TNA, Minute 5, 22nd meeting, 12 July 1955.

[147] CO 926/395 TNA, telegram 402 from Governor Armitage to Secretary of State, Colonial Office, 28 June 1955.

[148] Ibid., telegram 371, 29 June 1955.

[149] Ibid., telegram 411, 30 June 1955.

[150] Ibid., telegram 419, 4 July 1955.

[151] Ibid, telegram, 4 July 1955.

[152] Ibid., telegrams 425, 426, 6 July 1955.

administration in Cyprus. Cabinet agreed that this was the best way to proceed, but that the Secretary of State

> ... should satisfy himself that the Governor had ample evidence to justify the enactment of a measure of this kind – especially as the situation in Cyprus had become so much quieter since the announcement of the forthcoming conference. Even if such a law was still necessary, it was for consideration whether its application might not be limited to the organisation of acts of violence. Was it necessary that it should extend also to the conduct of revolutionary propaganda?[153]

The Secretary of State stated that he 'fully recognised the disadvantages of taking repressive action at this juncture' and that he would discuss the law and these issues further with the Governor.[154] The subsequent telegram correspondence advised replacing 'reasonable cause' with 'is satisfied that' so as to reduce the prospect of judicial challenge to the reasonableness of action in a particular case. The Governor was also advised to tighten up the grounds of detention so that the law would not catch mere intriguers such as the Greek Orthodox bishops or propagandists.[155] In the meantime, the Secretary of State visited the Island and met with the Governor and others. He reported back to Cabinet on his visit at its meeting on 12 July. He expressed himself fully satisfied of the necessity for the law and that the firm approach it represented would supplement the tripartite talks:

> There was ample evidence of a conspiracy to foment disorder by acts of violence, and the Governor could best defeat this by taking power to arrest and detain those responsible for organising it. The law which the Governor proposed to enact would be limited, in its application, to persons who had been active in the furtherance of an association which had been responsible for organising acts of violence directed against the administration of the Island.[156]

The Lord Chancellor stressed that high priority should be given to 'security and intelligence measures' and Cabinet approval was given for the enactment of the law. The Governor enacted it on 15 July 1955.[157] Like many of the 'emergency' or counter-terrorist powers examined in this book, it was ostensibly 'temporary' legislation. It came into force the next day, and was set to expire at the end of October 1955, unless renewed by order of the Governor (as it was throughout the Emergency) for a further six-month period or number of such periods.[158]

---

[153] CAB 128/29 TNA, Minute 1, 21st meeting, 7 July 1955.

[154] Ibid.

[155] CO 926/395 TNA, telegram 402 (Colonial Office to Governor), 7 July 1955.

[156] CAB 128/29 TNA, Minute 5, 22nd meeting, 12 July 1955; CO 926/395 TNA, Note for Secretary of State MED 30/1/03, paras 3, 4.

[157] Detention of Persons Law 1955 (Statute Laws of Cyprus No. 26 of 1955).

[158] s. 5.

Some of the pressures for and rationale of the law are set out in a note prepared by the Colonial Office as a basis for the Secretary of State to brief Cabinet on 12 July.[159] The law was said to be necessary because EOKA was responsible for recent outrages and were planning further terrorist acts against the police and others. A bomb had been thrown into a club used by soldiers. It would help restore morale among those Cypriots in the administration and the police subject to EOKA intimidation, the extent and nature of which had been conveyed in the Governor's telegrams. There had been further bombings during the Secretary of State's visit to the island in which he had met the Governor, Archbishop Makarios, and representatives of the Turkish Cypriot community. This last group had stressed in their meetings with him the need for firmer action. The paper expressed fear that unless this happened that community might itself resort to paramilitary action to protect against EOKA intimidation and attack, with the risk that such counter-terrorist action 'would spark off wider racial conflict'. Service chiefs had also called for firmer action. The terrorists, it was said, were known to have plans to assassinate outstanding Cypriot members of the police Special Branch (its vital intelligence arm) and other officers. Troops were concerned about the safety of wives and families living in dispersed villas. One paragraph stands out as resonating with current governmental concerns that it will be blamed for an Al Qaeda attack, one explanation for the Blair Government's seeking ever-greater security powers for the police and security services (the need to appear to be doing something) (see chapter 6):

> The Secretary of State argued that HMG would carry too heavy a responsibility if known terrorists were left at large. We have been incredibly fortunate so far in that only one person has been killed by bombs; but one serious incident involving the families of the police or Services would create a highly combustible situation. The morale of the Cypriot rank and file police will not long survive continued inaction against those who are threatening to murder them. The Secretary of State considered that we must now take limited but decisive action to neutralize the terrorists without waiting to be forced into this action by further loss of life.[160]

There was another reason why urgent action was now necessary. Ten EOKA operatives, including the second-in-command, had already been arrested and were held in the criminal process on remand. Without evidence which could be produced openly in court, Cypriot law was such that they would soon have to be released, although a number of adjournments had provided the authorities with some breathing space. Further remands were thought unlikely since the evidence available from security sources could probably not be produced in court because doing so would risk the safety of informers on whom the police relied for much of their intelligence. EOKA was now operating in small five-person cells to maximize

---

[159] CO 926/395 TNA, MED 30/1/03 on which the following account is largely based.
[160] Ibid., para. 5.

its security. Its membership was known to be increasing and there were thought to be EOKA members in the police service. EOKA left to act with impunity might, it was thought, created 'enotists' among previous 'middle of the roaders', and thus from a propaganda viewpoint render it important to bring EOKA quickly under control by means of the detention law. But there seems to have been no concern expressed that detention might prove the catalyst which would unite the Greek Cypriot community behind EOKA. Finally, the paper reiterated the Governor's view that the Government had to crush EOKA, otherwise the continued existence of its menace would be a reminder that the Government was not in control of the situation. While it was there, it could claim credit for any concessions made by the Government and thus increase its adherents. Until EOKA was crushed, progress on a constitution embodying a degree of self-government would be impossible. A secret Minute in the same file by the acting Colonial Secretary (Cyprus) dated 11 July 1955 makes some similar points. In particular, it stresses that magistrates, in the face of criticism from Press and public, were increasingly reluctant to grant further remands in custody so as to afford the police a sufficiently long time to build a criminal case. It also saw the recent arrests as evidence of police success in breaking into EOKA:

> it is known that by arresting the 10 people now in custody they have disrupted the Nicosia group and created confusion and suspicion in the organization. We believe that if we can drive the wedge home now and collect another 20 or 30 known members throughout the Island, the chances of crushing EOKA now are very much greater than they will be if we have to do it gradually over a long period by arresting a few individuals at a time.

The Governor had already stated that the release of the individuals so far arrested would enable them to go into hiding and for the organization to be remodelled.[161] The Minute also looks to the broader picture in terms of the forthcoming tripartite talks and the pressures from each community also embodied in the two opposing outside Governments which sought to protect and speak for them. Hence, while firm security action against EOKA would not be welcomed by the Greek Government at those talks,

> If we do not take firm measures it is equally certain that we shall be criticized by the Turks both here and in Turkey. One final warning, Turkish feeling is … running high, and if a Turk is killed by Greek terrorist action, that will provide just the spark that is needed to set off a conflagration of communal strife. If that happens the atmosphere in which inter-Governmental talks are to be held, if indeed they are held at all, will be, at least, strained.

---

[161]   CO 926/395 TNA, telegram 419 Governor to Secretary of State, dated 4 July 1955, attached to MED 30/1/03.

The mix of powers in the Detention of Persons Law 1955 in many ways resonates with those now available in the United Kingdom after the demise of ATCSA detention under derogating and non-derogating control orders in respect of involvement in terrorism in the Prevention of Terrorism Act 2005 (PTA 2005) (see chapter 7). Its formulation was, however, somewhat narrower than the very wide span the PTA 2005 affords the Home Secretary given the overbroad definition of 'terrorism' deployed by that Act. The Detention of Persons Law enabled the Governor to detain someone in such place and subject to such conditions as the Governor directed. This could be done if the Governor was satisfied that the person was or had been a member of, or was or had been active in the furtherance of the purposes of, an organization which the Governor was satisfied had been responsible for acts of violence directed to the overthrow by force or violence of the Government, or the destruction of Crown property, and that by reason of that the Governor was satisfied that it was necessary to exercise control over him/her.[162] The Governor could at any time cancel or vary the order.[163] He could also suspend its operation subject to such of the following conditions as he thought fit: prohibiting or restricting the possession or use by such persons of any specified article; imposing upon them such restrictions as might be specified in the direction in respect of their employment or business, the place of their residence, and their association or communication with other persons; prohibiting them from being out of doors between specified hours without written permission from a specified authority; requiring them to notify their movements in such manner and at such times as might be directed to a specified person or authority; and prohibiting travel save under the terms of permission granted by a specified authority.[164] Non-compliance with conditions could result in the suspension order being revoked and the individual being once more detained without trial. But whether or not that was the result, non-compliance was an imprisonable offence.[165] In addition, even where the subject of a suspended order fully complied with the conditions imposed, the Governor could revoke the suspension and re-detain without trial where he was satisfied that its continued suspension was not possible without detriment to the public safety or public order.[166] The parallel here with non-derogating control orders under the PTA 2005 is striking, although discretion to impose conditions is now broader than forty years ago, and a merely illustrative list is afforded in the legislation (the Cyprus model was a closed list). But the list in the PTA 2005 is rather longer, in part reflecting technological advances since 1955.

---

[162] s. 2(1).
[163] s. 2(3).
[164] s. 3(1).
[165] s. 3(2).
[166] s. 3(1).

The target of this Cypriot law was EOKA members and activists. The numbers detained were small initially (13 by the end of July).[167] Some of these had first been brought into the criminal process but their prosecutions were discontinued by the Attorney General. The numbers increased dramatically, however, so that by the end of 1955 the Governor reported that 211 detention orders had been made and 180 persons had been arrested under them (it was not always possible to serve orders since their subjects had fled to mountain hideouts). One hundred and forty were still detained, ten had escaped and 28 had been released (whether unconditionally or subject to restrictions is not clear). In comparison to Ireland (1916–22), Malaya or Kenya, these numbers seem very small. They must, however, be seen in the context of a small Cypriot population (less than 500,000) so that, as Foley commented (when only a hundred had been detained), 'it was as if ten thousand families had been deprived of a father or brother; and the allowances made to dependants did not replace the weekly pay packets'.[168] By early February 1956 almost 200 were detained, embracing a wide section of Greek Cypriot society. Along with the other emergency restrictions (curfews, collective punishments, but particularly corporal and capital punishment), the effect appears to have been one of cementing opposition to British rule and enhancing support for EOKA, Makarios and *enosis*. Foley put it strikingly:

> Dr Themistocles Dervis, Nicosia's noisy mayor, liked to tell his visitors that 'We are all Eoka!' and as time went on I began to wonder if he might not be right. The board of directors (all seven of them) from a large firm were arrested; a surgeon of international repute stitched up a final patient and stepped from his clinic into a waiting police car; a football club lost its captain and six players to a detention camp. Industrialists, artists, publicans and policemen were welded into freemasonry of anti-British feeling behind barbed wire.[169]

The TUC lobbied the Colonial Office in London about the detention of some trades unionists. At a meeting in mid-November 1955, they were told that the law was not aimed at trades unionists as such, but against terrorists, and the problem was that evidence could not be produced in court because of witness intimidation.[170] The position in terms of withdrawal of Greek Cypriot support for the Government worsened when, with Colonial Office approval, the Communist Party (AKEL) was proscribed and its members and supporters detained without trial under the Emergency Regulations.[171] Crawshaw (a journalist who, to write her account, was

---

[167] Telegram correspondence between the Governor and the Colonial Office in CO 926/396 TNA, on which the account given here is based.

[168] Foley (1964): 40.

[169] Ibid.: 41.

[170] CO 923/396 TNA, note of meeting of 9 November 1955.

[171] CO 923/562 TNA, telegram from Secretary of State to Governor No. 1072, 25 November 1955.

given access to governmental papers on a non-attributable basis)[172] saw the official basis (AKEL's involvement in violence) as not sustainable in 1955, although it would have been in 1948.[173] Most of AKEL's activities were lawful. Its oratory may have come close to sedition but was nowhere near as vicious or as loud as that of the Greek Cypriot ecclesiastics. AKEL's approach to nationalism indirectly helped the security forces. She saw another reason for the detention of Communists as being to silence this group of Archbishop Makarios's opponents in the hope that such an easing of pressure on him might give him more leeway for compromise in the ongoing and delicate political negotiations. Whatever the rationale, the effect was to increase sympathy for the leftists and help forge a united Greek Cypriot front. Trades unionists demonstrated throughout the island and workers engaged in building military bases and installations went on strike.

Once the State of Emergency was declared under powers in a 1939 United Kingdom Order in Council designed to give Colonial authorities a sufficiency and flexibility of powers to deal with the emergency that was the Second World War, the Governor could legislate without the formal approval from London required for primary legislation by Order in Council such as the Detention of Persons Law 1955.[174] Regulations 5 and 6 of the consequent Emergency Regulations gave him respectively powers to impose a variety of restrictions on an individual and the power to detain that person without trial, thus giving him much the same weapons as the Detention of Persons Law but capable of use against a broader range of targets. Regulation 3, which enabled the screening of suspects[175] and was to prove important in intelligence-gathering and in prevention of terrorism, gave the police and military acting in the course of their duty powers to arrest and detain for up to 48 hours any person who they had reasonable ground for suspecting to be acting, having acted or be about to act in any manner prejudicial to public safety or public order or to have committed, be committing or be about to commit an offence against the Regulations. The 48-hour 'ceiling' was raised to 16 days from 12 January 1956.[176] Regulation 5 afforded the Governor to restrict a person's activities and movements without resorting to detention without trial. It enabled the Governor to impose conditions on a person where satisfied that it was necessary to do so with a view to preventing him acting in a manner prejudicial to public safety or public order. The conditions imposable were similar to those that could be effected under the Detention of Persons Law by suspending the Detention order, considered earlier. The parallel with non-derogating control orders in the PTA 2005 is again striking. The Governor could make an Order for all or any of the following purposes: to keep a person out of a particular area in Cyprus save where

---

[172] Anderson (1994): 203 (n.1); Crawshaw (1978): 14–15.
[173] Crawshaw (1978): 151–2.
[174] Crawshaw (1978): 147.
[175] Simpson (2004): 944, citing the Greek Government's complaint against the United Kingdom under the ECHR.
[176] Simpson (2004): 1010.

permitted to do so by the competent authority; to prohibit or restrict their possession or use of specified articles or things; to require them to notify their movements in to the competent authority in a specified manner and at specified times; and to confine them to their residence or house. Anyone contravening an Order by being in a particular area or failing to leave it could be removed from it by a policeman or by any other person authorized to do so by the Governor.

The most draconian power, however, was that of indefinite detention without trial under Regulation 6. This was open to the Governor where he had reasonable cause to believe any person (a) to have been recently concerned in acts prejudicial to public safety or public order or in their preparation or instigation; (b) to be or have been a member of, or to be or have been active in the furtherance of the objects of an organization which is subject to foreign influence or control; or (c) to be an undesirable alien. He could make a detention order if he had reasonable cause to believe that by reason of any one or more of these things it was necessary to exercise control over the individual. A detention order could be suspended subject to such conditions or restrictions as the Governor thought fit, thus opening up the imposition of a broader range of restrictions than were imposable under Regulation 5. Failure to comply could result both in the revocation of the suspension (re-detention) and prosecution for an imprisonable offence under the Regulations. Once again, the parallels with control orders under the PTA 2005 and the range of measures used in respect of wartime (chapter two), the Irish question (chapter 3) and 'aliens' (chapter 4) are all marked.

As noted, the targets of this detention regime were communists. By mid-February 1956 175 detention orders had been made and 140 persons arrested. There were still 135 detained, two had escaped and one had been released. One hundred and thirty two were still detained in December 1955.[177] These are small numbers when set on a scale of comparative emergencies, but significant against a small close-knit population. Regulation 6, along with a number of other regulations, was revoked on 30 July 1957. It had not been used since 14 March 1957.[178] The Detention of Persons Law 1955 remained in force throughout the Emergency.[179]

Over the whole Emergency, under the two detention regimes, 3,458 detention orders were issued, 3,250 people were detained under them, 3,176 were released conditionally or unconditionally, there were 27 escapees, and 50 were moved into the criminal process and imprisoned. In addition, three subjects of detention orders were killed when resisting arrest. The peak of detentions (2,005) was reached in July 1958 in the face of inter-communal riots. Numbers ebbed and flowed in response to both the level of violence and the state of the delicate political negotiations on the future of the Island.[180] By 2 March 1957, 1,401 orders had been

---

[177] Simpson (2004): 909.
[178] CO 926/1082 TNA.
[179] Ibid.: Simpson (2004): 900–901.
[180] Simpson (2004): 909–10.

made, 1,322 were put into effect and 1,150 were actually detained. By February 1958, the number made had increased to 1,524, but only 656 remained in detention, the new Governor, Sir Hugh Foot having released many before Christmas 1957. By April, the number of detainees had dropped to 551, only to rise drastically to the peak of 2,005 after the inter-communal conflicts in July 1958.[181] To put the total figure in context, detention on the same scale in the United Kingdom at the time would have produced a figure in excess of 180,000. Detention in Cyprus thus 'had a very strong impact on local feeling. Very many Cypriots would know, or be related to, detainees'.[182] The vast majority of detainees over the period came from the Greek Cypriot community. Sometimes detention was used because criminal prosecution could not be attempted because of lack of evidence or the inability (through witness intimidation or the need to protect sources) to use it in court. But it was also used where prosecution had been attempted but had been discontinued or resulted in acquittal. This formed part of the Greek Government's complaint under the ECHR, considered later in this account.[183]

In its application against the United Kingdom under the ECHR, the Greek Government described the camps as 'concentration camps' and Cyprus as one 'huge concentration camp'.[184] Most detainees were held in camps. Some were held in prisons, including Kyrenia Castle, from which came the most dramatic escape, showing extreme laxity on the part of the personnel involved and reducing public confidence in the Cyprus Government, particularly among the Turkish minority.[185] To prevent future escapees leaving the Island, the passports of all detainees were impounded.[186] Red Cross inspection of the detention camps revealed conditions in the camps to be good.[187]

Deportation, expulsion and banishment The most dramatic use of powers of deportation and banishment during the Emergency was the exile to the Seychelles of four people: Archbishop Makarios, the Bishop of Kyrenia, another priest, and a journalist, all of whom were outspoken in their support for *enosis*. A number of questions fall to be answered here. Why use an executive measure rather than criminal prosecution, conviction and sentence? Why exile rather than detention without trial in Cyprus? Why not merely rely on deportation? There was also the question of which law to use to effect the banishment and the question which so often arose given the need to find a political settlement, of exactly when to deploy the power?

---

[181] Simpson (2004): 909, 931(n.33).

[182] Simpson (2004): 910.

[183] Simpson (2004): 944.

[184] Simpson (2004): 928, 931.

[185] Foley (1964):38; Crawshaw (1978): 139.

[186] CO 926/396 TNA, telegram 862 from Governor to Colonial Office, 19 October 1955.

[187] Simpson (2004): 909.

Criminal prosecution for sedition was, of course, one option for dealing with Archbishop Makarios and the other clerics, a possible attraction being that they would be proved guilty by fair trial processes of specific criminal acts. The width of the Cyprus sedition law has already been noted. It criminalized an intention to bring about a change in the sovereignty of the colony, thus arguably rendering criminal public advocacy of *enosis*, and was not limited to an intention to incite violence. The Bishop of Kyrenia had preached sermons openly advocating violence and praising the leader of EOKA.[188] Makarios, while clearly supporting *enosis*, was rather more circumspect. Conviction of either was thought by no means a certainty since witnesses might not be prepared to give evidence. An acquittal would, of course, have been a major propaganda coup. But even a conviction would have brought problems. Imprisonment on Cyprus would have made the prison locale a focus for demonstrations and of possible rescue or escape attempts, which if successful would afford another propaganda coup. Crawshaw identifies another fear. If (and this was unlikely) the Archbishop or the Bishop were found guilty of an offence attracting the death penalty, extending clemency to avoid martyrdom while denying it to so many EOKA fighters would also have been problematic.[189] The possibility of conviction followed by deportation as someone convicted of a criminal offence was also considered, but rejected because of fears of serious disorders during and after the trial and while any appeal was pending.[190] In short, so far as can be judged from available records, 'there was in reality no evidence capable of standing up in a court of law that Makarios was directly in control of terrorism'.[191]

Detention without trial on Cyprus, under either detention law but particularly Emergency Regulation 6, afforded another option for dealing with these troublesome clerics. But it posed the same risks to public order and the danger of rescue or escape as did imprisonment following criminal conviction.

Simple expulsion of the troublesome clerics from Cyprus was not possible under the Cyprus aliens and immigration legislation.[192] This formed part of the 'ordinary' law of Cyprus. It did, however, allow the Cyprus Government to refuse re-entry to anyone who had left, including a native of Cyprus, who on return would

---

[188] PREM 11/1248 TNA, telegram dated 10 September 1955 Attorney General to Secretary of State for Colonies.

[189] Crawshaw (1978): 155.

[190] PREM 11/1248 TNA, telegram dated 13 October 1955 Colonial Office to Prime Minister.

[191] Simpson (2004): 917.

[192] Aliens and Immigration Law, No. 13 of 1952.

... be likely to conduct himself so as to be dangerous to peace, good order, good government or public morals, or to excite enmity between the people of the Colony or to intrigue against Her Majesty's power and authority in the Colony.[193]

It would be particularly applicable to Archbishop Makarios, an inveterate traveller, but its timing would depend more on the chance of him going abroad rather than enabling the planned and decisive action an expulsion power would permit. It also raised the same problems as mere expulsion, considered below. The Aliens and immigration law was never used against Cypriots, but was deployed, possibly in conjunction with deportation under the Emergency Regulations, against 127 out of 147 teachers of Greek nationality who advocated *enosis*.[194]

For several months, Governor Armitage sought permission to deport Archbishop Makarios and the more extreme Bishop of Kyrenia. Doing so required a new legal base. The Colonial Office suggested amending the Detention of Persons Law 1955 to enable the deportation of those able to be detained under it.[195] This involved envisaging the clerics as active terrorists. The wording of that detention law would undoubtedly have covered the Bishop (who was or had been active in the furtherance of the purposes of EOKA) but less clearly the Archbishop who had advocated peaceful means rather than violence,[196] although the Archbishopric had been searched because it was thought to contain arms and explosives.[197] Then it was suggested that there be enacted a specific Expulsion of Persons Law, various drafts of which passed back and forth. 'Expulsion' was thought a better term since 'deportation' was 'less palatable internationally'.[198] Indeed, the Foreign Office favoured doing nothing.[199] Initially the wording of the proposed Law echoed that of section 2(1) of the Detention of Persons Law. Concern that it might not catch the Archbishop led to it being broadened. As finally approved, this would have enabled the Governor to deport if

... satisfied that any person is or has been conducting himself so as to excite enmity between the people of the Colony and Her Majesty, or is or has been intriguing against

---

[193] s. 6(1)(g).

[194] Simpson (2004): 898, incl. n. 76.

[195] PREM 11/1248 TNA, telegram No. 620 dated 9 September 1955, Secretary of State for Colonies to Cyprus Governor.

[196] PREM 11/1248 TNA, telegram dated 14 September 1955, Secretary of State for Colonies to Governor Armitage.

[197] PREM 11/1248 TNA, telegram dated 4 September 1995, Acting Governor Cyprus to Secretary of State for Colonies.

[198] PREM 11/1248 TNA, telegram dated 14 September 1955, Secretary of State for Colonies to Governor Armitage.

[199] Simpson (1996a): 394.

Her Majesty's power and authority in the Colony, or is or has otherwise been conducting himself so as to be a danger to peace, order or good government.[200]

The person could be kept in custody pending deportation and for non-compliance with the deportation order. There would be no provision for an appeal. The Governor would be empowered to appoint a custodian of the deportees' property and to have the deportees defray the expenses of their own removal and of their detention prior to it. But mere expulsion from Cyprus, leaving such people free to go where they will, whether London or Athens, was thought inappropriate since it would leave them free there to continue the very activities for which they had been deported. The British Embassy in Athens thought allowing the Bishop of Kyrenia to go to Athens would inflame feeling and create public order problems for the Greek Government.[201] Accordingly, it was decided to deport and detain them in the Seychelles (Kenya having been rejected as affording no suitable place of detention), thus keeping them out of sight and out of mind.[202]

As it was, the draft Expulsion of Persons Law remained just that. By the time it was decided to deport the clerics and detain them in the Seychelles, the State of Emergency had been declared in Cyprus. The deportations were effected therefore under Emergency Regulations 7–17. The scheme was drawn in terms of absolute discretion, most markedly in Regulation 7:

Deportation Orders

(1). The Governor may make an Order under his hand (in these Regulations referred to as a 'deportation Order') for the deportation of any person from the Colony.

(2). A deportation Order shall require the person in respect of whom it is made to leave and remain out of the Colony and it may be made subject to any condition which may be specified by the Governor in such order.

The people concerned could be detained pending removal and were legally obliged to comply with the Order. Removal would be effected on a ship or aircraft whose master or pilot could be compelled to take them. The deportee's money or personal property could be used to defray the expenses. If they were already serving a sentence of imprisonment, normally the order would only take effect after service of that sentence, unless the Governor otherwise directed. There was no appeal against an Order, although the Governor had power to vary it to enable return to Cyprus subject to conditions or to revoke it. Returning or attempting to return in

---

[200] PREM 11/1248 TNA, telegram dated 14 October 1955, Secretary of State for Colonies to Governor Harding.

[201] PREM 11/1248 TNA, telegram dated 15 September 1955, Embassy to Foreign Secretary.

[202] PREM 11/1248 TNA, telegram dated 13 October 1955, Colonial Office to Prime Minister; telegram dated 14 September 1955, Governor Armitage to Secretary of State for Colonies.

breach of the Order, or breaking a condition of return, were all rendered criminal offences punishable by imprisonment and also rendering the person liable to again be deported under the original Order. Knowingly harbouring or concealing such a returnee or person in breach of conditions was also criminal and punishable with imprisonment. There was no requirement to give reasons for the Order. Those in respect of the clerics simply recited that the Governor had decided that it was in the public interest that they be deported.[203]

The National Archive files surveyed by this author and by Simpson also show much debate on when action would be appropriate given the sensitive political discussions with Archbishop Makarios and proposed talks with Greece and Turkey. It also shows a softer approach with Archbishop Makarios than the more extreme Bishop of Kyrenia, but reveals a need to be able to justify why action was being taken against the latter rather than the former.[204] Thus a delay was called in order to see what the United States would do about having Cyprus removed from the UN Agenda.[205] It was then decided to postpone action while Harding replaced Armitage as Governor and further consideration was given to the matter of a State of Emergency.[206] This was put on hold while Harding held talks with Makarios, but in mid-October the new Governor preferred to have the Bishop of Kyrenia out of the way through banishment so as to leave Makarios freer to negotiate. Prime Minister Eden told Harding he thought it right to keep the Archbishop as a useful contact man until he was sure that he was not and requested the Governor not to take action to deport him without consulting Eden. Nor was he to deport any other high-ranking cleric without consultation unless 'there is some extreme urgency'. Politically, it was also vital that such drastic action as banishment should be avoided save in circumstances that could be defended on grounds of maintaining law and order, such as clear sedition or incitement. Later in October, the Prime Minister requested Harding to stay his hand until the Government saw what was happening with the Foreign Secretary's talks with Greece. Eden was fearful that enacting the Expulsion Law would unite the two prelates rather than drive them apart. On 26 October 1955, the Colonial Office advised that the talks were going well and enactment should be delayed. On 6 December 1955, in response to Harding's request to be able to deport the Bishop, Cabinet decided that, in spite of his continuing provocation, it would be unwise to accede for the time being since the deportation

---

[203] Found in CO 956/483 TNA (Papers on *Greece* v *United Kingdom* (1954–56).

[204] PREM 11/1248 TNA, telegram dated 13 September 1955, Secretary of State for Colonies to Governor Armitage.

[205] PREM 11/1248 TNA, telegram dated 17 September 1955, Secretary of State for Colonies to Governor Armitage.

[206] PREM 11/1248 TNA, telegram dated 24 September 1955, Secretary of State for Colonies to Governor Armitage.

... would, on balance, have an unfavourable effect on the Greek Government, and would make it even more difficult to bring about a resumption of the discussions between the Governor and Archbishop Makarios which might lead to a political settlement. The Archbishop could not afford publicly to dissociate himself from the Bishop of Kyrenia, and the Greek Government would be unwilling to condone the deportation of the latter, at any rate before the general election in Greece next March.[207]

The timing of the deportations also involved political considerations. Initially the Government wanted it done on 7 March 1956 to avoid a Parliamentary debate. The United States Secretary of State Dulles was only to be told an hour in advance, and there was concern that everything possible should be done to limit fall out at the UN. In fact the deportations took place on 9 March and questions were asked in the House of Commons on 12 March. The Commons were informed that generous allowances would be paid to the Archbishop and Bishop and that there was no question of recovering the expense from any of their personal property. They were held under a specifically enacted Seychelles' Political Prisoners' Detention Ordinance[208] at *Sans Souci*, the attractive summer home of the Governor of those islands. The Archbishop's parole was soon accepted, giving him a greater degree of freedom in that area of the island.

The matter of compliance with international law and, more specifically, the ECHR had also formed part of the decision-making process from September 1955 onwards. Simpson considers that 'this was in all probability, the very first occasion when the European Convention became a factor to be considered in determining policy'.[209] Even where deportation alone was in issue, this gave rise to some dispute among the Foreign Office legal advisers as to whether international law permitted a State to expel its own nationals. Matters became rather more complex when removal to detention outside Cyprus became the chosen option. Reliance on Art. 63(3) ECHR – the Convention was to be applied in the colonial territories to which its operation had been extended by the colonial Power with due regard to 'local requirements' – was not thought to justify the action. Art. 5(1)(f) ECHR permitted detention for deportation, thus covering arrest and detention in Cyprus. But detention in the Seychelles would need both a new law there and could only be justified by an Art. 15 derogation on grounds of a public emergency threatening the life of the nation. There was none in the idyllic and peaceful Seychelles. The view was taken, however, that the action could be based on the existence of one threatening the life of the Cypriot nation. Sir Gerald Fitzmaurice was, however, of the opinion that this might not be said to be 'strictly required by the exigencies of that emergency situation' since simple removal from Cyprus would suffice to counter subversive activities. Detention in the Seychelles would have to be

---

[207] PREM 11/1248, TNA CM (55) Conclusions, Minute 8, 6 December 1955.

[208] No. 1 of 1956.

[209] Simpson (1996a): 395. This, and TNA files containing the legal opinions, form the basis of the account given here.

justified on the basis of a public emergency there or one that affected the Empire as a whole. In other words, there were major ECHR problems in terms of the long-standing colonial remedy of banishing troublemakers to another part of the Empire. This caused 'panic' and 'overreaction' at the Foreign Office and it is clear from all the papers that the step of extending the ECHR to colonies was one very much regretted. Indeed the Foreign Secretary had not been aware of it having been done. In any event, the view was expressed that the argument of justification should be maintained even if the Government actually thought it to be 'bad law'. The opinion of the law officers (Attorney General and Solicitor General) was that the 'deportation' to the Seychelles might be supportable under Art. 5(1)(f) rather than being regarded as 'transportation' not covered by the provision and could only be justified under Art. 15 in terms of the public emergency threat to Cyprus, and not a threat to the Empire as a whole. They also thought it wise to keep the Council of Europe Secretary-General informed of the measures taken. This account is interesting for showing the limited role of the ECHR in decision–making. Government consideration was, however, to prove important since Greece on May 7 (but more in response to two imminent executions rather than the deportations) brought against the United Kingdom the first inter-State case under the ECHR. That was not the only effect of the deportations. There were violent demonstrations in Cyprus and Greece. Terrorism intensified though the insurrection Governor Harding feared did not occur. Greece withdrew its Ambassador from London and complained to the UN Security Council.[210] More importantly perhaps, 'Harding, by signing the deportation orders, had cut himself off from four fifths of the population'.[211] Finding Greek Cypriots prepared to help the police was rendered more difficult as was finding moderates in that community prepared to help take forward proposals towards a political settlement.[212] In late March 1957, when the European Commission of Human Rights was endeavouring to find a friendly settlement of the Geek complaint under the ECHR, Cabinet decided to release the exiles, but Makarios was not allowed to return to Cyprus.[213]

Security Measures: Administrative Challenge Machinery

The Emergency Regulations on deportation afforded those affected no right of administrative challenge, In contrast, each of the detention regimes enabled those detained to make representations to the Governor and to the appropriate Advisory Committee, the members of which were appointed by the Governor.[214] Neither regime stipulated requisite qualifications. In some Colonial Office material this

---

[210] Foley (1964): 49–50.
[211] Foley (1964); 51.
[212] Ibid.
[213] Simpson (2004): 969–70.
[214] Detention of Persons Law 1955, s. 4; Emergency Powers (Public Safety and Order) Regulations 1955, reg. 6(4).

Advisory Committee system is said to be based on that which had operated in the United Kingdom in respect of Regulation 18B detentions during the Second World War (see chapter 2). But the Advisory Committee under the Detention of Persons Law, while considering each case individually, did not function by way of personal hearings. The Government accepted that this should be so after Governor Harding had contrasted the fact that Regulation 18B Advisory Committee members operated in a friendly country and thus could be identified with safety, arguing that this was not the case in Cyprus and that following 18B processes would probably cause Advisory Committee members to resign.[215] The TUC, which had expressed concerns, were informed that the Advisory Committee was composed of Zekia J, Ackland–Hood, an assistant judge, and Dr Raeburn CBE DSO. The Advisory Committee under Emergency Powers (Public Safety and Order) Regulation 6 in contrast had power to allow detainees to appear in person and to take written representations from witnesses. Under both detention regimes, the chairman of the Advisory Committee had to provide the detainee with the grounds for his detention and with such particulars as the chairman considered necessary to enable the detainee to present his/her case. Legal representation was not, however, permitted. Information provided by Governor Harding to the Colonial Office shows that some detainees were released on the advice of the Committees, and several others had their orders suspended (release subject to conditions), but that many did not exercise their right to make representations.[216] In the course of proceedings on the Greek complaint under the ECHR, the United Kingdom undertook to conduct a new review of the cases of those detained.[217]

The Subcommission of the European Commission of Human Rights, which visited Cyprus early in 1958 in the course of its investigation of the complaint brought by Greece against the United Kingdom, took evidence from the then Chairman of the Advisory Committee under the Detention of Persons Law (Griffith Williams). It also examined ten of its files, selected by the Colonial Government from the 700 available. In addition, two leading Greek Cypriot lawyers gave evidence to it, complaining of the difficulties they faced in advising and assisting detainees and of the way in which the security authorities treated lawyers (said to be aggressive, tyrannical and humiliating). The majority of the Commission thought the Advisory Committee operated conscientiously and afforded an adequate safeguard in the circumstances, although its procedures as regards enabling detainees to present their case might possibly have been improved. The minority thought its procedures inadequate, the information on which decisions were based unreliable, and criticized its operation of a

---

[215] CO 926/396 TNA, interchange of telegram correspondence between Secretary of State and Governor Harding, telegrams 1009 (15 November 1955) and 1140 (30 November 1955).

[216] CO 926/396 TNA, telegram 1180, Governor Harding to Colonial Office, dated 5 December 1955.

[217] Simpson (2004): 963.

presumption of guilt which resulted in detention being over-used and catching people who were not really dangerous. For some unknown reason, no comparable investigation was made into the operation of Emergency Regulation 6.[218]

Legal Challenges: Cyprus Courts and the Judicial Committee of the Privy Council in London

In the Cyprus courts, there were a number of challenges to the admissibility of confessions obtained during interrogation.[219] There were also a number of appeals in death penalty cases to Cyprus' ultimate Court of Appeal, the Judicial Committee of the Privy Council in London.[220] In *Papaioannou v Superintendent of Prisons*,[221] in the Supreme Court, on a challenge to detention under Emergency Regulation 6 as AKEL members, both the judge at first instance and his brethren on appeal followed the wartime decisions of the House of Lords in *Liversidge v Anderson*[222] and *Greene v Home Secretary*.[223] The Supreme Court held that the maker of a detention order could not be required to disclose information as regards the sufficiency of the grounds on which the order was made, thus depriving habeas corpus or judicial review of any effective role. Zekia J, at first instance, noted that the applicants had in the light of those decisions rightly dropped at trial the argument that there was no evidence that the Governor had reasonable cause to believe. It was settled law that the Governor was not bound to disclose beyond the grounds on which he exercised the power 'his reasons, nature and source of information which had led him to order the detention of a person'.[224] His order was a complete and peremptory answer to the application.[225] He could not be questioned as to the sufficiency of the grounds on which he based his belief. It was legitimate to specify in the detention order more than one ground. Not specifying the place of detention in the detention order was a procedural defect not affecting the validity of the order. The Administrative Secretary could sign an order on the instructions of the Governor who, having considered the case and reports from others, had pronounced himself satisfied that it was appropriate to detain a person under the regulation. [226]

   The author has not been able to find any other reported cases on detention in the material surveyed in the National Archives or available sets of Law Reports of

---

[218] Simpson (2004): 1012–1014.
[219] Simpson (2004): 972–3, 1020–1021.
[220] See for example, CAB 128/30 TNA, Minute 3, Meeting 66, 18 September 1956.
[221] (1956) 21 Cyprus Law Reports 134.
[222] [1942] A.C. 206. See chapter 3.
[223] [1942] A.C. 284.
[224] (1956) 21 Cyprus Law Reports 134, at 139 (Zekia J).
[225] (1956) 21 Cyprus Law Reports 134, at 155 (Zekia J).
[226] (1956) 21 Cyprus Law Reports 134, at 155 (Hallinan J on appeal).

Cyprus cases.[227] No other cases are mentioned by Simpson. The lack of reported cases suggests either that no others were brought to court or that any which were brought were not thought fit to report as merely applying settled law which, as has been seen in all the areas surveyed so far, leaves matters squarely in the hands of the executive rather than the courts. Indeed, the same 'hands-off' judicial attitude exhibited in *Liversidge* v *Anderson* and the Cypriot case following it, was exemplified in *Ross-Clunis* v *Papadopoullos* in which individuals mounted an ultimately unsuccessful challenge to the validity of regulation 3 of the Emergency Powers (Collective Punishment) Regulations 1955.[228]

Human Rights Challenges under the ECHR

The ECHR had been extended to Cyprus as to other colonies without any searching appraisal of which laws might not be compatible with it. The United Kingdom Government, however, entered a notice of derogation under the public emergency clause in Art. 15. The reasons given for derogation provided on 7 October 1955, some three months after the introduction of the Detention of Persons Law 1955, were that certain emergency powers had been brought into operation in Cyprus on 16 July 1955 because of the commission of acts of violence including murder and sabotage and so as to prevent attempts to subvert the lawfully constituted Government. Settled policy meant that no further details were provided.[229] The declaration of the State of Emergency was not thought to warrant a further notice; the view was taken that most of the Emergency regulations could be supported under the 'clawback clauses' and 'exceptions' attached to particular ECHR rights and freedoms (for example, Articles 2, 8, 10). Detention without trial, only supportable by means of Art. 15 ECHR, was thought already covered by the original notice.[230] Although Government considered that deportation did not breach the ECHR, detention in the Seychelles might, so on 13 April 1956 a further derogation notice was entered to deal with the November Emergency powers and the banishment of the clerics, basing the emergency firmly in Cyprus itself.[231]

The two complaints made against the United Kingdom by Greece to the European Commission of Human Rights under the ECHR were but one element of a wider policy on the part of Greece and the Greek Cypriots to try to internationalize the Cyprus problem. Attempts were made to have it inscribed on the agenda of various UN bodies. There was some discussion at NATO meetings and an unsuccessful attempt was made to raise it in the Consultative Assembly of the Council of Europe.[232]

---

[227] The Cyprus Law reports for the 'emergency years' were surveyed.
[228] [1958] 1 WLR 546.
[229] Simpson (2004): 901–902.
[230] Simpson (2004): 912.
[231] Simpson (2004): 918–919.
[232] Simpson (2004): 924–9, 935–6, 953.

The first ECHR complaint dealt with the compatibility with the ECHR of various emergency laws and regulations, including the two regimes of detention without trial and the deportation and exile of Archbishop Makarios and the other enotist clerics. The second complaint dealt with allegations of an administrative practice of torture, inhuman or degrading treatment or punishment. Both have been examined in depth elsewhere.[233] Only an outline of the stages with respect to the first application and the Commission's eventual opinion on the merits of the detention and deportation aspects of it is required here.

The application was the first inter-State application under the ECHR. It raised interesting issues on the application to it of the requirement for exhaustion of domestic remedies. It was decided that the requirement had no application in an inter-State case where the object was not to secure compensation on behalf of named individuals but rather to put in issue whether particular legislative measures were compatible with the ECHR obligations of the State invoking them. Once declared admissible, the Commission then had two duties: to investigate and form an opinion on the merits of the application; and to place itself at the disposal of the Parties to try to secure a friendly settlement of the matter.[234] As regards the first, the Commission considered memorials and material submitted by the Parties and a Subcommission visited and took evidence on the island. As regards the second, the United Kingdom Government was at pains to confine the Commission to the legal issues raised by the application and prevent it trespassing into the wider political issues surrounding an overall settlement of the Cyprus question. As regards the merits, the Commission, without any suggestion of this by the Parties, propounded the doctrine that as regards the matters of derogation in times of public emergency under Art. 15 ECHR and the measures required to deal with it, the State concerned was entitled to a 'margin of appreciation'. Looking at the situation in Cyprus between April and November 1955, the majority of the Commission held that the United Kingdom had not exceeded its margin in deciding that a public emergency threatening the life of the nation existed. Moreover detention without trial could, applying that margin, be said to be a measure strictly required by the exigencies of a situation in which intimidation rendered ordinary criminal proceedings impossible. Moreover, it was accompanied by adequate safeguards (the Advisory Committee) against abuse. As regards deportation and exile, the majority of the Commission held that arrest and detention in Cyprus did not involve any violation. Nor did removal to the Seychelles, the Commission here drawing a distinction between the right to liberty of person (involving arrest and detention) and exile as raising matters of freedom of movement and the right to reside in a territory, matters not guaranteed by the ECHR. Detention in the Seychelles was in place of detention in Cyprus. Since detention in Cyprus, as noted above, was protected by Art. 15 ECHR, so was that in the Seychelles. Refusal to allow the deportees to return to Cyprus when released from exile in the Seychelles did not breach the

---

[233] Simpson (2004): chaps18, 19; Simpson (1996a): 400–404.
[234] Articles 28–31 ECHR.

ECHR since it does not guarantee a right to reside in the national territory. There was some criticism of the United Kingdom's failure to keep the Secretary-General of the Council of Europe fully informed as promptly as Art. 15(3) required. The Commission, while holding that breach of the reporting requirements might in an extreme case preclude reliance on the right of derogation, held that this was not such a case. The matter could not go to the Court since the United Kingdom had not recognized its jurisdiction. By the time the matter came before the other final decision-maker, the Committee of Ministers of the Council of Europe, a political body, the wider Cyprus question had effectively been settled by the Zurich agreement. The Committee simply took note of the Commission's Report and resolved that no further action was called for.[235]

In international law and under the ECHR, the proceedings were unprecedented, and, in terms of recognition of the Commission's jurisdictional competences, can be seen as a significant step forward in the idea of limiting state sovereignty by human rights considerations. However, as Simpson has stated,

> The general line taken by the majority in the report is no doubt understandable, but it can hardly be said that the outcome was a triumph for the international protection of human rights, and the adoption of the doctrine of the margin of appreciation in relation to their protection in times of internal crisis was the beginning of a process which seriously weakened the European Convention for the future. ...[T]he majority seemed determined to back the colonial government, come what may, so long as some justification could be contrived to support this. The decision began the process whereby, in defiance of its language, the convention was interpreted to deprive it of much of its significance in just those conditions in which government is most strongly tempted to violate the human rights of individuals in the name of the restoration of law and order.[236]

The case evoked a number of responses from the United Kingdom Government. There was regret at having without due thought extended the application of the ECHR to colonies. Receipt of the Greek application at the Foreign Office caused 'consternation'.[237] It was thought shocking that another State Party should arraign the United Kingdom, with its liberal traditions, before the Commission. Greece doing so was regarded as an abuse of the right of petition, but that admissibility condition applied only to individual petitions. There was hostility to the notion of the Subcommission visiting the island and taking evidence, a degree of reluctant co-operation with it while denying it jurisdiction in terms of involvement in the wider political issues, and some attempt to spin out proceedings. Some consideration was given to withdrawing from the ECHR, but this politically was out of the question. The result ultimately was to give

---

[235] For criticism, see Simpson (2004): 1048–1052.

[236] Simpson (2004): 1018–1019. See also criticism of the 'margin of appreciation' in chapter 1 and, in chapter 3, of the approach of the European Court of Human Rights in *Lawless* v *Ireland* (1961) and *Ireland* v *United Kingdom* (1978).

[237] Simpson (2004): 932.

compliance with the ECHR a higher, though not determinative, profile in governmental decision-making.[238] A more substantial notice of derogation, specifying in detail the legislation on detention, was made to the Secretary-General of the Council of Europe on 21 January 1959. It was withdrawn on 19 June 1959, the effective end, for the United Kingdom, of the Cyprus Emergency.[239] The practice of supplying more information on the need for derogation continued with other colonial emergencies and in response to further ECHR decisions against other States, but the need for promptness often seemed overlooked by those who had the responsibility for managing the conflicts that withdrawal from empire involved.[240]

The 'Hearts and Minds' and Constitutional Dimensions

While not keen for strategic reasons to relinquish control of Cyprus, the United Kingdom Government realized that with the attention of the world upon how they were dealing with the security problem posed by EOKA in a context in which self-determination was high on the agenda of the UN, it would have to try to find some political and constitutional solution to the different aspirations of the two communities in Cyprus and their protector governments, as well as deal with violence through security measures.[241] The two went hand in hand. As Governor Harding put it soon after taking up his post, there could be no way forward with the Greek Cypriots unless there was some mention of self-determination in the constitutional arrangements, but that no new Constitution could be operated until the law and order problems had been dealt with.[242] It has already been noted how the strategy on security, and the matters of when to introduce new laws, and when and against whom to implement them, were heavily influenced by the possible impact of such actions on sensitive and complex negotiations towards an overall settlement. This was particularly the case over the removal of Archbishop Makarios to the Seychelles. Equally the severity of the security measures polarized positions, with Archbishop Makarios condemning them from his pulpit as the imposition of a regime comparable to that of the fascists. As in Ireland, Northern Ireland and Kenya, a solution only proved possible by entering into negotiations with those previously described as 'terrorists', 'subversives' or 'the root of the problem', and the granting of amnesty.

There was a social and economic dimension to this attempt to win 'hearts and minds' with proposals for an economic development plan, including major

---

[238] Simpson (2004): chaps 18–20.

[239] Simpson (2004): 1058.

[240] Simpson (2004): 1059–61.

[241] The best account is in Holland (1998), the most readable is Crawshaw (1978). The brief account here draws on them and on the country record in the Library of Congress at <http://www.regiments.org/wars/20thcent/55cyprus.htm#links>.

[242] CAB 128/30 TNA, Meeting 41, 12 June 1956, Minute 6.

construction projects linked to the military bases and the building of a first-class port to boost the Cypriot economy and its prosperity as a trading hub in the eastern Mediterranean; for a new scheme of social insurance; and in respect of technical schools and other educational issues, There was also a crucial constitutional dimension, attempting to reconcile apparently irreconcialiable positions.

The Tripartite Conference, the setting up of which had precluded an earlier introduction of a State of Emergency, began in London on 29 August 1955. After stressing the United Kingdom's strategic needs in Cyprus and the inability to meet them by a leased base, Macmillan, then the Foreign Secretary who chaired the talks, stressed that a key aim was to introduce self-government in Cyprus, but without stating what form he had in mind. The statements from Greece and Turkey on subsequent days merely highlighted the irreconcilability of positions all round. It did, however, put a British plan on the table – a useful step for appeasing elements at the UN – but, by indicating that Cyprus might never be independent or ceded to another country, his plan alienated the Greeks and, while more appealing to the Turks, inaugurated a process of making British policy on Cyprus hostage to Turkish interests, and did not wholly satisfy the Turkish side since self-determination had not unequivocally been ruled out. Shortly afterwards, Field Marshal John Harding took up his position as Governor in October 1955. He immediately undertook talks with Archbishop Makarios, dangling the 'carrots' of a £38-million development plan and withdrawal of some emergency measures in return for acceptance of a plan for limited self-government and postponement of self-determination. Further talks between Governor and Archbishop early in 1956 began well but, degenerating into stalemate, collapsed in March, with each side accusing the other of bad faith and intransigence. Amnesties for EOKA fighters, removal of the security measures, the need for the Archbishop to use his influence to end violence and disorder, and self–determination, all proved stumbling blocks. The Archbishop was then exiled to the Seychelles. This had a counterproductive effect by limiting his restraining influence on EOKA and leaving more extreme forces in control. Its military commander, General Grivas, now had to combine his military with a political role. A general strike was called and there was an increased level of violence on Cyprus. The exile also attracted criticism of the United Kingdom abroad and from the Opposition parties at home, and inevitably limited political progress on the constitutional front.

In July 1956, to try to move forward on that front, Lord Radcliffe was appointed by the United Kingdom Government to consider the matter of constitutional reform in terms of principles of 'liberal democracy' and protection of diverse communities, but assuming retention of British sovereignty, the use of Cyprus as a base, and British control over defence, foreign affairs and internal security. His proposals, submitted by the end of the year, were a balanced package.[243] They envisaged a balanced legislature, but crucially also embodied the option of self-determination at some indeterminate time in the future and

---

[243] Radcliffe (1956).

safeguards for the Turkish Cypriot minority. Greece rejected the proposals outright. Archbishop Makarios would not even consider them while still in exile. Turkey accepted the plan. With EOKA declaring a ceasefire (which proved only temporary) if he were released, the Archbishop was allowed to leave the Seychelles in April 1957, but was not permitted to return to Cyprus, receiving instead a hero's welcome in Greece. EOKA's campaign continued through various raids and attacks, Archbishop Makarios went once again to New York to argue his case before the UN. Governor Harding was replaced in the Autumn of 1957 on his retirement by Hugh Foot. The security position in Cyprus worsened. Early 1958 saw inter-communal strife became severe for the first time, exacerbating tensions between Greece and Turkey. The Turkish Cypriots showed that they also had a paramilitary organization. It also raised the spectre of partition as Turkish Cypriots moved north and Greek Cypriots south. The Greek Cypriots were also divided amongst themselves. EOKA attempted enforcement of an island-wide boycott of British goods. Its sabotage attacks increased. Foot, however, sought to build bridges between divided communities and to differing degrees impressed both, but Turkey feared he was too pro-Greek.

In June 1958, the Macmillan Plan (put forward by the United Kingdom Prime Minister) suggested a seven-year partnership scheme of separate communal legislative bodies and separate municipalities. Greece and Greek Cypriots rejected it as tantamount to partition, something which attracted the Turkish side as an alternative to the status quo. The Plan did however lead to discussions of the Cyprus problem between Greece and Turkey from December 1958. For the first time the idea of an independent Cyprus (neither *enosis* nor partition) was on the agenda, since it was understood that Archbishop Makarios preferred this to the Macmillan Plan. Talks in Zurich in February 1959, between the foreign ministers of Greece and Turkey, produced an agreement supporting independence. The Greek and Turkish Government representatives were joined by representatives of the Greek Cypriots, the Turkish Cypriots, and the United Kingdom in London Makarios accepted the position papers, having failed to get Greek backing for his objections. The Zurich–London agreements were ratified by the official participants of this London Conference and became the basis for the Cyprus constitution of 1960. Britain's interests in Cyprus were waning and could be met by retention of bases. Under the Treaty of Establishment, the United Kingdom retained sovereign rights over two areas to be used as military bases (Akrotiri, Dhekelia). The Treaty of Alliance stipulated that contingents of Greek troops and Turkish troops were to provide for the defence of Cyprus and train its new army. The Treaty of Guarantee established that in the event of a threat to these newly established political arrangements in Cyprus, its signatories (Greece, Turkey, United Kingdom), were to consult on appropriate measures to safeguard or restore them. In addition, the signatories were granted the right to intervene together or, if concerted action proved impossible, to act unilaterally to uphold the settlement. As for EOKA, Grivas was allowed to go to Greece and other EOKA prisoners and detainees were released in March 1959.

These inherently complex constitutional arrangements broke down in 1964 because of the lack of goodwill between the two Cypriot communities. Instability and the Treaty of Guarantee came to provide the pretexts for repeated foreign intervention that severely undermined Cypriot security, and for Turkey's unilateral military action in 1974 allegedly in response to a coup instigated by Greece's ruling military *junta*, which led to the *de facto* partition of the island. This, despite Cyprus's membership of the EU and Turkey's desire to join, sadly continues today.[244]

The Kenyan Emergency

Kenya and its Importance

The scramble for Africa by the European colonial powers created a number of geo-political entities with boundaries which haphazardly cut across older tribal boundaries.[245] European settlement inevitably came at a cost in lives and land to the peoples already there. The Kikuyu, Kenya's largest ethnic grouping, were particularly hard hit. This land question is central to an understanding of the Kenyan Emergency which lasted from October 1952 until January 1960. The British had arrived in Kenya in 1897. Initially a protectorate, it became a colony in 1920. Its main rationale was to provide a rail route between landlocked Uganda – strategically situated at the head of the Nile and economically important – and the Indian Ocean coast. Building it brought the British into violent conflict with the Kikuyu. It also brought in an Asian community. Paying for the railway necessitated white settlement to develop Kenya. Settlers were promised abundant fertile land and a plentiful supply of African labour, the movement of which was regulated through a system of 'pass laws'. Certain lands (the White Highlands) were effectively reserved for whites and there were also tribal reserves. Despite this, white-settler farming was not a particular economic success. Such success as there was came about because of government restrictions on the marketing of the produce of African farmers. Farming in Kenya only became an economic success after the fall of Singapore in World War Two and the loss of the United Kingdom's South-East Asian Empire. The loss of India and Burma to independence after the war, however, rendered Kenya, situated on the Indian Ocean just south of the Horn of Africa, strategically important. Like Malaya, it was also seen as economically important to a beleaguered United Kingdom economy kept afloat by a large American loan. With the loss of India, Kenya became 'the jewel in the Crown'.[246] Principal exports were coffee, tea and sisal. Kenya's population in 1953, the year after the Emergency was declared, was some 5.5 million. This was composed of

---

[244]   Palley (2005): 13–23.
[245]   Elkins (2005): 4–5; Pakenham (1992).
[246]   Elkins (2005): 29.

some 42,200 whites, 131,000 Asians and 5.3 million Africans. The Kikuyu – the African tribe in which the causes of the Emergency were seen to be located and in which the violence was most keenly felt – comprised some 1.5 million.[247]

Nature of the Emergency

African grievances covered low wages, the pass laws and more general urban discontent, but principally centred on the question of land hunger and the eviction of squatters, all against an overarching issue, the lack of effective African representation in government. African politics had three strands: conservatives (principally chiefs and headmen through whom the small British Administration ruled African Kenya); constitutional nationalists (men like Jomo Kenyatta – later to be Kenya's first President – and the Kenyan African Union (KAU)) seeking change through peaceful means; and a militant element. The Emergency was declared to combat this growing militant element which emerged as Mau Mau. The United Kingdom Government, the Kenyan colonial Government and the white settlers, whose voices dominated the contemporary portrayal of the Mau Mau, saw it as a savage and bestial reversion to tribal barbarism, a form of sickness which corrupted its almost exclusively Kikuyu adherents, a violent reaction against modernization, in part explicable by having attempted African development too fast rather than too slow. With this perspective, it is easy to see why the heavily weeded public records now available in the National Archives at Kew convey the firm impression that in fighting to overcome Mau Mau terror and its corrosive effect the two Governments, their civil administrations and their security forces (regular army, police and reserves, and detention camp personnel) were engaged essentially in a 'civilizing' mission, protecting white settlers and loyal Africans alike.

Two recent scholarly histories provide a very different perspective: a 'dirty war' of terror and counter-terror, with the United Kingdom being fortunate, given the applicability of the ECHR to Kenya as to other dependencies, that, unlike Greece with Cyprus, no other State party stepped forward on behalf of Kenyans, and that it had not recognized the right of individual petition. Anderson, who has interwoven a narrative account with material from most of the capital trials of Mau Mau accused in the period of the Emergency, considers that

> The war against the Mau Mau was fought not just by the military, or by the police, but by the civil administration, in a pervasive campaign that sought to strip the rebels and their sympathizers of every possible human right, while at the same time maintaining the appearance of accountability, transparency and justice. Nowhere was this more apparent than in the Mau Mau trials.[248]

---

[247] Anderson (2005): 345 (Table 1.i); Elkins (2005): xiv.

[248] Anderson (2005): 6.

Elkins, in her controversial and Pulitzer Prize-winning study, makes use of a wider range of sources than those in official archives (criticizing their 'sanitation'), including oral and other published testimony from former Mau Mau adherents, white settlers and colonial officials. She focuses in particular on the mass use of detention without trial and a policy of enforced 'villagization' which she compares to those of Nazi and Soviet regimes (Britain's *gulag*) and contemporaries compared to the concentration camps of the Boer War. In her view,

> An integrated reading of all the sources – written, oral and visual – yields an astonishing portrait of destruction. I have come to believe that during the Mau Mau war British forces wielded their authority with a savagery that betrayed a perverse colonial logic: only by detaining nearly the entire Kikuyu population of 1.5 million people and physically and psychologically atomizing its men, women and children could colonial authority be restored and the civilizing mission re-instated.[249]

She refers to a 'murderous campaign', which Government attempted to cover up, 'to eliminate Kikuyu people'.[250] Her picture is one of deliberate governmental conspiracy and cover-up, one which risks being seen as overblown. Anderson, perhaps more convincingly, presents a similar picture of brutality on both sides, but conveys more of an impression of a London Government not wholly in control of the Governor and his policies and a Governor unable to control subordinates in some of the security forces and detention camps. The tension between policies of deployment of counter-terror and ones founded more firmly on the rule of law is palpable.

From these studies, but not altogether missing from extant public records, a rather different picture emerges of Mau Mau as a violent product of genuine African grievances which, had they been dealt with, might have avoided so savage a conflict. Only later in the Emergency was Mau Mau characterizable as isolated brigandage. While it was never a unified guerrilla army, Mau Mau had a fighter wing located in the forests from which units would emerge to carry out brutal raids on white farms and loyalist Kikuyu. By mid-1953, it was a 'significant fighting force'.[251] At its peak, it was some 24,000 strong, but units became increasingly isolated from each other as Government military forces moved into the forests. Mau Mau also had a passive wing both in the reserves and Nairobi, formed of both willing and intimidated 'supporters'. This wing was variously a source of supplies, intelligence (for example, the use of locals to guide fighters to targets) and recruits for the fighter wing. Jomo Kenyatta was identified wrongly by white settlers and the Governor as the mastermind behind the Mau Mau, despite Special Branch files that portrayed the rather more complex nature of African politics noted earlier.[252]

---

[249]   Elkins (2005): xiii.
[250]   Elkins (2005): xiv.
[251]   Anderson (2005): 244.
[252]   Anderson (2005): 41–4.

During the Emergency much more would have remained hidden from public view, but for a number of backbench Labour MPs (particularly Fenner Brockway and Barbara Castle) and (as in Boer War) of outspoken and concerned individuals. Although a rebellion against British power, it was not properly characterizable as a 'race' war. This is not to deny that white settlers (men, women and children) were brutally mutilated and murdered in Mau Mau attacks. They were, not as 'part of an overall plan, but as a method of obtaining arms and supplies, raising morale or for reasons of personal prestige'.[253] Only thirty two died. There were also less than 200 casualties among the British regiments and police who served in Kenya.[254] Elkins suggests that less than a hundred Europeans were killed.[255] Most fatalities and other casualties are found among the Kikuyu. Between 11,000 and 20,000 Mau Mau fighters were killed.[256] Elkins suggests thousands, perhaps hundreds of thousands, were killed in 'a murderous campaign to eliminate Kikuyu people'.[257] At least 1,800 African civilians (mostly Kikuyu) were killed by Mau Mau. Hundreds more were probably killed and their bodies never found. [258] The Mau Mau conflict was thus very much a civil war for control or dominance of the Kikuyu (Mau Mau versus the loyalists through whom the Government in Nairobi governed and to a degree enforced law in the tribal reserves). Mau Mau fighters and supporters were to be hunted down and punished. Loyalists (chiefs, headmen and their Home Guard) were to be rewarded with land, local political and judicial power and tax exemptions. The uneven contest was won by the colonial government through a variety of means in combination. Much can be attributed to the superior numbers and firepower of the military operating in aid of the civil power, rather than under martial law, with their legal powers being an admixture of those under the Emergency Regulations (ER) and common law.[259] Particularly important here was the abandonment of the 'reasonable' requirement with respect to use of lethal force in 'prohibited' areas.[260] These were areas (normally uninhabited forests and mountain areas but then home to Mau Mau fighters) where the security forces alone were entitled to be, and in which they could use their weapons freely and without the need for prior challenge. They thus operated on a 'straightforward war basis', secure in the knowledge that anyone else in the area must be an enemy.[261] Other areas in which troops operated on an offensive basis were designated 'special areas'. The prime basis there for the use of force was the common law one of reasonable force in the prevention of felony (serious crime).

---

[253] Erskine (1955): para. 5.
[254] Anderson (2005): 4.
[255] Elkins (2005): xiv.
[256] Anderson (2005): 4.
[257] Elkins (2005): xiv.
[258] Anderson (2005): 4.
[259] Erskine (1955): paras. 13,
[260] Reg. 22A.
[261] Erskine (1955): paras 14, 15; reg. 22B.

But in those areas the ER provided that anyone could be called upon to halt for the purpose of examination. Those who did not do so could be fired upon if that was reasonably necessary to effect an arrest or prevent their escape or rescue from arrest.[262] Defeating Mau Mau also involved a modified criminal prosecution approach as one means of dealing with captured or arrested Mau Mau personnel. [263] This produced large-scale use of the death penalty in trials of Mau Mau personnel at a time when the United Kingdom at home was coming closer to its abandonment. The campaign also involved the use of collective punishments and land/property confiscation.[264] It saw a very prominent deployment of executive measures: particularly detention without trial on a truly massive scale in what several authors have described as Britain's *gulag*; but also of internal exile and deportation.[265]

Concern at Mau Mau, growing steadily in the period after the Second World War, had resulted in it being declared an unlawful organization in August 1950. This brought members, adherents and organizers within a range of serious offences in the Criminal Code. A State of Emergency was not declared until 20 October 1952. The precipitating event for Governor Baring's Proclamation under the Emergency Powers Order in Council 1939 (he chose this rather than the local Emergency Powers Ordinance 1948[266]) was the murder by Mau Mau on 9 October of the loyalist senior Chief Warahiu. In the intervening period Baring's request to the Colonial Office to approve one had been the subject of correspondence by telegram and letter.[267] Baring's 'Top Secret' letter of 9 October to Lyttleton (Secretary of State for the Colonies in the Churchill Government) stressed a 'very serious' position; that Mau Mau was widespread among Kikuyu (but some 75 per cent only through coercion and intimidation); a deteriorating position in the Kikuyu Reserves rendering relaxation of precautions there dangerous; and that there was unanimity of opinion that Kenyatta and other KAU leaders were the instigators and planners of Mau Mau, a statement now shown not altogether to accord with material from Special Branch.[268] He was also concerned that inaction would lead to Europeans, chiefs and headmen taking the law into their own hands.[269] Lyttleton cabled his approval on 14 October.[270] The time gap between murder and Proclamation also enabled British troops to be moved to Kenya, and

---

[262] Erskine (1955): para. 16.

[263] See chapter 1.

[264] Williams (1953): 275 n. 5 criticized it as violating the principles that punishment was personal and that duress should exempt from punishment.

[265] Elkins (2005); Anderson (2005): 311; Clough (1998): 205.

[266] CO 822/443 TNA (Telegram No. 616, 10 October 1952).

[267] CO 822/444, TNA.

[268] Anderson (2005): 59–61.

[269] CO 822/443, TNA. (Telegram No. 616, 10 October 1952).

[270] CO 822/443 TNA (Telegram No. 658) following approval by Cabinet (CAB 128/25, TNA Meeting 85, minute 1).

plans to be agreed about detention of key Mau Mau figures under 'Operation Jock Scott'.[271] The Governor's broadcast justified the Proclamation on 'the prevalence of disorder in a part of Kenya':

> The grave step of proclaiming an emergency has been taken most unwillingly, and with great reluctance, by the Government of Kenya. But there was no alternative in the face of mounting lawlessness in a part of the Colony, and there was no other method of keeping the peace and protecting the lives and property of innocent men of all races. ... The measures taken by the Government are aimed at those, and at those only, who in the opinion of the Government, are responsible directly or indirectly for violence and the state of disorder in a part of the Colony. The Government have no intention of penalising anyone merely on account of his political view. Moreover the Government intend to support and protect the loyal and peaceable citizens of all races.[272]

The earlier statement of the Secretary of State for the Colonies to the House of Commons on the Kenya situation referred to the murder of Chief Warahiu, in respect of which a leading KAU member, John Koinage, had been charged, to other attacks and to the difficulties posed for the criminal process by Mau Mau intimidation of witnesses.[273]

The Emergency Regulations (ER) came immediately into effect. As seen elsewhere in this study, they did not form a complete legal code governing the response, but operated alongside other ordinances or laws (for example, the Criminal Code, the Immigration legislation), some of which had been amended in the period of tension prior to the Proclamation, shortly before Governor Baring's arrival in Kenya in September 1952. In that period the Acting Governor had feared a general Kikuyu revolt and was under pressure to act from the white-settler representatives in the Legislative Council. The measures enabled witness protection by the police; restriction of traffic movement at night; control of printing presses; and, crucially, a number of evidentiary rule changes, one of which, contrary to the usual rules of the Indian Evidence Act applied in Kenya, rendered admissible in court a confession made to a police officer. This change was to have a profound impact on the conduct of criminal trials of Mau Mau.[274] A number of key provisions in the ER (amended periodically throughout the Emergency) most pertinent to this account can usefully be highlighted here.[275]

Arrest was enabled on suspicion of an offence under the ER, or of contravening or failing to comply with an order or direction given under the ER, or of someone

---

[271] CO 822/444 TNA (Baring's telegrams Nos. 627, 630, 17 October 1952); CO 822/443, TNA (text of Baring's broadcast and Colonial Office Information Statement, both 20 October 1952).

[272] CO 822/443 TNA.

[273] HC Debs, Vol. 505, cols. 388–94 (16 October 1952).

[274] Anderson (2005): 53.

[275] This account is based on the consolidated text of Regulations as at 30 November 1953 found in CO 822/729 TNA.

who so acted as to endanger the public safety. The power was vested in magistrates, policemen (including those in the Reserve and the Tribal Police), the military, and appointed headmen under the Native Authority Ordinance.[276] A police officer also had power to stop and question any person as to identity and purpose of being somewhere. The officer could arrest and detain pending further inquiries anyone so questioned whom he reasonably suspected had acted or was about to act in a manner prejudicial to the public safety or the preservation of the peace or was about to commit an offence against the ER.[277] The Governor could order a person's arrest and detention without trial where satisfied that for the purpose of maintaining public order it was necessary to exercise control over him or her. He could also suspend its operation subject to conditions and restrictions on movement and travel, residence and employment, association with others, and curfew.[278] A regulation was soon added authorizing a District Officer to impose collective punishment in Native Lands under his jurisdiction by seizing cattle or vehicles, ordering the closure of specified shops, markets or trading centres for up to three months, or ordering that all or any dwellings be closed and unavailable for human habitation for periods of up to 14 days. He could do so in two situations. First of all, he could impose any or all of these punishments where it appeared to him that certain specified crimes had been committed (for example, murder, manslaughter, managing an unlawful society) and that the inhabitants of the affected area had failed to take reasonable steps to prevent the commission of the crime or to prevent the escape of any person they had reasonable cause to believe to be its perpetrator. Secondly, collective punishment could be imposed where it appeared to the officer that the inhabitants or a substantial number of them in the affected area were members of or were or had been recently active in the furtherance of the objectives of Mau Mau or to have recently consorted with or harboured any member of Mau Mau. The circumstances of seizure of cattle or vehicles had as soon as possible to be reported to the Governor so that he could consider the exercise of his powers with respect to their release, forfeiture, disposal or sale. No rights of challenge appear to have been afforded those affected. The proceeds of sale could be used to compensate those in the area injured at the hands of Mau Mau.[279]

In a sense, there were two 'wars': one against Mau Mau fighters in the forests; the other against Mau Mau supporters in the city or reserves. Both were won by use of military, criminal and executive or security measures. But overall success came ultimately only by increasing moves to self-government and independence with governing power going to those once condemned as terrorists. The ebb and flow of the Emergency is well documented in the two recent historical studies and in reports from the then military commanders with respect to their 'watch' during

---

[276] Reg. 28.
[277] Reg. 3.
[278] Reg. 2.
[279] Reg. 4A.

the Emergency.[280] This study focuses instead on some key operations, giving a flavour of the whole campaign against Mau Mau and enabling an appreciation of the interaction of military methods, the modified criminal prosecution approach and the use of executive measures. The operations are: 'Operation Jock Scott' (the arrest of Kenyatta and other supposed leaders of Mau Mau leadership); 'forest operations' (taking on Mau Mau fighters and dealing with its 'passive' wing or support operations in the Kikuyu reserves and on the forest fringes); and 'Operation Anvil' (destroying the Mau Mau 'passive' wing and support network in Nairobi). In all three, both the modified criminal prosecution approach and executive measures had prominent roles to play, although the precise mix varied.

'Operation Jock Scott', the Modified Criminal Prosecution Approach, Special Assize Courts, and the Death Penalty.

'Operation Jock Scott', designed to decapitate Mau Mau,[281] was executed at the same time as, and was a prime rationale of, the Proclamation of Emergency. It involved the arrest and detention under the ER of Kenyatta and a number of other leaders in the KAU thought prominent in Mau Mau. Kenyatta and five others were selected to stand trial for managing an unlawful organization, an offence in the Criminal Code. The trial was held in a remote area and has been characterized as a rigged, 'show' trial, with the judge carefully selected and defence lawyers placed at some disadvantage,[282] and possible perjury by the Crown's main witness.[283] The convictions were, however, upheld by the East African Court of Appeal and the Judicial Committee of the Privy Council. Kenyatta and the others convicted with him served their sentence in a remote and somewhat arid area of Kenya, and it was clear that exile there would continue under the ER after sentence had been served. Others arrested were detained without trial under the ER. As shall be seen below, detention without trial was deployed on a large scale in the Emergency. But so was the criminal process, modified in a number of respects to enable its effective deployment.

This involved more than the already examined extension of powers of arrest. Resident Magistrates were upgraded to Supreme Court Justices to increase manpower to try serious criminal offences and retired judges were brought in from London.[284] Special Assize courts were established to deal with the increased numbers of offenders under the ER. The authorities were able to deploy the criminal process more effectively because of an alteration of Kenya's evidence rules (Kenyan legislation applied the Indian Evidence Act) to admit confessions made to a police officer. That Act was in any event more protective of informers

---

[280] Erskine (1955); Lathbury (1956).

[281] Anderson (2005): 62.

[282] Elkins (2005): 37–46; Anderson (2005): 63–8.

[283] Elkins (2005): 357.

[284] Anderson (2005): 152–3.

than was the case in England and Wales. It embodied mandatory non-disclosure of the informer's identity, with none of the exceptions applicable in England and Wales.[285] Just prior to the Proclamation of Emergency, the law had been amended also to enable better police protection through protective custody of witnesses. Crucially, the ER introduced a number of offences, conviction of which eventually carrying a mandatory death penalty, which a prosecution found easier to prove whether from confessions, accomplice evidence, witness evidence and the accused simply being caught in the act, whether in forest, reserve or city. The offences covered the carrying, possession or manufacture without lawful authority (the burden of proving which lay on the defence) of explosives, firearms and ammunition;[286] administering or participating in Mau Mau oath-taking; and membership of a Mau Mau gang likely to carry out acts prejudicial to public order. It was also a capital offence to consort with another who was in possession of firearms, ammunition or explosives in circumstances raising a reasonable presumption that he or she intended to act, had acted or was about to act with that other in a manner prejudicial to public safety or the maintenance of public order.[287] The sale of arms, etc., in circumstances raising a same reasonable presumption that the seller knew the other person intended or was about to use it for a purpose prejudicial to public safety, was also capital.[288] So was demanding, collecting or receiving supplies for such a prejudicial purpose.[289] There were other related and similar offences punishable with long terms of imprisonment.[290] Once again, service of sentence did not necessarily mean release. Those who had 'done their time' might well be transferred to the executive regime of indefinite detention without trial,[291] just as were many of those acquitted.[292]

The most striking feature of this criminal process was the sheer scale of application of the death penalty, 'ruthlessly deployed in the suppression of the rebellion'.[293] Over the period April 1953–December 1956, the Special Assize Courts in 1,211 trials tried 2,609 Kikuyu on capital charges relating to Mau Mau offences. Some 40 per cent were acquitted, but 1,574 were sentenced to hang. Government resisted white settler calls for speedy public executions. During the eight years of the Emergency, 160 of those convicted of capital offences were successful on appeal against conviction,[294] but

---

[285]   *Singh* v *R* (1951) 18 EALR 283.

[286]   Reg. 8A.

[287]   Reg. 8C(1).

[288]   Reg. 8B.

[289]   Reg. 8F.

[290]   Regs 8B (offensive weapons), 8C(2) (knowingly consorting with someone in possession of a firearm, explosive or ammunition).

[291]   Elkins (2005): 131–2.

[292]   Anderson (2005): 7.

[293]   Anderson (2005): 291.

[294]   Anderson (2005): 291.

1,090 Kikuyu [went] to the gallows for Mau Mau crimes. In no other place and at no other time in the history of British imperialism, was state execution used on such a scale as this. This was more than double the number of executions carried out [by the French] against convicted terrorists in Algeria, and many more than in all the other British colonial emergencies of the post-war period – in Palestine, Malaya, Cyprus and Aden.[295]

This also occurred at a time when the authorities in the United Kingdom – despite ECHR endorsement of the death penalty – were seriously debating the abolition of capital punishment in the United Kingdom. Executions in the United Kingdom annually rarely in modern times reached far into double figures and there was a moratorium for 18 months in 1956–57.[296] Of the 1,090, only 346 were convicted of murder. The remainder were convicted of capital offences under the ER: 210 for consorting with terrorists; 62 for participating in the administration of a Mau Mau oath; and 472 for possession of arms or ammunition.[297] The thirty women sentenced to hang were among the 240 reprieved. Others convicted but under 18 years of age also escaped the death sentence.[298] Over the same period, 247 'ordinary' murderers were convicted and sentenced to hang. Thirty–six won their appeals, five escaped the noose when certified insane, and in 106 cases the Governor commuted the death sentence to life imprisonment. In contrast, only 27 Mau Mau on death row were granted clemency by the Governor.[299] The prospect of clemency was sometimes used to gain the accused's co-operation in helping the military to locate their erstwhile colleagues or to persuade them to surrender, but co-operation did not invariably save the individual from the gallows.[300] Concern expressed by Prime Minister Churchill about the impact of mass executions on public opinion[301] was dealt with eschewing simultaneous execution of the type portrayed on the cover of Gatrell's classic study, although some executions were semi-public on a portable gallows.[302] Execution instead took place sometimes in series, one after another at 200-minute intervals. But the scale of execution is the more worrying, given the degree of coercion and brutality in the interrogation process and the ability of prosecution witnesses (loyal Kikuyu) to be able to settle longer-standing scores or grievances through the results of their evidence.[303] Corruption in the Home Guard and native police suggests that claims that evidence had been planted may not always have been wide of the mark.[304]

---

[295] Anderson (2005): 7.
[296] Anderson (2005): 291–2.
[297] Anderson (2005): 291.
[298] Anderson (2005): 7.
[299] Anderson (2005): 291.
[300] Anderson (2005): 234–5 (General China pardoned but later detained without trial), 276–7 (Ngemwe hanged).
[301] CAB 128/26 TNA (Meeting 33, minute 1, 21 May 1953).
[302] Gatrell (1996); Simpson (1996b): 666.
[303] Anderson (2005): chap. 4.
[304] Anderson (2005): 210–211.

Combating Mau Mau Fighters in the Forests and Support Networks in the Reserves

Here military might ultimately proved dominant, but those Mau Mau captured rather than killed could readily be processed through the Special Assize Courts given the terms of the capital offences under the ER. Sometimes a magistrate accompanied an Army mobile column so that those captured could be tried and sentenced, as far as possible, on the same day.[305] Those involved in support networks could be criminally prosecuted or detained without trial, depending on the available evidence.

Mau Mau never became an effective unified guerrilla force, in part because the State of Emergency came before it was ready for armed conflict, probably a year too soon.[306] Nonetheless it was dominant in the period up to June 1953 and fighting remained intense until June 1954, with the initiative beginning to swing towards the Army by the end of 1953.[307] Thereafter, particularly in the wake of 'Operation Anvil' which destroyed its support base in Nairobi, the security forces reduced Mau Mau largely to brigandage.[308] By May 1955, the Mau Mau Emergency had entered its 'last phase'.[309] A variety of military operations ('Carnation', 'Buttercup', 'Grouse', 'Hammer', 'First Flute'), aiming to move militarily from the defensive onto the offensive, saw the Army win superiority through larger troop numbers, better equipment and firepower and the use of aerial reconnaissance to identify gangs and aerial bombardment to drive Mau Mau fighters towards troops, and of aircraft to drop supplies to Army units in the forests[310] Pursuing and engaging Mau Mau armed bands was aided by the construction by the Public Works Department and later 39 Corps Engineer Regiment of wide roads into the forests to enable a rapid mechanized response.[311] Captured and 'turned' Mau Mau were used to target their erstwhile colleagues. The security forces also used special 'pseudo gangs' (security forces disguised as Mau Mau) initially to capture, later to physically eliminate Mau Mau fighters.[312] The forest areas were ones permitting an at-will use of lethal force on sight.[313] A number of partial amnesty 'surrender' offers (only actual murderers would face the gallows or later no one would face the death penalty) saw some fighters turn themselves in to face imprisonment or

---

[305] Erskine (1955): para. 34.
[306] Anderson (2005): 236.
[307] Erskine (1955): para. 3.
[308] Anderson (2005): 252.
[309] Erskine (1955): para. 125.
[310] Erskine (1955): 82–7.
[311] Erskine (1955): para. 32.
[312] Kitson (1960).
[313] Erskine (1955): para.14.

detention without trial ('Operation Green Branch'), but another failed when the Mau Mau gangs in question wrongly thought they had been lured into a trap.[314]

It was also vital to separate forest fighters from food, intelligence and other support from those Mau Mau supporters forming in the initial period at least the bulk of the population of the Kikuyu Reserves. This was achieved through clearing areas between jungle and 'reserves' (in which area security forces could shoot after challenge) to hinder communication. Those thought to be part of the 'passive wing' could after screening and interrogation operations be detained or prosecuted as could their 'fighting wing' contacts. Men often fled to the forests to avoid this, thus swelling the Mau Mau bands there. The strategy also demanded enforced 'villagization' (emulating Malaya). Women, children and the elderly were herded into villages protected by a ditch with spikes and barbed wire fencing. Loyalists thus received protection, in part through a Home Guard post, and exercised police powers over other Kikuyu. Elkins rightly sees this for non-loyalists as an integral part of a wider detention '*gulag*'. It has been identified by others as the major element in defeat of Mau Mau outside Nairobi.[315] A Farm Guard helped by reducing stock thefts by Mau Mau.[316] Collective punishments also aimed to deter provision of support and encourage a flow of information to the authorities. It was, however, 'Operation Anvil' which 'sealed the fate of the forest fighters. Supplies from Nairobi no longer reached the camps and the stream of recruits dried up'.[317] The ER combined with better intelligence meant that the authorities now had the ability through screening and detention to destroy the passive wing of Mau Mau in the capital.

'*Operation Anvil*': Managing Mau Mau in Nairobi

'Operation Anvil' consisted of a surrounding and flooding with troops and police of African areas of Nairobi. The operation had been planned for several months. It was executed as from dawn on 24 April 1954 ('D day'). A main concern of it, as of the other military operations, was to stop the spread of Mau Mau to other tribes.[318] Its legal bases were the ER and the Emergency (Control of Nairobi) Regulations 1954. The 'Nairobi' Regulations enabled the Governor to make Evacuation Orders (initially valid for six months, but later extended for a further four months) enabling communal removal and detention in a Reception Centre for purposes of assessing who were involved in Mau Mau.

The authorities saw 'Anvil' as a selective sweep.[319] Its execution seems closer to the wartime 'collar the lot' approach, one that was capricious and afforded no

---

[314] Erskine (1955): paras. 35, 48–55, 104–8.
[315] Anderson (2005): 294, citing Sorensen; Lathbury (1956): para. 5.
[316] Lathbury (1956): para. 6.
[317] Anderson (2005): 268.
[318] Erskine (1955): paras. 34–7, 56–64.
[319] Erskine (1955): para. 40.

room for according the benefit of the doubt. [320] By the end of the operation on 26 May more than 50,000 had been arrested and detained for screening purposes. Hooded informers and loyalists were used to identify Mau Mau suspects. A crude grading system, similar to that used in Allied dealings with Germans at the end of the Second World War identified those in respect of whom action was to be taken. Category 'White' were those to be released into the city or compulsorily repatriated to the Reserves (some 2,150 women and 4,000 children). In practice the former initially were only those known to be Home Guard members or in other branches of the security forces, and those in other trusted government service, but the category broadened as screening went on. Category 'Grey' was formed of passive Mau Mau supporters in respect of whom there was no immediate evidence either of loyalty or misdemeanour. Category 'Black' embodied those thought to be active or dangerous terrorists identified by the hooded informers or on the Special Branch lists. Some identified may have been prosecuted. Most ended up in the detention without trial 'pipeline', a series of punitive work camps designed to 'rehabilitate' or 're-educate' those 'infected' by Mau Mau. The idea was that as a detainee's commitment to Mau Mau declined, he or she would be moved along the 'pipeline' to a better camp and on to eventual release to the Reserves. It was envisaged that detention might be permanent for the 'hard core'. It is quite clear from the exhaustively researched accounts by Anderson and Elkins that brutality and ill-treatment were a pervasive feature of screening, interrogation and detention in Kenya, with scandals revealed by the small number of courts martial, criminal trials of Home Guard members, and the official reports occasioned by the Hola incident in 1959,[321] being very much the tip of a large iceberg.

Longer-term detention, and detention other than in 'Operation Anvil', was effected under one of two types of indefinite detention order. Those made by the Governor (GDO) were for the most serious cases. Most were dealt with by a Delegated Detention Order (DDO) based on a low level of suspicion, affording an opportunity for old scores to be settled by hooded informers or loyalists. At least 80,000 were detained as a result of Operation Anvil and other earlier and later operations (for example, 'Pepperpot' in Nairobi). The actual number with some experience of detention was likely to be closer to double that. Some were exiled to remote parts of Kenya and some consideration was given to transportation to other parts of the Empire. Women, children and the elderly were repatriated – some compulsorily, others allegedly 'at their own request' –to the reserves and 'villagization'. A number of foreign 'agitators' (including an Irish lawyer) were deported and some lawyers were refused entry to Kenya. The State of Emergency formally ended on 12 January 1960. Some 1,000 remained in detention or internal exile, including Kenyatta. The demise of the ER saw the base for this transferred

---

[320] The account of 'Anvil' here is based on Anderson (2005): 200–214; Elkins (2005): chap. 5; Erskine (1955): paras 37–40, 56–64.

[321] Anderson (2005): 326–7; Elkins (2005): chap. 10; Secretary of State for the Colonies, Memorandum for Cabinet C (59) 92, 2 June 1959 TNA.

on 11 December 1960 to that of regulations made under an *ad hoc* ordinance.[322] These enabled detention or restriction of a 'specified' person where the Governor was satisfied that it was necessary to exercise control over him or her for securing the public safety and the maintenance of order. Those detained or restricted had a right of recourse to a reviewing authority appointed by the Governor.[323]

Administrative Challenge Mechanisms

The ER afforded detainees a right of recourse to an Advisory Committee, one for GDOs and another for DDOs.[324] These travelled from camp to camp, hearing representations but not permitting legal representation. Nor was there effective access to legal advice. Elkins dismisses them as 'window-dressing', 'an exercise in futility' for most detainees.[325] Some official material survives in the public records, including the Committee decision with respect to the only Asian detainee (Antonio Pinto). The committee recommended his detention for the period of the emergency. That file shows the dominant effect of Special Branch assessment, the Committee's views on the demeanour of the detainee, their not being impressed by the giving of his evidence, and recourse to detention rather than prosecution in order to maximize protection of a Special Branch agent.[326] The other material suggests that the Advisory Committee accelerated the moving of detainees along the 'pipeline' rather than immediately to outright release, but the figures indicate something like a 4 per cent success rate.[327] This may say as much about the weakness of the initial detention case as it does about the efficacy of the Committee.

Challenges in Courts

The author's researches in the National Archives, and in various libraries among the available sets of law reports covering the period of the Emergency, produced no cases on detention, banishment or deportation. Nor are any such cases or legal challenges mentioned by Anderson, Elkins or Simpson, The East African Court of Appeal did affirm, however, in a case on rent control, that some Emergency Regulations could have retrospective effect.[328] Commentators have noted lack of legislative control over the regulations and have considered that it was not really possible to challenge their validity in the courts.[329] Most of the reported cases deal

---

[322] CO 822/1334 TNA; the Detained and Restricted Persons (Special Provisions) Ordinance 1960; See also the Preservation of Public Security Ordinance 1960.

[323] CO 936/536 TNA.

[324] Reg. 2; CO 822/1234 TNA.

[325] Elkins (2005): 219.

[326] CO 822/1234 TNA (Petition No. 564).

[327] CO 822/1234 TNA (letter from Colonial Secretary MacLeod to Dingle Foot QC, MP, 4 January 1960).

[328] *Corbett* v *Floyd* [1958] EA 389.

[329] Ghai and McAuslan (1970): 411.

with the modified criminal process; with evidential issues such as admissibility of confessions and rules on accomplice evidence. One, which concerned the admission of improperly obtained physical evidence (ammunition) went all the way to the Judicial Committee of the Privy Council in London.[330] So too did a number of death penalty appeals, mostly without success. Some 160 appeals in capital cases were, however, successful in the East African Court of Appeal.[331] Other cases deal with whether and when a home-made 'gun' constituted a firearm under the ER.

ECHR and International Involvement

The ECHR had been extended to Kenya as to other colonies without any searching appraisal of which laws might not be compatible with it. On 24 May 1954, the United Kingdom Government belatedly entered a notice of derogation under Art. 15 in respect of Kenya and several other dependencies, dealing with detention and obligations under Art. 5. As regards Kenya the reasons for it were stated:

> ... owing to the crimes of violence, including murder and mutilation, and the attempted subversion of the lawfully constituted Government by terrorists known by the name of Mau Mau.[332]

Other than mentioning detention, no further information was provided. The notice was not amended to cover 'Operation Anvil'. The right of individual petition was not accorded. No other State Party stepped forward, but two were reported to be considering doing so as concerned Kenyans sought to internationalize the issues. Government knew it was vulnerable in respect of compulsory labour in the camps and more generally in Kenya both under Art. 4 ECHR, the Forced Labour Convention 1930 and other International Labour Organization agreements. But it pressed on regardless, dismissing the breaches as merely 'technical', not offending against the 'spirit' of Art. 4 ECHR or the 1930 Convention. [333] There were a number of visits to camps by the International Committee of the Red Cross, after a period in which Government had resisted visits. Some concern was expressed over corporal punishment, the lack of provision of underclothing for women detainees and other aspects of hygiene.[334] The non-public reports from the international Committee of the Red Cross seem merely quietly to have been shelved.[335] Officials and Ministers grappled once more with the terms and reach of Art. 15 ECHR as the

---

[330] *Kuruma* v *R* [1955] A.C. 197.

[331] Anderson (2005): 291.

[332] Simpson (2004): 878.

[333] CAB 129/65 TNA (Colonial Secretary's Memoranda for Cabinet C (54) 50, and C (59) 97).

[334] CO 822/1258, TNA; Elkins (2005): 331; Anderson (2005): 321–2.

[335] Anderson (2005): 322.

policy imperative became one of formally ending the State of Emergency. It was accepted that its ending could not coincide with a withdrawal of the derogation, since the 'temporary', 'post-emergency' detention measures could only comply with obligations under Art. 5 ECHR pursuant to a valid derogation from the Convention under Art. 15 of it.[336]

'Hearts and Minds' and Constitutional Dimensions

The need to win 'hearts and minds' and to make progress in the constitutional field, seen to be so important in Malaya, Cyprus and later in Northern Ireland (see chapter 3), was not ignored in the Kenyan context. When Prime Minister, Winston Churchill had wanted negotiations to settle the matter from a very early stage. Rehabilitation as conceived by some in the colonial government was meant to work as it had in Malaya, but in Kenya its punitive aspect predominated and it proved difficult, given the fears of loyalists, to provide the same link between detainee and those who controlled the Reserves enabling release and support after release. As well as preventing aid to Mau Mau and forming part of the detention '*gulag*', protected villages supported and protected the loyalist Kikuyu and other affected tribes. Well-intentioned farming projects also brought benefits to loyalists. From 1954, the Secretary of State for the Colonies (Lyttleton followed by Lennox-Boyd) made it clear that there would have to be greater African involvement in Government. The debate in the House of Commons on the Hola Camp incident saw Enoch Powell, a right-wing Conservative MP, attack the Government for its operation of 'double standards' in respect of its African subjects. Further moves to multi-racial government (a 'parliamentary democracy based on universal franchise') were announced at talks at Lancaster House in London in January 1960.[337] It became abundantly clear if progress was to be made that Jomo Kenyatta, despite opposition from the Governor and white settlers, had to be brought into the picture. The new Colonial Secretary of State in the Macmillan Government was Iain MacLeod. He did just that in August 1961. He had support from his Prime Minister, Harold Macmillan, but the policy attracted vilification from the right of the Conservative Party. Kenyatta was dramatically re-invented in the official presentation as the moderate he in retrospect seems always to have been.[338] The Government aim was to secure transfer of power to a conservative administration. This was achieved when Kenya attained independence on 12 December 1963. Kenyatta, popularly known as the Reconciler, became its first President. There was 'deafening silence' about Mau Mau in the new Kenya. The new President was soon signing detention orders against former Mau Mau at the same desk at which Governor Baring had signed his order against Kenyatta.[339]

---

[336] CO 822/1334 TNA.
[337] Elkins (2005): 356.
[338] Elkins: (2005): 357–8.
[339] Elkins (2005): 354–5.

President Kenyatta, like the former colonial government, saw Mau Mau as a disease to be eradicated and erased from memory.[340]

---

[340] Anderson (2005): 330–336.

PART III

After 9/11: Have the Rules of the Game Changed?

Chapter 6

After 9/11: Overview and Context

Introduction

This chapter seeks to place the various executive measures used since 9/11 in the context of the Government's counter-terrorism strategy at the beginning of this twenty first century and the revisions to it after 9/11 and 7/7. It affords this contextual overview the better to enable the reader to appreciate and digest the detailed examination of those executive measures undertaken in subsequent chapters. Chapter 7 subjects to close scrutiny the nature and use of the executive measures deployed: indefinite detention without trial under the Anti-terrorism, Crime and Security Act 2001 (ATCSA); control orders under the Prevention of Terrorism Act 2005 (PTA 2005), restricting movement and liberty and security of person and a variety of privacy, communication, association and property rights; exclusion and deportation on national security grounds; and the range of changes in citizenship and immigration law designed to increase the numbers of individuals amenable to powers applicable only to foreign nationals through deprivation of British citizenship or the right of abode enjoyed by some Commonwealth citizens. It also delineates the very real concerns such controversial measures have generated. Chapter 8 considers the nature of the challenge mechanisms open to those subjected to these executive measures: appeals to the Special Immigration Appeals Commission (SIAC) as regards ATCSA detentions and immigration and citizenship matters; and the role of the High Court in respect of control orders. It also considers the role of applications for judicial review. It delineates the powers of SIAC and the High Court and the ways in which the schemes seek to reconcile competing interests of protection of security material and sources, on the one hand, and due process and individual rights to a fair hearing, on the other. The processes involve dealing with material in 'open' and' closed' sessions, with the latter excluding from participation the individual and their legal team. The SIAC or the High Court examines the material relied on by the Home Secretary aided in this task by a lawyer appointed as a Special Advocate to promote the interests of the individual without being subject to the latter's instructions or a part of his/her legal team. Those processes are controversial and it is argued by some that they are not compatible with the 'fair hearing' requirements of the ECHR. Chapter 9, in turn, considers how that matter and other concerns about the powers, have translated into legal challenges and examines their outcome and what those challenges tell us about the changed role of the courts faced with security powers in the HRA era. Finally, chapter 10 looks back to some of the themes and issues outlined in chapter

1 and reflects on the proper role of the courts in a liberal democracy when considering the impact on fundamental rights and freedoms of executive measures thought by Executive and Legislature essential for the protection of the public and of national security.

Anti-terrorist Powers for the Twenty-first Century: the Terrorism Act 2000

The Terrorism Act 2000 (TA 2000) was enacted following the Government's acceptance[1] of most of the recommendations of an inquiry by Lord Lloyd of Berwick,[2] established in 1995 by the previous Conservative Government to consider whether there would be any necessity for the United Kingdom to have specific counter-terrorism legislation in the United Kingdom in the event of a lasting peace in Northern Ireland.[3] Lord Lloyd reported that there would remain a need for permanent counter-terrorism legislation.[4]

The Act, stated by the Government to be fully Convention compliant, sought to provide powers sufficient to deal with a number of terrorist threats to the United Kingdom. First of all, there remained the residual threat from terrorism connected with Northern Ireland affairs from groups not 'on ceasefire' as part of the ongoing Northern Ireland peace process. Secondly, its powers were designed to enable the authorities to deal with a range of other threats from domestic terrorist groups: Scottish and Welsh nationalists; extreme elements of the animal rights and environmentalist lobbies; and the danger that pro-Life, anti-abortion groups might follow the path to violence of their American counterparts. But the most potent threat it was created to deal with was the increasing one from international terrorism which had and would continue to have a significant impact. A growing part of international terrorism was that motivated by religious fanaticism.[5] Neither Al Qaeda nor Osama Bin Laden find specific mention in the Report or in its supporting Evidence Volume.[6] In hindsight that will seem surprising, but at the time that material was prepared they had only just begun to appear on the radar of United States' investigative agencies, with Bin Laden perceived principally as a financier of terrorism, and the FBI just beginning to look over CIA intelligence material to see if there was an investigation worth pursuing. It only became aware of Al Qaeda late in 1996, after Bin Laden's fatwa against the United States from a cave in Afghanistan.[7]

---

[1] Cm 4178 (1998).
[2] Cm 3420 (1996a).
[3] Cm 4178 (1998): 'Introduction', para. 3
[4] Cm 3420 (1996a) para.
[5] Cm 4178 (1998): chap. 2.and chap. 3, paras 3.9–3.12.
[6] Cm 3420 (1996b).
[7] Wright (2006): 3.

The Act introduced new definitions of 'terrorism' and 'terrorist', considered in chapter 1. Fortunately, given their vagueness and overbreadth, they do not represent as such criminal offences. Rather, they help determine the scope of subsequent powers in this Act and because of incorporation by reference in later anti-terrorist legislation (ATCSA; PTA 2005 and the Terrorism Act 2006 (TA 2006)), the scope of powers in those Acts. This definition accords with but was not created in response to that in the EU Council Framework Decision on Combating Terrorism.[8] The central anti-terrorism approach in the Act is that of the modified criminal prosecution model: providing the police with extended powers of arrest and extended detention without charge of terrorist suspects (at the time of writing, permitting detention for up to 28 days with judicial approval);[9] and adding to the scope of the criminal law a further battery of specific offences dealing with such matters as the financing of terror,[10] the provision of terrorist training, and intelligence or information gathering for terrorist purposes.[11] It did further extend, beyond terrorism connected with Northern Ireland affairs, the executive power to proscribe organizations involved in terrorism,[12] but the principal rationale of that was to bring members and supporters within a range of serious criminal offences concerning the political, financial and material support dimensions of terrorism.[13] It also afforded the authorities a range of preventative powers of stop and search[14] and of travel control on journeys by air or sea[15] to hamper terrorist movements, and a range of controls on parking, the better to guard against terrorist acts such as car bombs.[16] It further honed investigative powers as regards financial and material support of terrorism and the ability to confiscate the assets of terrorism.[17]

In contrast, the role of the executive measures as a supplement or alternative to the criminal process on which this book focuses was deliberately reduced. Powers enabling the exclusion from all or part of the United Kingdom of terrorist suspects connected with Northern Ireland affairs, a centrepiece of successive Prevention of Terrorism (Temporary Provisions) Acts since 1974, were lapsed after 21 March 1998, while remaining on the statute book, rapidly re-invocable, should the need arise, by executive order subject to parliamentary approval.[18] The powers were not brought into the Terrorism Bill. The Government believed

---

[8] Peers (2003): 227.
[9] TA 2000, ss. 40, 41 and Sched. 8.
[10] TA 2000, Part III.
[11] TA 2000, Part. VI.
[12] TA 2000, Part I.
[13] Cm 4178 (1998): chap 4.
[14] TA 2000, ss. 44–47.
[15] TA 2000, s. 53 and Sched. 7.
[16] TA 2000, ss. 48–52.
[17] TA 2000, Part IV and Scheds 5, 6.
[18] Cm 4178 (1998): para. 5.3. On the powers and their use, see further chapter 3.

... that although the powers have been useful, their utility is limited. More importantly
... the powers are fundamentally objectionable in so far as they may be used to exclude
British citizens by executive order from part of the national territory.[19]

As part of the ongoing Northern Ireland peace process, the hated power of
internment[20] was deleted from the statute book rather than being kept as a reserve
emergency power for rapid invocation should that process go badly wrong and
violence return to previously high levels. In its Consultation Paper which preceded
the enactment of the TA 2000,[21] the Government noted:

> The Northern Ireland (Emergency Provisions) Act 1998 removed the power for the
> Secretary of State for Northern Ireland to introduce detention without trial (internment).
> The Government took that step because it doubted whether internment could ever be
> effectively introduced. Since the Omagh bombing, there have been a number of calls to
> reinstate that power (as well as some to take a further step and introduce internment
> itself).
>   The Government recognises the reasons behind these calls. It does not rule out for all
> time the reintroduction of the power to intern, but the setting aside of the criminal law in
> favour of executive action could only be contemplated exceptionally, where the
> Government were convinced that the measure was likely to prove effective; and it would
> require the Government to enter a derogation under article 15 of the European
> Convention on Human Rights (ECHR). Joint action by the UK and Irish Governments
> might increase the likelihood of effectiveness, but the Government remains to be
> convinced of the practical merits of such a measure. At present, the Government has no
> plans to reintroduce the power of internment.

Of this book's trio of executive measures, refusal of entry and deportation on
national security grounds alone remained. That measure's decision-making and
judicial challenge processes had heavily been revised by the Special Immigration
Appeals Commission Act 1997 in response to the adverse decision of the European
Court of Human Rights in *Chahal* v *United Kingdom*.[22] As has been seen in
chapter 4, the first tests of that process in the courts in *Secretary of State for the
Home Department* v *Rehman*[23] saw the Court of Appeal and the House of Lords
limit the impact of the process. Those courts reduced the powers of the Special
Immigration Appeals Commission (SIAC) to those at the review rather than
appellate end of the spectrum; propounded a very wide notion of national security
threat; and affirmed the tradition of extreme judicial deference to executive
knowledge in the national security field. Their Lordships' opinions were written
before but delivered after the terrorist attacks on the United States that have come
to be known by the date of their occurrence (11 September 2001) as 9/11. Two

---

[19] Cm 4178 (1998): para. 5.5.
[20] See chapter 3.
[21] Cm 4178 (1998).
[22] (1997) 23 EHRR 413. See further chapter 4.
[23] [2002] 1 All ER 122.

Law Lords specifically referred to this. Lord Steyn considered Lord Woolf MR's formulation of the Home Secretary's difficult task of evaluating the risk an individual poses to national security. The Master of the Rolls had stated:

> In any national security case the Secretary of State is entitled to make a decision to deport not only on the basis that the individual has in fact endangered national security but that he is a *danger* to national security. When the case is being put in this way, it is necessary not to look only at the individual allegations and ask whether they have been proved. It is also necessary to examine the case as a whole against an individual and then ask whether on a global approach that individual is a danger to national security, taking into account the executive's policy with regard to national security. When this is done, the cumulative effect may establish that the individual is to be treated as a danger, although it cannot be proved to a high degree of probability that he has performed any individual act which would justify this conclusion. ... It is the danger which he constitutes to national security which is to be balanced against his own personal interests.

Approving that, Lord Steyn thought that the dynamics of the role of the Secretary of State, charged with the power and duty to consider deportation on grounds of national security, irresistibly supported Lord Woolf MR's analysis. While Lord Steyn had come to this conclusion by the end of the hearing of the appeal, the tragic events of 11 September 2001 in New York reinforced compellingly that no other approach was possible.[24] Lord Hoffman commented that those events

> are a reminder that in matters of national security, the cost of failure can be high. This seems to me to underline the need for the judicial arm of government to respect the decisions of ministers of the Crown on the question of whether support for terrorist activities in a foreign country constitutes a threat to national security. It is not only that the executive has access to special information and expertise in these matters. It is also that such decisions, with serious potential results for the community, require a legitimacy which can be conferred only by entrusting them to persons responsible to the community through the democratic process. If the people are to accept the consequences of such decisions, they must be made by persons whom the people have elected and whom they can remove.[25]

9/11 changed the Government's counter-terrorism strategy.

---

[24] [2002] 1 All ER 122, para. 29.
[25] [2002] 1 All ER 122, para. 62.

The Horrific and Catalytic Events of 9/11

The events of 9/11 have been analysed in copious detail elsewhere.[26] Nineteen Al Qaeda operatives boarded and hijacked in the United States a number of aircraft. Two (American 11 and United 175) were flown respectively into the North and South twin skyscraper towers of the World Trade Center in New York, causing their collapse some 90 minutes later. Another (American 77) was crashed into the Pentagon, headquarters of the United States' Defence department in Arlington Virginia. The fourth (United 173), thought to be bound for the Capitol or the White House in Washington DC, was brought down in southern Pennsylvania as a result of an onboard struggle between hijackers and passengers. In all, some 2,800 died at the World Trade Centre; 125 at the Pentagon; and 256 on the aircraft involved. The death toll exceeded that in the attack on Pearl Harbor in 1941 which brought the United States into the Second World War. The criminal trial of one plotter, Zacaria Moussaoui, indicated a possibility that there was intended to be a fifth plane targeted at the White House, the home and office of the President of the United States in Washington DC.[27]

The International and EU Response

The attacks were the next day condemned by the UN Security Council in Resolution 1368 (2001) and characterized in UN Security Council Resolution 1773 (2001), like other acts of international terrorism, as a threat to international peace and security. The Council there re-affirmed the need to combat all such acts by all means available.[28] At an extraordinary meeting on 21 September, the European Council prioritized as an objective the fight against terrorism and approved a plan of action on: enhanced police and judicial cooperation; the strengthening of air security; coordination of the EU's global action; attacking the funding of terrorism; and developing and implementing international anti-terrorist legal agreements. The catalyst of 9/11 accelerated an EU policy on terrorism, which had been in preparation for some time.[29] When the United Kingdom government responded with new legislation, it was marching in the 'war on terrorism' to the beat of drums other than the purely national.[30]

---

[26] National Commission (2004).
[27] Goldenberg and Dodd (2006).
[28] S/RES/1373 (2001) 28 September 2001.
[29] Bonner (2004): 93–4 and sources cited there.
[30] Ibid.

Nature of, and Problems with, the United Kingdom Response to 9/11

Anti-terrorism, Crime and Security Act 2001 (ATCSA)

The United Kingdom governmental response was to procure the relatively rapid enactment of ATCSA as an emergency measure. This, responding to UN and EU initiatives, further enhanced powers to attack terrorist finances. It sought to ensure that government departments and agencies could collect and share information required for countering the terrorist threat. It attempted to ensure the security of the nuclear and aviation industries, and to improve the security of dangerous substances (chemical, nuclear and biological weapons, pathogens or toxins) that might be targeted or used by terrorists. It sought to enable the government to meet European obligations in the area of police and judicial co-operation and international obligations to counter bribery and corruption. It enhanced police powers of fingerprinting and photographing and gave a new power to compel the removal of disguises. In many respects, it thus sought to improve the existing 'modified criminal prosecution approach' model.[31]

ATCSA's most controversial and draconian aspect lay in Part 4. This enabled the indefinite detention without trial, under immigration powers which would otherwise be time-limited, of those foreign national terrorist suspects who could not for a variety of reasons, be prosecuted, but who could also not be deported for some practical reason or because their removal would violate the United Kingdom's obligation under Art. 3 ECHR not to remove someone to a country where there were substantial grounds for believing that if returned there the suspect would face a real risk of subjection to torture, inhuman or degrading treatment or punishment, whether at the hands of state or non-State actors. In addition, section 33 (replaced with the same effect by legislation in 2005) precluded resort to the proper substantive determination of an asylum claim if it was deemed that the exclusion clauses in the Convention on Refugees applied or if the person concerned was considered to be a danger to national security in accordance with Art. 33(2) of that Convention. The Home Secretary could certify that the asylum claimant's removal would be conducive to the public good and that he or she was not entitled to protection from *refoulement* because of Art. 33(2) or Art. 1F. In such a case, SIAC (the sole route of appeal in this streamlined asylum process) could only consider the statements made in the Home Secretary's certificate and not the substantive asylum claim (whether the person has a well-founded fear of persecution).

---

[31] See Bonner (2002); Fenwick(2002); Tomkins (2002).

A and Others: Incompatibility with Convention Rights of ATCSA Detention without Trial

In a decision showing a very welcome departure from a constitutional and legal tradition of undue judicial deference to Executive opinion in times of emergency or when the Executive then or otherwise intones the mantra of national security, the House of Lords on 16 December 2004 issued a declaration under section 4 of the HRA that section 23 of ATCSA, the key provision in the indefinite detention without trial scheme, was incompatible with Convention Rights.[32] It was, firstly, incompatible with Art. 5 (liberty and security of person) read with Art. 15 ECHR (derogation) as going beyond what was necessitated by the exigencies of a public emergency threatening the life of the nation (disproportionate). Secondly, it was incompatible with Art. 14 (discrimination) read with Art. 5 ECHR; it was unjustifiably discriminatory on grounds of nationality/national origin.

The Governmental Response to the Declaration of Incompatibility: the PTA 2005

Their Lordships' decision neither procured the release of the detainees, nor an immediate change in the law. Consistent with the United Kingdom's key constitutional principle of parliamentary sovereignty, a declaration of incompatibility cannot invalidate a provision of an Act of Parliament or deprive it of legal effect. It remains fully in force. Rather, the declaration, directed to the law-makers (the executive/legislature partnership), exerts pressure on them in the political arena to respond to it by repealing the offending provision(s), in this case the detention scheme. The law-makers were not obliged to do so, and could have done nothing, leaving the individuals to pursue their case in Strasbourg. Instead, Home Secretary Clarke on 16 January 2005 announced to the House of Commons that he would seek renewal of the detention powers in March only for so long as necessary to procure from Parliament legislation replacing the detention scheme with one empowering him to impose on any terrorist suspect, whatever their nationality and whatever the terrorism involved, a control order, capable of embodying a spectrum of controls ranging from reporting to the police at one end to house arrest at the other.[33] This system of non-derogating and derogating control orders was enacted in the PTA 2005. There is no derogation under Art. 15 ECHR, so only the former are operative. Breach of a control order is a criminal offence. The remaining ATCSA detainees were immediately made the subject of non-derogating control orders.

---

[32] *A and Others* v *Secretary of State for the Home Department* [2004] UKHL 56.
[33] HC Debs, Vol. 430, cols. 305–324.

The Attacks of 7/7: Another Catalyst for Change

An attack on the United Kingdom had long been expected. The then Metropolitan Police Commissioner, Sir John Stevens, thought one 'inevitable'. Reportedly, several had been foiled.[34] On 7 July 2006 four young Muslim men attacked London's transport network.[35] Three, all second-generation British citizens with parents of Pakistani origin, were from Leeds: Mohammed Siddique Khan (30), Shazad Tanweer (22) and Hasib Hussain (18). The other, Jermaine Lindsay (19), a convert to Islam, was a British citizen of West Indian origin, born in Jamaica, who lived for most of his life in Huddersfield and moved after marriage to Aylesbury. Three of them detonated bombs almost simultaneously at around 8.50 a.m. in different places on the Underground: the first in a Circle Line tunnel between Liverpool Street and Aldgate stations (Tanweer); the second on the Circle Line just outside Edgeware Road station (Khan); and the third in a Piccadilly Line tunnel between Kings Cross and Russell Square stations (Lindsay). At 9.47 a.m. another explosion occurred above ground on the upper deck of a No. 30 bus in Tavistock Square (Hussain). The explosions killed the suicide bombers and 52 others and injured more than 700.

The bombings caused horror and outrage. The Government's national crisis management facility (COBRA) was activated and the Home Secretary chaired a meeting there at 10 a.m. The attacks were condemned by the Prime Minister, the Home Secretary and the Mayor of London and in a unanimous UN Security Council Resolution. As the Joint Committee on Human Rights stated, the attacks:

... constitute gross violations of human rights ... [and] ... of the foundational values of democracy and the rule of law on which human rights law is built. They can never be justified by invoking the language of human rights, for it is well established in human rights law that invoking human rights to justify the destruction of other human rights is an abuse of rights and never attracts protection. Human rights law is unequivocal in its condemnation of these atrocities. Human rights law ... imposes onerous positive obligations on states to take steps to protect the lives and physical integrity of everyone within their jurisdiction against the threat of terrorist attack. Moreover, those steps must be effective in providing such protection. The increasing recognition of the rights of victims also entails a corresponding obligation on states to do everything possible to bring to justice suspected perpetrators, organisers and sponsors of terrorist acts.[36]

It was thought there might be an Al Qaeda connection, and that remains under investigation, but the thrust of the official reports indicate that the attack was in fact home-grown rather than directed from abroad, planned on a shoestring budget from information on the internet, that there was no 'fifth-bomber' and no direct

[34] Carlile (2005): para. 24.

[35] The account here attempts to meld material from two official inquiries into 7/7: Cm 6785 (2006); and HC 1087 (2006).

[36] JHRC 3rd (2005): paras 4, 5.

support from Al Qaeda, although two of the bombers had visited Pakistan, and its deputy leader later claimed responsibility for the attacks as part of Mohammed Siddique Khan's video message aired on 1 September 2005 by the Arabic television station Al Jazeera. The role played by the Iraq war in radicalizing them is a matter of controversy. Nothing in the evidence suggested that the attacks were in any way linked to the G8 summit then taking place in Scotland.

The attacks catalysed ongoing government planning into public promises of action and legislative proposals. In their aftermath and that of the failed attacks a fortnight later, the Prime Minister made clear that the 'rules of the game' had changed. He announced a 12-point plan of action on 5 August 2005[37] under which the government would deal with terrorist suspects in a number of ways noted in chapter 1. Some of this was new, some formed part of an existing but unpublished strategy from early 2003. That strategy was published in July 2006 and must now be examined.[38]

The Government's Counter-terrorism Strategy: a Re-emerging Prominence of Executive Measures

The Government's counter-terrorism strategy has a number of strands: *Prevent*, *Pursue*, *Protect* and *Prepare*. Only the first three are centrally relevant to this book.

Prevent is the 'hearts and minds' dimension. It involves inhibiting the radicalization of individuals by tackling disadvantage at home and abroad and pursuing reform; engaging in a battle of ideas in part to encourage moderates in Islam to challenge its extremists; and changing the environment in which extremists and those who radicalize others can operate. This last element overlaps with *Pursue*, since it involves deterring those who facilitate terrorism and those who encourage others to become terrorists. Deterrence is, of course, a prime role of the criminal law. But there is also a role for executive measures here. Hence aspects of *Pursue* involve gathering intelligence so as to identify and understand the terrorist threat and working with other countries both to strengthen that intelligence effort and to secure disruption of terrorists and their networks overseas. But a central strand in *Pursue* is the disruption of terrorist activity; 'taking action to frustrate terrorist attacks and to bring terrorists to justice through prosecution and other means, including strengthening the legal framework against terrorism, for example, by introducing legislation to deport those who are judged not to be conducive to the public good' on grounds of national security or unacceptable behaviour, or through use of other executive measures (control orders; deprivation of citizenship or the right of abode; denying acquisition of

---

[37] Prime Minister's Press Conference 5 August 2005 <http://www.number-10.gov.uk/output/Page8041.asp>.

[38] Cm 6888 (2006).

citizenship through voluntary act to those not of good character). Here *Pursue* begins to shade into *Protect*. This facet is very much about 'target hardening': taking physical security measures in conjunction with the private sector to protect key public utilities; reducing the risk and impact of attacks on transport networks through enhanced security and technological advances; and protecting (for example, through an enhanced police presence) crowded places so as to protect people going about their daily lives. But it also involves strengthening border security by better intelligence and international co-operation, through enhanced identity management (use of biometrics)[39] 'so that terrorists and those who inspire them can be prevented from travelling here'. This brings into sharp focus the exclusion aspect of immigration powers, encountered earlier in the chapter on undesirable 'aliens': the ability of the Home Secretary and the immigration service to deny admission to someone whose presence here is not conducive to the public good.

Prepare is concerned with ensuring that the country is as ready as it can be to deal with the consequences of a terrorist attack. It involves a number of key elements; a continual evaluation and reappraisal of our preparedness; identifying and assessing the potential impact of potential risks; and building the necessary capabilities for responding to terrorist attacks. It is very much the province of contingency planners and the emergency and medical services.

The Government's Perception of the Terrorist Threat

After 9/11, the threat was seen to emanate from Islamist groups linked to Al Qaeda and, essentially, to be a threat to the United Kingdom posed by foreign nationals, a misperception at the heart of the litigation over ATCSA detentions. The principal threat gradually came to be perceived as one from all Islamist terrorists:

> ... radicalised individuals who are using a distorted and unrepresentative version of the Islamic faith to justify violence ... a tiny minority within the Muslim communities here and abroad. Muslim communities themselves do not threaten our security; indeed they make a great contribution to our country. The Government is therefore working in partnership with Muslim communities to help them prevent extremists gaining influence there. The current threat from Islamist terrorism is serious and sustained. It is genuinely international in scope, involving a variety of groups, networks and individuals who are driven by particular violent and extremist beliefs. It is indiscriminate – aiming to cause mass casualties, regardless of the age, nationality, or religion of their victims; and the terrorists are often prepared to commit suicide to kill others. Overall, we judge that the scale of the threat is potentially still increasing and is not likely to diminish significantly for some years.[40]

---

[39] Fingerprints, iris scans.

[40] Cm 6888 (2006): para. 3.

The misperception that the problem was one of foreign nationals is only too graphically highlighted by 7/7 and the disruption on 10 August 2006 in the wake of a plot simultaneously to blow up over the Atlantic or American cities a number of aircraft bound for the United States, a plot foiled in an intelligence-led operation resulting in 18 arrests, with the principal suspects being British-born.[41]

Prevent: the Hearts and Minds Dimension

The 'hearts and minds' dimension, seen elsewhere in this book as a vital part of an anti-terrorist campaign, has received some, but until recently rather muted attention, with government, initially at least, identifying major difficulties in its application to the current terrorist threat. It has been stressed that Muslims are not a target and are not being unfairly targeted by anti-terrorism laws. Steps have been taken to consult the Muslim community in terms of a preventing extremism policy and to outlaw incitement to religious as well as racial hatred. The Counter-terrorism Strategy document is replete with measures, strategies and initiatives, such as the Commission on Integration and Cohesion and an increased level of United Kingdom and international support for regionally led reform in the Muslim world. There can be no negotiation on matters negating the values of Western liberal democracy: on the re-creation of the caliphate; on the imposition of sharia law; on equality between the sexes; or on the ending of free speech. But there is also governmental perception that British policy in respect of the Middle East (the Israeli/Palestinian/Lebanon conflicts) and the United Kingdom's close links with the USA in the 'war' on terrorism have a radicalizing effect. Government, however, despite mounting evidence, seems less willing to accept the same in respect of the war in Iraq, confusing explanation of the problem with justification of terrorism.[42]

Prevent and *Pursue* – a Hierarchy of Responses: the Interaction of the Criminal Process and Executive Measures

In preventing extremism and deterring those who would encourage others to support or become terrorists as part of *Prevent*, the criminal law and process and executive measures also have a role to play, albeit that their principal role is as part of *Pursue*: disrupting terrorist activity and protecting the public by removing dangerous individuals from circulation in the community. It is clear that here there is a hierarchy of preferred responses. The criminal law and process, even after 9/11 and 7/7, was stated to remain the primary response. But the supplemental and

---

[41] See Home Secretary's statement 10 August 2006 found at <http://www.homeoffice.gov.uk/about-us/news/373144>.
[42] Cm 6888 (2006): para. 48.

alternative executive measures on which this book focuses have once again come very much to the fore. Setting the executive measures fully in context requires us first to recall some of the reasons why the criminal process is not thought to suffice, despite the enhancement of the battery of criminal offences effected by recent anti-terrorism legislation and the development in recent years by the courts of a variety of methods to protect witnesses (anonymity, giving evidence from behind a screen or even these plus voice disguise by a scrambler device). It is also necessary to consider the government's reasons for rejecting a key measure which might make more cases amenable to the criminal process and at least reduce the need for executive measures: the admission as evidence in criminal proceedings of material from intercepted communications.

As was shown in chapter 1, when times are normal, the principal mechanism employed by the State against those who threaten its national security, the public peace and public order, is indeed that of the criminal law – which may well have draconian elements – backed up by coercive police powers and the criminal trial process and its range of punitive sanctions.[43] An effective counter-terrorism or counter-insurgency strategy is intelligence-led, and is increasingly the realm of a State's security and intelligence services, as well as of its police. That strategy involves human intelligence sources and a variety of covert surveillance techniques. It thrives on protecting those sources from disclosure and keeping methods of surveillance under wraps to avoid educating the targets in avoidance strategies. The interest in protecting methods of surveillance has meant that legislation still precludes the admissibility in court of communications' intercept evidence.[44] Concern has traditionally been to protect security methods and sources from disclosure in court, rather than with rights of suspects (as with SIAC, the PTA 2005 specifically provides that the prohibition on use of intercept material does not apply in control order proceedings).[45] It is unclear whether the concern flows from MI5 or the Home Office and whether it now rather reflects concerns about the diversion of personnel and resources into transcription of material for court. But the preclusion is increasingly under attack from a varied body of critics within and outside government.[46]

The TA 2006 has nonetheless made several important changes offering potential for more prosecutions.[47] It fits very much within the 'modified criminal prosecution approach' model. It has extended the reach of anti-terrorist criminal law with controversial offences such as encouragement of terrorism,[48] the giving

[43] Simpson (2004): 54.
[44] Regulation of Investigatory Powers Act 2000 (RIPA), s. 17.
[45] PTA 2005, s. 11, Sched., para. 9. On SIAC, see RIPA, ss. 17, 18(1)(e).
[46] *The Guardian*, 19 February 2007 (Lord Carlile), 6 February 2007 (Shadow Home Secretary), 25 January 2007 (DPP), 20 November 2006 (Attorney General).
[47] Carlile (2007): paras 4, 5.
[48] TA 2006, s. 1.

and receiving of terrorist training,[49] and the preparation of acts of terrorism,[50] which significantly alter the scope of the criminal law extending beyond the scope of traditional concepts of incitement, conspiracy and attempts. It extends ability to hold preparatory hearings in criminal trials, currently applicable to serious fraud cases, into the sphere of terrorist crime.[51]

The traditional paradigm of the criminal law and the criminal trial process, and the problems it poses for protection of sensitive evidence, sources and methods of detection, were considered in chapter 1. It was shown that the authorities must first make a decision whether or not to proceed with a prosecution at all and, if proceeding, to decide whether to abandon the attempt should securing a conviction mean sacrificing the source. And, despite the expansion of witness and source protection methods in courts, the 'bottom line' at criminal trial remains: if the identity of the source or the witness is crucial to the issue of guilt/innocence, it must be disclosed. Given all this, it is perhaps unsurprising that another strategy to protect sensitive evidence is often used: avoiding criminal trial and deploying against the suspect a range of other security options: indefinite detention without trial under ATCSA; control orders under the PTA 2005, restricting movement and liberty and security of person and a variety of privacy, communication, association and property rights; exclusion and deportation on national security grounds; and the range of changes in citizenship and immigration law designed to increase the numbers of individuals amenable to powers applicable only to foreign through deprivation of British citizenship or the right of abode enjoyed by some Commonwealth citizens. A hierarchy operates here too in that, where prosecution is not possible, the next resort for dealing with foreign national terrorist suspects is their deportation from the United Kingdom. For them, a control order is a last resort option, to be brought into play only where the foreign national cannot be deported without breaching international human rights obligations (in particular where there is a real risk of torture). But the processes also enable severe restrictions to be imposed on those against whom there is insufficient evidence for any prosecution, not just those where there is enough evidence but its sensitivity precludes use in court.

With that overview and context in mind, it is to the nature and use of these options that attention must now turn.

---

[49] TA 2006, ss. 6, 8.

[50] TA 2006, s.5.

[51] TA 2006, s.5.

Chapter 7

Executive Measures after 9/11: the Powers and their Use

Introduction and Overview

The context of operation of the executive measures deployed after 9/11 and their role in the Government's counter-terrorism strategy has just been explored. This chapter has a different focus. It constitutes an in-depth examination of those powers, their rationale and competing claims on their use or misuse. It begins with the ATCSA regime of indefinite detention without trial of foreign national terrorist suspects, the most obvious and draconian legislative response in the United Kingdom to the events of 9/11. It then considers, in turn, control orders under PTA 2005; national security deportations; issues of removal of citizenship and the right of abode; and detention in Iraq and Afghanistan. The powers are extensive. All make inroads into important human rights and civil liberties and have generated controversy and concern. Much relates to the substance and use of these powers and is examined in this chapter. A good part centres on the decision-making and appeal processes, the subject of chapter 8. Insofar as concerns have generated litigation, its nature and outcomes form the subject matter of chapter 9. It will become clear that some individuals have been subjected in turn to more than one of the executive measures (have had their lives seriously disrupted for more than five years without being found guilty of criminal conduct) as Government strives to deal in ways that are compatible with ECHR rights and freedoms with those it cannot or is unwilling to prosecute.

ATCSA Detention Without Trial

The Powers and their Rationale

This was the Government's principal and most draconian response to the threat perceived as posed to the United Kingdom, an ally of the United States in the 'war on terror', in the wake of the 9/11 attacks. The threat was characterized by Government as one amounting to a public emergency threatening the life of the nation, warranting derogation under Art. 15 ECHR, to the extent strictly required by the exigencies of that emergency situation, from its obligations under Art. 5 ECHR. The Notice of Derogation, communicated to the Secretary-General of the

Council of Europe as Art. 15(3) demands, was annexed to the Derogation Order, approved by Parliament under the HRA. The Notice justified the derogation by reference to the 9/11 attacks, to the UN Security Council Resolutions in consequence characterizing the attacks and other international terrorism as a threat to peace and security, and because of

> ... a terrorist threat to the United Kingdom from persons suspected of involvement in international terrorism. In particular, there are foreign nationals present in the United Kingdom who are suspected of being concerned in the commission, preparation or instigation of acts of international terrorism, of being members of organisations or groups which are so concerned or of having links with members of such organisations or groups, and who are a threat to the national security of the United Kingdom.[1]

In short, the problem was perceived, as in the Gulf War (see chapter 4), as one posed by 'undesirable aliens', who could not always be prosecuted. Many could not be deported even on national security grounds because of the *Chahal* principle (real risk of torture etc. in their national state).[2] Their detention for deportation was permissible under national law[3] and the ECHR only for so long as deportation was a realistic prospect.[4] Accordingly, Part 4 of ATCSA enabled, under a range of immigration provisions the effect of which would otherwise be limited temporally,[5] the indefinite detention without trial of someone, not a British citizen or with the legal right of abode in the United Kingdom, whom the Home Secretary certified as a suspected international terrorist threat to national security, and who could not be deported for a legal reason (typically Art. 3 ECHR, its ICCPR and UNCAT equivalents) or a practical one.[6] The Home Secretary could so certify such a person where he reasonably both believed that the person's presence in the United Kingdom was a risk to national security, and suspected that the person was a terrorist.[7] For these purposes, a 'terrorist' was someone who was or had been concerned in the commission, preparation or instigation of acts of international terrorism, was a member of or belonged to an international terrorist group, or had links with an international terrorist group in the sense that he or she supported or assisted it.[8] An international terrorist group was one subject to the control or influence of persons outside the United Kingdom, where the Home Secretary suspected that the group was concerned in the commission, preparation or

---

[1] The Human Rights Act 1998 (Designated Derogation) Order 2001 (SI 2001/3644), Art. 2 and Sch.
[2] *Chahal* v *United Kingdom* (1996) 23 EHRR 413; see chapter 4, above.
[3] *R* v *Governor of Durham Prison, ex parte Singh* [1984] All ER 983.
[4] Art. 5(1)(f) ECHR; *Chahal* v *United Kingdom* (1996) 23 EHRR 413, para.112).
[5] Listed in ATCSA, s. 23(2).
[6] ATCSA, ss. 21, 23.
[7] ATCSA, s. 21(1).
[8] ATCSA, s. 21(2), (4).

instigation of acts of international terrorism.[9] ATCSA deployed the definition of 'terrorism' embodied in the Terrorism Act 2000 considered in chapter 1. Certification enabled a range of actions to be taken against the persons notwithstanding the inability to remove them,[10] but more importantly in present context it enabled their indefinite detention without trial under specified detention powers under immigration law.[11]

The Use of the Powers

The Newton Committee considered the circumstances in which there would be resort to ATCSA detention, and also its interrelationship with criminal prosecution and national security deportation.[12] It noted that the police and the Security Service consider the options open for action against a foreign national (including referring a case to the Crown Prosecution Service) if available intelligence suggests involvement in international terrorism. In deciding whether to resort to ATCSA detention, the authorities have regard not just to the likelihood of securing a conviction, but also consider the extent to which the likely sentence would address the potential threat posed by the suspect. For example, if the successful conviction of a terrorist suspect for credit card fraud was likely to lead to detention for a matter of months, the authorities might still pursue certification and detention under Part 4. Where the person concerned was considered to be a threat to national security but successful prosecution was unlikely, or the potential sentence was thought insufficient, MI5 might instead recommend a national security deportation. Where appropriate, if deportation was not possible, it would also recommend certification and detention under ATCSA Part 4. The decision whether to recommend certification to the Home Secretary was made by the Home Office in consultation with the intelligence agencies, the police and Foreign and Commonwealth Office.

Despite the gravity of the perceived threat, not all of those who might fall within the scope of ATCSA Part 4 were detained:

> It would depend on such matters as the strength of the intelligence case, the prospect and gravity of any criminal proceedings, possible length of sentence, the management of the risk whether defensively or to obtain information, the prospect of deportation, and the significance of the threat which they were assessed to pose and whether detention was proportionate to that threat. Resources for detention [were] relevant. It was unlikely, if

---

[9] ATCSA, s. 21(3).

[10] ATCSA, s. 22.

[11] ATCSA, s. 23.

[12] Newton Committee (2003): paras 180–182.

the danger warranted detention, that compassionate or family circumstances would prevent it.[13]

Only 16 persons were ever certificated and detained. Eight were detained in December 2001, one in February 2002, two in April 2002, one in October 2002, one in November 2002, two in January 2003 and one in October 2003. Another was certified in August 2003 but detained under other powers. Two certificates were revoked when the individuals voluntarily left the country rather than be detained (Ajouaou and F), on the basis that the Home Secretary considered he could not properly regard someone's presence in the country to be a threat to national security where in fact the person was not present in the country.[14] One appeal against certification was allowed (M). Several others were admitted to bail on appeal. Detention (but not certification) of two others under ATCSA ended when their mental condition became such that they were instead detained under mental health legislation (Abu Rideh, P). The certification and detention of another (D) was revoked by the Home Secretary in April 2004 for reasons unknown to SIAC, and he was released without conditions. Between December 2001 and March 2005, the detainees were held in a number of maximum security jails: principally HMP Belmarsh, but also HMP Woodhill. At the end of January 2005, Lord Carlile reported, only seven were held in prison solely under Part 4 of ATCSA. The number of detentions had been reduced by a few being charged with conventional crime and transferred to remand status pending Crown Court trial, one released on bail subject to strict conditions amounting to house arrest, an unconditional release, and the two transfers to secure hospitals. That number was reduced further by the government's decision not to oppose bail (albeit under stringent conditions including house arrest in some cases) in relation to all eleven remaining detainees.[15] But these were then made subject to non-derogating control orders on 11 March 2005. On 11 August 2005 eight were revoked and replaced by notice of deportation on security grounds. Some of those were released on stringent bail conditions, others detained pending deportation. In short, a number of the same people moved from one regime to another, so that, by mid-2006 they had been in one form of custody (including house arrest or significant restriction under a control order) since 2001.

Lord Carlile undertook three reviews of the operation of the scheme and throughout was of the view that, on the material he had seen, each of the detainees was a suitable candidate for certification and detention. The detainees had several things in common aside from foreign national status. All are male. All are Islamists. Their connection is with countries in the Middle East or North Africa. The identity of some of them is known (Ajouaou, Abu Rideh, Abu Qatada). Others

---

[13] SIAC Generic Judgment 29 October 2003. SIAC files and determinations are found at < http://www.hmcourts-service.gov.uk/legalprof/judgments/siac/siac.htm#top >.
[14] *A and Others No. 2 (torture/merits case)* [2004] EWCA Civ 1123, para. 188.
[15] Carlile (2005): para. 31.

have been referred to only by letter of the alphabet (A, B, C, D, E, F, G, H, I, K, M, P, S). The nature of the bases of ATCSA certification and the difficulties of challenging the decision to detain are conveyed graphically by setting out some details of each of the individual cases. Those details are an amalgam of material from decisions of SIAC on appeal, on the issue of bail and on first or subsequent reviews of certification. The limitations of the information here presented must be stressed. The material represents what SIAC found on the basis of evidence and intelligence submitted by the Home Secretary in 'open' and 'closed' session. Much of it was contested vigorously by appellants denied the full case against them. In other cases, the appellants maintained a general denial of the Home Secretary's contentions, but otherwise took no real part in what they saw as unfair proceedings. Some refused legal representation. Where possible, SIAC had an advantage over the Home Secretary, namely, the benefit of the evidence and intelligence being probed by the forensic skills of the Special Advocates. Finally, the standard to be satisfied falls far short of the criminal standard of proof beyond reasonable doubt or even the civil standard of balance of probabilities. The question for SIAC was whether at the date of the hearing there were reasonable grounds (a) to suspect the person to be an international terrorist with links to Al Qaeda or associates and (b) to believe in consequence their presence in the United Kingdom to be a risk to national security.

A is an Algerian in the United Kingdom since 1989. In 1992 he was deported to Sweden as an overstayer, but was returned by the Swedish authorities to this country. A subsequent asylum application was refused and the refusal upheld on appeal. His claim for indefinite leave to remain on the basis of children living here for more than seven years was rejected. On 17 December 2001 he was certificated under ATCSA on the basis of active support in the United Kingdom of a proscribed terrorist group (GSPC) and of the objectives of Osama bin Laden and Al Qaeda. SIAC found the GSPC to be an international terrorist group active in pursuit of both a national agenda, including fighting the Algerian regime and the Zouabri-led GIA, and a wider anti-Western agenda. It rejected the suggestion that its attention was confined to Algeria or that it could be regarded as not part of the Al Qaeda–linked threat because it did not target civilians. There was no evidence at all to support the proposition that GSPC terrorism excluded any civilian targets, or that attacks on non–civilian targets in the West are excluded from the scope of the emergency. There was evidence, particularly in closed session, about GSPC-linked civilian attacks outside Algeria, in France and Niger. The GSPC was also linked to Al Qaeda through training, and funding and in other ways. Its being on the UN list added to the weight of evidence as to those links. Like the GIA, the GSPC was controlled or influenced by people outside the United Kingdom. In contrast, however, while the GIA was a functioning terrorist organization, it had no current 'organizational level' links with Al Qaeda. Posing no threat to Western interests outside Algeria; it was not truly part of the Al Qaeda-linked emergency. Its significance in the story was as the precursor to the GSPC, or as the original terrorist group supported by those said now to be significantly connected to other looser networks, and in that different way linked to Al Qaeda. More specifically the case against A was support of the GSPC through his involvement in credit card fraud, its main source of income in the United Kingdom. He had also been heavily involved in the procurement of telecommunications equipment, giving assistance to a terrorist called Abu Doha, who was arrested at Heathrow Airport as he tried to flee the United Kingdom. Abu Doha headed or inspired 'the Abu Doha Group'. SIAC considered there to be ample evidence that this group fell within the Act, had links to Al Qaeda and was thus a very important part of the emergency. Not a group with an exclusive membership, its members or supporters or some of them may form part of other networks or groups, as well. It was the paradigm group, loosely co-ordinated but overlapping with other groups or cells of North African, principally Algerian, extremists. It may have overlapped with groups centred on Abu Qatada or Beghal. It too was controlled or influenced by people outside the United Kingdom. On these bases, SIAC held that there were reasonable grounds to suspect that A was an international terrorist and a threat to this country's national security. It dismissed also his outstanding appeals against the Home Secretary's decisions not to revoke the deportation order and to refuse him indefinite leave to remain in the United Kingdom. On 2 July 2004 and 28 February 2005, SIAC on review held justified the continuing certification. In March 2005 he was made the subject of a control order and in August that year was again detained for purposes of deportation and his appeal against it dismissed in March 2006.

Abu Qatada, known also by other names, is a Jordanian national, a successful asylum seeker with a family in the United Kingdom and an appeal for indefinite leave to remain was still pending when ATCSA came into force. He would have been certified and detained then, but had gone into hiding. On 23 October 2002, his hiding place having been discovered, he was certificated under ATCSA, his application for indefinite leave was refused, a national security deportation decision was issued, and he was detained. Abu Quatada has had a number of involvements with the criminal process both in Jordan and the United Kingdom. He was convicted in his absence in Jordan for his involvement in terrorist attacks there in March and April 1998 and in relation to a plot to plant bombs to coincide with the Millennium. Art. 3 ECHR precluded his return there. He had been arrested in February 2001 by the police on suspicion of involvement with a cell in Frankfurt responsible for plotting to cause explosions at the Strasbourg Christmas market. It was decided that there was insufficient admissible evidence to sustain a prosecution and so no charges were preferred. Sterling and foreign currency to a value in excess of £170,000 was found in his possession; £805 was in an envelope which recorded that it was 'for the mujahidin in Chechnya'. He chose not to attend the SIAC hearing or to participate in it in any way. Considering the case on its merits, SIAC issued a damning condemnation in finding the case against him established to the relatively low level ATCSA required:

> Indeed, were the standard higher than reasonable suspicion, we would have had no doubt that it was established. The appellant was heavily involved, indeed was at the

centre in the United Kingdom of terrorist activities associated with Al Qaida. He is a truly dangerous individual and these appeals are dismissed.[16]

In February 2007, SIAC held that Art. 3 ECHR did not bar deportation to Jordan.

Abu Rideh (also known as Abu Ramsi) was born in Jordan to stateless Palestinian parents. and arrived in the United Kingdom with a Jordanian passport in January 1995. In 1998 he was granted indefinite leave to remain in the United Kingdom as a refugee. On 17 December 2001 the Secretary of State issued a certificate under ATCSA. He saw Abu Rideh as actively supporting (including through fund-raising) various international terrorist groups, including those with links to Osama Bin Laden's terrorist network. In July 2002, because of mental health problems, he was transferred to Broadmoor from HMP Belmarsh. SIAC upheld his certification, on the basis mainly of closed material. He had told deliberate lies about important matters, and had been a very successful fund-raiser able to get money out to Afghanistan. It was accepted that some of the fund-raising was for charitable purposes. On 2 July 2004, SIAC on review of his case maintained the certificate. On 28 January 2005, in part in view of his mental health, SIAC admitted him to bail, to be reviewed every three months. Balancing the diminished and continuing risks, the effect of the constraints imposed by the bail conditions and the further detention which he would face for a breach, against the effect on him of past and continued detention, SIAC held that his continued detention was disproportionate to the risk in view of other methods of control which could be put in place. He is now subject to a control order.

Ajouaou is from Morocco. In 1988 he was granted indefinite leave to remain on the basis of his marriage to a British citizen, which marriage broke up shortly afterwards. He made two applications for naturalization as a British citizen, in 1990 and 1997. The latter remains to be formally determined. In 2000 he re-married, again to a British citizen, and there is a child of the marriage. On 17 December 2001 the Secretary of State decided to make a deportation order against Ajouaou, and also to certify him under ATCSA s. 25. Ajouaou lodged appeals to SIAC against both decisions. But on 22 December 2001 he left the United Kingdom and has remained in Morocco since that date. The Secretary of State revoked the certificate on 16 January 2003, purportedly with effect from 22 December 2001, the date of Ajouaou's departure from the United Kingdom because he took the view 'that he could not properly believe that a person's *"presence in the United Kingdom"* was a risk to national security if the person was not present in the United Kingdom'. His case against Ajouaou was that he had links with both the GIA and GSPC and was a close associate of extremists who themselves were linked with Al Qaeda or Bin Laden; he had been involved in preparing or instigating acts of international terrorism by procuring high-tech equipment for the GSPC and/or Islamic extremists in Chechnya; and he had supported one or more extremist factions in Chechnya by his involvement in fraud

---

[16] SIAC File No. SC/15/2002, 8 March 2004, para. 20.

which facilitated the provision of funds, and the storing and handling of propaganda videos promoting the jihad. He was also a close associate of Abu Doha. The fraud case depended effectively entirely on closed material. SIAC was entirely satisfied that Ajouaou supported or assisted the GIA, the GSPC, and the looser group based around Abu Doha, and at any time Ajouaou is in the United Kingdom his presence here is a risk to national security.

B is another Algerian whose asylum claim was rejected in 1996. He was detained pending removal. He then made a further asylum claim, was granted temporary release, was re-arrested and then released again. He served two short sentences of imprisonment for driving while disqualified and associated offences. On 5 February 2002 the Secretary of State decided to make a deportation order against B, and also to certify under ATCSA. On the same day he also issued a certificate under ATCSA to the effect that B was not entitled to the protection of Art. 33(1) of the Refugee Convention because Art. 1F or 33(2) applied to him. The Home Secretary's open case against him was that he had belonged to the GSPC since 1997 or 1998 having contacts with leading members of the GSPC in the United Kingdom, and in 2000 had played an important role in procuring telecommunications equipment and providing logistical support. The Home Secretary's assessment was that the equipment was for use by Chechyen Mujahaddin extremists and the GSPC in Algeria. B appealed to SIAC both against the ATCSA certificate and the decision to deport him. He did not attend the appeal hearing and the short statement he put in was cast in the most general terms. So there was really nothing to displace the Home Secretary's evidence. SIAC found that B worked with Abu Doha and used a false name in purchasing telecommunications equipment. The closed material rendered the Secretary of State's conclusions 'even more reasonable'. B's appeals were dismissed. On 2 July 2004, SIAC on review of certification accepted that the GSPC remained an active terrorist organization linked to the state of emergency and that there remained at large associates of B. B was a trusted and senior member of the GSPC, who was not deterred by previous periods of detention from carrying on his terrorist support activities and he would be able and willing to resume those activities should he be released. There were contacts with whom he would link up. The certificate was properly maintained

C, in contrast, is an Egyptian who claimed asylum in the United Kingdom in 2000. Despite his false accounts of his earlier movements in his asylum interview and in an interview with the Security Service, he was accorded refugee status in March 2001 and granted indefinite leave to remain. On 18 December 2001 he was certificated because the Home Secretary saw him as an active supporter of the proscribed organization Egyptian Islamic Jihad (EIJ). He had been sentenced in his absence to fifteen years imprisonment by an Egyptian military court for his role in trying to recruit serving Egyptian Army officers for the EIJ and in planning operations on behalf of the EIJ, both in Egypt and abroad. C's appeal involved consideration of the EIJ, described by the Home Secretary as a proscribed terrorist group, aiming to overthrow the Egyptian Government. It had mounted a number of high profile attacks up to the mid-1990s and had merged in some form or other with Al Qaeda in 2001. Indeed, from the late 1990s its leadership had been closely associated with Osama Bin Laden. For example, in February 1998 Al Zawahiri, its then leader, was the second signatory to the Bin Laden fatwa and he was one of Bin Laden's closest associates. There were now organizational links, well established between the EIJ and Al Qaeda. The majority of the group was fully merged with it. EIJ members were on Al Qaeda's ruling council and assisted with terrorist attacks. The EIJ was a good example of a terrorist group which had had originally a national agenda, but which had become a close supporter of the global agenda, which is capable of being pursued alongside or as an inseparable part of a national agenda. C did not give evidence but his two submitted statements were regarded by SIAC as entirely unreliable. SIAC were wholly satisfied that there were reasonable grounds for suspecting that C has a senior leadership role in the EIJ in the United Kingdom, and dismissed his appeal. On first review in July 2004, it upheld continuing certification.

D is another Algerian. His 1999 application for asylum was refused on 13 February 2001. His appeal had not been determined when on 18 December 2001 the Home Secretary both certificated and decided to deport D as an active supporter of the GIA, who had used false documents, and was involved with other extremists whom the Secretary of State named. D gave evidence and was cross-examined. SIAC regarded D as a practised and accomplished liar, and did not believe his excuses, his claims to ignorance, his attempts to distance himself from other terrorist suspects, or his assertions that he has nothing to do with the GIA or other terrorist organizations, networks or activities:

> [S]ome of [D's] relationships, in particular that with Beghal, had a social content. But that was not all. Taken as a whole, the evidence we have seen is sufficient to support the Secretary of State's case that D's extensive contacts with those who were involved at various levels in terrorist planning and activity did not arise primarily or solely for social reasons: he had contact with these individuals because he was himself supporting international terrorism in various ways. ... his association with the GIA would be formally sufficient to justify the certificate, but would not be '*within the derogation*'. His support of the looser network of North African terrorists is, however, sufficient for both purposes. His appeal against the certificate is dismissed.[17]

SIAC on review upheld continued certification on 2 July 2004.

E is from Tunisia. He is a failed asylum seeker, nonetheless granted exceptional leave to remain until 2005. The Home Secretary certificated E on 18 December 2001. He considered him to be an active supporter of the Tunisian Fighting Group (TFG), a terrorist organization with close links to Al Qaida, and to have provided direct assistance to a number of active terrorists. E raised an issue as to the very existence of this group. As to that SIAC entertained no doubt: it accepted that the

---

[17] SIAC appeal No SC/06/2002, para. 11.

TFG had its origins in the Tunisian Islamic Front (FIT); its ultimate aim was the establishment of an Islamic State in Tunisia; and both it and the FIT had links with Al Qaeda. SIAC were satisfied that E was a member of the TFG and so had links with an international terrorist group, the TFG itself being an international terrorist organization within the meaning of ATCSA. Their reasons rested largely on closed material, but SIAC stated in its open specific judgment that it had been careful only to rely on material which could not have an innocent explanation. The issue relating to evidence having been obtained by torture or other treatment in violation of ECHR Art. 3 first arose in E's case. SIAC rejected the submission. On 2 July 2004 it upheld continued certification as justified. Although a number of other extremists with whom he worked had been detained there were still many at large and the networks which they operated still existed. There was further material to support the conclusion that, if released, E would have no difficulty in re-establishing his connections to extremist Islamic networks. He was admitted to bail in March 2005 and soon subject to a control order, quashed by Beatson J in February 2007 but reinstated by the Court of Appeal in May 2007.[18]

F is another Algerian who related that he first arrived in the United Kingdom in 1994 on a false Spanish passport. In 1997 he was charged alongside others with offences contrary to the PTA 1989. He claimed asylum in December 1997. On 3 March 2000 the case against him and his co-defendants was abandoned. On 15 March 2000 he was granted a right of residence until March 2005 on account of his French wife's status as an EEA resident. On 17 December 2001 the Secretary of State certificated him on grounds that F had provided active support to the proscribed organization GIA. His activities on behalf of international terrorists included the procurement of terrorism-related materials and equipment and the provision of false documentation. F was detained pursuant to the certificate but, having become a French national in 2001, he went to France in March 2002 where he remains. As in *Ajouaou* and for the same reasons, the Secretary of State revoked the certificate. SIAC acknowledged that there would have been no basis for a certificate in May 1997 (had ATCSA then been in force) when F had been charged with terrorist offences, since, for want of links with Al Qaeda, the GIA and its activities would not have fallen within the scope of the Art. 15 derogation. SIAC was satisfied that F had continued to associate with GSPC affiliates, and had provided false documentation for its members and for the mujahadin in Chechnya. He had been properly certificated.

G is also from Algeria. His claim for asylum on arrival in 1995 was rejected. His marriage to a French national, however, led to a residence permit valid for five years from 2001. ATCSA certification in his case was based on his being an active supporter of the GSPC. SIAC found there to be reasonable suspicion that G was an international terrorist and reasonable belief that his presence in the United Kingdom constituted a risk to national security. It had no doubt that he had been involved in the production of false documentation, had facilitated young Muslims

---

[18] See chapter 9.

travelling to Afghanistan to train for jihad, had actively assisted terrorists who have links with Al Qaeda, and had actively assisted the GSPC. Because of a severe mental condition, G was released on bail in May 2004 on strict conditions, amounting to house arrest with further controls.[19] On 2 July 2004, SIAC upheld his continuing certification. In March 2005 a control order was served on him and in August that year he was again held pending deportation on national security grounds. His appeal against deportation was dismissed by SIAC in February 2007 and his return sanctioned to Algeria.

H is also an Algerian. He supported the FIS, which won the elections in Algeria in 1991, leading to a military coup. Later it was banned. He went to Afghanistan in 1992. He arrived in the United Kingdom in August 1993 and claimed asylum on the ground that as a supporter of FIS he would be persecuted if returned to Algeria. In 2000 he was granted indefinite leave to remain in the United Kingdom as a refugee. The Home Secretary certificated him on 22 April 2002 as an active supporter of the proscribed organisation, GSPC, which has links to Osama Bin Laden's terrorist network. His activities on behalf of the group included fund-raising and distribution of propaganda. Unlike most of the other appellants, H gave evidence before SIAC and contested the case with some vigour. SIAC found some of his evidence unsatisfactory, not least that relating to certain documents. Relying in part on closed material, SIAC were satisfied that H was an international terrorist and that his detention was proportionate. On review SIAC on 2 July 2004 found justified continuing certification. He has since withdrawn his appeal against deportation and returned to Algeria.

I (who has a number of aliases) is an Algerian citizen, an asylum seeker granted exceptional leave to remain in May 2000 as part of attempts to deal with the asylum backlog. He was given a Home Office travel document. On 22 April 2002 the Home Secretary decided to deport him as a threat to national security and certificate him under ATCSA. The basis for both decisions was the Home Secretary's view that I was undertaking a range of support activities on behalf of various international terrorist groups including networks associated with Osama Bin Laden, including fund-raising and the maintenance of support activities, such as the provision of safe houses for the Abu Doha group. It was claimed that I had received mujahidin training in Afghanistan in 1998 and during 1999, had expertise in the manufacture of electrical explosives, and was involved in credit card fraud both in London and Leicester. I was an associate of a number of other extreme Islamists many of whom had either been convicted for terrorist offences, were awaiting trial for terrorist offences, had been linked to disrupted terrorist attacks both in the United Kingdom and overseas and/or were themselves detained under the 2001 Act. His association with these individuals was consistent with I himself being part of the networks, still engaged in active terrorist support and planning, which posed the threat giving rise to the public emergency. I had also been brought into the criminal process. Following his arrest on terrorist charges on 17 January

---

[19] SIAC Bail Application SCB10G.

2002 his home in Leicester was searched. The recovered equipment included a credit card reader-writer with 300 credit card numbers stored in it. Other recovered equipment could be used to produce false documentation. The terrorist charges were not pursued, but I was charged on 29 August 2002 with six counts alleging dishonesty of various kinds including conspiracy to defraud. He pleaded guilty to conspiracy to defraud. The Crown submitted that the figure realised was £250,000. The remaining counts were left on the file. I chose not to give evidence to SIAC, contending that its processes were unfair. SIAC found that the closed evidence reinforced the already powerful case against I upon the basis of that material, and the connection with the Abu Doha group. It rejected his appeals.

K (another known by several names) is also an Algerian citizen, and a failed asylum seeker who had admittedly travelled on a series of false passports. His certification and the decision to deport on national security grounds were based on the Home Secretary's view that K, a senior member of a group of mujahidin engaged in active support for various international terrorist groups, including networks associated with Osama Bin Laden, was engaged in a variety of activities on behalf of Islamist networks. Those activities included facilitation of travel for mujahidin, in particular from Abu Doha's group, to and from Afghanistan, Pakistan and the Caucasus. K had also attempted to join Ibn Khattab's Arab mujahidin in Chechnya in order to fight. He held a senior position within Abu Doha's group and provided active support for a network of extreme Islamists planning to carry out attacks in the United Kingdom and Western Europe including the use of toxic poisons. There was material linking him both to the GIA and GSPC. K denied all this, contested the nature of his interrogations, and claimed to be involved in humanitarian fund-raising for Chechnya. Training in Afghanistan was solely for the purpose of him being able to help defend Chechnya by fighting there. He did not attend the appeal but his solicitor, Gareth Pierce, made statements on his behalf, ultimately stating that K did not wish to take part in unfair proceedings or be represented by a lawyer. SIAC found that the open material supported reasonable grounds for the certification and deportation decisions. Taking the totality of the open and closed material, SIAC had no doubt that K was a senior, and active member of the Abu Doha group. K later withdrew an appeal against deportation and returned to Algeria.

M's proved a rather different case. M is Libyan, opposed to the Qaddafi regime there, and a failed asylum seeker. Despite that claim's failure the Home Secretary accepted that M could not safely be returned to Libya. K's ATCSA certification on 23 November 2002 (accompanied by a decision to deport on national security grounds and detention) was founded on the assertion of him being a member of a group of mujahidin engaged in active support for various international terrorist groups, including networks associated with Osama Bin Laden. K's activities on behalf of these networks were said to include the provision of material support. K admitted association with the LIFG, opposing Qaddafi, but argued that group had no Al Qaeda connections. SIAC did not doubt that M was a terrorist, but doubted the claimed Al Qaeda connection. Accordingly it allowed both the appeal against certification and that against deportation. Its right to do so was endorsed by the Court of Appeal (see chapter 8).

P, in contrast, appealed unsuccessfully against certification and a national security deportation decision. P, a failed asylum seeker, is another Algerian national. Criminal charges, some of a terrorist nature, were brought but not proceeded with. Certification and deportation were founded on the view that P was an associate of Algerian extremists engaged in active support (including the supply of false documents) for various international terrorist groups, including nationals associated with Osama Bin Laden. P's written statement to SIAC was a robust denial of the allegations, but he declined further to participate in an unfair appeal process. There was a connection with the Finsbury Park Mosque and the radical preacher, Abu Hamza. SIAC found P to pose a danger which could not be dealt with by restrictive bail conditions. It rejected him falling within ATCSA section 21(2)(a) as involved in the preparation of a terrorist attack or within (b) as a member of the Abu Doha group. It found he fell within (c), a link with a terrorist group in the sense that he supported or assisted it. Both in July 2004 and February 2005, SIAC on first and second review respectively maintained the certification. Between first and second review, in view of a deteriorating mental condition, P was detained in Broadmoor under the Mental Health Act 1983. He later withdrew his appeal against deportation and returned to Algeria.

S (another known under many names) is an Algerian citizen, another failed asylum seeker, earlier jailed for passport fraud. Terrorist criminal charges were brought, but not proceeded with. On release from custody in respect of those charges in May 2001, he was detained pending resolution of an extradition request from France. Certification and deportation decisions were made on 7 August 2003, but detention remained founded on the extradition request. The decisions were based on the Home Secretary's claim that S was a member of a group of mujahidin engaged in a variety of active support for various international terrorist groups, including networks associated with Osama Bin Laden. His activities on behalf of Islamist networks were said to include: involvement in criminal activities by the Fateh Kamel network in Canada to raise funds assessed to be for extreme Islamist causes; training at terrorist training camps which are associated with Bin Laden; planning to take part in Ahmed Ressam's terrorist cell which intended to carry out an attack on Los Angeles Airport over the Millenium, only being prevented from joining the cell when arrested at Heathrow Airport in November 1998 whilst attempting to board a flight for Toronto on a false Belgian passport; provision of support for a terrorist cell linked to the Abu Doha group which intended to attack the Christmas market in Strasbourg at the end of 2000; and the supply of false documents. S's written statement to SIAC denied all this, criticized the extradition proceedings, and raised concerns about his mental state. A statement by his solicitor at the SIAC hearing said S would welcome a fair criminal trial but would not participate in the unjust SIAC procedures. SIAC were satisfied upon the basis of the open material alone that there were substantial grounds for believing that S was a senior and trusted figure in the Abu Doha group in the United Kingdom and in other terrorist networks linked to Al Qaeda, and that he played a significant role in their terrorist activities. Considering the entirety of both open and closed material, there could be no real doubt that S was a senior member of the Abu Doha and other terrorist groups linked to Al Qaeda and directly involved in planning terrorist attacks. S was extradited after court proceedings.[20]

Concerns about the Use of ATCSA Detention

A number of very proper concerns have been raised about ATCSA detention and its decision-making and judicial supervision regimes, since the Bill that became ATCSA was first published. Those concerns, both in terms of human rights and the efficacy in security terms of the regime, have been raised both by scrutiny/review individuals or bodies and by NGOs and other organizations giving evidence to them or in briefing papers for press, MPs and peers. Insofar as these concerns have translated into litigation, they are examined in depth in chapter 9.

A pervading concern has been the lack of 'equality of arms' in the decision-making process, its subordination of due process to security concerns, and the use which might be made of evidence or material obtained through torture, something more fully explored in chapters 8 (challenge mechanisms) and 9 (legal and human rights challenges).[21] There was also concern that the powers were both disproportionate to the exigencies of the public emergency and discriminatory on grounds of national origin,[22] concerns vindicated by their Lordship's declaration of incompatibility in *A and Others* (see chapter 9). Given that the threat came also from British nationals, the Newton Committee was troubled about the efficacy of detention only of foreign nationals. It questioned the security value of allowing those detainees who wished to do so to go to another country, 'given the risk of exporting terrorism' and an associated risk that they might return to the United Kingdom undetected by the authorities.[23] That only the United Kingdom had derogated from the ECHR was seen by that Committee as puzzling, given that other European 'countries face considerable threats from terrorists within their borders'.[24] It remained concerned that insufficient consideration was being given to enhancing existing surveillance through the imposition of lesser restrictions such as electronic tagging, curfews, daily reporting to a police station, limits on communications and use of financial services.[25] The lengthy delays in the appellate and review processes (almost two years in some cases) generated concern because this was equivalent (in real terms) to a significant custodial sentence, with

---

[20] See SIAC Determination SC/29/2004, 19 May 2006, para. 53.

[21] Newton Committee (2003): para. 187.

[22] Ibid., para. 194.

[23] Ibid., para. 195.

[24] Ibid., para. 189.

[25] Ibid., para. 251; Carlile (2003): para. 6.13; JHRC 18th (2003–04), paras 75–80 and submission of *Justice*.

detainees held in high security conditions, without having been proven guilty of any criminal offence.[26] The existence and uncertainty about the powers had led to understandable disquiet in the Muslim community.[27] While the limited use of detention accorded with Lord Carlile's view that it was 'desirable that as few persons as possible should be subject to non-criminal sanctions without a conviction by a criminal court'[28] and might thus be welcomed, the Newton Committee rightly warned, citing a United States Supreme Court Justice, that

> nothing opens the door to arbitrary action so effectively as to allow ... officials to pick and choose only a few to whom they will apply legislation and thus to escape the political retribution that might be visited upon them if larger numbers were affected.[29]

The conditions and unlimited nature of detention, and the adverse effects on physical and mental health of the detainees, were very much the subject of adverse comment and concern. Lord Carlile commented:

> HMP Belmarsh is an unattractive and unpleasant place. The detainees I saw there and at Woodhill are held in very high category conditions. Woodhill is a less unpleasant prison, with natural light and space to move around even in the high security setting. As last year, the detainees to whom I spoke in Woodhill appeared more relaxed, a natural consequence of the altogether more benign environment. Last year all complained to me of the fact that they were treated in the same way as men convicted of the most serious crimes, indeed were locked up alongside such men. Some complained then of worse treatment, including the use of solitary confinement, restricted opportunities to contact family, and insensitivity to religious observance. Generally they have the opportunity to fraternise with each other, an opportunity that would not necessarily be permitted in all other countries. However, their position and status is unenviable. All told me of the real and, in my view understandable, difficulty of dealing with incarceration without either trial, conviction or an indication of when if ever it would come to an end. The 2006 closure date for the legislation does not reassure them. Some contrasted their position unfavourably with that of life sentence prisoners, who at least know their tariff and when they will be considered for parole. They have no remission, and no parole.[30]

In response the Home Office made available conditions comparable to remand prisoners but the Newton Committee recorded that the detainees had refused to use them.[31]

The Commons/Lords Joint Human Rights Select Committee (JHRC) reported that it had received a number of representations about the impact of indefinite

[26] Newton Committee (2003): para. 197; Lord Carlile, *Anti–Terrorism, Crime and Security Act 2001 Part IV Section 28 Review 2003*, paras 50–57.

[27] Newton Committee (2003) para. 196.

[28] Carlile (2005): para. 32.

[29] Newton Committee (2003): para. 191.

[30] Carlile (2005): paras. 99–100.

[31] Newton Committee (2003): para. 199.

detention on the mental health of detainees.[32] There had been cause for serious concern over the mental health of two of the detainees. One had been transferred to Broadmoor and released on bail, effectively to house arrest, because of those concerns. The British Psychological Society had expressed concern that serious harm was being done to the mental well-being of ATCSA detainees, mainly because of the psychological impact of indefinite detention without charge or trial without being informed of the evidence against them, or even being subjected to interrogation or questioning. It was particularly concerned about the impact on vulnerable groups such as the young, those who have previously experienced torture and detention in their country of origins, and those with existing mental health problems or physical or learning disabilities. In addition, the Mental Health Act Commission submitted that, where an ATCSA detainee was transferred to hospital under the Mental Health Act 1983, the review mechanisms of the Mental Health Review Tribunal and SIAC were inadequate in not affording an opportunity to make a fair challenge to decisions over the appropriate level of security provision. The JHRC noted that in its report on its visit to the ATCSA detainees in February 2002, the European Committee for the Prevention of Torture and Inhuman or Degrading Treatment found that the indefinite nature of their detention, and the belief that they had no means to contest the broad accusations made against them, were a source of considerable distress to the detainees. Amnesty International considered this had a debilitating effect on the mental and physical health of the detainees.[33] It was open to question whether the conditions amounted to inhuman or degrading treatment contrary to Art. 3 ECHR (see chapter 9).

PTA 2005 Control Orders

The Powers and their Rationale

The control order scheme embodied in the PTA 2005 represents the response of Government and Parliament to the House of Lords' declaration that detention without trial of foreign nationals under ATCSA was not compatible with Convention Rights. It takes on board also Lord Hoffman's statement that detention without trial of all terrorist suspects was not to be the answer. Indeed Home Secretary Blunkett had much earlier characterized such an extension as disproportionate.[34] Instead as Home Secretary Clarke informed the Commons in January 2005,

---

[32] JHRC 18th (2003–04): paras 33–37.

[33] JHRC 18th (2003–04): submission from Amnesty International, para. 13.

[34] Cm 6147 (2004), para. 36.

We intend that [control] orders be capable of general application to any suspected terrorist irrespective of nationality or, for most controls, of the nature of the terrorist activity – whether international or domestic – and that they should enable us to impose conditions constraining the ability of those subject to the orders to engage in terrorist-related activities. Control orders would be used only in serious cases. The controls imposed would be proportionate to the threat that each individual posed. Such orders would be preventive and designed to disrupt those seeking to carry out attacks – whether here or elsewhere – or who are planning or otherwise supporting such activities. They would be designed to address directly two of the Law Lords' concerns: discrimination and proportionality. .... The Secretary of State would consider whether, on the basis of an intelligence assessment provided by the Security Service, there are reasonable grounds for suspecting that an individual is, or has been, concerned with terrorism. If the answer to that question is yes, and if the Secretary of State considers such action necessary for the purposes of protecting the public from terrorist-related activities, he or she would impose controls on that individual. There would be a range of controls restricting movement and association or other communication with named individuals; the imposition of curfews and/or tagging; and restrictions on access to telecommunications, the internet and other technology. At the top end, control orders would include a requirement to remain at their premises. The controls to be imposed under the new scheme will not include detention in prison, although I intend that breach of a control order should be a criminal offence, triable in the usual way through the criminal courts and punishable by imprisonment.

Indeed, as Lord Carlile put it in his first annual review of the operation of the PTA 2005:

> The intention is that conditions imposed under a control order should be specific and tailored to the individual. The aim is to secure the safety of the State by the minimum measures needed to ensure effective disruption and prevention of terrorist activity.[35]

However, the Government has submitted, in its intervention in a case before the European Court of Human Rights, that the control order system inevitably can only provide a partial protection to the public.[36]

The main provisions of the PTA 2005 entered into force on royal assent on 11 March 2005. ATCSA 2001 sections 21–32 (detention without trial) were repealed with effect from 14 March 2005, without prejudice to ongoing appeals or claims for compensation.[37] Instead the PTA 2005 established a regime of 'non–derogating' and 'derogating' control orders. The distinction between them reflects the fact that ECHR jurisprudence distinguishes between interferences with freedom of movement (guaranteed by Protocol Four ECHR, to which the United Kingdom

[35] Carlile (2006): para. 10.
[36] Application 2524/05, *Observations of the Governments of Lithuania, Portugal, Slovakia and the United Kingdom*, para. 20. cited at <http://www.liberty–human–rights.org.uk/resources/policy-papers/2006/pta-renewal-for-jchr-.PDF>.
[37] PTA 2005, s. 16(2)–(4).

is not a party)[38] and situations where the degree of restriction, moving nearer to the 'close confinement' or 'imprisonment' end of the spectrum, constitutes a deprivation of liberty and security of person guaranteed by Art. 5 ECHR. That stipulates an exhaustive range of permissible heads of legitimate interference with that crucial freedom.[39] Only derogating control orders can impose restrictions amounting to a deprivation of liberty within the meaning of Art. 5. Those imposed by non-derogating orders must fall short of that or be invalid. The line between the two situations and orders – movement/non-derogating control order, on the one hand, and liberty/derogating control orders – is a fine and imprecise one, as the Home Secretary learned to his cost in the High Court and Court of Appeal.

'Derogating' control orders, which would enable, for example, 'house arrest', have not yet been invoked. They require parliamentary approval of an Art. 15 ECHR designated derogation order under the HRA 1998.[40] As yet, the Government has not considered one necessary, but in May 2007 the Home Secretary indicated that the derogation option might be used should the House of Lords uphold restrictive limitations on non-derogating control orders.[41]

The obligations imposable under either type of control order are those that the Home Secretary or the court (as may be) 'considers necessary for purposes connected with preventing or restricting involvement by that individual in terrorism-related activity'.[42] A non-exhaustive list of obligations includes a prohibition or restriction on possession of certain articles; restrictions on association or communication with others; electronic tagging; curfews; restrictions on movement within the United Kingdom; a requirement that the person remain in a particular place. [43] Embodied in a derogating control order, this could amount to detention without trial; as Home Secretary Clarke informed the Commons in moving the Second Reading,

> At the top end, the obligations that could be imposed could include *a requirement for the individual to remain in a particular place at all times*, or some similar measure that amounted to a deprivation of liberty. The place in question will vary with the threat posed by the individual. It could be the individual's own home, or his or her parents' home. It could even, in certain circumstances, be *in accommodation owned and*

---

[38] Even if it were bound by it, then, subject to 'proportionality' in each case, the range of restrictions available under a 'non-derogating control order' might well comply with the legitimate restrictions on freedom of movement within a State set out in the Protocol. See further the sources cited in the next note.

[39] *Guzzardi* v *Italy* (1981) 3 EHRR 333; Ovey and White (2006): 103–105 [Art. 5] and chap. 18 [Protocol Four].

[40] PTA 2005, ss. 1(10), 4(3)(c), (7)(c), (10)(c); HRA, s. 14(1).

[41] *The Guardian*, 25 May 2007, 1-2.

[42] PTA 2005, s. 1(3).

[43] PTA 2005, s. 1(4)–(8). HC Debs, Vol 431, col. 152 (February 22, 2005).

managed by the Government. However, such severe forms of control order would require a derogation from Art. 5 of the ECHR before they could be implemented.[44]

The Home Secretary and/or the High Court will have to decide at what point in any case the degree of restriction shades from one on freedom of movement into one amounting to a deprivation of liberty and security protected by Art. 5 ECHR, so that a non–derogating order is impermissible and a derogating control order must be sought.[45]

If he/she considers that the involvement in terrorism-related activity of which an individual is suspected may have involved the commission of an investigable offence relating to terrorism, the Home Secretary must, before making, or applying for the making of, a control order, consult the relevant chief officer of police about whether there is evidence available that could realistically be used to prosecute the individual for an offence relating to terrorism.[46] After an order is made, he/she must inform the relevant chief officer of that, so that the chief officer, consulting the prosecuting authorities as appropriate, can secure that investigation of the individual's conduct with a view to prosecuting the latter for an offence relating to terrorism, keeping this under review, and consulting throughout the period during which the control order has effect.[47] Breach of a control order is an arrestable and imprisonable offence.[48] All this is consistent with the policy of prosecution where possible. The duties under this section can be reviewed by the High Court in control order proceedings. In *Secretary of State for the Home Department* v *E*, Beatson J held that the Home Secretary's duty to consult the chief officer is not a condition precedent to his ability to make a control order (and he had in fact consulted properly), but that officer's failure to fulfil his post-order duties could taint the Home Secretary's maintaining the order in force. In addition, the Home Secretary's breach of his own continuing duty to keep the matter of prosecution under review, flowing from the general requirement for the order to be necessary, in this case invalidated his order. The Court of Appeal, however, held that the Home Secretary's clear breach did not have an invalidating effect; the duty was not a condition precedent to the making or renewal of a control order. Beatson J should have further analysed the consequences of the breach.[49]

Just as the degree of restrictions that may be imposed varies as between 'non-derogating' and 'derogating' control orders, so does the applicable decision-maker, the process for making them, and the relative degree of judicial control of their imposition. The whole process has become much more 'judicialized', with the Home Secretary who wants a control order against an individual largely having to

---

[44] HC Debs, Vol 431, col. 152 (February 22, 2005) (emphasis supplied).
[45] See further chapter 9.
[46] PTA 2005, s. 8(1), (2).
[47] PTA 2005, s. 8(3)–(7).
[48] PTA 2005, s. 9.
[49] [2007] EWHC (Admin) 233; [2007] EWCA Civ 459.

seek the issue of one from the High Court or permission to make one, rather than making one of his own volition and having to defend it in court later. But, legal formalities aside, it is very clear that in reality, non–derogating orders are much more the province of the Home Secretary than is the case with derogating control orders, since the scheme affords that court less room to intervene than with the latter. The Home Secretary remains more in control of the process, and needs to satisfy the court to a much lower standard, so long as the restrictions imposed under a non–derogating control order do not amount to a deprivation of liberty within the meaning of Art. 5 ECHR. In contrast, were the Home Secretary to need a derogating control order (able to support restrictions which did restrict liberty and security of person), control of the process begins to slip from his/her hands. Each House must approve a designated derogation order giving effect under the HRA to an Art. 15 ECHR notice of derogation. In addition, the High Court will only make a lasting order where it is satisfied, *on the balance of probabilities* (a much higher test than that applicable to ATCSA detention, national security deportation or non-derogating control orders) that the controlee is someone who is or has been involved in terrorism-related activity and *it considers* that imposing on them obligations ranking as deprivation of liberty is necessary for purposes connected with protecting the public from a risk of terrorism arising out of, or associated with, the public emergency in that designated derogation order. Given that the danger to the country is said to have increased since the House of Lords accepted the existence of such an emergency in *A and Others* in December 2004, this loss of effective control helps explain why there has been no such derogation and no resort to derogating control orders. Rather the Home Secretary has sought instead to push the restrictions in non-derogating orders to their limits (and beyond) and to again resort to detention for purposes of national security deportation in respect of foreign nationals (many of whom are former ATCSA detainees) where 'no ill-treatment' Memoranda of Understanding (MOU) are seen to re-open a channel once thought closed by the *Chahal* ruling. The deportation route also has the advantage that SIAC has been persuaded to impose bail restrictions amounting to effective house arrest (as an alternative to detention in prison) and the Home Secretary has in those cases secured ends otherwise only attainable under the PTA 2005 by derogating under Art. 15 ECHR with all the drawbacks that involves for him. But this has deprived the individual of the high level of judicial scrutiny that would be available to him were the PTA 2005 route taken.

The test for making a 'non-derogating' control order is whether there are reasonable grounds for suspecting that the individual is or has been involved in terrorism-related activity and the decision-maker (Home Secretary or the court, as the case may be) further considers it necessary, for purposes connected with protecting members of the public from a risk of terrorism, to make a control order imposing obligations on that individual.[50] A 'non-derogating control order is one whose restrictions are not of sufficient degree to amount to a deprivation of liberty

---

[50] PTA 2005, s.2 (1).

guaranteed by Art. 5 ECHR as opposed to limiting free movement guaranteed by Protocol Four by which the United Kingdom is not bound. Such an order can be made by the Home Secretary (subject to court challenge after the event) only in two circumstances: where in his/her opinion the urgency of the situation precludes the seeking of court permission to issue the order or the order was made before 14 March 2005 against an individual who, at the time it was made, was an individual in respect of whom a certificate under section 21(1) of ATCSA was in force (the existing 'Belmarsh' detainees).[51] Otherwise, having decided that there are grounds to make such an order against that individual, he/she must apply to the High Court for permission to make the order. That hearing will generally be *ex parte* (with no representations from the suspect who will generally not even know of the application). The court may only refuse permission to issue an order where it considers that the Home Secretary's decision to go for one on the basis that the test was met was 'obviously flawed' in terms of the principles applicable on judicial review. If permission is granted, the order is made and executed. The court must arrange for a full hearing on the order in which the individual and their lawyer, subject to the security considerations mentioned above, can participate and challenge the order. At that hearing, the court must confirm the order unless satisfied that the decision to make it at all and/or the restrictions to impose is flawed in the light of the principles of judicial review, in which case it can quash it or one or more of the obligations imposed by it, or give directions to the Secretary of State for the revocation of the order or for the modification of the obligations it imposes.[52]

A 'derogating control' order will require an Art. 15 designated derogation order under the HRA approved by both Houses of Parliament.[53] Judicial control is tighter here. The Home Secretary must apply to the High Court for a 'derogating' control order against that person.[54] The Act provides that the putative subject can be arrested and detained by the police where it is thought necessary to ensure that they are available to be given notice of the order if it is made. The person can be so held for up to 48 hours, and the usual rights granted to those arrested under the Terrorism Act 2000, of access to a lawyer and to have someone informed of the detention, apply here without ability to postpone their exercise.[55] Detention thereafter is a matter for the High Court.[56] The court must hold an immediate preliminary hearing on the application (which may be held without the suspect being notified, present or allowed to make representations) to decide whether to make such an order and, if so, to direct the holding of a full hearing to determine whether to confirm the order (with or without modifications). The test to be applied

---

[51] PTA 2005, s. 3(1).

[52] PTA 2005, s. 3(10), (11)

[53] PTA 2005, ss.4 , 6; HRA, s.14(1).

[54] PTA 2005, s. 4

[55] PTA 2005, s. 5(1)–(3)

[56] PTA 2005, s. 5.

by the High Court varies according to whether it is considering the matter at the preliminary hearing of the Home Secretary's application for such an order, or considering at the later full hearing whether to confirm the order issued at that earlier stage. The standard for confirmation is more stringent than for the initial issuing of the order.

At the preliminary hearing, the court in essence

> ... considers whether there is a *prima facie* case for the making of an order ... whether there is a case to answer ... a low threshold for the making of a judicial order which deprives the individual of liberty, particularly when one bears in mind the width of the definition of conduct which is capable of amounting to involvement in terrorism-related activity. It falls far short of a requirement that the court be satisfied itself of the necessity for an individual to be deprived of their liberty.[57]

To delineate more fully the court's powers at this stage, the court may make a control order against the individual in question if it appears to the court (a) that there is material which (if not disproved) is capable of being relied on by the court as establishing that the individual is or has been involved in terrorism-related activity (the *prima facie* case aspect); (b) that there are reasonable grounds for believing that the imposition of obligations on that individual is necessary for purposes connected with protecting members of the public from a risk of terrorism; (c) that the risk arises out of, or is associated with, a public emergency in respect of which there is a designated derogation from the whole or a part of Art. 5 of the ECHR; and (d) that the obligations are or include derogating obligations of a description set out for the purposes of the designated derogation in the designation order. The obligations that may be imposed by a derogating control order at this stage include any obligations which the court has reasonable grounds for considering are necessary for purposes connected with preventing or restricting involvement by that individual in terrorism-related activity.[58]

At the full hearing, higher standards are rightly applicable. The court may confirm the control order (with or without modifications) only if (a) it is satisfied *on the balance of probabilities* that the controlled person is an individual who is or has been involved in terrorism-related activity; (b) *it considers* that the imposition of obligations on the controlled person is necessary for purposes connected with protecting members of the public from a risk of terrorism; (c) it appears to the court that the risk is one arising out of, or is associated with, a public emergency in respect of which there is a designated derogation from the whole or a part of Art. 5 of the ECHR; and (d) the obligations to be imposed by the order or (as the case may be) by the order as modified are or include derogating obligations of a description set out for the purposes of the designated derogation in the designation

---

[57] JHRC 10th (2004–05): para.6.
[58] PTA 2005, s. 4(3), (4).

order. Otherwise it must revoke the order made at the preliminary hearing.[59] A 'derogating' control order lasts for up to six months, unless revoked earlier, but can be renewed for further periods of up to six months.[60]

Use of the Powers: Numbers and Nature of Controlees

Lord Carlile reported that by the end of 2005 18 control orders had been made. The controlees were all male. Only one was a British citizen. By that time, however, there were only nine orders subsisting, only one of which related to a British citizen. Lord Carlile's analysis maintains controlee anonymity, but does so by number, whereas the High Court system of reference deploys letters, as does SIAC for both ATCSA detainees and putative national security deportees. The different systems of reference renders more difficult following through individual subjects, the case against whom has already been encountered when dealing with ATCSA detention, but in what follows some attempt is made to do so. Eight of the 18 controlees were served on 11 August 2005 with notice of intention to deport. Those eight were formerly detainees under ATCSA (A, Abu Quatada (also known as Othman), B, G, H, I, P, K). Their control orders were revoked on 31 August 2005 after their detention for deportation purposes. Four of the eight (A, G, H are identifiable as former ATCSA detainees from SIAC deportation hearings) were later admitted to bail by SIAC using its deportation jurisdiction. Bail was subject to conditions similar to rigorous non-derogating control order obligations. Two former ATCSA detainees (Abu Rideh, E), remained subject to control orders but had not been served with deportation notices. As at 17 May, 2006, 12 orders were in place, four against British citizens. By mid-June, the picture was 14, five of which were in respect of British citizens.[61] By July 2006, 15 control orders were operative. Nine were in respect of foreign nationals while six covered British citizens.[62] As at 16 January 2007 18 orders were operative. Three subjects had by then absconded, three others later.[63] A partial picture of the case against some of the controlees emerges from the three High Court challenges to date. The controlees' denials of, and factual disputes about, that case must be kept in mind, as must the low level of judicial scrutiny involved. Here, even more than with ATCSA, this is in two cases still the Home Secretary's unproven case. The exposition is undertaken merely to give a flavour of the bases on which control order decisions are made and the difficulties in challenging an adverse decision.

In *Re MB*, the controlee was a naturalized British citizen, whose mother had indefinite leave to remain in the United Kingdom. He currently resided with an adult sister. Having considered the papers and met with relevant officials, the

---

[59] PTA 2005, s. 4(5).

[60] PTA 2005, s. 4(5) – (9).

[61] HC Debs, 12 June 2006, col 48WS.

[62] Cm 6888 (2006), para. 77.

[63] Carlile (2007): 8–9; *The Times*, 24 May 2007, 15.

Home Secretary concluded that there were reasonable grounds for suspecting MB to be or have been involved in terrorism-related activity and that a control order was necessary for purposes connected with protecting members of the public against terrorism. Consultations with the Chief Constable of South Yorkshire Police had shown that MB could not successfully be prosecuted for a terrorist offence. The order, insofar as it might interfere with his or his sister's ECHR rights was, moreover, thought by the Home Secretary to be a proportionate restriction on any rights affected. MI5 had assessed MB as an Islamist extremist who had in 2005 attempted to travel to Syria and the Yemen, with a view, MI5 thought, to travel to Iraq to fight against coalition forces. His passport had been confiscated by police when he was detained for examination at Heathrow Airport, having been stopped under the TA 2000 before boarding his flight to the Yemen. Having decided that there were grounds for a non-derogating control order, the Home Secretary applied for and was granted permission to make one in a without notice hearing in the High Court before Ouseley J. At the adversarial hearing Sullivan J considered himself compelled by the terms of the Act and the United Kingdom's legal order to uphold the order, but granted a declaration that the decision-making scheme for non-derogating control orders was incompatible with the fair hearing requirements of the ECHR. The Court of Appeal, however, held that he had underestimated the degree of judicial scrutiny possible and had been wrong to make the declaration of incompatibility.[64]

In *Re JJ and Others*, Sullivan J at the adversarial stage considered the cases of six controlees, all identified (presumably to distinguish them from former ATCSA detainees) by a double letter of the alphabet: JJ, KK, GG, HH, NN, LL. All were subject (with minor variations) to the same set of severe restrictions, set out later. Sullivan J held those restrictions in their totality to amount to a deprivation of liberty and thus not be validly imposed under a non-derogating control order.[65] His decision was upheld as 'compelling' by the Court of Appeal and the Home Secretary's appeal was 'without merit', the degree of restriction – particularly the 18-hour curfew – were clearly on the wrong side of the dividing line between deprivation of liberty (not permissible under a non-derogating control order) and restriction on movement (the proper ambit of such an order).[66] The Court of Appeal refused the Home Secretary leave to appeal to the House of Lords but he successfully petitioned their lordships for leave and the case will be heard later in 2007.[67] So far the focus has solely been on the Convention rights aspect and full details of the case against the six controlees have yet to emerge. They are all single men, live alone, and have no family in the United Kingdom. Five are Iraqi asylum

---

[64] *Secretary of State for the Home Department* v *MB* [2006] EWCA Civ 1140. See chapter 9.

[65] *Secretary of State for the Home Department* v *JJ and Others* [2006] EWHC 1623 (Admin), Annex II (Statement of Agreed Facts).

[66] *Secretary of State for the Home Department* v *JJ and Others* [2006] EWCA Civ 1141.

[67] Ford (2006).

seekers thought by the Home Secretary to have come to the United Kingdom to perpetrate terrorist attacks on civilians.[68] It is unclear whether the sixth is an Iranian or Iraqi national.[69]

E, a Tunisian, is a former ATCSA detainee subject to a non-derogating control order since March 2005. His degree of restriction was less extensive than those in *Re JJ and Others*. In February 2007 Beatson J found the national security case against him established to the low standard required by the PTA scheme. But he quashed the order as an illegitimate restriction on liberty not permitted in a non-derogating control order. He stayed his quashing order to allow the Home Secretary time to consider an appeal, leave for which Beatson J was minded to grant.[70] The appeal was heard by the Court of Appeal late in April 2007. Judgment was awaited at the time of going to press.

Use of Non-derogating Control Orders: the Severity of the Restrictions Imposed

Most, but not all controlees, have, with minor variations, been subject to a severe range of restrictions. These were successfully impugned in respect of six controlees (PTA 14–19 in Lord Carlile's system) in *Re JJ and Others* as incompatible with the protection afforded deprivation of liberty by Art. 5 ECHR (and thus needing either modification of their severity or embodiment in a derogating control order).[71] Lord Carlile had viewed them as on the cusp of needing a derogating control order. The JHRC presciently thought the line had been crossed. Similar but less extensive restrictions (with his curfew hours reduced to 12 after that decision) were successfully challenged in *Secretary of State for the Home Department v E*.[72] Backing up these obligations, it will be recalled that contravention of an obligation in a control order, without reasonable excuse, is a serious criminal offence.[73]

The restrictions applicable to most controlees require the fitting and wearing at all times of an electronic monitoring tag. Such a controlee must reside at a specified address (sometimes their own home, but often a flat nominated by the Home Office) and is subject to curfew rules in that they have to remain *inside* that house or flat for 18 hours per day (now reduced to 10–14) except between the hours of 10 a.m. and 4 p.m. If the place of 'residence' is a flat, they cannot during those hours use the communal spaces in the block to which outsiders (non-residents in the block) might have unrestricted access or, if the residence was a house or bungalow, they cannot during the curfew hours use its outside space. Every day, they must report by a specially provided telephone line to the identified

---

[68] *Secretary of State for the Home Department v JJ and others* [2006] EWCA Civ 1141, para. 3; Travis (2006); Morris (2006).

[69] [2006] EWCA Civ 1141, para. 3.

[70] [2007] EWHC (Admin) 233.

[71] See chapter 9.

[72] [2007 EWHC (Admin) 233.

[73] PTA 2005, s. 9.

monitoring company on the first occasion they leave the residence after the curfew is over and on the last occasion that day when they return to it before the curfew period recommences. Of the six cases considered in *Re JJ*, only GG remained in his own home, a one-bedroom council flat. The others lived in one-bedroom flats to which the authorities took them. They were between 11 and 20 miles from previous homes.[74]

There are restrictions on having visitors to the residence. The controlee can permit, without specific Home Office approval, the entry of their nominated legal adviser (as notified to the Home Office), anyone required to be given access under the tenancy agreement for the residence (a copy of which agreement has to be supplied to the Home Office), and, but only in an emergency, healthcare or social work professionals or members of the emergency services. Such persons can bring a mobile phone with them, provided that it remains switched off at all times when the controlee is in the residence; if it remains on the controlee breaches their obligations with respect to communications' equipment, examined later. Otherwise, no other visitor is allowed save with the prior approval of the Home Office. Once 'approved', that visitor does not need prior Home Office approval for subsequent visits, but the Home Office can withdraw 'approved' status at any time. To gain a visitor that status, the controlee must supply the Home Office with the would-be visitor's name, address, date of birth and photographic identity. Before permission is granted, presumably that individual will be vetted and 'cleared' by the police and Security Service.

There are restrictions on pre-arranged meetings outside the residence in the non-curfew period. The controlee cannot by prior arrangement meet anyone outside the residence apart from their legal adviser (already named to the Home Office) or for health and welfare purposes someone at an establishment on a list provided to and agreed with the Home Office in advance of the first visit there. It is made clear that a meeting outside the residence takes place even where only someone other than the controlee is outside (for example, communicating through a window or a door). Nor can the controlee without prior Home Office agreement attend any pre-arranged meetings or gatherings save attending group prayers at a mosque. A number of controlees[75] are specifically prohibited from leading prayers at a mosque. In either case, the choice of mosque is limited to the one approved by the Home Office prior to the controlee's first visit.

Communication or association whether direct or indirect, at any time or in any way, with certain named individuals is prohibited. Thus JJ, KK, GG, HH and NN were each prohibited from communicating or associating with the other four, while the order against LL identified the other five. For monitoring purposes, a controlee must permit entry (on proper identification) to the residence to police officers, persons authorized by the Home Secretary or by the monitoring company, so that

---

[74] [2006] EWHC 1623 (Admin), Annex II (Statement of Agreed Facts).

[75] Certainly HH and GG: see *Secretary of State for the Home Department* v *JJ and Others* [2006] EWHC 1623 (Admin), Annex I.

such officers or persons can verify the controlee's presence there and/or ensure his/her compliance with the obligations imposed by the control order. A non-exhaustive definition of 'monitoring' includes: a search of the residence; photographing the controlee (presumably to make for up-to-date records of changed appearance); removal of any item; inspection, modification or removal for such inspection or modification of any article to ensure that it does not breach the obligations imposed by the control order; and permitting the installation of such equipment (CCTV or sound-detecting devices, for example) as may be considered necessary to ensure compliance with those obligations.

To restrict communication with the outside world or prohibited individuals, a controlee cannot bring into or permit in the residence any communications equipment or equipment capable of connecting to the internet or components thereof (including but not limited to mobile phones, fax machines, pagers, computers and public telephone and/or internet facilities). Nor can they use or keep, directly or indirectly, any such equipment, whether in or outside the residence. This would prohibit use of a phone box, a payphone in a restaurant or of an internet cafe. However, apart from the dedicated line maintained by the monitoring company, they are permitted to maintain and use no more than one fixed telephone line, but that telephone must on request be delivered up to someone authorized by the Home Secretary for inspection and approval prior to it being permitted to be in or remain in the residence. It is emphasized that the controlee must not connect to or use by any means directly or indirectly the internet at any time. Nor may they use or keep, nor whilst they are is in the residence permit any person to use, any mobile phone in the residence.

The controlee is subject to tight restriction with respect to bank accounts, the transfer of money and the sending of documents or goods. They can only maintain a single account with a bank or other approved financial institution within the United Kingdom. They must supply the authorities with a variety of information depending on precise financial circumstances: with details of all accounts held at the time of service of the control order, within two days of such service; with closing statements relating to any accounts additional to the one permitted account, within 14 days of service of the control order; or, if no account is held at the time of service of the control order but one is opened subsequently, with details of that account, within two days of its opening. In addition, statements of the permitted account on a monthly basis must be provided within seven days of receipt. They cannot transfer any money, or send any documents or goods to a destination outside the United Kingdom (whether themselves or through an intermediary) without the prior agreement of the Home Office.

There are also extensive travel restrictions. All passports, identity cards or other travel documents must be surrendered to the authorities within 24 hours of service of the control order. An exception is made for any genuine passport issued by the Iraqi authorities, but any such passport in the controlee's possession or available for their use must be notified to the Home Office. In addition, prior notification must be given to the Home Office before the controlee may apply for or have in their possession any passport, identity card, travel document(s) or travel ticket which would enable them to travel outside the United Kingdom. A controlee is banned from entering or being present at any airport, sea port, or any part of a railway station that provides access to an international rail service, unless in each case they have prior permission from the Home Office. Such restrictions are, of course, directed to travelling overseas, to leaving the country. In addition, however, a controlee may not go outside the boundaries of a defined geographical area, indicated on a map forming Annex A to the control order, within the United Kingdom. In terms of the six individuals considered by Sullivan J in *Re JJ*, those areas varied in size (41 sq kms [JJ], 32.5 sq kms [KK], 60 sq kms [GG], 62 sq kms [HH] and 72 sq kms [NN]). In each case the areas contain at least a mosque and a hospital, primary care facilities, shops and entertainment and sporting facilities.[76]

A number of controlees have been subject to a lesser range of restrictions. Male 1 (to use Lord Carlile's reference system), one of the former ATCSA detainees subjected to a control order immediately the PTA 2005 entered into force (1 March 2005), had his tagging obligation removed after entering an appeal about it. Male 12 (MB), a British citizen, was not subject to curfew or tag, and was allowed to work normal hours. His obligations under the control order (as modified in minor respects for clarification purposes by Ouseley J at the without notice hearing) are: to reside at [address given] ('the residence') and give the Home Office at least seven days' prior notice of any change of residence; to report in person to his local police station (the location of which was notified in writing to him at the imposition of the order) each day at a time notified in writing by his contact officer according to written details provided on service of the order; to surrender passport, identity card or any other travel document to a police officer or persons authorized by the Secretary of State within 24 hours; not to apply for or have in his possession any passport, identity card, travel document(s) or travel ticket which would enable him to travel abroad; not to leave the country; not to enter or be present at any airport or sea port or any part of a railway station that provides access to an international rail service; at any time to allow into the residence, on production of identification, police officers and persons authorized by the Secretary of State, to verify his presence at the residence and/or to ensure that he can comply with and his complying with the obligations imposed by the control order. Such monitoring may include but is not limited to a search of the residence, removal of any item to ensure compliance with the remainder of the obligations in these orders, and the taking of his photograph.[77]

A number of very proper concerns have been raised about control orders and their decision-making and judicial supervision regimes, since the Bill that became the PTA 2005 was first published, both by scrutiny/review individuals or bodies and by NGOs and other organizations giving evidence to them or in briefing papers for press, MPs and peers. Insofar as these concerns have translated into litigation,

---

[76] [2006] EWHC 1623 (Admin), Annex II (Statement of Agreed Facts).

[77] *Re MB* [2006] EWHC 1000 (Admin), para. 18.

they are examined in depth in chapter 9. A pervading concern is the lack of 'equality of arms' in the decision–making process, its subordination of due process to security concerns, something more fully explored in chapters 8 (powers and process) and 9 (legal and human rights challenges).[78] But concern with 'fair hearing' issues embraces here, more obviously than with ATCSA detention or national security deportation, issues of an ineffective level of judicial scrutiny, particularly with respect to non-derogating control orders and the 'without notice' (preliminary hearing) stage with respect to derogating ones.[79] Another concern is the imposition of restrictions amounting to deprivation of liberty in non-derogating control orders; when coupled with the delays in the system of adversarial hearings and further appeals, this may well mean restriction, akin to imprisonment in an Open Prison, under an 'invalid' order for several years. Even if invalidity is confirmed by the House of Lords, the process of restriction could continue in 'cat and mouse' fashion by reducing the degree of restriction or transferring the controlee to the deportation sector. After the Court of Appeal upheld Sullivan J's invalidation of the control orders in *Re JJ and others* and refused the Home Secretary leave to appeal to the Lords, the Home Secretary reluctantly reduced the curfew to 14 hours and relaxed some of the restrictions on visitors, while indicating that he would seek leave to appeal from the House of Lords itself. It remains arguable that even these reduced restrictions fall on the wrong side of the deprivation of liberty line, the Court of Appeal in its judgment having referred to ECHR jurisprudence upholding a 12-hour curfew coupled with a curfew throughout the weekend.[80] And the option remains, if all else fails, of validating in a derogating control order yet more extensive restrictions by derogating from Art. 5 ECHR. Even where restrictions fall short of deprivation of liberty, one can readily see from the survey of those imposed, varying degrees of interference with a number of other ECHR rights; not just those of the controlee but of their family and associates: the right of the individual, their partner and any children to respect for family life (Art. 8); the right of those and single controlees to respect for home, private life (social relationships) and correspondence (Art. 8); freedom of conscience and religion (restrictions on worship but particularly leading prayers) (Art. 9); freedom of expression (worship, leading prayers, communication – the right to impart and receive information and ideas) (Art. 10); freedom of assembly and association (restrictions on visitors, on communicating with named persons, on attending gatherings or pre-arranged meetings) (Art. 11); property rights (entry to the home, removal of equipment, restrictions on bank accounts) (Art. 1 of Protocol One ECHR).[81] None of these, of course, are absolute rights, but the terms of

---

[78] JHRC 12th (2005–06): App. 7, paras (c), (d) (Liberty).

[79] Ibid, paras. 63–68; App. 5, paras 4–5, 11–21 (Justice); App. 6, pp. 49–50 (The Law Society); App. 7, paras (c), (d) (Liberty).

[80] Travis (2006). '

[81] JHRC 12th (2005–06): para. 85; App. 4, pp. 38–9 (Campaign Against Criminalising Communities); App. 5, para. 5 (Justice); App. 6, pp. 48–9 (The Law Society); App. 7, pp.

permissible restriction under the ECHR raise issues of proportionality between legitimate aim (protection of the rights of others, national security) and means (the degree of restriction – no more than necessary or overkill). The prohibition of discrimination (Art. 14) continues to be relevant even though the powers, unlike those successfully impugned in ATCSA, can and are being used against both British and foreign nationals. The JHRC in mid-February 2006 noted that the limited use against British nationals (then only one out of 18 orders) raised that spectre.[82] Moreover, even enhanced use against British nationals does not remove the possibility of discrimination: all controlees are male, all are Islamic.[83] There are again grave concerns in terms of the physical and mental health effects on the controlee and their family, with several lawyers and NGO's raising again the issue of possible inhuman and degrading treatment contrary to Art. 3 ECHR.[84] Issues under Arts 3 and 8 ECHR were considered by Beatson J in February 2007 in *Secretary of State for the Home Department* v *E*.[85] He found neither breached.[86]

Immigration Powers: Refusal of Entry and Deportation; Limiting Asylum Rights in Respect of the Refugee Convention

The terms of the Home Secretary's powers under immigration law to refuse entry to the country or deport from it undesirable 'aliens', including those who threaten national security, remained unchanged after 9/11. He/she and his/her immigration officers can refuse entry to those whose presence would not be conducive to the public good, and can remove those whose deportation is deemed conducive to the public good. Adding, as would be usual in terrorism or national security cases, that the decision to deport was for reasons of national security, international relations with another state or international organization, or for other reasons of a political nature is, in legal terms, effective merely for removing appellate scrutiny from the standard immigration appeals system and placing the matter instead in the hands of SIAC. In terms of legal change as regards appellate challenge, the trend has also been in the direction of curtailing in-country rights of appeal and narrowing the

---

53–7 (Liberty); App 7, pp. 70–8 (Liberty – redacted witness Statement by Gareth Pierce, Solicitor for many of the former ATCSA detainees); App. 9 (Ann Alexander, Scotland Against Criminalising Communities); App. 10 (Tyndalwoods Solicitors, evidence from a controlee).

[82] Ibid, paras 87–8.

[83] Art. 14 ECHR covers discrimination on any ground including sex and religion. The matter raises comparable issues to those about the use of stop and search powers under the TA 2000, on which see HAC 6th (2004–05): chap. 6. For the Government's response see Cm 6593 (2005).

[84] JHRC 12th (2005–06): paras 79–84; App.7, para. 11(a) and paras 37–9 of Annex 3 (Liberty).

[85] [2007] EWHC (Admin) 233.

[86] See chapter 9.

grounds on which an appellate authority can overturn an executive decision in this area of security and asylum.

A deportation order requires its subject to leave the United Kingdom and enables their detention until removed. It also prohibits them from re–entering the country for as long as it is in force and invalidates any leave to enter or remain in the United Kingdom given them before the Order is made or while it is in force. Detention pending deportation is only valid so long as deportation is a feasible prospect and being diligently pursued. Removing someone from the country to another state by turning them away at a port or airport or by deporting them there cannot be effected where there are substantial grounds for believing that if returned there they face a real risk of treatment contrary to Art. 3 ECHR (torture, inhuman or degrading treatment or punishment) whether at the hands of State or non-State actors (the *Chahal* principle). Nor can removal be effected without breaching Convention Rights if they face the death penalty there.

Where criminal prosecution is not possible, deportation remains a central plank in the *Prevent* and *Pursue* strands of Government's counter-terrorism strategy.[87] It is thought important not only in ensuring public safety by thus disrupting terrorist activity, but also by deterring those who would come to the United Kingdom for terrorist purposes by sending a strong signal that foreign nationals who threaten its security by facilitating or engaging in terrorism, will, if they manage to gain entry, be removed. Persons outside the United Kingdom who threaten its security will normally be excluded from obtaining a visa, entry clearance or entry to the United Kingdom.[88]

The formal Immigration Rules have never elaborated very much on the behaviour which will render someone's presence in the United Kingdom 'not conducive to the public good' or render their deportation from the country 'conducive to the public good'. As regards refusal of entry, the Rules merely note that entry clearance (including visa) or entry to the United Kingdom is to be refused to a person (a) where the Home Secretary has personally directed that the exclusion of that person from the United Kingdom is conducive to the public good,[89] or (b) where, from information available to the Immigration Officer, it seems right to refuse leave to enter on the ground that exclusion from the United Kingdom is conducive to the public good; if, for example, in the light of the character, conduct or associations of the person seeking leave to enter it is undesirable to give them leave to enter.[90] With respect to deportation, the Rules elaborate only on process: while each case will be considered on its merits, where a person is liable to deportation the presumption shall be that the public interest requires deportation. The Home Secretary will consider all relevant factors in considering whether the presumption is outweighed in any particular case,

---

[87] See chapter 9.
[88] Cm 6888 (2006): pp. 12, 18.
[89] Rule 320.6.
[90] Rule 320.19.

although it will only be in exceptional circumstances that the public interest in deportation will be outweighed in a case where to deport would not be contrary to the ECHR and the Convention and Protocol relating to the Status of Refugees. The aim is an exercise of the power of deportation which is consistent and fair as between one person and another, although one case will rarely be identical with another in all material respects.[91] However, a deportation order will not be made against any person if their removal in pursuance of the order would be contrary to the United Kingdom's obligations under the Convention and Protocol relating to the Status of Refugees or the ECHR.[92] Past practice showed that deportation on public good grounds was effected with respect to persons convicted of criminal offences, who posed threats to public order or national security, including suspected terrorists (see chapter 4). After 7/7, however, it was decided to broaden the range of behaviours by producing a supplementary list of unacceptable behaviours likely to result in exclusion or deportation on public good grounds. That list embraces any non-British citizen who uses any medium to express views which: foment, justify or glorify terrorist violence in furtherance of particular beliefs; seek to provoke others to terrorist acts; foment other serious criminal activity or seek to provoke others to serious criminal acts; or foster hatred which might lead to inter-community violence in the United Kingdom. 'Any medium' includes: writing, producing, publishing or distributing material; public speaking including preaching; running a website; or using a position of responsibility such as teacher, community or youth leader.[93]

The number of national security deportations has always been small, and they have over the years been high profile and controversial cases (see chapter 4). The Newton Committee, when reviewing ATCSA detention, noted in 2003 that 'there have been no successful deportations on national security grounds since 1997'.[94]

In its July 2006 counter-terrorism strategy document, Government reported that since August 2005, 36 foreign nationals had been excluded (banned from, or refused, entry) on grounds of such unacceptable behaviour. In another case a decision in principle had been made to deport on the basis of such unacceptable behaviour and four other cases were under consideration.[95] Since 7/7, 38 foreign nationals have been detained pending deportation on national security grounds and another person, in custody prior to 7/7, also awaits such deportation. Two of the 38 have already been deported to Algeria, four are facing criminal prosecution and another six (JJ, KK, GG, HH, NN and LL) were instead made the subject of non-derogating control orders after it was decided that their deportation was not a realistic prospect. As at July 2006, there were thus 26 individuals facing national security deportation. Some were in custody, others subject to effective house arrest

---

[91] Rule 364.

[92] Rule 380.

[93] Cm 6888 (2006): para 50.

[94] Newton Committee (2003): para. 197 (n.99).

[95] Cm 6888 (2006): para 50.

under bail conditions more restrictive than those imposable under a non-derogating control order. Since then SIAC has upheld the deportation of BB, Y and G to Algeria and approved that of Abu Qatada to Jordan.[96]

We have so far identified a number of those facing deportation as former ATCSA detainees. Although appeals in respect of national security deportations are still in progress, some information on the nature of the case against the others emerges from the open judgments of SIAC so far available. That information is provided here subject to the same caveats as governed that on ATCSA detainees and PTA controlees.

MK was born in Algeria in 1973 but became a French citizen. He was served with a deportation order on 23 September 2004 and was from then detained under immigration legislation, pending deportation to France on national security grounds, until his admission to bail by SIAC on 24 May 2005. SIAC considered that the threat to national security and any danger of absconding could be met by release on bail subject to strict conditions comparable to a modified version of those imposed in the control order on Abu Rideh. There was thus no restriction on his going into an enclosed garden if there was one with his house. His curfew-free hours are from 10a.m. until 4 p.m., but he has to report daily to a specific police station between noon and 2 p.m., and he is subject to a SIAC-defined area limit outside of which he must not move without specific Home Office consent. Bail was subject to two sureties. The passport condition applied and he must not to apply for any travel tickets enabling him to travel outside the restricted area without Home Office consent. As regards the national security case against MK, SIAC rejected his appeal. Having considered the open and closed material, it concluded that on the open material alone, there were substantial grounds for believing he was a member (but not a prominent member) of the Abu Doha group as originally formed and as subsequently reconstituted. It was not able to decide what precise role he played nor precisely what activities he engaged in, but considered that there were substantial grounds for believing he used or allowed his passport to be used for activities connected with the 'group', that he had links with and associates with active extremists (including several ATCSA detainees and others now held for deportation) and that it could be inferred from his long residence in the United Kingdom that he acted as a link man and supporter for extremists in the United Kingdom. There was no evidence in the open material to establish that he travelled, using his passport, for terrorist activities. However, it was satisfied that one of the reasons why he achieved membership of and sustained such a long association with a group of extremists was the use to which he could put his passport. He had breached some of his bail conditions in terms of pre-arranged meetings and going outside the restricted area without permission. A factual basis had been established as regards allegations that he had undergone military training in Afghanistan at a terrorist training camp; travelled to Pakistan and Afghanistan for terrorist purposes; had been a member of, associated with, and

---

[96] See chapter 9.

thereby supported, a network of extremists operating in the United Kingdom and providing logistical support to terrorists in Afghanistan, Algeria and Chechnya; had been a member of, associated with, and thereby supported, a network of extremists operating in the United Kingdom who had obtained funds to support terrorist activities, including those involved with the ricin plot in the United Kingdom and in the plots to bomb the Los Angeles airport and the Strasbourg Christmas market. SIAC was not, however, satisfied that he had engaged in fraudulent activity other than by allowing others to use his passport. [97]

T, an Algerian, came to the United Kingdom on a forged French passport. He is a failed asylum seeker, with an Algerian wife (also a failed asylum seeker) and children in the United Kingdom. He was not certificated or detained under ATCSA. Nor was he a PTA 2005 controlee. That national security case against him is more generalized than some of the others. It rests on association with P, an ATCSA detainee and subsequent PTA 2005 controlee who was part of the Abu Doha group, and with individuals convicted of or awaiting trial on terrorism charges. The Home Secretary also alleged that T received terrorist training in Afghanistan. SIAC admitted him to bail on 20 October 2005.[98] His 'merits' appeal awaits determination.

Q had been certificated under ATCSA, but his appeal against it was adjourned pending the resolution of criminal proceedings in which he was convicted and sentenced to a total of three years on fraud charges. He was released on licence in January 2005 into SIAC detention pending deportation and remained on licence until 23 October 2005. During the licence period he married a Slovak citizen resident in the United Kingdom. The substance of the national security case against him concerns alleged involvement in logistical support (fraudulent fund-raising, the procurement of false documents) for a variety of Islamic terrorist networks and facilitating travel to Afghanistan for terrorist training. He was said to have been involved with those acquitted of the ricin plot. SIAC refused to grant him bail on 20 October 2005. His 'merits' appeal was later withdrawn and he has returned to Algeria.

BB is an Algerian who left Algeria in 1992. He arrived in the United Kingdom in 1995 with six months' leave. Contact with him was lost until he was arrested on some other basis in 1999, whereupon he claimed political asylum, a claim as yet unresolved. He was arrested in September 2003 on Terrorism Act charges (later withdrawn) and other charges. He pleaded guilty to false passport charges, was sentenced to three months' imprisonment on those, and was released in mid-July 2004 on temporary admission on the expiry of his sentence. He was on weekly and then monthly reporting until his arrest following the notice of intention to deport on 30 September 2003. He has an Algerian wife (a failed asylum seeker) and three children aged 3, 2 and about 6 months. Without disclosing the nature of the

---

[97] SIAC Appeal No: SC/29/2004: judgment (bail) 24 May 2005; judgment (merits) 19 May.

[98] SIAC Appeal Nos. SC/33–39/2005.

national security case, SIAC on 20 December 2005 declined to admit him to bail given the strength of that case and the danger of absconding.[99] On 5 December 2006 SIAC decided there were reasonable grounds for regarding him as a threat to national security and sanctioned his deportation to Algeria.[100]

PP arrived in the United Kingdom around September 2003, using a genuine French passport but one to which he was not entitled in his true identity. He was using a false identity. He gave an account of how that came about and how he acquired the genuine French passport. He has continued to use the false identity contained in that French passport in the United Kingdom since his arrival. He used it in the Islamic marriage ceremony that he went through in April 2004 in this country to a Dutch citizen of Somali origin (deceiving her as to his true identity) and continued to use it through his life with her and her son. He returned to Algeria in September/October 2005 for a visit which was said to be to an unwell mother and returned to the United Kingdom using the same genuine passport that did not reflect, again, his true identity. He was again travelling on a false identity. His true identity only came out when he was questioned by the Immigration Service and Special Branch. It was claimed that he posed a risk to national security because of his use of a false identity and his links to a group of Algerian extremists in France, including links to his brothers, one of whom is in custody (apparently because he cannot get a surety), the other of whom has been released pending trial because it is not thought that the charges leading to conviction would warrant any significant custodial sentence. He claimed asylum following his return from Algeria on the grounds that he fears the GIA in Algeria, because of extortion threats and payments made by him to them under duress in the past, and is now said also to fear the Algerian Government, because of the detention on national security and the claims by the Secretary of State. The decision on that claim was awaited when SIAC refused to admit him to bail in March 2006.[101]

OO is a Jordanian national who arrived in the UK in 1997, followed by his wife who is now a British citizen, as are their eight children, the youngest of whom, aged 16, 11 and 9, live at home. OO was arrested on 26 January 2006, the Secretary of State giving notice of intention to deport him to Jordan. He was taken to HMP Belmarsh. Despite his poor health, bail was refused by SIAC on 10 April 2006 because of the strength of the national security case (not elaborated on) and danger of absconding.[102]

Y, a 33-year-old Algerian, said to have come to the United Kingdom on a false passport, is a successful asylum seeker, given on appeal indefinite leave to remain in 2001. He was arrested in 2003 in respect of the ricin plot but acquitted and released from custody in April 2005. He was on bail for five months living in National Asylum Support Service (NASS) accommodation and complied with the

---

[99] SIAC Appeal No. SC/39/05.
[100] See chapter 9.
[101] SIAC Appeal No. SCB/34/05 (Ref TRS 147/06).
[102] SIAC Appeal No. SC/51/2006 (Ref TRS 159/06).

limited bail requirements then imposed. He was not made subject of a control order. He is not married, but is engaged to a fiancée he met during the trial. According to the Home Secretary, he is subject to two sentences of life imprisonment and one of death passed in Algeria in his absence, following convictions in his absence for terrorist-related offences. His extradition is, apparently, sought. Medical evidence supported allegations of torture in Algeria. He suffers from low mood and a sense of helplessness. On 16 December 2005, SIAC considered that the threat to national security and the danger of absconding could be adequately met by bail conditions.[103] On 14 August 2006, SIAC found him to be a threat to national security and permitted his deportation to Algeria.[104] On 29 September 2006 it refused to admit him to bail.

X arrived in the United Kingdom in 1995 on false French documents. He is a failed asylum seeker, who gained exceptional leave to remain on medical and compassionate grounds. He had indefinite leave to remain since 9 December 2002. He married in February 2004 an Algerian national, who arrived in the United Kingdom in 2004 and made a claim, not yet determined, to stay as the dependant of her brother. They have no children. He has lived for the last two years at the same local authority address. Medical reports suggest that he is obese or considerably overweight and has been for some time. There is some evidence of past acts of self-harm, though he is not at present on suicide watch. He is vulnerable to stress and anxiety and very fearful of return to Algeria. He has had a psychiatric illness for ten years. The national security case against him relates to his alleged involvement in the ricin plot, although the criminal case against him was abandoned in October 2003. It also relates to other groups with whom he is allegedly involved and to the contacts that he has. SIAC thought it ill–advised to express particular views about that second part of the national security case, but indicated that, in so far as it relies on the ricin plot and evidence from Meguerba (an alleged participant in the plot), it had some doubts. Nonetheless the danger that if bailed he would engage in acts prejudicial to national security grounded SIAC's refusal of bail on 16 December 2005.

AA (Sihali) is also an Algerian, who initially entered the United Kingdom on false documents and re-entered, having failed to get into Spain, using a false name and a relative's French passport. He was brought into the criminal process in 2002 on charges of possession of false documents for terrorist purposes (most of which were later dropped) and in connection with the ricin poison plot. He was acquitted of the conspiracy but he pleaded guilty to two counts of possession of false passports. He was sentenced to 15 months' imprisonment, which led to his immediate release following the acquittals in April 2005. He was then detained under immigration law while his outstanding asylum claim was determined. He was granted immigration bail on not very onerous terms, there being no suggestion then that he posed a threat to national security. He was detained again in

---

[103] SIAC Appeal No. SC/33 to 38, 41/2005.
[104] See chapter 9.

September 2005 when the Home Secretary decided to make a deportation order based on the expectation of the conclusion of an appropriate Memorandum of Understanding so as to permit his return to Algeria. On 16 December 2005, SIAC decided that conditional bail would suffice to deal with the national security threat. SIAC allowed his 'merits' appeal in May 2007, finding insignificant any threat he could pose to national security. It also held that deportation to Algeria would not have been barred by ECHR obligations.[105]

Z, an overstayer, is another Algerian, with an Algerian wife and two young children in the United Kingdom. Although his solicitor claimed he was living openly, SIAC rejected that evidence and proceeded on the basis that he had gone into hiding when ATCSA was enacted and retained the ability to abscond. Given that, and a strong national security case against him based on GIA connections, it refused him bail on 16 December 2005. In May 2007, SIAC held deportation to Algeria was not precluded by ECHR obligations.

W is a 34-year-old Algerian, an illegal entrant whose asylum claim had still to determined when SIAC admitted him to bail in December 2005. He had been brought into the criminal process in connection with the ricin plot, but was acquitted as part of the second group of defendants following the jury verdicts of not guilty on the first group in April 2005, whereupon he was detained under immigration law but in May was admitted to immigration bail. He was re-arrested in September 2005 but no control order was made. Although there was a national security case to answer, SIAC considered that the dangers of absconding could be met by bail conditions, and suggested that the address he should live at not be one near the Finsbury Park mosque. In May 2007, SIAC held deportation to Algeria was not precluded by ECHR obligations.

V's identity and nationality are uncertain. The first time he sought entry and asylum he claimed to be Palestinian. The second time he sought entry having been returned from Ireland on false French identity papers, he made an unsuccessful asylum claim as a Libyan. Nonetheless he was granted exceptional leave to remain until December 2002. In January 2003 he was arrested in connection with the ricin plot. He remained in the criminal process in custody until released into immigration detention in April 2005, when he was acquitted as part of the second group of defendants. He was released on immigration bail in May 2005. He went through the asylum claim, trial process and application for immigration bail as a Libyan national. Shortly afterwards, he said in an attempt to make a clear breast of his position, that he was someone called V, an Algerian. It is not accepted yet or denied by the Secretary of State that he is that man. He was taken into detention again on 15 September 2005 on notice of intention to make a deportation order covering both identities and both nationalities. The uncertainty over identity and an ability to gain access to false documents and to funds meant a real risk of absconding. This, coupled with a national security case founded on 'closed' material persuaded SIAC, in this marginal case, not to grant bail. Interesting

---

[105] SC/38/2005 (judgment 14 May 2007).

questions will arise in his outstanding appeals both on that national security case and on fear of return to Algeria or Libya.

CC is a 46-year-old Libyan, with indefinite leave to remain as a refugee. His wife appears stateless, one of his three children is a British citizen and another entitled to register as such. He was arrested in October 2005, on the basis of the Home Secretary's notice of detention to deport. A Memorandum of Understanding was concluded between Libya and the UK on 18 October 2005. The Libyan Islamic Fighting Group of which the Secretary of State says the applicant is a prominent member was proscribed on 14 October 2005. CC has never been subject to ATCSA certification or detention or to a control order. His good record of compliance with immigration requirements throughout his period in the United Kingdom, and his strong interest in making a successful appeal on the 'merits', 'family life' and 'fear of return' aspects of his appeal caused SIAC to admit him to bail on 16 December 2005.

Refugee Status: Solely an Executive Decision?

It will have been noted that a number of ATCSA detainees, PTA controlees and putative national security deportees have made asylum claims, some successful, some not. ATCSA, section 33 – now repealed and replaced in terms by section 55 of the Immigration, Nationality and Asylum Act 2006 – impacted significantly on asylum claims, essentially preventing the proper substantive determination of an asylum claim if it is deemed that the exclusion clauses apply or if the person concerned is considered to be a danger to national security in accordance with Art. 33(2) of the Refugee Convention. Further restriction was effected by section 72 of the Nationality, Immigration and Asylum Act 2002, subsection (2) of which stipulates that someone shall be presumed to have been convicted by a final judgment of a particularly serious crime and to constitute a danger to the community of the United Kingdom if they are (a) convicted in the United Kingdom of an offence, and (b) sentenced to a period of imprisonment of at least two years. Subsection (4) is more far-reaching in not requiring such a sentence. It states that a person will also 'be presumed to have been convicted by a final judgment of a particularly serious crime and to constitute a danger to the community of the United Kingdom if ... convicted of an offence specified by order of the Secretary of State'. The Home has specified a raft of specific offences under the anti-terrorist legislation. In addition, section 54 of the Immigration, Nationality and Asylum Act 2006 dictates an interpretation of Art. 1F (c) of the Refugee Convention relating to the Status of Refugees, by specifying that 'acts contrary to the purposes and principles of the United Nations' which will result in exclusion from asylum include acts of committing, preparing or instigating terrorism and acts of encouraging or inducing others to commit, prepare or instigate terrorism. All of these provisions are open to the criticism that they may deprive someone of refugee protection for relatively minor offences, such as the destruction of identity documents without reasonable excuse (an offence punishable with up to two years' imprisonment) and criminal damage and minor theft, which are specified offences. The Refugee Convention, unlike Art. 3 ECHR, does not afford absolute protection when faced with claims about risks to national security or engagement in terrorism, heightening the important role of that Article for those facing national security deportation.

Section 33 ATCSA empowered the Home Secretary to certify that the asylum claimant was not entitled to protection from *refoulement* under Art. 33(1) of the Refugee Convention because of Art. 1F and Art. 33(2) and that removal from the United Kingdom would be conducive to the public good. In such a case, the individual may only appeal to SIAC. It can only consider the statements made in the Home Secretary's certificate and not the substantive asylum claim (whether the person has a well-founded fear of persecution). If SIAC upholds the certificate, the Home Secretary can proceed to remove the person concerned from the UK, but if SIAC concludes that the certificate is unjustified then the Home Secretary is required to consider the substance of the claim. Information about the kind of reasons used to make such certificates can be gleaned from the cases of ATCSA detainees (B, C) examined in that section of this chapter. As Cholewinski points out, this system thus leaving the decision on the substance of the asylum application to executive discretion 'is inconsistent with the structure of the Convention, the UNHCR Handbook and the subsequent 2003 Guidelines on Application of the Exclusion Clauses as well as previous authority in the UK, which all point to the need to consider the substantive claim first before a view is taken regarding exclusion'.[106] The section removed the need to strike a balance between the nature of the offence presumed to have been committed by the applicant and the degree of persecution feared. As Blake and Husain point out, these provisions reversed the modest restraints available previously and articulated in the Court of Appeal's judgment in *Chahal* where the Home Secretary had to weigh up national security interests with the gravity of the harm faced if the individual had been excluded from protection. The centrality of Art. 3 ECHR and the *Chahal* principle is thus confirmed, both for the Home Secretary who seeks national security deportation and the putative deportees seeking to prevent return to a country where they fear they will face death, torture, inhuman or degrading treatment or punishment. In-country appeals are now confined to this sole issue. Other aspects of the appeal can only be dealt with after removal.[107]

Complying with or Changing the Chahal Principle

This, it will be recalled, states that a State will breach its Art. 3 ECHR obligations if it removes someone to a country where there are substantial grounds for believing that, if returned there, they face a real risk of torture, inhuman or

---

[106] Bonner and Cholewinski (2006): 171.

[107] Nationality, Immigration and Asylum Act 2002, s. 97A inserted by Immigration, Asylum and Nationality Act 2006, s. 7.

degrading treatment or punishment, whether at the hands of State or non-State actors. It is absolute and permits of no exception for national security. It affords the individual greater protection than the Refugee Convention. But it is regarded by the Government as an unjustified impediment to the Home Secretary seeking to protect the public by turning back at a port or airport or deporting someone in the United Kingdom, on national security grounds. Government has sought to tackle this in two ways. First it has concluded 'no ill-treatment' agreements – Memoranda of Understanding – with proposed destination States in the Middle East and North Africa in the hope that their existence, backed by independent monitoring, and specific assurances in the individual case, will together defeat challenge on *Chahal* grounds by obviating the risk of maltreatment or reducing it below the level of the 'real risk' that test requires. Its second mode of dealing with the 'problem' has been to try to secure by a number of routes the relaxation of this preclusionary principle: by threatening to legislate to amend the HRA so that United Kingdom courts have to balance the risk to the individual against the degree of risk to the State; possibly by seeking at international level to confine Art. 3 ECHR to torture; and, finally, by intervening with a number of other Governments in a national security deportation case brought against the Netherlands, in the hope that the European Court of Human Rights will itself modify the absolute nature of the *Chahal* principle.

In its counter-terrorism strategy document,[108] published in July 2006, the Government reported that it had concluded Memoranda of Understanding with Jordan, Lebanon and Libya. Bodies to monitor the agreements had been appointed in Jordan and Libya and an agreement in principle had been reached with such a body in Lebanon. Negotiations were ongoing with a number of other countries in the Middle East and North Africa. Moreover, unspecified separate arrangements were in place to deal with deportations to Algeria. The memorandum concluded with Jordan provides:

Application and Scope

This arrangement will apply to any person accepted by the receiving state for admission to its territory following a written request by the sending state under the terms of this arrangement. …

Such a request may be made in respect of any citizen of the receiving state who is to be returned to that country by the sending state on the grounds that he is not entitled, or is no longer entitled, to remain in the sending state according to the immigration laws of that state.

Requests under this arrangement may include requests for further specific assurances by the receiving state if appropriate in an individual case.

---

[108]   Cm 6888 (2006): para. 74.

Understandings

It is understood that the authorities of the United Kingdom and of Jordan will comply with their human rights obligations under international law regarding a person returned under this arrangement. Where someone has been accepted under the terms of this arrangement, the conditions set out in the following paragraphs (numbered 1–8) will apply, together with any further specific assurances provided by the receiving state.

1. If arrested, detained or imprisoned following his return, a returned person will be afforded adequate accommodation, nourishment, and medical treatment, and will be treated in a humane and proper manner, in accordance with internationally accepted standards.

2. A returned person who is arrested or detained will be brought promptly before a judge or other officer authorised by law to exercise judicial power in order that the lawfulness of his detention may be decided.

3. A returned person who is arrested or detained will be informed promptly by the authorities of the receiving state of the reasons for his arrest or detention, and of any charge against him.

4. If the returned person is arrested, detained or imprisoned within 3 years of the date of his return, he will be entitled to contact, and then have prompt and regular visits from the representative of an independent body nominated jointly by the UK and Jordanian authorities. Such visits will be permitted at least once a fortnight, and whether or not the returned person has been convicted, and will include the opportunity for private interviews with the returned person. The nominated body will give a report of its visits to the authorities of the sending state.

5. Except where the returned person is arrested, detained or imprisoned, the receiving state will not impede, limit, restrict or otherwise prevent access by a returned person to the consular posts of the sending state during normal working hours. However, the receiving state is not obliged to facilitate such access by providing transport free of charge or at discounted rates.

6. A returned person will be allowed to follow his religious observance following his return, including while under arrest, or while detained or imprisoned.

7. A returned person who is charged with an offence following his return will receive a fair and public hearing without undue delay by a competent, independent and impartial tribunal established by law. Judgment will be pronounced publicly, but the press and public may be excluded from all or part of the trial in the interests of morals, public order or national security in a democratic society, where the interests of juveniles or the protection of the private life of the parties so require, or to the extent strictly necessary in the opinion of the court in special circumstances where publicity would prejudice the interests of justice.

8. A returned person who is charged with an offence following his return will be allowed adequate time and facilities to prepare his defence, and will be permitted to examine or have examined the witnesses against him and to call and have examined witnesses on his behalf. He will be allowed to defend himself in person or through legal assistance of his own choosing, or, if he has not sufficient means to pay for legal assistance, to be given it free when the interests of justice so require.[109]

Those with Libya and Lebanon are in essentially the same terms, although both in addition contain provisions on re-trial for those convicted *in absentia* and more detailed provisions on contact with, regular visits by and review by the monitoring body.[110]

On a number of occasions, the Prime Minister has indicated a willingness to amend the HRA so that the minority principle in *Chahal* (enabling a balance between risk to the individual and the risk to national security) would be the one to be applied by United Kingdom courts.[111] The Home Secretary has now categorically assured the JHRC that this path is not one to pursue[112] and recently the Lord Chancellor's review has rejected outright modification of the HRA or withdrawal from the ECHR. Both are a welcome reaffirmation of the commitment to that key element in the constitutional settlement. They are also sensible since merely modifying the HRA could not preclude recourse to the Strasbourg Court where the majority principle in *Chahal* would be applied, and neither it, nor partial withdrawal from the ECHR (full withdrawal not being feasible given that EU membership is contingent on adherence to the ECHR) would affect obligations under UNCAT, albeit that they cover the risk of torture only and not inhuman or degrading treatment or punishment. Instead, Government has taken a more rational course of seeking to have the European Court of Human Rights itself modify the *Chahal* principle by the Government's intervention in a national security deportation case brought against the Netherlands. Were the Court to do that (which is thought highly unlikely), the modification would effectively bind United Kingdom courts.

National Security Deportation: Concerns about Effectiveness and Human Rights

The Newton Committee, in its review of ATCSA, questioned the efficacy of deportation in dealing with international terrorism:

> *Seeking to deport terrorist suspects does not seem to us to be a satisfactory response, given the risk of exporting terrorism.* If people in the UK are contributing to the terrorist

---

[109] JHRC 19th (2005–06b): Ev. 78–79.
[110] JHRC 19th (2005–06b): 79–84.
[111] JHRC 19th (2005–06b): 106 (Submission of Amnesty International) 121 (British Irish Rights Watch); *Prime Minister's press conference* 05.08.05 found at <http://www.number10.gov.uk/output/Page8041.asp>.
[112] JHRC 3rd (2005): 152.

effort here or abroad, they should be dealt with here. While deporting such people might free up British police, intelligence, security and prison service resources, it would not necessarily reduce the threat to British interests abroad, or make the world a safer place more generally. Indeed, there is a risk that the suspects might even return without the authorities being aware of it.[113]

The JHRC in two reports and a raft of NGOs giving evidence to it were sceptical in the light of experience of the value of 'no ill-treatment agreements' or specific case diplomatic assurances from States with a bad record on torture.[114] So have been the Council of Europe High Commissioner on Human Rights and the UN Special Rapporteur on Torture.[115] While the concern about 'fair trial' issues pervading all of the executive measures also arises here, some criticisms by immigration lawyers were more muted, since the SIAC process constituted a great improvement on the previous advisory panel system. There were also concerns about detention for deportation amounting to effective detention without trial and the imposition of bail conditions of a severity that, if imposed as a control order under the PTA 2005 would have had to be embodied in a derogating control order supportable only by an Art. 15 ECHR derogation approved by both Houses of Parliament.

Deprivation of, and Refusal to Accord, British Citizenship

British citizenship brought with it immunity from deportation and from ATCSA detention. The 'citizenship' strand of the Government's counter-terrorism strategy is designed to make 'undesirable' dual nationals amenable to ATCSA detention or to deportation.[116] It also has an impact on the individual's ability to seek from the Government its diplomatic protection in respect of his/her maltreatment by another State.[117]

Deprivation of British Citizenship

The United Kingdom's nationality and citizenship laws have for a long time enabled the Home Secretary to deprive someone who acquired their status through voluntary act (naturalization or registration) on the grounds of fraud or

---

[113] Newton Committee (2003): para. 195.

[114] JHRC 19th (2005–06a): paras 110–131; JHRC 19th (2005–06b): 105–110 (Amnesty International), 110–138 (British Irish Rights Watch), 145–50 (Human Rights Watch), 153–59 (Liberty and Justice).

[115] JHRC 19th (2005–06a): para. 131.

[116] Cm 6888 (2006): para. 74

[117] On attempts to use the courts to compel Government to exercise its right of diplomatic protection in respect of British citizens detained by the United States at Guantanamo Bay, and to intervene on an analogous basis in respect of long-standing residents of the United Kingdom, see chapter 9.

misrepresentation or specific acts of treason or disloyalty after acquisition. Protection was accorded to prevent statelessness. In 2002, the ability to deprive of British citizenship was extended, but always subject to the overarching principle precluding deployment which would render an individual stateless. The Home Secretary acquired power to strip a dual national of British citizenship *however acquired* where he was satisfied that the person had done something prejudicial to the vital interests of the United Kingdom. Presented as a power taken to enable ratification of the European Convention on Citizenship, from which the key phrase is taken, the real target of the measure were British citizens thought to be a terrorist threat, such as the radical cleric Abu Hamza, opening them up to deportation powers and the ability under ATCSA to detain them without trial if deportation was not legally or practically feasible. That deprivation power, wide in itself, was replaced from July 2006 by a broader power; deprivation of a dual national's citizenship on the grounds that the Home Secretary is satisfied that such deprivation is conducive to the public good.[118] The expansion of relevant behaviours seen with deportation will also apply here. Where deprivation is effected on grounds of national security (terrorism or otherwise), the focus of this book, appeal lies to SIAC, with its ability to protect security material through its use of 'closed' sessions employing 'special advocates'. Otherwise appeal lies to the Asylum and Immigration Tribunal (AIT).

Acquisition of British Citizenship

This can be acquired by birth in the United Kingdom, to a British citizen parent or someone 'settled' here; by descent from a British citizen parent; or by adoption by a British citizen. It can also be acquired by an individual, whether with another citizenship or stateless, through voluntary act. The Home Secretary grants citizenship through the process of naturalization to foreign national applicants and through a registration process to Commonwealth citizens or to them or other nationals seeking to acquire British citizenship on the basis of marriage to a British citizen. The naturalization process is discretionary, does not require the Home Secretary to assign reasons for refusal, and embodies a 'good character' requirement. It has thus long enabled refusal on security grounds. In contrast, however, until recently there has been no 'good character' requirement for individuals seeking registration and the process is more 'rights-based' than discretionary. Since July 2006, however, a 'good character' requisite has been introduced for most of those seeking registration.[119]

---

[118] British Nationality Act 1981, s. 40, as amended by Immigration, Asylum and Nationality Act 2006, s. 56.

[119] Immigration, Asylum and Nationality Act 2006 (IANA), s. 58. A number of groups are exempt: those whose entitlement to register is based on the Statelessness Convention; those under 10 on the date of application; and certain British Overseas citizens, British subjects or British protected persons without any other citizenship.

Removal of a Commonwealth Citizen's Right of Abode in the United Kingdom on Security Grounds

Some Commonwealth citizens with a parental or marital connection to the United Kingdom, typically citizens from the 'white' Commonwealth (Australia, Canada, New Zealand or South Africa), while not British citizens, nonetheless enjoy under United Kingdom law a full right of abode in the United Kingdom. They do not require leave or government permission to be here. That precludes exercise of the refusal of entry, curtailment of leave or deportation powers under the immigration legislation and prevented their detention under the ATCSA regime. With effect from July 2006, the Home Secretary can remove that right of abode where he considers it conducive to the public good.[120] Where the basis for this is national security (terrorism or otherwise), the area on which this book focuses, appeal lies to SIAC, with its ability to protect security material through its use of 'closed' sessions employing 'special advocates'. Otherwise appeal lies to the AIT.[121]

Detention in Iraq and Afghanistan

Intervention in Afghanistan was very much designed to deal with its role as a safe haven for international terrorism, particularly Al Qaeda, and the matter of opium production and drug trafficking, but the security position has worsened.[122] It has been seen that a number of those subject to one or more of the executive measures examined in this Part (ATCSA detention, deportation or control orders) are said by the Home Secretary to have gone there for terrorist training. The legal basis for the relatively few British detentions in Afghanistan rested on a series of United Nations Security Council Resolutions, most recently UNSCR 1623 (2005), and by agreement with the Government of Afghanistan. ISAF (International Security Assistance Force) policy, agreed by NATO, is that individuals should be transferred to the Afghan authorities at the first opportunity and within 96 hours, or released.[123] The responsibilities of United Kingdom forces to detainees are said by government to be clear and its procedures governing the handling of detainees to be consistent with the principles of the Geneva Conventions, whether detaining as part of an International Security Assistance force (ISAF) operation or of Operation Enduring Freedom (OEF). The Government also has a Memorandum of Understanding on detention with the Afghan Government, setting out the responsibilities of United Kingdom Armed Forces towards detainees in the period prior to their handover to Afghan security forces or release.[124]

---

[120] IANA, s. 57(1).
[121] IANA, s. 57(2).
[122] FAC 4th (2005–06): chap. 8.
[123] Defence 5th (2005–06): para. 74.
[124] Defence 6th (2005–06): paras 33–4, 36.

There is little other information on detention in Afghanistan, the focus of reports being much more on Iraq. The invasion of Iraq was justified by Government and endorsed by the House of Commons on other grounds, infamously the ultimately elusive 'weapons of mass destruction'. It has come increasingly to be seen by government as part of the 'war' on terror, although it seems likely that most of the international terrorists now there are a product rather than a cause of the invasion. It has been seen that control orders under the PTA 2005 have been used to deal with an individual thought to be going to Iraq to assist the insurgents. In Iraq, British forces have resorted to detention without trial for imperative reasons of security as permitted by international law to a belligerent power, and, after the war was over, under the authority of the Fourth Geneva Convention as extended by UN Security Council Resolution 1546 and the exchange of letters with the Prime Minister of the Iraqi interim government.[125] This power would lapse once a permanent Iraqi government was established and the power of internment would be reconsidered at that stage.[126] The Commons Defence Committee recorded that British forces initially operated a facility to house internees near Umm Qasr, which was subsumed into the US Camp Bucca on 10 April 2003. The United Kingdom was represented at that camp by its Prisoner of War Registration Unit and Prisoner Monitoring Team. There was another British Divisional Temporary Detention Facility (DTDF) in Shaiba Logistics Base. After 15 December 2003, all the internees who were originally taken into custody by British forces were transferred there. As of 10 February 2004, British forces held 108 detainees.[127] In May 2004 the DTDF 127 held internees; but by December 2004 there were only eighteen internees (a mixture of former Ba'athists, suspected terrorists and a few 'ordinary' criminals). British policy on internment was to detain those representing an imperative threat to security, as defined in the Security Council. Where someone appeared guilty of criminality, he or she would be handed over to the Iraqi authorities. Otherwise, those picked up would be released.[128] The committee expressed the hope that this draconian power of internment would be dispensed with once operational needs permitted and that until then its use should continue to be limited with increasing priority given to helping the Iraqis secure prosecutions.[129] The FAC reported that there were some 40 detainees held by British forces early in 2006 (compared with 14,000 held by the United States).[130] It recommended that whenever and wherever possible these be handed over to the Iraqi government for trial, and called for better information on the current number and status of detainees held by British forces.[131] While the

---

[125] Defence 6th (2004–05): paras. 92–101.
[126] Defence 1st (2005–06): para. 12.
[127] FAC 4th (2003–04): para. 82.
[128] Defence 6th (2004–05): paras. 95–97.
[129] Ibid., para. 101.
[130] FAC 4th (2005–06): para. 246.
[131] Ibid., para. 247.

scale of detainee abuse never reached the scale perpetrated by its United States' ally, nonetheless, in its report in the previous session, the Committee had concluded

> ... that some British personnel have committed grave violations of human rights of persons held in detention facilities in Iraq, which are unacceptable. We recommend that all further allegations of mistreatment of detainees by British troops in Iraq, Afghanistan or elsewhere be investigated thoroughly and transparently. We conclude that it is essential that wherever there are overseas detention facilities, those responsible for detainees must have adequate training. We recommend that the Government review its training of and guidance to agency personnel, officers, NCOs and other ranks on the treatment of detainees to ensure that there is no ambiguity on what is permissible.[132]

Earlier, Amnesty International raised doubts about the current legal structure in Iraq, effectively a two-tier penal system, in which suspects arrested and detained by coalition forces have fewer rights than those arrested and detained by Iraqi officials.[133] The Intelligence and Security Committee examined British participation in the interrogation of prisoners in Afghanistan, Iraq and at Guantanamo Bay. It reported in March 2005 that British personnel had witnessed or conducted just over 2,000 interviews. It found that there were less than 15 occasions when United Kingdom intelligence personnel reported actual or potential breaches of international law or United Kingdom policy in respect of those interviews, and was assured that here were no other occasions.[134] It recommended better training of such personnel and prompt investigation of and action on such reports of breach of standards.[135] There remains, however, strong concern at the apparent use in Iraq of methods (hooding and use of stress positions) condemned as contrary to Art. 3 ECHR by the European Court of Human Rights in *Ireland* v *United Kingdom*, methods which the then Conservative Government had in 1972 said would not in future be used.[136]

---

[132] FAC 6th (2004–05): para. 76.

[133] FAC 4th (2003–04): para. 86.

[134] Cm 6469 (2005), para. 110.

[135] Ibid., paras 121, 125–26.

[136] *The Observer* 27 May 2007; JHRC Press Notice No. 39 (2006–07), 23 May 2007 found at <http://www.parliament.uk/parliamentary_committees/joint_committee_on_human_righ ts/jchrpn39_230507.cfm>.

Chapter 8

Challenge Mechanisms

Introduction

This chapter considers the nature of the challenge mechanisms open to those subjected to the executive measures deployed after 9/11. It deals with appeals to the Special Immigration Appeals Commission (SIAC) as regards immigration, asylum and citizenship matters, and in respect of ATCSA detentions. It analyses the comparable role of the High Court in respect of the Home Secretary's application for a control order, the controlee's responses to that and the controlee seeking the revocation or modification of his or her order. It delineates the various jurisdictions and powers of SIAC and the High Court and surveys the processes and rules by which the schemes seek to reconcile competing interests of protection of security material and sources, on the one hand, and due process and rights to a fair hearing, on the other. Those processes involve dealing with material in 'open' and 'closed' sessions. The latter exclude from participation the individual and their legal team. In 'closed' sessions, SIAC or the High Court examine the material relied on by the Home Secretary. They are aided to do so by a lawyer appointed as a Special Advocate to promote the interests of the individual without being subject to the latter's instructions or a part of their legal team. The role of the Special Advocate and criticism of it are considered in some depth. Those processes are controversial. It is arguable that they are not compatible with the 'fair hearing' requirements of the ECHR. The material in this chapter thus lays a base for consideration in chapter 9 of the litigation that issue has generated. One aspect of that question concerns the sufficiency of the level of judicial scrutiny afforded. Accordingly, the nature and terms of each of the jurisdictions must separately be considered.

Powers and Jurisdictions: SIAC

In *Chahal* neither the adviser system of challenge nor judicial review in the High Court in respect of national security deportation decisions satisfied the fair hearing requirements of Art. 5(4) ECHR. Nor did either provide the effective remedy required by Art. 13 ECHR. The European Court of Human Rights there drew attention to one version of a Canadian mechanism for reconciling due process and security interests. Accordingly, the Government proposed and Parliament approved the creation through the Special Immigration Appeals Commission Act 1997

(SIACA) of a modified version of that system to govern challenges to national security decisions in the immigration sphere. The Government was confident, and not unreasonably so, given the Court's apparent 'steer', that the scheme would satisfy the 'fair hearing' and the 'effective remedy' requirements of the ECHR. As will be seen in chapter 9, the European Court of Human Rights, while continuing to draw attention to a SIAC type scheme as a possible reconciler of due process and security interests, has declined to confirm in national security cases in other contexts that SIAC is compatible with Articles 5(4), 6 and 13 ECHR. Since enactment of SIACA, moreover, Government counter-terrorism strategy since 9/11 has been to reduce the scope of asylum appeals and, as regards national security deportation, to limit the range of matters appealable while in the country. SIAC, created as an independent judicial tribunal, has, since 2001, been a superior court of record equivalent to the High Court.[1] It was set up to hear appeals against immigration and asylum decisions where, because of national security or other public interest considerations, some of the evidence on which the decision is based cannot be disclosed to the appellant. It is presided over by a High Court judge. Its decisions are not amenable to judicial review and can only be challenged by way of appeal on a point of law to the Court of Appeal as provided in SIACA[2] or ATCSA.[3] Its members are appointed by the Lord Chancellor and have all been security-vetted.[4] Although there have been changes to the precise terms of its composition reflective of a bewildering range of change in the immigration and asylum appeals area, essentially it hears proceedings as a three-member panel, chaired by a member who holds or has held high judicial office (usually a High Court judge). Specialist expertise in immigration, intelligence and security issues is provided by the other two members. One must be or have been a legally qualified member of the Asylum and Immigration Tribunal (AIT).[5] The other will be a lay member. When the House of Commons Constitutional Affairs Committee (CAC) reported in 2005 on SIAC and its roles, Ouseley J was the chair of SIAC. It then had 22 judicial members, 13 legal members and 13 lay members.[6]

SIAC operates in controversial areas and risks attracting criticism whatever it does in the exercise of its independent decision-making functions. As will be seen in chapter 9, sometimes it has upheld the decisions of the Home Secretary. At other times, it has decided matters against him or her and has roundly been criticized by the Home Secretary. Lawyers for the individual, however, have sometimes thought it too deferential to the Home Secretary's views on security issues. Its expert status has attracted a degree of respect from higher courts.

---

[1] ATCSA, s. 35.
[2] s. 7.
[3] s. 30(5)(a).
[4] CAC 7th (2004–05b): Ev 48, para. 16 (Department of Constitutional Affairs).
[5] Prior to 4 April 2005, this member had to be or have been the Chief Adjudicator or a legally qualified member of the IAT.
[6] CAC 7th (2004–05a): para. 25.

SIAC: the Immigration and Asylum Jurisdiction

Broadly speaking, there is a right of appeal to SIAC against an immigration or asylum decision where the Home Secretary has certified under section 97 of the Nationality, Immigration and Asylum Act 2002 (NIAA 2002) that the decision has been taken in the interests of national security; in the interests of the relationship between the United Kingdom and another country; or otherwise in the public interest. It thus covers both refusal of entry to the United Kingdom and deportation from it on such grounds, as well as refusal to revoke a deportation order made on such grounds.[7] Appeals against banning from, or refusal of, entry are perforce are conducted with the appellant out of the country. Until July 2006, appeals in respect of deportation took place with the appellant in the country, either in detention or on bail. With respect to an appeal lodged after that, however, the normal course will be for the appeal to be brought after removal from outside the country. Where the appellant has made a human rights claim, however, the appeal can be brought 'in country', precluding removal until resolved, unless the Home Secretary certifies that removal would not breach the ECHR. An 'in country' appeal lies to SIAC in respect of such a certification. If that appeal was unsuccessful, the appeal against deportation would then be conducted after removal.[8]

Essentially, SIAC must allow an appeal in so far as it thinks that the decision appealed against does not accord with law (including any immigration rules), or that a discretion exercised in making the decision should have been exercised differently.[9] The fullness of those terms has, however, to be read in the light of the dictates of the House of Lords in *Rehman* which arguably have defeated Parliament's intention and reduced SIAC's role more to one of judicial review.[10] In addition SIAC also has power to admit to bail someone detained as a result of an immigration or asylum decision.[11]

In asylum cases, the range of issues to be considered by SIAC has been narrowed. Moreover, statute stipulates definitions of relevant key terms in the Refugee Convention. As regards refusal of asylum, ATCSA, section 33 – now repealed and replaced in terms by section 55 of the Immigration, Asylum and Nationality Act 2006 (IANA 2006) – essentially prevented the proper substantive determination of an asylum appeal if it was deemed that the exclusion clauses apply or if the person concerned was considered to be a danger to national security in accordance with Art. 33(2) of the Refugee Convention. Further restriction was effected by section 72 of NIAA 2002, subsection (2) of which stipulates that someone shall be presumed to have been convicted by a final judgment of a

---

[7] SIACA s. 2; Nationality Immigration and Asylum Act 2002 (NIAA 2002), s. 97.

[8] NIAA 2002, s. 97A, inserted by Immigration, Asylum and Nationality Act 2006 (IANA 2006), s. 7.

[9] NIAA 2002, s. 86(3), applicable through SIACA, s. 2(2)(g).

[10] See chapter 4.

[11] IA 1971, Sch. 2 as modified by SIACA, Sch. 3.

particularly serious crime and to constitute a danger to the community of the United Kingdom if he is (a) convicted in the United Kingdom of an offence, and (b) sentenced to a period of imprisonment of at least two years. Subsection (4) is more far-reaching in not requiring such a sentence. It states that a person will also 'be presumed to have been convicted by a final judgment of a particularly serious crime and to constitute a danger to the community of the United Kingdom if (a) he is convicted of an offence specified by order of the Secretary of State'. The Home has specified a raft of specific offences under the anti-terrorist legislation. These provisions are open to the criticism that they may deprive someone of refugee protection for relatively minor offences, such as the destruction of identity documents without reasonable excuse (an offence punishable with up to two years' imprisonment) and criminal damage and minor theft, which are specified offences. In addition, section 54 of IANA 2006 dictates an interpretation of Art. 1F (c) of the Refugee Convention, by specifying that 'acts contrary to the purposes and principles of the United Nations' which will result in exclusion from asylum include acts of committing, preparing or instigating terrorism and acts of encouraging or inducing others to commit, prepare or instigate terrorism.

Evidence from the Department of Constitutional Affairs to the CAC indicated 10 deportation appeals and one exclusion appeal in the period 1998–2005. One appeal remained pending. The appeal against exclusion saw the Home Secretary lift the exclusion. SIAC upheld a decision not to revoke a deportation order. Two appellants withdrew their appeals. Another was abandoned. Two decisions to deport were withdrawn. Another three were upheld by SIAC on the deportation issue but in two of these SIAC held that removal was precluded by Art. 3 ECHR, and in the other (Rehman), the individual was not removed because by the end of the appeal process (which continued all the way to the House of Lords) he was no longer regarded as a national security threat.[12]

SIAC: the Citizenship and 'Right of Abode' Jurisdiction

The NIAA 2002 enabled the Home Secretary to deprive a British citizen with dual nationality of their British citizenship, however acquired, where he or she was satisfied that the person had done something prejudicial to the vital interests of the United Kingdom. That deprivation power, wide in itself, was replaced from July 2006 by a broader power; deprivation of a dual national's citizenship on the grounds that the Home Secretary is satisfied that such deprivation is conducive to the public good, a concept covering a much broader range of behaviour than before.[13] Where deprivation is on grounds of national security (terrorism or otherwise), appeal lies to SIAC.[14] Similarly, the right of abode in the United

---

[12] CAC 7th (2004–05b): Ev 52, Annex B.

[13] British Nationality Act 1981, s. 40(2), as amended by IANA 2006, s. 56. See further chapter 8.

[14] SIACA, s. 2B.

Kingdom possessed by some (mainly white) Commonwealth citizens prevents their deportation or (while in operation) ATCSA detention. With effect from July 2006, the Home Secretary can remove that right of abode where he or she considers it conducive to the public good.[15] Where the basis for this is national security (terrorism or otherwise), appeal lies to SIAC.[16]

Whether the deprivation is of citizenship or the right of abode, SIAC must allow an appeal in so far as it thinks that the decision appealed against does not accord with law or a discretion exercised in making the decision should have been exercised differently.[17]

There appears only to have been one appeal against deprivation of citizenship – the case of the radical cleric, Abu Hamza. He was detained initially in respect of extradition proceedings by the United States and then in respect of criminal charges (incitement to murder and incitement to racial hatred) in respect of which he was convicted and imprisoned. The 'citizenship' appeal was stayed at his request.[18]

SIAC: the ATCSA Detention Jurisdiction

ATCSA empowered the Home Secretary to detain someone, without the right of abode in the United Kingdom, whom he or she had certified as an international terrorist suspect who posed a threat to national security.[19] That person had a right to appeal to SIAC against certification. SIAC had to cancel the certificate if, on the basis of all the material available as at the date of the hearing, it considered either (a) that there were not reasonable grounds for suspecting the person to be a terrorist or for believing them to threaten national security, or (b) that for some other reason the certificate should not have been issued. Cancellation resulted in the certificate being treated as never having been made.[20] In addition, whether or not the person certificated appealed, SIAC had regularly to review the certificate. On a review the Commission had to cancel the certificate if it considered, on the basis of the material as at the time of review, that there were no reasonable grounds for the requisite belief or suspicion. Otherwise it could not make any order except as to leave to appeal. A certificate ceased to have effect at the end of the day on which SIAC's order on review cancelling it was made.[21] In addition, SIAC also had power to admit a detainee to bail.[22]

Whether on appeal or on periodic review, SIAC considered the cases of all 17 persons certificated under ATCSA. Two were admitted to bail. Only one certificate

---

[15] IANA 2006, s. 57(1).
[16] NIAA 2002, s. 82(2)(ib) inserted by IANA 2006, s. 57(2).
[17] NIAA 2002, s. 86(3), applicable through SIACA, s. 2(2)(g).
[18] CAC 7th (2004–05a): para. 29.
[19] ATCSA, ss. 21, 23.
[20] ATCSA, s. 25.
[21] ATCSA, s. 26.
[22] ATCSA. s. 24.

was cancelled as a result of an appeal. On the other appeals and reviews, SIAC upheld certification. Concerns were expressed both about the level of the scrutiny applied by SIAC and the matter of deference on security issues to the Home Secretary. Some aspects of this are noted further below when considering 'closed' sessions and the role of the Special Advocate. The litigation which those concerns produced is examined in chapter 9.

Powers and Jurisdictions: the High Court and Control Orders under the PTA 2005

The PTA 2005 empowers the making of two types of control order: non-derogating control orders and derogating control orders. Just as the degree of restrictions that may be imposed varies by type of order, so does the applicable decision-maker, the process for making them, and the terms governing judicial control of their imposition. The whole process has become much more 'judicialized', with the Home Secretary who wants a control order against an individual, in effect largely having to seek the issue of one from the High Court rather than making one of his or her own volition and having to defend it in court later.

A 'non–derogating' control order can be made by the Home Secretary (subject to court challenge after the event) only in two circumstances: where in his/her opinion the urgency of the situation precludes his/her seeking court permission to issue the order; or where the order was made before 14 March 2005 against an individual who, at the time it was made, was an individual in respect of whom a certificate under section 21(1) of ATCSA was in force (the existing 'Belmarsh' detainees).[23] Otherwise, having decided that there are grounds to make such an order against that individual, he/she must apply to the High Court for permission to make the order.

The test for making a 'non-derogating' control order is whether there are reasonable grounds for suspecting that the individual is or has been involved in terrorism-related activity and the decision-maker (Home Secretary or the court, as the case may be) further considers it necessary, for purposes connected with protecting members of the public from a risk of terrorism, to make a control order imposing obligations on that individual.[24] There are here two stages in court proceedings.

The 'first stage' 'permission' hearing will generally be *ex parte* (with no representations from the suspect who will generally not even know of the application). The court may only refuse permission to issue an order where it considers that the Home Secretary's decision to go for one on the basis that the test was met was 'obviously flawed' in terms of the principles applicable on judicial review. If permission is granted, the order is made and executed. The court must

---

[23] PTA 2005, s. 3(1).
[24] PTA 2005, s. 2(1).

arrange for a full hearing on the order – a process envisaged as beginning within seven days of the initial approval of the order – in which the individual and their lawyer, subject to the security considerations mentioned above, can participate and challenge the order. At that hearing, the court must confirm the order unless it is satisfied on the material available to it as at the date of this 'second stage' hearing that the decision to make it at all and/or the restrictions to impose is flawed in the light of the principles of judicial review, in which case it can quash it or one or more of the obligations imposed by it, or give directions to the Secretary of State for the revocation of the order or for the modification of the obligations it imposes.[25]

A 'derogating control' order (one interfering because of the degree of its restrictions with 'liberty and security of person' protected by Art. 5 ECHR, for example, house arrest) will require an Art. 15 designated derogation order approved by both Houses of Parliament.[26] Judicial control is tighter here. The Home Secretary must apply to the High Court for a 'derogating' control order against that person.[27] The Act provides that the putative subject can be arrested and detained by the police where it is thought necessary to ensure that they are available to be given notice of the order if it is made. The person can be so held for up to 48 hours, and the usual rights granted to those arrested under the TA 2000 of access to a lawyer and to have someone informed of the detention apply here without ability to postpone their exercise.[28] Detention thereafter is a matter for the High Court.[29] Again, the court process has two stages. At the first stage, the court must hold an immediate preliminary hearing on the application (which may be held without the suspect being notified, present or allowed to make representations) to decide whether to make such an order and, if so, to direct the holding of a full hearing (the second stage) to determine whether to confirm the order (with or without modifications). The test to be applied by the High Court varies according to whether it is considering the matter at the preliminary hearing of the Home Secretary's application for such an order, or considering at the later full hearing whether to confirm the order issued at that earlier stage. The standard for confirmation is more stringent than for the initial issuing of the order.

At the 'first stage' or preliminary hearing, the court in essence

> ... considers whether there is a *prima facie* case for the making of an order ... It falls far short of a requirement that the court be satisfied itself of the necessity for an individual to be deprived of their liberty.[30]

---

[25] PTA 2005, s. 3(10), (11).
[26] PTA 2005, ss. 4, 6; s. 14(1).
[27] PTA 2005, s. 4
[28] PTA 2005, s. 5(1)–(3).
[29] PTA 2005, s. 5.
[30] JHRC 10th (2004–05): para. 6.

To delineate more fully the court's powers at this stage, the court may make a control order against the individual in question if it appears to the court (a) that there is material which (if not disproved) is capable of being relied on by the court as establishing that the individual is or has been involved in terrorism-related activity (the *prima facie* case aspect); (b) that there are reasonable grounds for believing that the imposition of obligations on that individual is necessary for purposes connected with protecting members of the public from a risk of terrorism; (c) that the risk arises out of, or is associated with, a public emergency in respect of which there is a designated derogation from the whole or a part of Art. 5 of the ECHR; and (d) that the obligations are or include derogating obligations of a description set out for the purposes of the designated derogation in the designation order. The obligations that may be imposed by a derogating control order at this stage are those which the court has reasonable grounds for considering are necessary for purposes connected with preventing or restricting involvement by that individual in terrorism-related activity.[31] At the full hearing, higher standards are rightly applicable. The court may confirm the control order (with or without modifications) only if (a) it is satisfied, *on the balance of probabilities*, that the controlled person is an individual who is or has been involved in terrorism-related activity; (b) *it considers* that the imposition of obligations on the controlled person is necessary for purposes connected with protecting members of the public from a risk of terrorism; (c) it appears to the court that the risk is one arising out of, or is associated with, a public emergency in respect of which there is a designated derogation from the whole or a part of Art. 5 of the ECHR; and (d) the obligations to be imposed by the order, or (as the case may be) by the order as modified, are or include derogating obligations of a description set out for the purposes of the designated derogation in the designation order. Otherwise the court must revoke the order made at the preliminary hearing.[32] A 'derogating' control order lasts for up to six months, unless revoked earlier, but can be renewed for further periods of up to six months.[33]

Processes and Procedures

These are essentially the same for each court (SIAC/High Court), despite being founded on different legal bases.[34] Broadly speaking, the processes and procedures are designed to mirror those applicable, respectively, to ordinary immigration and

---

[31] PTA 2005, s. 4(3), (4).

[32] PTA 2005, s. 4(5).

[33] PTA 2005, s.4 (5)–(9).

[34] SIACA and the Special Immigration Appeals Commission (Procedure) Rules 2003 (SI 2003 No. 1034)('SIAC Rules'); PTA 2005 and Civil Procedure Rules (CPR), Part 76, inserted by the Civil Procedure (Amendment No. 2) Rules 2005 (SI 2005 No. 656) ('High Court PTA Rules').

asylum appeals (SIAC compared to AIT/IAT) and other civil proceedings (High Court). The crucial difference between these and ordinary processes, however, lies in the making of special provisions to enable the Home Secretary to rely on material without disclosing it to the appellant or their representative, where to do so would be contrary to the public interest. Both courts are duty bound to secure that information is not disclosed contrary to the interests of national security, the international relations of the United Kingdom, the detection and prevention of crime, or in any other circumstances where disclosure is likely to harm the public interest. But subject to that, they must be satisfied that the available material enables proper determination of the proceedings.[35] Unlike the position in public interest immunity proceedings where one party (often the Crown or at its behest) seeks to withhold material from another, neither SIAC nor the High Court has power to decide that the harm disclosure might cause to those interests is outweighed by the benefit to the public interest in the fair administration of justice.[36] They are also required to exclude the appellant and their representative from a hearing or part of a hearing if they consider it necessary in order to ensure that information is not disclosed contrary to the public interest.[37] The relevant law officer (in England and Wales the Attorney General) may appoint a special advocate to represent the interests of appellants in any proceedings from which they and their legal representative are excluded.[38] Although this is a discretion rather than a duty to appoint a special advocate, one will invariably be appointed, since the Home Secretary cannot rely on material which has not been disclosed to the appellant or their representative unless a special advocate has been appointed.

Since SIAC was the initial model, a delineation of its processes with respect to appeals is set out first, since this conveys most readily the nature of the process. Some variations flowing from the 'reverse' nature of the PTA 2005 process (the Home Secretary as applicant for permission to make a non-derogating control order or for a derogating control order itself) will then be noted.

The appellant must give notice of the appeal. This is made by sending a completed form to SIAC by hand, post or fax. A copy of that notice and any documents must be served at the same time on the Home Secretary. Upon receipt SIAC will issue an appeal number and acknowledge receipt to the parties. If the Home Secretary is going to respond to the appeal he/she must provide SIAC with a summary of the facts relating to the decision being appealed. Reasons for the decision must also be given, plus the grounds on which the appeal is opposed and supportive evidence. If he/she objects to any of this material being disclosed to the appellant then the SIAC must be informed of the reasons for that objection. At this stage contact the Attorney General's office must be contacted so that a Special Advocate may be appointed. Once appointed the Special Advocate will contact the

---

[35] SIAC Rules, r. 4; High Court PTA Rules, r. 76.2.

[36] CAC 7th (2004–05a): para. 58.

[37] SIAC Rules, rr. 37, 38 and 43; High Court PTA Rules, r. 76.22.

[38] SIAC Rules, r. 34; High Court PTA Rules, r. 76.23.

appellant and their representatives. The Home Secretary must make available to the Special Advocate any material provided to SIAC and must also supply the appellant with any material that is not contrary to the public interest. There is no time limit within the rules for the Home Secretary to oppose the appeal so SIAC may call a directions hearing to specify a time for him/her to oppose the appeal and to serve the 'closed' material on the Special Advocate. SIAC can also convene a directions hearing at any stage in order to issue directions for the conduct of proceedings. All parties are usually involved. Unlike other stages before SIAC, this can be chaired by a single member of SIAC. Once the Special Advocate has had sight of the 'closed' material (any relevant material that the Home Secretary objects to disclosing to the appellant and their legal representative) they may no longer communicate directly or indirectly with the appellant or their representative. Upon seeing the 'closed' material the Special Advocate may make submissions as to why the material should be disclosed to the appellant. The Secretary of State has the opportunity to respond. The Special Advocate and Secretary of State may meet to try to resolve issues of disclosure. If there remain any issues which the Secretary of State and the Special Advocate are unable to resolve then these will be decided by SIAC at a hearing. Neither the appellant nor their representative is permitted to attend that hearing. The Commission will make a ruling on all remaining issues of disclosure. It may call a directions hearing to provide a timetable for the submission of skeleton arguments, evidence and witness statements prior to the hearing of the appeal. All parties are given written notice of the date, time and place of the hearing by SIAC. The United Kingdom representative of the UNHCR is also notified of the hearing. The proceedings will be 'open' except where SIAC has to consider 'closed' evidence in which case only the Special Advocate and the Home Secretary's representatives will be present. At the conclusion of the hearing SIAC will reserve judgement and will normally set a date for delivery of its determination. SIAC must record its decision in writing and may produce an 'open' and 'closed' version of its determination.

It was noted earlier that the processes with respect to control orders were two-stage. Proceedings by the Home Secretary for a control order in the High Court operate in much the same way as a SIAC appeal as regards the second 'with notice' stage of full hearings. So do proceedings brought by the controlee for revocation of an order or modification of obligations imposed by it. The initial stage of application for permission to make a non-derogating control order or of application for a derogating one is, of course, without notice, and accordingly rather different. As regards 'first stage' proceedings, for either type of order, the Home Secretary must file with the Court a draft of the order sought; a statement of reasons to support the application for making that order and for imposing each of the obligations imposed by it; all relevant material; and any written submissions. The Court will grant or refuse permission/the order on that basis. There will be no controlee or Special Advocate involvement.

Neither SIAC nor the High Court are bound by the strict rules of evidence applicable to other civil and criminal courts. SIAC's rules empower it to receive evidence that would not be admissible in a court of law.[39] Those for the High Court similarly stipulate that 'the court may receive evidence that would not, but for this rule, be admissible in a court of law'.[40] Unlike the criminal trial or civil proceedings, the processes of 'closed' session used both by SIAC and the High Court enable (at no little cost to the rights of the 'defence') the protection of informants, intelligence agents and operatives, other witnesses fearful of reprisals, and the secrecy or security of methods of investigation. Consequently, as regards both courts the statutory restriction on non-admissibility of communications intercept material is lifted.[41] This does not mean that there are no evidentiary rules. As will be seen in the next chapter, statements obtained through torture, but not physical evidence, probative in itself, obtained as a result of statements so obtained, are absolutely precluded. Nor is acquittal at criminal trial seen as proof of innocence. That the matter went to court or that the trial judge left the case to the jury can both be taken into account in assessing someone's involvement in terrorism or threat to national security.[42] SIAC and the High Court can receive evidence in documentary or any other form.[43] Their procedural rules stipulate that the evidence of a witness may be given orally or in writing.[44] Witnesses can be required to give evidence on oath.[45] All parties to proceedings are entitled to adduce evidence and to cross-examine witnesses during any part of a hearing from which the individual and their legal representatives are not excluded.[46] The nature of the material seen by SIAC and the operation of 'closed' sessions in which material never disclosed to the individual or their lawyer is considered in proceedings from which they are both excluded – a 'Kafkaesque' world – has obviously been controversial. The more far-reaching matter of whether the processes concerned comply with the 'fair hearing' dictates of the ECHR is considered in chapter 9. Here we consider the operation of 'closed' sessions and the nature and role of the Special Advocates in respect of which a number of criticisms and suggestions for reform have been proffered by Select Committees, bodies and persons appointed to review the operation of the relevant legislation, by NGOs and others (including a former SIAC member) giving evidence to them, and, not least, by those eminent lawyers appointed as Special Advocates.

---

[39] SIAC Rules, r. 44.

[40] High Court PTA Rules, r. 76.26(4).

[41] PTA 2005, s. 11, Sched, para. 9. On SIAC, see Regulation of Investigatory Powers Act 2000, ss. 17, 18(1)(e).

[42] SIAC Appeal SC/36/2005, judgment 24 August, *Y* v *Secretary of State for the Home Department*, para. 72.

[43] SIAC Rules, r. 44; High Court PTA Rules, r. 76.26.

[44] Ibid.

[45] Ibid.

[46] Ibid.

Evidence, 'Closed' Sessions and Special Advocates

The paradigm of a fair, adversarial legal hearing of a dispute is one which enables the court or tribunal to deal with the case justly, in a context in which, so far as is practicable, the parties to the dispute are on an equal footing. They will have equal rights in relation to evidence and to examination and cross-examination of identifiable witnesses in full view of the parties and the judge, with rights to legal representation of their own choice. Typically in the United Kingdom with its divided legal profession, this will entail the services of both solicitor and barrister (counsel). Counsel for the individual will be instructed by another legal expert, the solicitor, fully conversant with the case and the client, and with the resources and ability to have investigated appropriate lines of inquiry and gather appropriate evidence, including expert evidence, to mount a proper challenge to the case made by the other side. Both counsel and solicitor will be in constant contact with their client to take instructions and thoughts and responses on material to be dealt with, throughout with the protective coverage of legal professional privilege. The proceedings are characterized by transparency and openness in that there is full disclosure to both parties of all relevant evidence. The ideal is not always achievable in practice, of course, since the financial resources of the respective parties may be very different and one side may be able to afford or attract the services of better lawyers and experts than the other. Moreover, as has been seen, the transparency features of that paradigm have precluded in many cases resort even to a criminal process modified in some degree to reflect witness and evidential protection needs in respect of terrorist cases, and have necessitated the use of executive measures with the different challenge arrangements and processes just delineated. Openness, transparency and full disclosure have been 'trumped' in these arrangements and processes by security concerns in terms of 'closed' material not being revealed to individuals or their legal teams, and with them being excluded from the 'closed' sessions in which the relevant court deals with that material. The 'fair hearing' counterbalance, to enable a degree of probing and testing of the 'closed' material in the interests of the individual and of assisting the relevant court to deal with the case justly and effectively, is said to be provided by the role of the Special Advocate. It is acutely clear that individuals and their legal teams are at a very significant disadvantage. It is equally clear that the Special Advocates, in dealing with the 'closed' material, are by no means on an equal footing with their counterparts acting for the Home Secretary. Indeed the Special Advocate is faced sometimes by the principal Government Law Officer, the Attorney General, and always by an expert legal team backed by all the resources of a great Department of State and the Government legal service, not least of Treasury Solicitor's office. Special Advocates are hampered in part in that they cannot have the usual relationship with the person in whose interests they are acting or with that person's legal team. They do not take instructions from that person, who is not a 'client' in any real sense, nor are they a part of their legal team able to interact with an instructing solicitor representing the appellants. They are, moreover, backed by few institutional resources in terms of investigating lines of inquiry, assembling expert or other witnesses, or maintaining a database of relevant legal decisions of SIAC or the High Court.

The Government is firmly of the view that

> These procedures provide an appellant with a fair and effective means of challenging decisions while ensuring that sensitive information is protected from disclosure, and that the composition of SIAC provides it with the expertise necessary both to assess intelligence material, and to consider and decide appeals within its jurisdiction. Immigration and nationality matters do not fall under the head of civil rights and obligations, and the provisions of Article 6 of the ECHR therefore do not apply. However, if they did, the Government considers that SIAC's present procedures fully meet the requirements of that Article as they relate to civil procedures.[47]

While the Court of Appeal, as shall be seen, certainly thought that the processes enabled the achievement of a substantial measure of justice for the individual,[48] the evidence of Special Advocates themselves has firmly been couched in terms of making it clear that their participation in proceedings should not be read as giving them a seal of approval in terms of affording justice. Some have withdrawn from participation in protest in respect of ATCSA proceedings, one to avoid giving a 'fig leaf of respectability and legitimacy to a process' he found 'odious',[49] while those who have continued have done so on the basis that they can do some good in, but none out.[50]

The Home Secretary's case against an individual will be made up of both 'open' material and 'closed' material. 'Open' material is that which is disclosed to individuals and their lawyers and which features strongly in the open judgments of SIAC and the High Court. Much of it consists of assertions, the evidential base for which is contained in 'closed' material.[51] 'Closed material' covers any relevant material that the Home Secretary objects to disclosing to individuals and their legal teams.[52] Apparently, in each case so far the Home Secretary has relied on some such material, necessitating therefore the appointment by the Solicitor General in each case of a Special Advocate.[53] The open judgments of SIAC and of the High Court on PTA control orders and the evidence to the CAC inquiry into SIAC and its operation, together afford some insight into the nature of the 'closed' material. It will typically consist of intelligence assessments prepared by the security and intelligence services on the situation in a particular country, on particular groups

---

[47] CAC 7th (2004–05b): Ev. 50, para. 25 (Department for Constitutional Affairs).

[48] *M* v *Secretary of State for the Home Department* [2004] 2 All ER 863, paras. 13, 34.

[49] CAC 7th (2004–05b): Ev. 1, answer to Q. 1 (Ian MacDonald QC).

[50] CAC 7th (2004–05b): Ev. 2, answer to Q. 4 and Ev. 4 answer to Q.10 (both Neil Garnham QC); Ev. 54–5, para. 7 (a number of Special Advocates).

[51] Ibid, Ev. 45, para. 8 (Amnesty International).

[52] High Court PTA Rules, r. 76.1.

[53] CAC 7th (2004–05b): Ev. 53, para. 1 (a number of Special Advocates).

and their links with each other and to Al Qaeda. There may be documentary evidence from and oral testimony by members of those agencies or other experts called by the Home Secretary. Some material may be derived from agents and informers. Some may derive from allied intelligence services. The mode of its obtaining has raised the issue of the admissibility of material derived from torture. This is explored in more depth in the coverage in the next chapter of the relevant litigation and its outcome. But, on a more basic level, some material may originally have been in a foreign language and issues may arise as to its proper translation. Other material may consist of or be the product of communications intercepts, admissible here but not in the 'ordinary' courts. The material may focus on the person's links with others thought to be involved in terrorism or themselves the subject of SIAC/High Court proceedings by the Home Secretary, raising a spectre of guilt by association, and helping interfere with the private and family life of individuals and their families by contributing to a reluctance of family, friends and neighbours to visit those in detention or subject to a control order. A variety of references to criminal proceedings resulting in acquittal has also been seen to figure in the open judgments of SIAC. Some of the 'closed' material may consist of unproven and untested allegations or suspicions of past criminal conduct, putting in stark context the issue of the standard of proof, considered below. Some may well be in the public domain already (for example, used elsewhere in legal proceedings or part of material leaked to the press here or in another country).

'Closed' material (the evidentiary base for the assertions in the 'open' material (all individuals know of the case against them)) is considered by SIAC or the High Court in 'closed' sessions from which individuals and their chosen legal team are excluded. As Amnesty International put it, they 'are denied disclosure of the most important 'evidence' against them … [something in Amnesty's view] contrary to Article 6(3)(a)–(c) of the ECHR and Article 14(3)(a), (b) and (d) of the ICCPR'.[54] As regards this material, the Special Advocate has two roles: a 'disclosure' role and a 'representation' role. Before explaining and appraising each, it is appropriate to further consider the appointment and general task of the Special Advocate and his/her relationship with the individual and their legal team.

Where (apparently invariably) the Home Secretary proposes to rely on 'closed' material, he or she must notify the Attorney General to procure the appointment of a Special Advocate.[55] If one were not appointed, the Home Secretary would be unable to rely on any 'closed' material in the proceedings.[56] Statutorily, the task of the Special Advocate is to represent the interests of an appellant in any proceedings before SIAC (or the High Court) from which the appellant (or the actual or putative controlee) and any of their legal representatives are excluded.[57] The Special Advocate's functions are to represent those interests by making submissions to the

---

[54] CAC 7th (2004–05b): Ev. 45, para. 8.
[55] SIAC Rules, r. 34; High Court PTA Rules, r. 76.23.
[56] SIAC Rules, r. 37(2); High Court PTA Rules, r. 76.28(1)(b).
[57] SIACA, s. 6(1); PTA 2005. s. 11(5), Sch., para. 7.

Commission or Court at any hearings from which the individual and their legal representatives are excluded; cross–examining witnesses at any such hearings; and making written submissions to the Commission or Court.[58] While the Attorney General is specified as the appointer, that function has properly been delegated to the Solicitor General, since not only is the Attorney General a chief legal officer of the Government of the day, he or she may well lead for the Home Secretary in the proceedings before SIAC (as was done in the generic ATCSA proceedings before SIAC and in the House of Lords in the derogation case, *A and Others*) or the High Court.[59] In England and Wales, the Special Advocate must hold a general legal qualification, and typically is a barrister.[60] Many, but not all, Special Advocates are members of the three civil panels of junior counsel to the Crown approved to do Government legal work. From these panels, the Treasury Solicitor's department recommends to the Attorney General a potential list of candidates with appropriate experience. Those selected are then security-vetted. The resulting 'pool' can then be drawn on, subject to any conflict of interest, to act for either the Crown or as Special Advocate for affected individuals. A number of leading members of the Bar regarded as having 'good claimant experience and expertise have also been appointed'. Initially, given the immigration 'bent' of SIAC's jurisdiction, Special Advocates typically were public lawyers often with immigration law experience. The Special Advocates themselves thought this too narrow a range on which to draw. They suggested that

> The principal requirement for a Special Advocate in proceedings before SIAC is the ability to absorb and analyse information that may be in voluminous documents, and to cross–examine effectively on the basis of this. Such abilities are not confined to public law practitioners. While public law issues do sometimes arise in relation to closed material, the nature of the work may also require skills which those such as criminal lawyers, or those with experience of handling witnesses in civil cases, would be equally if not better qualified to perform.

The CAC recommended broadening the pool,[61] and the Government moved quickly to advertise so as to get Advocates with that wider range of experience.[62] Too limited a pool has another consequence – delay – since in this system, with restrictions on communication once the Special Advocate has seen 'closed' material, each individual needs a different Special Advocate.

---

[58] SIAC Rules, r. 35; High Court PTA Rules, r. 76.24.

[59] CAC 7th (2004–05a): para. 69.

[60] SIAC, s.6 (3); PTA 2005, s. 11, Sch., para. 7(3), (4); CAC 7th (2004–05a): para. 44. On Scotland and Northern Ireland, see SIAC, s.6 (2), (3) and PTA 2005, s. 11, Sch., para. 7(3), (4), (6), (7). The appointment is respectively by the Lord Advocate and the Attorney General for Northern Ireland.

[61] CAC 7th (2004–05a): para. 74.

[62] Cm 6596 (2005): 6.

As regards the relationship of the Special Advocate to the individual and their legal team, the legislation specifically provides that he or she is 'not to be responsible to the person whose interests he is appointed to represent'.[63] There is no normal adviser-client relationship here. The individual has no unfettered choice of who should act as Special Advocate, although the process has evolved, in part because of the CAC Inquiry, so that, with the wider pool referred to above, the intention is that the individual will have greater choice so long as it does not produce a conflict with any other appeal in which that Special Advocate is or has acted, but, more importantly given the security rationale of this whole process, the chosen Special Advocate must not have had prior access to the 'closed' material.[64] This is because there are very specific rules about their communications with the individual and their legal team after such access. Communication with them is permitted at any time before service of 'closed' material by the Home Secretary. Thereafter, he/she cannot communicate without specific direction from SIAC or the High Court. He/she can request such direction, but any such request must be notified to the Home Secretary to enable an objection. The Special Advocates indicated in evidence to the CAC inquiry that in practice the power to enable communication was as a result 'almost never used' since in effect it meant that the Special Advocate could communicate with the individual and their lawyers 'only if the precise form of the communication has been approved by his opponent in the proceedings. Such a requirement precludes communicating even on matters of pure legal strategy (matters unrelated to the particular factual sensitivities of a case).'[65] As Lord Bingham noted in another context in respect of which a Special Advocate regime was sought to be used, appointment of a lawyer to act as Special Advocate raised ethical problems because

> A lawyer who cannot take full instructions from his client, nor report to his client, who is not responsible to his client and whose relationship with the client lacks the quality of confidence inherent in any ordinary lawyer–client relationship, is acting in a way hitherto unknown to the legal profession. While not insuperable, these problems should not be ignored, since neither the defendant nor the public will be fully aware of what is being done.[66]

The awkwardness of the Special Advocate's position manifested itself where the individual and their legal team withdrew in protest from proceedings. What, in such a case, should the Advocate do? *Justice* thought he or she should follow the individual's lead.[67] Some had done that.[68] But one Special Advocate thought it important to exercise an independent judgment about whether staying on in the

---

[63] SIACA, s. 6(4); PTA 2005, s. 11, Sch., para. 7(5).

[64] Cm 6596 (2005): 6.

[65] CAC 7th (2004–05b): Ev. 55, para. 9.

[66] *R v H and C* [2004] UKHL 3, cited in CAC 7th (2004–05a): para. 63.

[67] CAC 7th (2004–05b): Ev. 68, para. 38.

[68] Ibid, para. 36.

'closed' proceedings might advance the individual's case and thus be acting in their best interests.[69]

The Special Advocate has two functions: the 'disclosure' function; and the 'representation' function. Having set the necessary context on appointment and the general task of the Special Advocate and their relationship with the individual and their legal team, these can now be analysed in turn.

The CAC encapsulated the 'disclosure' function as one of testing in 'closed' session

> ... to the full the cogency of the case put forward by the Home Secretary for non-disclosure of material. The Special Advocate examines closed passages in statements and closed documents to ascertain whether, for example, no possible or no real harm could arise from disclosure, or the material in question is already in the public domain (for example, as a result of a Governmental press release, disclosure in a foreign case, material leaked to the press etc). This stage can be extremely time-consuming, as it tends to operate by means of an iterative process using a series of exchanges between the Special Advocate and Home Secretary (usually in the form of a schedule of objections with reasons, responded to in Schedule form), culminating in points of dispute that are brought before SIAC for its adjudication.[70]

It is essential

> ... that as much information as possible be made available to the appellant and his or her representative. ... information should only be withheld from the client where it can be clearly demonstrated that disclosure would result in a serious or credible risk to national security. Not only is disclosure essential to protect the human rights of the appellant, it is also crucial that SIAC has the best possible evidence before it when determining matters of national security. That in turn requires evidence from one party to be subject to challenges by the other.

The more material available to the individual and their legal team, the better they are able to prepare their own case, which will be considered in 'open' sessions. But also, the more they know, the better they can aid the Special Advocate, during the period before he or she is served with 'closed' material, by suggesting points to consider, lines of inquiry and the like, as regards that material in 'closed' session. Ensuring maximum possible disclosure consonant with genuine security needs is the role both of the Special Advocate and the relevant court. But both are hampered in attaining this limited ideal. The process does not operate like a normal civil disclosure one in which a party has to disclose all relevant material, whether supporting or undermining their case. In SIAC or in High Court control order proceedings, the Home Secretary effectively decides what he or she will and will not disclose and supplies only edited materials. The limited powers of the relevant

---

[69] Neil Garnham QC, cited in CAC 7th (2004–05a): para. 98.
[70] CAC 7th (2004–05a): para. 58.

court and the severe imbalance of resources as between the Special Advocate and the Home Secretary inhibit the end of attaining as full a disclosure as is consonant with genuine security needs. Those limitations and that imbalance place a premium on the integrity and capabilities of the Home Secretary's advisers, security and intelligence staff, and his/her legal team.

Where the Home Secretary proposes to rely on 'closed' material, he or she must file with SIAC or the High Court, and serve the Special Advocate with, a copy of that material, and a statement of the reasons for objecting to the disclosure of that material to the individual and their legal team. A statement of the material must also be filed and served in a form which can be served on the individual and their legal team, if and to the extent that is possible without disclosing information contrary to the public interest, and serve it also on them.[71] If the Home Secretary and the Special Advocate cannot agree on disclosure, the dispute will be dealt with by way of hearing by SIAC or the High Court, as may be.[72] There are some problems in identifying relevant and, particularly, exculpatory material. Those bodies ostensibly can overrule the Home Secretary's objections to disclosure. They can also direct him/her to serve material on the individual and his legal team either in the form it was filed with the SIAC or the Court or in a different form. The force of those powers is somewhat blunted, however, because the Home Secretary can avoid disclosure and service on the individual by deciding to proceed without relying on that material and resting his or her case on material that remains 'closed'.[73] The PTA 2005 and the High Court 'control order' rules, however, place on the Home Secretary a duty to make a reasonable search for and to disclose to the Special Advocate and the Court all material available to him or her and relevant to the matters under consideration in the proceedings or to the reasons for decisions to which those proceedings relate.[74] No similar duties are expressed in SIACA, ATCSA or the SIAC Procedure Rules, but a similar practice operated apparently reflective of the public law duty at common law to act fairly in a procedural sense.[75] The idea is that evidence is assembled so far as possible in a non-partisan, balanced manner. Material connected to the individual concerned, but on which the Home Secretary does not propose to rely, is nevertheless scrutinized by counsel to the Home Secretary to see if it contains any exculpatory material. Any identified will be disclosed to the Special Advocate. The problem here is that neither SIAC nor the High Court nor the Special Advocate possesses any means of knowing that this has been done or how well. The process relies heavily on the integrity and professionalism of counsel to the Home Secretary. Yet neither that counsel, with their legal training, nor intelligence officers preparing the assessments in the closed material, lacking that training, can operate in the same way as would a lawyer

---

[71] SIAC Rules, r. 37; High Court PTA Rules, r. 76.28.

[72] SIAC Rules, r. 38; High Court PTA Rules, r. 76.29.

[73] SIAC Rules, r. 38(6), (7); High Court PTA Rules, r. 76.29(6)–(8).

[74] PTA 2005, Sch., para. 4; High Court PTA Rules, r. 76.27.

[75] CAC 7th (2004–05a): para. 92.

trying to construct a defence. They may, because of the different ways in which they might approach the material, not identify any linkages that could prove exculpatory. Nor can Special Advocates readily act as would defence lawyers in civil or criminal cases. Once served with 'closed' material, they cannot discuss matters with the individual and their legal team and obtain their assistance in identifying lines of inquiry. Nor, lacking the services of an instructing solicitor and their investigative team (private detectives, security consultants), are they able, faced with a mass of detailed material, to assemble translators to check translation or possible other meanings, to gather expert witnesses with scientific or technical expertise or specific regional or country or terrorist group expertise. Nor have they the tools to assemble any witnesses. A fundamental problem is that they can only deal with the material identified as potentially exculpatory by the 'other side'. They have no opportunity to 'consider all the material held by the Home Secretary to decide whether it is potentially exculpatory'.[76] And, even were such an opportunity afforded, they lack the resources to do so effectively.

A number of suggestions have been made to move towards redressing the imbalance in the Special Advocate's resources when set against the support available to the Home Secretary. These will be examined below, after consideration of the Special Advocate's other function – that of 'representation', since they encompass both functions.

As the CAC saw it,

> The representation function is to represent the Appellant's interests in relation to that part of the hearing held *in camera*, which entails making the best case possible from all the available evidence–both open and closed–but without informed instructions from the appellant.[77]

The nature of the material relied on by the Home Secretary makes this a difficult task, particularly since the individual and their legal team are left very much in the dark about the case against them and because of the inability of the Special Advocate to discuss matters with them once served with the 'closed' material. Even where efforts succeed in securing a greater disclosure to the individual and their legal team of relevant material than the Home Secretary intended originally, this may not help much because the two parties cannot discuss matters once the Special Advocate has been served with 'closed' material. Thee individual and their legal team can communicate with the Special Advocate (and the latter can acknowledge receipt) but there can be no dialogue about the significance of that newly disclosed material or on what leads or lines of questioning or inquiry usefully to pursue. As a number of Special Advocates put it:

---

[76] Ibid., para. 61.
[77] Ibid., para. 58.

... the Special Advocates have no means of pursuing or deploying evidence in reply. If they put forward a positive case in response to the closed allegations, that positive case is inevitably based on conjecture. They have no way of knowing whether it is the case that the appellant himself would wish to advance. The inability to take instructions on the closed material fundamentally limits the extent to which the Special Advocates can play a meaningful part in any appeal.[78]

Their main role is thus to identify through submissions and cross-examination the respects in which the Home Secretary's case is unsupported by the evidence relied on and to check for and highlight inconsistencies in it.[79] But they are also frustrated by the nature of the material before SIAC and the High Court and the *Rehman* – supported lack in such proceedings (other than those in respect of the yet-to-be-invoked derogating control orders) of any meaningful concept of a standard of proof. The Special Advocates reported in their evidence on the following type of cross examination in 'closed' session:

Special Advocate: Do you accept that document A, though consistent with the sinister explanation you attribute to it, is equally consistent with another completely innocent explanation?

Witness: Yes.

Special Advocate: So, the sinister explanation is no more than conjecture?

Witness: No. Document A has to be considered alongside documents B, C, D and E. When viewed as a whole, on a global approach, the sinister explanation is plausible.

Special Advocate: But you have already admitted that documents B, C, D and E are in exactly the same category: each of them is equally consistent with an innocent explanation and with a sinister one.

Witness: Yes, but when viewed together they justify the assessment that the sinister explanation is plausible and form the basis of a reasonable suspicion.[80]

They, like the Law Society, suggested a threshold of balance of probabilities.[81] That applies as regards derogating control orders, but not as regards immigration and citizenship issues or non-derogating control orders, the only ones currently deployed. In such situations, how relevant a particular piece of material is will depend on assessment by members of the security and intelligence services. Following *Rehman*, SIAC had to show deference on the issue of risk to national

---

[78] CAC 7th (2004–05b): Ev. 55, para. 10.
[79] Ibid.
[80] Ibid., Ev. 58, para. 27.
[81] Ibid., Ev. 58, para. 28 (Special Advocates); Ev. 42.

security. But (for ATCSA detentions and control orders) in respect of the reasonableness of the Home Secretary's suspicion that the individual was a terrorist, the Special Advocates contended that, despite its claims to the contrary, SIAC accorded undue regard and respect to the experience and expertise of the member giving evidence:

> When faced with (for example) a coded conversation which is said to bear a particular meaning or a question about the reliability of a source, SIAC treats the assessment of the Security Service witness as a judge in civil proceedings would treat (for example) the evidence of a doctor or surveyor or engineer giving expert evidence. Unlike in ordinary civil litigation, however, the Special Advocate has no opportunity to call expert evidence in reply.[82]

What might or has been done to try to reduce the imbalance? Lord Carlile (the official independent reviewer of the operation of ATCSA and PTA 2005) suggested (and the CAC supported this) 'that Special Advocates be provided with seconded and specially trained intelligence officers' to help probe for relevant material and help the Special Advocate fully to understand it and its potential weaknesses.[83] Government was unwilling to second serving officers because the role was not consistent with their duties of confidence and loyalty.[84] It confirmed, however, that such officers

> ... remain willing (as they have been in the past) to assist the Special Advocates with specific enquiries or, even more generally, to understand the nature of intelligence material. This includes the provision of secure internet faculties for the purposes of conducting searches of material in the public domain. The Special Advocates are being provided with a training pack which includes, in classified form, explanations of closed material to assist with that understanding.[85]

Government pointed out that its provision of instructing solicitors (see further below) (which the Special Advocates had argued for)[86] would further aid this. Moreover, consideration was being given to the feasibility of providing a 'short induction into intelligence assessments'.[87] The Special Advocates' call for the ability to draw on independent expertise[88] would be looked at on a case-by-case basis.[89] The CAC's call for the establishment of a body to support Special Advocates[90] has been met in part by the establishment in May 2005 of the Special

---

[82] Ibid, para. 29.
[83] CAC 7th (2004–05a): paras 77, 93.
[84] Cm 6596 (2005): 10.
[85] Ibid.
[86] CAC 7th (2004–05b): Ev. 56, paras 12–14.
[87] Cm 6596 (2005): 10.
[88] CAC 7th (2004–05b): Ev. 57, paras 18–19.
[89] Cm 6596 (2005): 10. The expert would have to be security cleared.
[90] CAC 7th (2004–05a): paras 108, 109, 112.

Advocates Support Office (SASO). Located in the Treasury Solicitor's Department, SASO, Government said, would operate 'entirely independently' of the immigration team acting for the Home Secretary.[91] SASO is made up of three security-vetted government lawyers to act as the Special Advocates' substantive instructing solicitors. Each will be able 'to see the closed material, engage with the substance of the case and provide administrative support to the Special Advocate'[92] who will also have the assistance of a procedural instructing solicitor who would not necessarily be security cleared. His/her role would be to 'deliver the initial brief to the Special Advocate with any open material, as well as engaging in correspondence with the parties and, for example, attending directions hearings and liaising in relation to listing'.[93] These are welcome measures. The CAC, however, doubted whether SASO would be enough, and instead recommended an 'Office of the Special Advocate'. This should be backed by adequate resources and staffing and 'should include security-cleared staff to assist in research and assessment of controlled material'.[94]

Some staff could surely come from retired but experienced security service personnel. Government rejected this as unnecessarily bureaucratic and involving disproportionate public expenditure.[95] It also considered that the current rules permitted a greater degree of contact with the suspect and their legal team after 'closed' material had been served on the Special Advocate, than had been used. It saw some of the Special Advocate's difficulties in such communication as attributable to the suspect's unwillingness to engage with the 'open' parts of the appeal process.[96] But that, of course, stems in great part from their perception, shared with others, that the process cannot afford them a 'fair hearing'.[97]

A Raft of Questions to Consider

It has been seen that there are a variety of views on whether the processes examined here afford a fair hearing. There seems a measure of agreement that the SIAC process represents in the immigration sphere a marked improvement on the previous 'adviser' system. There remain grave doubts, however, on whether such processes and the low level of 'proof' involved are apt for dealing with detention without trial and control orders. Whether the processes comply with the fair

---

[91] Cm 6596 (2005): 11.

[92] Ibid.

[93] Ibid.

[94] CAC 7th (2004–05a): paras 108, 109, 112.

[95] Cm 6596 (2005): 12.

[96] Ibid., pp. 8–9.

[97] CAC 7th (2004–05b): Ev. 54–5, para. 7 (Special Advocates); Ev. 64, paras 19–20 (Justice); Ev. 76, paras. 9–11 (Liberty); Ev., p. 40–41 (Anver Jeevanjee, former member, IAT).

hearing requirements of the ECHR remains an open question. Do they represent (particularly since the 2005 reforms) the best achievable compromise between security interests and those of due process in a situation of perceived danger to the public and to national security in which a criminal process alone cannot suffice? Or are they an attempt to give an undeserved 'fig leaf' of respectability to counterproductive and unnecessary processes likely to bring our courts into disrepute?[98] Have SIAC and the High Court abdicated their proper function and been unduly deferential to executive opinion? Or have they rather endangered security and the public by inappropriately fettering the Home Secretary, police and security services seeking to protect both? What do challenges in this area tell us about the proper role of courts in the security context in the HRA era? These are some of questions to be pondered by the reader in the light of the foregoing exposition of the schemes and processes of challenge. Some are considered in the next two chapters dealing respectively with litigation in respect of human rights and other legal matters (chapter 9), and broader matters of summation and reflection (chapter 10).

---

[98] Baroness Kennedy, HL Debs, Vol 670, cols. 195–6 (1 March 2005).

Chapter 9

Legal Challenges and Human Rights Issues

Introduction and Overview

This chapter explores the ways in which some of the concerns identified in this Part of the book have translated into the outcome of a range of legal challenges, including those raising human rights issues, in respect of the use of executive measures since 9/11. In a number of instances, where powers have yet to be invoked or challenges are pending, the chapter suggests what the outcomes might be.

Each of the security regimes of executive measures since 9/11 affords a right of appeal from the executive decision-maker, either to SIAC (ATCSA detention and national security immigration/citizenship matters) or to the High Court (control orders under the PTA 2005). From those courts lies a further appeal, on a point of law only, to the Court of Appeal (or its Scottish and Northern Ireland equivalents) and the House of Lords. For other regimes (detention in Iraq; issues surrounding the United Kingdom Government's response to detainees in Guantanamo), there is the avenue of judicial review. This chapter notes judicial review in those spheres. but mainly examines the use made of these appellate modes of challenge, focusing particularly on matters of human rights compliance. In the past such matters were very much the domain of the organs of the regional system of human rights protection, the European Convention on Human Rights (ECHR). The period since 9/11, in contrast, falls in the era of the HRA, and these matters have instead to date solely been the province of United Kingdom courts, with recourse to Strasbourg as a yet-to-be-needed longstop. The initial appellate modes of challenge are set in motion by the aggrieved individual, seeking to overturn the executive decision to detain, subject to a control order, exclude, deport or deprive of citizenship, as the case may be. But the further recourse to higher courts has been used by both sides. The executive uses it to seek to overturn a SIAC or High Court ruling that some aspect of the scheme in question is not Convention-compliant and to have restored the Government view on that issue. The individual uses those appeal rights to overturn SIAC/High Court/Court of Appeal validation of the executive decision limiting his/her rights and freedoms. Moreover, on human rights issues, other actors appear on the stage. Constitutional and human rights litigation typically sees the court being aided on the matter by the intervention of a number of interested parties. Going beyond national courts to the European Court of Human Rights is, of course, a direct route of challenge open only to the aggrieved individual. The State cannot be a victim of a human rights violation, merely a respondent in a case brought against it, or an applicant bringing a case against another state, as in *Greece* v *United Kingdom* or *Ireland* v *United Kingdom*. To date, the United Kingdom has only ever featured as a respondent. The deportation context, however, shows the United Kingdom Government intervening in a case before that Court in which an individual is contesting the human rights compliance of a decision of the Netherlands to deport him on security grounds.[1] The Government's objective here is an aspect of its wider strategy of trying to secure a change in one of the 'rules of the game', namely a modification of the absolute preclusion of deportation afforded by the *Chahal* principle. In effect, the Government is seeking to have adopted the view of the minority in *Chahal*,[2] a view which seems to have prevailed – at least in very exceptional circumstances – in the Canadian Supreme Court applying the Canadian Charter of Rights and Freedoms.[3] The Home Secretary explained in a speech to the European Parliament that it is

> ... necessary to balance very important rights for individuals against the collective right for security against those who attack us through terrorist violence. Our strengthening of human rights needs to acknowledge a truth which we should all accept, that the right to be protected from torture and ill-treatment must be considered side by side with the right to be protected from the death and destruction caused by indiscriminate terrorism, sometimes caused, instigated or fomented by nationals from countries outside the EU. ... The view of my Government is that this balance is not right for the circumstances which we now face ... and that it needs to be closely examined in that context.[4]

The legal challenges (actual or potential) have covered, or could cover, a number of areas. They have embraced (or could embrace) matters of substantive compliance with a number of ECHR rights and freedoms: freedom from torture, inhuman or degrading treatment and punishment; the right to liberty and security of person (freedom from arbitrary arrest and detention), the right to respect for private and family life, home and correspondence, as well as the interrelated freedoms of thought, conscience and religion, and of expression, association and assembly. They have also raised matters of the material or evidence on which SIAC and/or the High Court can act, and the standards of scrutiny they must apply, unfortunately varying (with not a great deal of justification for that variance) as between each decision-making context. Finally a central focus of actual and potential litigation concerns the matter of whether the systems for challenging adverse executive decisions themselves, and their attempts to reconcile due process and security, meet ECHR requirements of a fair hearing. Discussion is divided

---

[1] *Ramzy* v *Netherlands* Application no. 25424/05.

[2] JHRC 3rd (2005): para. 148.

[3] *Suresh* v *Minister of Citizenship and Immigration and the Attorney General of Canada (Suresh* v *Canada)* [2002] 1 SCR 3.

[4] Quoted in JHRC 3rd (2005): para. 148.

accordingly and, because of varying levels of review, sometimes by reference to the particular scheme.

Substantive Compliance with Fundamental Rights and Freedoms

ATCSA Detention: the Derogation Litigation

From the outset, Government was clear that its scheme of indefinite detention without trial of foreign national terrorist suspects, unable to be prosecuted or deported, was incompatible with the guarantee of liberty and security of person afforded by Art. 5 ECHR, as normally applicable. It accordingly entered a protective derogation under Art. 15 ECHR, arguing that, in accordance with that provision, the scheme was a justified, necessary and proportionate response to a public emergency threatening the life of the nation. It did not go beyond what the exigencies of that emergency strictly required. It was, moreover, consistent with the country's other international obligations. As an immigration measure, to deal with a threat posed by foreign nationals, it was furthermore not discriminatory contrary to Art. 14 ECHR, but instead rationally distinguished between citizens and aliens, as that provision and international law permitted.

This characterization of the scheme was the first subject of challenge by the ATCSA detainees before SIAC, with the matter of whether they were properly detained under the legislation being adjourned pending resolution of the derogation issues and the general Convention compliance of the ATCSA scheme.

The challenge to this Convention rights aspect was initially upheld by SIAC on 20 July 2002. SIAC is the only court to examine in detail all the 'security evidence' seen by and presented to it on behalf of the Home Secretary. Moreover, SIAC also had the advantage, not possessed by him, of having that material carefully probed, on its and the applicants' behalf, by the Special Advocates in their 'devil's advocate' role. Applying to that material thus thoroughly scrutinized the Art. 15 tests propounded by the European Court of Human Rights in *Lawless* v *Ireland*, SIAC, paying the due deference to executive opinion that *Rehman* and the traditional judicial approach required, held that there existed in the United Kingdom an imminent public emergency threatening the life of the nation. It did so not because an attack was imminent, but rather because of the devastation possible if a 9/11 type attack by Al Qaeda operatives was not prevented.[5] That conclusion was thought to be reinforced since the United Kingdom, standing 'shoulder to shoulder' with the United States in the 'war on terrorism', was as a result at greater risk than other European States.[6] It also regarded the response as proportionate. SIAC declared the relevant ATCSA provisions incompatible with Art. 5 read with Art. 14 ECHR as discriminatory on grounds of national origin, since those terrorist

---

[5] [2003] 1 All ER 816, at paras 33–35, 83–90.

[6] Ibid.

suspects threatening security who held British citizenship could not be detained. Art. 14 ECHR was not the subject of derogation, and had to be read in its normal application. In SIAC's view, the material before the Home Secretary did not show the threat as solely arising from foreign nationals.

The Home Secretary successfully appealed the decision to the Court of Appeal. On 25 October 2002, the Court – paying due deference to his assessment and to that of SIAC as the only court which had seen the 'security' evidence' – upheld the decision on imminent public emergency. Again paying the required due deference to executive opinion, like SIAC, the Court of Appeal held that the detention measures taken did not go beyond the exigencies of that emergency situation required. They were not disproportionate and the deprivation of liberty imposed was subject to adequate safeguards, because of the availability of SIAC appeal and review options.[7] The decision on the adequacy of safeguards is supportable, but the former finding on proportionality may be criticized since neither court explored the viability of less restrictive alternatives which might be sustainable under the ECHR without an Art. 15 derogation. These perforce would have to fall well short of effective 'house arrest' (for example, electronic tagging, physical and other electronic surveillance), and would have significant privacy implications and resource costs.[8] SIAC's decision on discrimination, however, was overturned by the Court of Appeal.[9] The Court regarded the proper pigeonhole for the legislative scheme as 'immigration' which of necessity distinguishes, as recognized in international law, between citizens and aliens. Moreover the greater threat to security (paying the due deference to executive opinion required by law)[10] came from foreign nationals, so that the detention only of such nationals was not discrimination contrary to Art. 14 ECHR. The two groups were not similarly situated for purposes of comparison.

The applicants appealed to the House of Lords. The constitutional importance of the challenge was reflected in that the House sat in a bench of nine Law Lords. Lord Steyn, in the light of views he had expressed extra-judicially, had agreed not to be part of it. Argument was heard over four days in October 2004. The nine opinions in the seminal decision of the House of Lords were delivered on 16 December, 2004. The decision represents a marked but welcome departure from a traditional judicial attitude of extreme deference to executive opinion when the red flag of national security is waved. Given that established constitutional and legal tradition of deference, and given the weak-willed approach of the European Court of Human Rights to Art. 15 ECHR, the Home Secretary might be forgiven for thinking legal challenge an irritant but not a particular problem; especially so, when, as has been seen, the House of Lords in *Rehman*, in opinions written before but delivered after 9/11, had castigated SIAC for too narrow an approach to

---

[7]   *A and Others* [2003] 1 All ER 816, at 831–6, 844–6.

[8]   Bonner (2002): 517–520.

[9]   *A and Others* v *Secretary of State for the Home Department* [2003] 1 All ER 816.

[10]   *Secretary of State for the Home Department* v *Rehman* [2002] 1 All ER 122.

national security and for insufficient deference to the Home Secretary's expertise in security matters. The deferential tradition was, moreover, very much to the fore in the Court of Appeal decision on the derogation issues, the decision the subject of this, the ATCSA detainees', appeal to their Lordships' House. Put shortly, the House issued a declaration under section 4 of the HRA that section 23 of ATCSA, the key provision in the indefinite detention without trial scheme, was incompatible with Art. 5 (liberty and security of person) read with Art. 15 ECHR (derogation) as going beyond what was necessitated by the exigencies of a public emergency threatening the life of the nation (disproportionate) and was incompatible with Art. 14 (discrimination) read with Art. 5 ECHR, as being unjustifiably discriminatory on grounds of nationality/national origin.

Closer analysis is required of the opinions in these 'difficult and important appeals',[11] 'one of the most important cases which the House has had to decide in recent years'.[12] The analysis shows that in the Human Rights Act era, the rules of the game have indeed changed as regards judicial scrutiny of executive and legislative action in the national security/public emergency area. Consideration is best approached by separating out the three matters the House had to consider: (a) the threshold issue, whether there was a public emergency threatening the life of the nation; (b) the necessity/proportionality issue, whether the measures taken were strictly required by the exigencies of that public emergency; and (c) whether the measures, by focusing solely on foreign national terrorist suspects, breached the ECHR requirement in Art. 14 that interferences with the protected rights and freedoms be non-discriminatory.

The 'threshold', public emergency, issue SIAC found that an imminent emergency existed, not because an attack was imminent, but because of the devastation that could occur if one took place. The House of Lords held by eight to one (Lord Hoffman dissenting on this issue) that SIAC had not erred in law in that finding, so their Lordships were not empowered to overturn that. 'Public emergency' was regarded as a question primarily if not exclusively a matter for the Executive rather than the judiciary. This did not mean that the judges had simply to accept whatever the Government said on the issue. Baroness Hale put very well both the powers of the court on the issue and the limited nature of the courts' ability to deal with it:

> The courts' power to rule on the validity of the derogation is another of the safeguards enacted by Parliament in this carefully constructed package. It would be meaningless if we could only rubber-stamp what the Home Secretary and Parliament have done. But any sensible court ... recognises the limits of its expertise. Assessing the strength of a general threat to the life of the nation is, or should be, within the expertise of the Government and its advisers. They may, as recent events have shown, not always get it

---

[11] [2004] UKHL 56, para. 191 (Lord Walker).

[12] [2004] UKHL 56, para. 86 (Lord Hoffman). Baroness Hale characterized it 'the most important case to come before the House since I have been a member' (para. 219).

right. But courts too do not always get things right. It would be very surprising if the courts were better able to make that sort of judgment than the Government. ... That does not mean that the courts could never intervene. Unwarranted declarations of emergency are a familiar tool of tyranny. If a Government were to declare a public emergency where patently there was no such thing, it would be the duty of the court to say so. But we are here considering the immediate aftermath of the unforgettable events of 11 September 2001. The attacks launched on the United States on that date were clearly intended to threaten the life of that nation. SIAC were satisfied that the open and closed material before them justified the conclusion that there was also a public emergency threatening the life of this nation. I, for one, would not feel qualified or even inclined to disagree.[13]

Lord Hoffman's much-reported dissent – doubtless reflective of his South African experience – unfortunately attracted most headlines. It was the subject of the Prime Minister's derisory approach to judges in statements after the 7/7 attacks. Lord Hoffman stated in ringing terms:

This is one of the most important cases which the House has had to decide in recent years. It calls into question the very existence of an ancient liberty of which this country has until now been very proud: freedom from arbitrary arrest and detention. The power which the Home Secretary seeks to uphold is a power to detain people indefinitely without charge or trial. Nothing could be more antithetical to the instincts and traditions of the people of the United Kingdom. ... The Home Secretary has adduced evidence, both open and secret, to the existence of a threat of serious terrorist outrages. The Attorney General did not invite us to examine the secret evidence, but despite the widespread scepticism which has attached to intelligence assessments since the fiasco over Iraqi weapons of mass destruction, I am willing to accept that credible evidence of such plots exist. The events of 11 September 2001 in New York and Washington and 11 March 2003 in Madrid make it entirely likely that the threat of similar atrocities in the United Kingdom is a real one. But the question is whether such a threat is a threat to the life of the nation. The Attorney General's submissions and the judgment of the Special Immigration Appeals Commission treated a threat of serious physical damage and loss of life as necessarily involving a threat to the life of the nation. But in my opinion this shows a misunderstanding of what is meant by 'threatening the life of the nation'. Of course the government has a duty to protect the lives and property of its citizens. But that is a duty which it owes all the time and which it must discharge without destroying our constitutional freedoms. There may be some nations too fragile or fissiparous to withstand a serious act of violence. But that is not the case in the United Kingdom. ... This is a nation which has been tested in adversity, which has survived physical destruction and catastrophic loss of life. I do not underestimate the ability of fanatical groups of terrorists to kill and destroy, but they do not threaten the life of the nation. Whether we would survive Hitler hung in the balance, but there is no doubt that we shall survive Al Qaeda. ... Terrorist violence, serious as it is, does not threaten our institutions of government or our existence as a civil community. For these reasons I think that the Special Immigration Appeals Commission made an error of law ... In my

---

[13] [2004] UKHL 56, para. 226.

opinion, [indefinite detention without trial] in any form is not compatible with our constitution. The real threat to the life of the nation, in the sense of a people living in accordance with its traditional laws and political values, comes not from terrorism but from laws such as these.[14]

Its tone is reminiscent of Lord Atkin's famous dissent in *Liversidge* v *Anderson* and that of Lord Shaw in *ex parte Zadig*. It also adopts the 'strict scrutiny' approach that arguably should be that of the European Court of Human Rights.[15] Despite this, it is open to a number of criticisms. First of all, it takes insufficient account of the Strasbourg jurisprudence, as section 2 of the HRA mandates courts to do. Lord Hoffman merely characterized that case law as unhelpful and as stressing the wide margin of appreciation it afforded a State. For him, Strasbourg case law meant that a United Kingdom court had to decide the matter for itself. His opinion thus fails to relate the Court's definitions to the context of the cases in which they were propounded. It shows no appreciation for the low level of violence and anti-State activity accepted[16] and the 'not very high' threshold[17] set by the Court in *Lawless* v *Ireland* and in *Marshall* v *United Kingdom* as a basis for derogation, something analysed more fully in the opinions of Lords Rodger,[18] Walker,[19] and, particularly, Lord Bingham, who also explored material in respect of the United Kingdom's obligations under the 'public emergency clause' in Art. 4 ICCPR, statements from the Council of Europe's Commissioner for Human Rights, the Newton Review of ATCSA and reports on it by the JHRC.[20] Lord Hoffman had read in draft Lord Bingham's opinion, but adopted it only as a 'statement of the background to this case and the issues which it raises'. Nor does Lord Hoffman's opinion consider the analogy between that case and the situation under appeal of terrorists using one country as a base to attack another. Lord Hoffman's opinion is difficult to reconcile with the deferential approach he set out for SIAC in *Rehman* immediately after 9/11. Indeed his colleague Lord Hope expressly relied on Lord Hoffman's opinion in *Rehman* to stress that in 'the domestic legal order also great weight must be given to the views of the executive', so that 'that the questions whether there is an emergency and whether it threatens the life of the nation are pre-eminently for the executive and for Parliament. The judgment that has to be formed on these issues lies outside the expertise of the courts, including SIAC in the exercise of the jurisdiction that has been given to it by Part 4 of the 2001 Act.'[21]

---

[14] [2004] UKHL 56, paras 86, 94–7.
[15] Goss and Ni Aolá.in (2001): 637–649
[16] [2004] UKHL 56, paras 17, 28 (Lord Bingham).
[17] [2004] UKHL 56, para. 208 (Lord Walker).
[18] [2004] UKHL 56, paras 165–6.
[19] [2004] UKHL 56, para. 208.
[20] [2004] UKHL 56, paras 16–29.
[21] [2004] UKHL 56, para. 112.

While unwilling to regard the SIAC finding as erroneous in law, some of Lord Hoffman's colleagues nevertheless put on record misgivings about the decision they felt compelled to reach on the public emergency issue, a degree of scepticism about the Government's claims in respect of it, and some indication of the wider political and constitutional context fuelling that scepticism.

Lord Bingham decided the issue against the detainees, not without misgiving enhanced by reading Lord Hoffman's opinion.[22] Lord Walker, similarly, in light of that dissenting opinion, rejected the applicants' 'no emergency' submission 'not without some hesitation'.[23] Lord Scott gave the Government the benefit of the doubt in deciding the threshold issue in its favour. But he also alluded to the effect of the controversy over the intelligence and WMD debacle in respect of going to war in Iraq:

> The Secretary of State's case that this threshold criterion has been met is based upon the horrific example of the 11 September attack on the Twin Towers in New York, on the belief that those responsible may target allies of the United States for similar atrocities (a belief given credibility by the recent attack in Madrid) and on the assertion that available intelligence indicates the reality and imminence of a comparable terrorist attack on the United Kingdom. The Secretary of State is unfortunate in the timing of the judicial examination in these proceedings of the 'public emergency' that he postulates. It is certainly true that the judiciary must in general defer to the executive's assessment of what constitutes a threat to national security or to 'the life of the nation'. But judicial memories are no shorter than those of the public and the public have not forgotten the faulty intelligence assessments on the basis of which United Kingdom forces were sent to take part, and are still taking part, in the hostilities in Iraq. For my part I do not doubt that there is a terrorist threat to this country and I do not doubt that great vigilance is necessary, not only on the part of the security forces but also on the part of individual members of the public, to guard against terrorist attacks. But I do have very great doubt whether the 'public emergency' is one that justifies the description of 'threatening the life of the nation'.[24]

The necessity/proportionality issue Here the question was whether the measures of indefinite detention – applicable only to foreign national terrorist suspects – were strictly required by the exigencies of that public emergency. Strasbourg jurisprudence shows this to embody a number of matters. First of all, could any lesser measures suffice? Secondly, if not, were the measures in question subject to adequate safeguards against abuse? The opinions of those in the majority on this issue deal only with the first of these. Lord Walker, dissenting on the necessity and proportionality of the measures, dealt with both matters. He thought that SIAC had not erred in law in finding the measures necessary and proportionate:

[22] [2004] UKHL 56, para. 26.
[23] [2004] UKHL 56, para. 165.
[24] [2004] UKHL 56, para. 154.

the detention without trial of non-national suspected terrorists is a cause of grave concern. But the judgment of Parliament and of the Secretary of State is that these measures were necessary, and the 2001 Act contains several important safeguards against oppression. ... Moreover the legislation is temporary in nature. Any decision to prolong it is anxiously considered by the legislature. While it is in force there is detailed scrutiny of the operation of sections 21 to 23 by the individual (at present Lord Carlile QC) appointed under section 28. There is also a wider review by the Committee of Privy Councillors appointed under section 122. All these safeguards seem to me to show a genuine determination that the 2001 Act, and especially Part 4, should not be used to encroach on human rights any more than is strictly necessary. ... is also significant that in a period of nearly three years no more than seventeen individuals have been certified ... every single detention without trial is a matter of concern, but in the context of national security the number of persons actually detained ... is to my mind relevant to the issue of proportionality. Liberty ... appears to rely on the small number of certifications as evidence that there is not a sufficiently grave emergency. That is, I think, a striking illustration of the dilemma facing a democratic government in protecting national security.[25]

The difference between Lord Walker and his colleagues is ultimately more one of judgment and appreciation than a fundamental one of approach. He saw the issue of detention without trial as probably the most crucial instance of the difficulties of reconciling individual human rights with the interests of the community, and of determining the proper functions, in this process, of the various branches or organs of government. He cited, with approval, Lord Hoffman's approach to that matter in *Rehman*. But, like the others, he recognized that the area of liberty and security of person was such as to require the courts to subject the decision of executive or legislature to very close scrutiny:

> Safeguarding national security is (with the possible exception of some questions of macro-economic policy and allocation of resources) the area of policy in which the courts are most reluctant to question or interfere with the judgment of the executive or (a fortiori) the enacted will of the legislature. Nevertheless the courts have a special duty to look very closely at any questionable deprivation of individual liberty. Measures which result in the indefinite detention in a high-security prison of individuals who have not been tried for (or even charged with) any offence, and who may be innocent of any crime, plainly invite judicial scrutiny of considerable intensity.[26]

This was so, in part, because history showed that national security can be the tyrant's last refuge, 'a cloak for arbitrary and oppressive action on the part of government.'[27]

His fellow Law Lords all supported the need for very close scrutiny in an area vitally affecting the fundamental right to liberty and security of person. Moreover,

---

[25] [2004] UKHL 56, paras 192, 217–218.

[26] [2004] UKHL 56, para. 192.

[27] Ibid.

they considered that courts were not required to show so much 'deference' or 'margin of discretion' to executive or legislative judgment on this necessity/proportionality issue as on the public emergency issue. They based that on a variety of factors and considerations, some legislative, some flowing from their view of the constitutional relationship between the courts and the other organs of government, and on the implications of the vertical relationship between national courts and authorities and the jurisdiction and approach of the European Court of Human Rights.

The task of the courts, said Lord Bingham, is to protect liberty and thus to subject the Home Secretary's decision to use detention to very close scrutiny.[28] This was warranted in part because the European Court of Human Rights' accordance of a wide margin of appreciation to States in this area – an aspect of 'the principle of the subsidiarity of the protection of Convention rights' – was predicated on a proper judicial review in national courts.[29] He also drew on the point made by the House in *Daly*, that where proportionality questions are at issue, the intensity of review by the courts is greater than when applying traditional *Wednesbury* irrationality scrutiny, even under the heightened scrutiny approach there appropriate when considering interference with a fundamental right or freedom. Lord Bingham took note of the warning from the *Korematsu* decision of the Supreme Court on the internment during the Second World War in the United States of American citizens of Japanese origin. That decision in 1942 upheld executive action on the basis of necessity. In another *Korematsu* case in 1984 Patel J, a federal judge, characterized the earlier case as a caution that in times of distress the shield of military necessity and national security must not be used to protect governmental actions from close scrutiny and accountability. Adding to that mix of considerations, the legislative mandate conferred by the HRA accentuated the need for close judicial scrutiny; Lord Bingham considered that

> The courts are not effectively precluded by any doctrine of deference from scrutinising the issues raised. ... I do not accept the full breadth of the Attorney General's submissions. I do not in particular accept the distinction which he drew between democratic institutions and the courts. ... the judges in this country are not elected and are not answerable to Parliament. ... Parliament, the executive and the courts have different functions. But the function of independent judges charged to interpret and apply the law is universally recognised as a cardinal feature of the modern democratic state, a cornerstone of the rule of law itself. The Attorney General is fully entitled to insist on the proper limits of judicial authority, but he is wrong to stigmatise judicial decision-making as in some way undemocratic. It is particularly inappropriate in a case such as the present in which Parliament has expressly legislated in section 6 of the 1998 Act to render unlawful any act of a public authority, including a court, incompatible with a Convention right, has required courts (in section 2) to take account of relevant

---

[28] [2004] UKHL 56, paras 36–44, esp. 42, para. 177 (Lord Scott),
[29] [2004] UKHL 56, para. 40, citing the European Commissioner for Human Rights in Opinion 1/2002, para. 9.

Strasbourg jurisprudence, has (in section 3) required courts, so far as possible, to give effect to Convention rights and has conferred a right of appeal on derogation issues. The effect is not ... to override the sovereign legislative authority of ... Parliament, since if primary legislation is declared to be incompatible the validity of the legislation is unaffected (section 4(6)) and the remedy lies with the appropriate minister (section 10), who is answerable to Parliament. The 1998 Act gives the courts a very specific, wholly democratic, mandate.[30]

As Lord Nicholls saw it, the HRA imposed a particular responsibility on courts to check that legislation and ministerial decisions do not overlook the human rights of individuals adversely affected. Courts should accord the other organs of government a proper degree of latitude which will

... vary according to the subject matter under consideration, the importance of the human right in question, and the extent of the encroachment upon that right. The courts will intervene only when it is apparent that, in balancing the various considerations involved, the primary decision–maker must have given insufficient weight to the human rights factor.

Here, the subject matter being national security would normally involve 'substantial latitude', but that was drastically reduced where, as here,

The right to individual liberty is one of the most fundamental of human rights. Indefinite detention without trial wholly negates that right for an indefinite period. With one exception all the individuals currently detained have been imprisoned now for three years and there is no prospect of imminent release. It is true that those detained may at any time walk away from their place of detention if they leave this country. Their prison, it is said, has only three walls. But this freedom is more theoretical than real. This is demonstrated by the continuing presence in Belmarsh of most of those detained. They prefer to stay in prison rather than face the prospect of ill treatment in any country willing to admit them.[31]

For Lord Hope it was 'impossible ever to overstate the importance of the right to liberty in a democracy' and the threat to it of indefinite detention on executive stated grounds of public interest.[32] Since ECHR rights belonged to everyone within a State's jurisdiction, the court had to subject ATCSA detention of foreign nationals to 'the same degree of scrutiny as it would have to be given if it had been designed to deprive British nationals of their right to liberty'.[33] The court should accord the executive and legislature the appropriate 'margin of discretion', which

---

[30] [2004] UKHL 56, para. 42.

[31] [2004] UKHL 56, para. 81.

[32] [2004] UKHL 56, para. 100.

[33] [2004] UKHL 56, para. 106.

will vary according to the context, the right at stake and the relevant stage of analysis in the questions that arise under Art. 15 ECHR.[34]

As regards the necessity/proportionality issue, he thought that the inclusion of 'strictly' invited close scrutiny of the action that has been taken. Where the rights of the individual are in issue the nature of the emergency must first be identified, and then compared with the effects on the individual of depriving him or her of those rights. The proper function of the judiciary was to subject the government's reasoning on these matters in this case to very close analysis, keeping in mind that what the exigencies of the situation require depends on what constitutes the emergency.[35] There was a difference between what was 'desirable' and what was 'strictly required'. Lord Rodger founded his opinion on ATCSA making SIAC the initial appellate body for dealing with legal proceedings on derogation. If that was to have real meaning, deference to the views of the other organs of government on the issues could not be taken too far. Even where national security was involved, deference was not to be equated with abasement before those views. The legitimacy of scrutiny by SIAC and appellate courts of these issues was undoubted, the more so given that, as Lord Bingham had also noted, the wide margin of appreciation granted by the Strasbourg Court pre–supposed national courts policing the limits set by Art. 15 ECHR. Adequate scrutiny by the courts also guarded against the risk that national security was used as a pretext, as in Nazi Germany, to justify repressive measures taken in reality for very different reasons. Proper scrutiny was also necessary because of the simple danger that a measure thought justified by executive and parliament on the basis of national security, might on closer examination by the courts be revealed as going too far. The example given by his Lordship here was the 'collar the lot' approach taken in 1940 to German and Italian enemy aliens, many of them refugees from the Axis powers.[36] Hence, he continued, moving matters to specific context,

> SIAC and the appellate courts have a limited, but none the less important, duty to check whether, as Art. 15(1) stipulates, the measure was strictly required by the exigencies of the situation. In discharging that duty British courts are performing their traditional role of watching over the liberty of everyone within their jurisdiction, regardless of nationality. In the words of La Forest J in *RJR-MacDonald Inc v Attorney General of Canada* [1995] 3 SCR 199, 277, 'Courts are specialists in the protection of liberty....' Here the exercise happens to take the particular form of examining the grounds for the derogation from the basic guarantees in Art. 5 of the Convention, which aim to secure the right of individuals in a democracy to be free from arbitrary detention at the hands of the authorities … In performing this role and checking whether detention of the foreign suspects, such as the appellants, was strictly required, the courts are entitled to have regard to the extent of the inroad which it makes into the liberty of those foreign suspects: the greater the inroad, the greater the care with which the justification for it

---

[34] [2004] UKHL 56, paras 107–8.
[35] [2004] UKHL 56, para. 116.
[36] See chapter 2.

must be examined. On any view, the inroad into the appellants' liberty is far-reaching. ... the reality is that they have already been detained for three years and their detention is likely to continue for at least two more years. In fact it is likely to go on for even longer if the legislation is renewed in 2006 ... The acute question is whether the exigencies of the situation strictly required a small number of foreign suspects to endure indefinite detention of this kind while, in the judgment of the Government and Parliament, an undisclosed number of British suspects could safely be allowed to remain at liberty.[37]

For the majority of their lordships, this differential treatment of foreign national and British terrorist suspects was the nub of the matter. It obviously is crucial to the matter of discrimination, yet to be examined. But it was also central to the necessity/proportionality issue now under consideration. As has been seen, the Government approached the problem essentially as one of immigration law, creating in ATCSA Part 4 a detention regime to deal with the fact that deportation on security grounds, the traditional way of disposing of undesirable 'aliens' (see chapter 4), in this case terrorist suspects, was closed off in many cases because of the *Chahal* ruling; that is, that government would breach Art. 3 were it to return a suspect to a State where there were substantial grounds for believing that if returned there he faced a real risk of torture, inhuman or degrading treatment or punishment within the meaning of Art. 3 ECHR. That same preclusion is found also in the Human Rights Committee's jurisprudence on Art. 7 ICCPR and, in respect of torture only, Art. 3 UNCAT. It asserted in its derogation notice that the threat constituting the public emergency came in particular from

> foreign nationals present in the United Kingdom who are suspected of being concerned in the commission, preparation or instigation of acts of international terrorism, of being members of organizations or groups which are so concerned or of having links with members of such organizations or groups, and who are a threat to the national security of the United Kingdom.[38]

Elsewhere, and before the House of Lords, the position was maintained that the threat came predominantly (although not exclusively) and more immediately from foreign nationals. Each of their Lordships considered a range of material on this crucial point: the findings of the Newton Committee; Lord Carlile's reviews; and reports of the JHRC. The findings of fact by SIAC, which saw and appraised with the benefit of Special Advocate analysis and criticism all the security evidence seen by the Home Secretary, were, however, to prove crucial to their Lordships' decision. SIAC, the decision of which was in essence if not in strict legal form, under appeal to their Lordships' House, found that

---

[37] [2004] UKHL 56, paras. 177–8.
[38] Cited in [2004] UKHL 56, para. 11.

the evidence before us demonstrates beyond argument that the threat is [not confined to the alien section of the population]. There are many British nationals already identified – mostly in detention abroad – who fall within the definition of 'suspected international terrorists,' and it was clear from the submissions made to us that in the opinion of the [Home Secretary] there are others at liberty in the United Kingdom who could be similarly defined.[39]

Lord Bingham emphasized:

This finding has not been challenged, and since SIAC is the responsible fact-finding tribunal it is unnecessary to examine the basis of it. There was however evidence before SIAC that 'upwards of a thousand individuals from the UK are estimated on the basis of intelligence to have attended training camps in Afghanistan in the last five years,' that some British citizens are said to have planned to return from Afghanistan to the United Kingdom and that 'The backgrounds of those detained show the high level of involvement of British citizens and those otherwise connected with the United Kingdom in the terrorist networks.' It seems plain that the threat to the United Kingdom did not derive solely from foreign nationals or from foreign nationals whom it was unlawful to deport.[40]

The threat from British nationals, while smaller, was not qualitatively different from that posed by foreign nationals.[41] Lord Nicholls thought that the legislature had given insufficient weight to the human rights of foreign nationals.[42] Security considerations had not resulted in a similar deprivation of liberty for British citizens posing a similar security risk and the Home Secretary had indeed specifically rejected such a response as too draconian.[43] Lord Hope saw two questions to be answered. The first was the effects of ATCSA detention on those affected. Secondly, given those effects and the way in which similar British citizen security threats were dealt with, could derogating from the right of those foreign nationals to liberty be said to be strictly necessary or instead to go beyond what was demanded by the exigencies of the public emergency?

It is acknowledged that there are some British nationals who are thought also to present a threat to the life of the nation because they too are suspected of involvement in international terrorism. The Attorney General accepted that there may be others whom the powers … cannot touch because … they have a right to remain in this country. These include people whom … the government is unable or unwilling to prosecute. They too cannot be removed to third countries. Yet it was decided not to introduce measures for their detention. In their case such measures, it must be assumed, were not thought to be strictly required by the exigencies of the situation that had been identified. If the threat

---

[39] Cited in [2004] UKHL 56, para. 32.
[40] [2004] UKHL 56, para. 32.
[41] [2004] UKHL 56, para. 33.
[42] [2004] UKHL 56, para. 81.
[43] [2004] UKHL 56, para. 83.

was such that their detention was strictly required, a measure would have had to be introduced to provide for this. But that step has not been taken. ... The Attorney General ... said that a number of measures were in place for the protection of the public, and that those involved were being prosecuted where possible. He explained that any response which provided for the indefinite detention of those people would have had to have been a different response, as they were not subject to immigration control. The distinction which was drawn between their case and that of the foreign nationals was that the foreign nationals had no right to be here. For British nationals the measure would have had to have provided for a form of detention that had four walls. It would have had to have been more draconian. *But that answer, while true, does not meet the objection that the indefinite detention without trial of foreign nationals cannot be said to be strictly required to meet the exigencies of the situation, if the indefinite detention without trial of those who present a threat to the life of the nation because they are suspected of involvement in international terrorism is not thought to be required in the case of British nationals* ... But the derogation is from the right to liberty. The right to liberty is the same for each group. If derogation is not strictly required in the case of one group, it cannot be strictly required in the case of the other group that presents the same threat. ... If the threat is as potent as the Secretary of State suggests, it is absurd to confine the measures intended to deal with it so that they do not apply to British nationals, however strong the suspicion and however grave the damage it is feared they may cause.[44]

In short, the central complaint of the applicants on the necessity/proportionality issue was thus sustained by an overwhelming majority in the House of Lords. Given its findings on the evidence on the nature of the terrorist/security threat, SIAC had erred in law in deciding that the measures were strictly required by the exigencies of the emergency situation. It was not a conclusion to which it could properly come.[45] ATCSA part 4 was not strictly required – it was unnecessary and disproportionate because if British citizen terrorist threats could be dealt with by measures short of detention, so could foreign nationals in the United Kingdom. Moreover, it was hard to see that the detainees were so very dangerous given that the United Kingdom was happy to let them go to any country that would take them.[46]

Lord Scott based his finding on SIAC's failure to require the Home Secretary to demonstrate that lesser measures would have sufficed. The measures he had in mind were monitoring arrangements or movement restrictions less severe than incarceration in prison. This was perhaps something drawn on by the Home Office when formulating the PTA 2005, the response to their Lordships' declaration of incompatibility in respect of ATCSA, section 23.

Lord Hoffman, given his decision on public emergency, declined to express an opinion on either the necessity/proportionality issue or that of discrimination.[47] But, in a remark which points up his colleagues' findings on these issues, he stated

---

[44] [2004] UKHL 56, paras 124, 126, 129 (emphasis supplied).
[45] [2004] UKHL 56, paras 44 (Lord Bingham), 189 (Lord Rodger), 228 (Baroness Hale).
[46] [2004] UKHL 56, paras 33, 44 (Lord Bingham).
[47] [2004] UKHL 56, para. 97.

that he wished to avoid the impression that all that was necessary was to extend indefinite detention to British citizen terrorist threats.[48] The view taken by the present author is that a legitimate reading of their Lordships' findings on proportionality/necessity is that a proportionate response to the level of threat considered by the House would have been to subject foreign nationals to the restrictions *then* legally applied to British national terrorist suspects (for example, to the physical or electronic surveillance that the law then permitted). Such a reading has implications for the question whether control orders (the PTA 2005 response to the declaration of incompatibility) represent a proportionate interference with the ECHR rights and freedoms affected.

The discrimination issue There is some apparent interconnection with the previous issue, in that the evidentiary material and the conclusions to draw from it also have relevance to the question of discrimination. There is, however, a legal difference in that Art. 14 ECHR, the Convention's discrimination provision tied to the areas covered by the rights and freedoms protected elsewhere in the Convention, was not an explicit subject of the Art. 15 Derogation Order. Moreover, an argument, maintained by government before SIAC, that it was subject to an implied derogation, was not pursued before either the Court of Appeal or the House of Lords.[49]

Art. 14 ECHR stipulates that the enjoyment of the rights and freedoms in the ECHR must be secured without discrimination on any ground such as sex, race, colour, language, religion, political or other opinion, national or social origin, association with a national minority, property, birth or other status. The House (Lord Walker dissenting and Lord Hoffman declining to express a view) further held that the measures were discriminatory on grounds of nationality/national origin contrary to Art. 14 read with Art. 5 ECHR. Non-discrimination demands that 'like cases be treated alike'. The key problem lies in setting the parameters for the appropriate grouping warranting equal treatment. This depends on the perspective or context in which one views the subject matter. If it is that of 'immigration', this produces no problems in terms of discrimination, since as the Government argued and the Court of Appeal accepted, national and international law on immigration (copiously analysed in Lord Bingham's opinion) clearly permits differentiation between nationals and non-nationals. But if, as SIAC and House of Lords correctly thought, the proper perspective is that of 'security', the position changes. The key matter is identifying those warranting similar treatment as being similarly situated. The House held that the group similarly situated was composed of all those terrorist suspects threatening national security who could not be prosecuted and who could not *for one legal reason or another* be removed from the United Kingdom. That group comprised both British citizens and foreign nationals. National and international law says that one cannot deport one's own

---

[48] Ibid.

[49] [2004] UKHL 56, para. 47 (Lord Bingham). SIAC had rejected the argument.

citizens (one legal reason). The group also comprises foreign nationals whose removal is precluded by Art. 3 ECHR or its ICCPR equivalent (another legal reason). Since only the latter could be detained, this was unjustifiable discrimination.[50] Baroness Hale encapsulated it well:

> The foreigners have no right to be here and we would expel them if we could. We only have to allow them to stay to protect them from an even worse invasion of their human rights. Hence, he argued, the true comparison is not with suspected international terrorists who are British nationals but with foreign suspected international terrorists who can be deported. This cannot be right. The foreigners who can be deported are not like the foreigners who cannot. These foreigners are only being detained because they cannot be deported. They are just like a British national who cannot be deported. The relevant circumstances making the two cases alike for this purpose are the same three which constitute the problem: a suspected international terrorist, who for a variety of reasons cannot be successfully prosecuted, and who for a variety of reasons cannot be deported or expelled. Even then, the difference in treatment might have an objective justification. But to do so it must serve a legitimate aim and be proportionate to that aim. Once again, the fact that it is sometimes permissible to treat foreigners differently does not mean that every difference in treatment serves a legitimate aim. If the situation really is so serious, and the threat so severe, that people may be detained indefinitely without trial, what possible legitimate aim could be served by only having power to lock up some of the people who present that threat? This is even more so, of course, if the necessity to lock people up in this way has not been shown.

ATCSA Detention: the Scope of the Derogation

Although on its face ATCSA did not specifically limit the international terrorism covered or the groups concerned to Al Qaeda and associates, the Court of Appeal held that it was so limited as a matter of law. In *M*, Lord Woolf CJ said:

> It is common ground that the Secretary of State's powers under the 2001 Act are limited by the terms of the Human Rights Act 1998 (Designated Derogation) Order 2001, by which the United Kingdom derogated from Art. 5 of the ECHR. Accordingly, those powers cannot be exercised (except in accordance with the derogation) in respect of someone whom he does not reasonably suspect or believe to be a risk to national security because of his connection to the public emergency threatening the life of the nation — namely the threat posed by Al Qa'ida and its associated networks. Thus it is not enough that the person detained may have had connections with a terrorist organisation. It must be a terrorist organisation which has links with Al Qa'ida.[51]

---

[50] [2004] UKHL 56.

[51] [2004] EWCA Civ 324, para. 11.

He had made the same point on narrowing an over-inclusive statutory provision in *A and Others (the derogation issue)*, supported by Brooke and Chadwick LJJ.[52] Brooke LJ confined the powers 'to the threat posed by Al Qaeda and its associate networks *(and no one else)*'.[53] In *A and Others (the torture/merits issue)*,[54] Pill LJ read the italicized words in Brooke LJ's statement as merely confirming that the ATCSA detention scheme could not be deployed against foreign nationals belonging to other terrorist organizations, such as ETA or the Real IRA, and not as denoting anything about the notion of the requisite level of link to Al Qaeda. In that 'torture' case, the appeal from SIAC's decision on the 'merits' of the detentions, the Court of Appeal held that SIAC had approached correctly, in a broad fashion consistent with the policy and rationale of ATCSA and the threat it sought to counter, this aspect of the appeals: groups covered and the necessary degree of link. The matter had to be dealt with in such a way as to reflect the reality of the way in which Al Qaeda operated.[55] In consequence, a broad approach had to be taken to the meaning of the word 'group', to cover not just those with a formal structure but also informal, ad hoc groups, formed for temporary expediency, and to embrace the concept of networks.[56] SIAC had thus correctly accepted the nature of Al Qaeda as a series of loosely connected operational and support cells. It accepted a general schematic diagrammatic description of this:

> At the centre of an oval was Al Qu'eda, linked by arrows to the cardinal points where were marked four distinct but interlinked entities: the strategic decision-making structure, the base force for guerilla warfare in Afghanistan, the loose coalition of transnational terrorist and guerilla groups and the global terrorist network. Links around the circumference of the oval connected to those groups.[57]

In line with the policy and objects of ATCSA, SIAC had rightly rejected as too narrow the submission by the appellant detainees that the requisite link demanded support for the Al Qaeda aim of global jihad, expressed in the indiscriminate killing of civilians, or the core aims of global jihad against the West by terrorist means. Given an interdependent world and the international nature of the terrorist problem, the Court found that SIAC, like the House of Lords in *Rehman*, rightly accepted that the nation's life could be threatened by attacks on friends, allies or countries forming a vital source of material, like oil, for the economy. The threat could be direct in the form of the disruption from attacks. It could also be indirect in terms of the strength gained by terrorists from such an attack. Consequently, as SIAC correctly characterized it,

---

[52] [2002] EWCA Civ 1502, paras 42, 98, 149.

[53] [2002] EWCA Civ 1502, para. 98 (emphasis supplied).

[54] [2004] EWCA Civ 1123.

[55] [2004] EWCA Civ 1123, para. 217 (Laws LJ),

[56] [2004] EWCA Civ 1123, paras 375–7 (Neuberger LJ).

[57] SIAC Generic Judgment, paras 98–9, cited in [2004] EWCA Civ 1123, para. 218.

The threat to the nation, which underlies the derogation, is posed by any of the various activities of Al Qaeda and those who are associated with it, whether or not they agree with all aspects of his global agenda or with the indiscriminate killing of civilians as a means or end. ... The 'international terrorist group' contemplated by section 21 is Al Qaeda or a group associated with it, provided it is recognised that the very nature of the groups associated with Al Qaeda encompasses informal, even ad hoc, groups which can as easily or better be described as overlapping, loosely co-ordinated groupings or networks. Their purposes may overlap in part but not in whole, and they may not agree with all the means which another would use; but that does not prevent them being part of the threat to the life of the nation as a matter of principle or law. It is that connection to Al Qaeda which provides the threat.[58]

Given the nature of Al Qaeda, the legislature could not have intended a relatively narrow meaning of 'group'.[59] It was thus not possible to define the requisite connection between groups in terms of more than one remove or link being insufficient connection.[60] The Court endorsed SIAC's findings on the overlapping groups or cells at issue in the appeals:

We accept the broad assessment by the Respondent that there is a network, largely of North African extremists, in this country which makes up a number of groups or cells with overlapping members or supporters. They usually have origins in groups which had or may still have a national agenda, but whether that originating group does or does not have a national agenda, whether or not it has direct Al Qaeda links, whether or not the factions are at war in the country of origin, such as the GIA and GSPC in Algeria, those individuals now work together here. They co-operate in order to pursue at least in part an anti-West terrorist agenda. Those less formal groups are connected back to Al Qaeda, either through the group from which they came which is part of what can be described as the Al Qaeda network, or from other extremist individuals connected to Al Qa'eda who can be described as part of Al Qaeda itself or associated with it. They are at least influenced from outside the United Kingdom. These informal, ad-hoc, overlapping networks, cells or groups constitute 'groups' for the purpose of the 2001 Act.[61]

For similar reasons, hard and fast distinctions should not be made for ATCSA purposes between membership, support and assistance.[62] This line of analysis enables SIAC to take an approach differentiating between terrorist groups. So in *M*, the Court upheld SIAC's right to conclude that while M was an international terrorist within the meaning of ATCSA, he could not be detained under that Act because there was no reasonable suspicion linking him with Al Qaeda or an associated group.[63] The same would have been true of the connection of F and

---

[58] SIAC Generic Judgment, paras 108–9, cited in [2004] EWCA Civ 1123, para. 219.

[59] [2004] EWCA Civ 1123, para. 377 (Neuberger LJ).

[60] SIAC Generic Judgment, para. 112, cited in [2004] EWCA Civ 1123, para. 62.

[61] SIAC Generic Judgment, paras 302–303, cited in [2004] EWCA Civ 1123, para. 63.

[62] [2004] EWCA Civ 1123, para. 378 (Neuberger LJ).

[63] [2004] EWCA Civ 324, paras 30–34.

Ajouaou, two of the appellants in *A and Others (the torture/merits case)*, to the Algerian group, GIA. But in each case detention was upheld because SIAC was satisfied also of their links with another Al Qaeda-connected group, the GSPC, and the similarly connected looser group based around Abu Doha, a terrorist with Al Qaeda links.[64]

ATCSA Detention: Scrutiny of the Merits, the Proper Approach to Matters of Proof and Due Deference

To certificate a foreign national under the scheme the Home Secretary had to both reasonably suspect that the person was a terrorist and reasonably believe that their presence in the United Kingdom was a threat to national security.[65] Their indefinite detention could then be authorized if removal was prevented by international obligation or some practical reason.[66] In line (as they saw it) with judicial pronouncements in *Rehman* and the greater impact on rights that detention had, the detainees argued in *A and Others (the torture/merits case)*[67] that a very high standard of scrutiny had to be applied by SIAC, at the very least in terms of the factual basis for the allegation that the individual was a terrorist. They argued that substantial investigation was required to ground reasonable suspicion. In stating that the standard the Secretary of State had to meet was not a demanding one, SIAC erred in law. The Court of Appeal did not accept that. They relied on *M*,[68] another Court of Appeal decision in which SIAC's quashing of the certificate was upheld. In *M*, Lord Woolf stated that the task of SIAC

> ... is not to review or 'second–guess' the decision of the Secretary of State but to come to its own judgment in respect of the issue identified in section 25 of the 2001 Act. ... SIAC is required to come to its decision as to whether or not reasonable grounds exist for the Secretary of State's belief or suspicion. Use of the word 'reasonable' means that SIAC has to come to an objective judgment. The objective judgment has however to be reached against all the circumstances in which the judgment is made. There has to be taken into account the danger to the public which can result from a person who should be detained not being detained. There are also to be taken into account the consequences to the person who has been detained. To be detained without being charged or tried or even knowing the evidence against you is a grave intrusion on an individual's rights. Although, therefore, the test is an objective one, it is also one which involves a value judgment as to what is properly to be considered reasonable in those circumstances.[69]

---

[64] [2004] EWCA Civ 1123, paras 175–6, 187–196.

[65] ATCSA, 21(1).

[66] ATCSA, s. 23.

[67] [2004] EWCA Civ 1123.

[68] [2004] EWCA Civ 324.

[69] [2004] EWCA Civ 324, paras 15, 16, approved and applied in [2004] EWCA Civ 1123, paras. 46 (Pill LJ), 236 (Laws LJ), 339 (Neuberger LJ).

SIAC's composition and experience, and its examination of all the security evidence relied on by the Home Secretary, probed and tested by the Special Advocate in a way not possible before the Home Secretary, all combined to make SIAC qualified to make the value judgments involved. Those judgments had to be made in light of the material available at the date of the hearing.[70] In *A and Others*, the Court of Appeal, following *Rehman*, rejected the utility of notions of burden of proof. SIAC's 'unfortunate' statement on standard was characterized as one trying to draw comparison with those provided in other judicial proceedings rather than a departure from the test in ATCSA. Although the context (indefinite detention without trial) was different from *Rehman* (deportation), Pill LJ adopted Lord Hoffman's approach in that case: the matters were ones of evaluation and judgment. While in some circumstances specific acts might have to be proved, what really mattered was SIAC's own assessment of the whole picture.[71] SIAC did not have to be satisfied on the balance of probabilities that the detainee was either a threat to national security or a terrorist. The matter of whether there are reasonable grounds respectively to believe or suspect those things was one of 'assessment'.[72] It was clear that SIAC had been aware of the need for a 'close and penetrating analysis of the material including the assessments and inferences' and had undertaken that.[73] As regards the *Rehman* requirement of due deference in a national security context, the Court held that SIAC got this right by according due weight, not unquestioning adherence to the Home Secretary's views and assessments.[74]

The points made on due deference, applying *Rehman*, span the national security spectrum of decision-making. *Rehman* sets the standard of review for SIAC and national security deportations. Those set in *A and others* and *M* on the standard of scrutiny are at first sight context-specific, dealing with the wording of SIAC's powers under ATCSA. Given similar wording they would apply also to the role of the High Court in dealing with derogating control orders, where the High Court again has to make its own decision on the basis of material as at the date of the relevant hearing (without notice or adversarial/contested). An attenuated standard is, however, applicable when that Court deals with the matter of the making of a non-derogating control order. That level of review was criticized as deficient by the JHRC, and by a number of bodies giving evidence to it.[75] The scope of that standard of court supervision and its compatibility with ECHR requirements were dealt with recently by Sullivan J and the Court of Appeal in *MB*, with the latter

---

[70] *M* [2004] EWCA Civ 324, paras 15, 16, 34(v); *A and Others* [2004] EWCA Civ 1123, paras 342 (Neuberger LJ).

[71] [2004] EWCA Civ 1123, para. 49.

[72] [2004] EWCA Civ 1123, paras 364, 371.

[73] [2004] EWCA Civ 1123, para. 50.

[74] [2004] EWCA Civ 1123, paras 40, 48–52 (Pill LJ), 226 (Laws LJ).

[75] See JHRC 9th (2004–05): paras 15–17; JHRC 10th (2004–05): paras 11–17; JHRC 12th (2005–06): paras 67–78, Ev 45–7 (Justice), 48–9 (Law Society), 52–4 (Liberty).

rather enhancing the High Court's powers in order to effect compatibility with Convention Rights. The case is examined later in the context of 'fair trial' issues.

PTA 2005: Policing the Line between Non-derogating and Derogating Control Orders

Under the PTA 2005 a clear distinction in law is made between 'non-derogating' and 'derogating' control orders. The former can encompass only restrictions falling short of a deprivation of liberty within the meaning of Art. 5 ECHR. The decision to go for one is made initially by the Home Secretary who must then apply for permission to make one to the Administrative Court (the branch of the High Court which deals with the matter) which is empowered only to reject them if the decision to make one was obviously flawed in the light of the principles of judicial review.[76] This is a much lower empowerment of the court when contrasted with that under ATCSA or national security deportation. It is also significantly lower than that applicable to derogating control orders.

There is an uncertain line between restrictions on freedom of movement (the proper ambit of non-derogating orders) and a deprivation of liberty (the area reserved to derogating control orders). Lord Carlile who reviews the operation of the PTA 2005 thought that the range of restrictions imposed in a number of derogating control orders came close to the line.[77] The JHRC Human Rights thought that they crossed the line.[78] In its reply to concerns expressed on the matter by the Council of Europe's Human Rights Commissioner, the Government made clear that if the Administrative Court (or one of the appellate courts) considered that the totality of a particular set of restrictions embodied in a purported non-derogating control order had strayed across that boundary to amount to a deprivation of liberty, the court could quash that purported order as invalid.[79] It would then be open to the Secretary of State either to make a new order with such a lesser degree of restriction as to fall on the right side of that uncertain line or, alternatively, to persuade Parliament to approve a designated derogation order under the HRA derogating under Art. 15 from Art. 5 ECHR and ask the Administrative Court to approve restrictions amounting to a deprivation of liberty embodied this time in a derogating control order.

The matter of whether the line had been crossed in particular orders came before Sullivan J in *Re JJ and Others*.[80] Other issues were raised by the respondents, but he confined consideration to whether, on agreed facts or those

---

[76] PTA 2005, s. 3.

[77] Carlile (2006): Annex 2 and paras 42–3: 'they fall not very short of house arrest and certainly inhibit normal life considerably'.

[78] JHRC 12th (2005–06): para. 38.

[79] For the Commissioner's Report see Council of Europe Document Comm DH (2005) 6 (8 June 2005). For the Government's reply see Appendix to that Report, p. 63.

[80] [2006] EWHC 1623 (Admin) (28 June 2006).

apparent on the face of the orders, the restrictions amounted to a deprivation of liberty under Art. 5 ECHR. He considered pertinent ECHR case law, in particular *Guzzardi v Italy*[81] and *HL v United Kingdom*.[82] He also reflected on the decision of the House of Lords in *Gillan* in which the House confirmed that the exercise by the police of the random stop and search powers afforded them in the TA 2000 did not amount to a deprivation of liberty under Art. 5.[83] He also noted coverage of the issue in parallel areas of restrictions imposed by a mental health tribunal in a mental health case,[84] and ones embodied in a supervision licence applied to a young offender released from custody prior to full release into the community.[85] All these authorities made clear that all the circumstances had closely to be examined. The distinction between restrictions on movement and ones depriving of liberty was one of degree or intensity rather than nature or substance. The starting point for a decision was the concrete situation of each individual concerned and account had to be taken of a non-exhaustive range of factors: the type, duration, effects and manner of implementation of the measure concerned. Also relevant were the purpose of the measure and whether it was for the benefit of the person subjected to it. It was not a matter of a mechanistic comparison between the circumstances of the ECHR cases and the cases before him. The relevant restrictions in the cases before him were extensive: electronic tagging; remaining inside a designated residence for 18 hours a day, with no access to the internet, or a mobile telephone, but only a single landline and the telephone for communicating with the 'tagging' company; approved visitors only with Home Office permission obtainable only by providing intrusive detail about the visitor; and restriction to a limited geographic area with restrictions on where one could go or what one could do. Sullivan J had little difficulty in finding the degree of restriction to be a deprivation of liberty:

> ... bearing in mind the type, duration, effects and manner of implementation of the obligations in these control orders, ... the cumulative effect of the obligations has been to deprive the respondents of their liberty in breach of Art. 5 of the Convention. I do not consider that this is a borderline case. The collective impact of the obligations in Annex I could not sensibly be described as a mere restriction upon the respondents' liberty of movement. In terms of the length of the curfew period (18 hours), the extent of the obligations, and their intrusive impact on the respondents' ability to lead anything resembling a normal life, whether inside their residences within the curfew period, or for the 6-hour period outside it, these control orders go far beyond the restrictions in those cases where the European Court of Human Rights has concluded that there has been a

---

[81] (1980) 3 EHRR 333, paras 92–3.

[82] (2004) 40 EHRR 761, para. 89.

[83] *R (Gillan and Another)* v *Commissioner of Police of the Metropolis* [2006] 2 WLR 537.

[84] *Secretary of State for the Home Department* v *Mental Health Review Tribunal and PH* [2002] EWCA Civ 1868.

[85] *Davies v Secretary of State for the Home Department* [2004] EWHC 3113 (Admin).

restriction upon but not a deprivation of liberty. The respondents' 'concrete situation' is the antithesis of liberty, and is more akin to detention in an open prison,[86]

Accordingly he quashed the purported non-derogating control order as a nullity, something made without power to do so. He suspended the quashing order, however, for seven days to give the Home Secretary time to consider whether to appeal to the Court of Appeal and seek a further stay of the order pending the hearing of that appeal.[87] His decision was castigated by the Government in customary style,[88] indeed elevated to the status of a constitutional crisis,[89] but, as Sullivan J put it, the trap into which the order fell was one of the Government's own making.[90] The orders in question remained in force pending the hearing of an appeal, and non-derogating control orders could still be made.[91] On 1 August 2006, the Court of Appeal upheld Sullivan J's decision as compelling and found the Home Secretary's appeal to be without merit. The degree of restrictions clearly fell on the wrong side of the line between deprivation of liberty and freedom of movement. The orders were quashed and the Home Secretary reduced the curfew period to 14 hours and relaxed some of the restrictions on visitors, opening up the possibility of challenge to that degree of restriction as falling on the wrong side of the line. He now has leave to appeal from the House of Lords itself and the case will be heard later in 2007.[92]

In *Secretary of State for the Home Department* v *E*, restrictions akin to but less restrictive than those in *Re JJ* had been imposed. Beatson J, while considering E's case to be more finely balanced, considered that their cumulative effect deprived E of his liberty in breach of Art. 5 ECHR. On 17 May 2007, however, the Court of Appeal held the control order to be valid; the restrictions fell far short of deprivation of liberty.[93] The case is likely to go to the Lords in due course. Beatson J earlier in April had quashed on the same basis as in his decision in *E* the order against Abu Rideh (12-hour curfew).[94] Following Beatson J's approach in *E*, Ouseley J quashed the order against AF (a 14-hour curfew) as a deprivation of liberty. The restrictions were less severe than in JJ but comparable to those in E.[95] He also held that decisions on a control order did not have to be made personally by the Home Secretary, but could be ones made by a Minister of State.[96]

---

[86] [2006] EWHC 1623 (Admin), paras 73–4.

[87] [2006] EWHC 1623 (Admin), paras 92–8.

[88] Travis and Norton Taylor (2006); Travis and Gillan (2006).

[89] Leader, *The Guardian*, 30 June 2006; *The Independent*, 30 June 2006.

[90] [2006] EWHC 1623 (Admin), para. 93.

[91] Cm 6888 (2006): para. 77.

[92] *Secretary of State for the Home Department* v *JJ and Others* [2006] EWCA Civ 1141; Ford (2006).

[93] [2007] EWHC (Admin) 233; [2007] EWCA Civ 459.

[94] [2007] EWHC 804 (Admin).

[95] [2007] EWHC 651 (Admin), paras 62–91.

[96] [2007] EWHC 651 (Admin), paras 94–107.

Control Orders: Impact on Families

The impact of control orders on members of the controlee's family has been a matter of concern raised by pressure groups and lawyers. In S*ecretary of State for the Home Department* v *E*, Beatson J considered the impact on the children under Art. 3 ECHR. He recognized the vulnerability of children. He took on board one child's bedwetting and evidence that the long-term impact of the situation on their mental health was 'likely to be significant and detrimental'. But he concluded that this was not a case where the restrictions posed such a risk to their mental health as to constitute 'inhuman and degrading treatment by humiliating and debasing them or breaking their moral resistance'.[97] He examined the impact on the family as a whole under Art. 8 ECHR. The interference with private and family life was significant, so had the Home Secretary established that it was proportionate to a legitimate aim in the context of the national security case against E? Beatson J had held that the low threshold required in respect of non-derogating control orders was crossed by a 'substantial margin on the basis of the open material alone' – there were substantial grounds for believing E to be a 'senior terrorist recruiter and facilitator' and that the risk he posed to national security was ongoing.[98] He concluded that the weight of the interests of the State and the public in preventing or restricting involvement in terrorism-related activity was such as to justify the serious interference with the rights of E's wife and children. The Court of Appeal upheld his finding that the control order was not in this respect disproportionate.[99]

What if Derogating Control Orders were to be Used?

If a derogating control order was used, the restrictions would raise similar issues under the same range of ECHR provisions as non-derogating ones. In addition, they would raise ones of deprivation of liberty under Art. 5 ECHR. 'House arrest', for example, like ATCSA detention without trial, would not be supportable by any of the permissible heads of deprivation of liberty afforded by that Article, and, to be Convention-compliant, would have to be justified by derogation under the public emergency clause, Art. 15 ECHR. In short, the same issues would arise as in *A and Others* which saw the demise of ATCSA detention. Any claim that there was no public emergency seems doomed to failure, given their Lordships' acceptance in that decision of the existence of one in mid-December 2004, the events of 7/7, and any other catalytic event precipitating the derogation. The key issue would thus be whether, given the nature of that emergency, derogating control orders – applicable irrespective of nationality – were a proportionate response to its exigencies and accompanied by adequate safeguards against abuse.

---

[97] [2007] EWHC (Admin) 233, paras 307–309.

[98] [2007] EWHC (Admin) 233, paras 82, 96.

[99] [2007] EWHC (Admin) 233, para. 280; [2007] EWCA Civ 459.

It is difficult to see the Government losing on that issue, given that the orders can apply to all constituting the threat, regardless of nationality and the findings to date that the lesser degree of judicial scrutiny afforded in non-derogating cases and the processes concerned satisfied the 'fair trial' dictates of the ECHR. The matter of discrimination contrary to Art. 14 ECHR read with another ECHR provision could again arise, despite applicability regardless of nationality, especially were the exclusively male and Islamic focus seen with non-derogating control orders also to form a feature of resort to their derogating counterparts. The question then would be one of identifying groups requiring similar treatment and of whether there was a reasonable and rational relationship of proportionality between the threat constituting the emergency and the identity of the group(s) singled out for subjection to a derogating control order.

National Security Deportations

These have raised issues of compatibility with the ECHR and of EU law on freedom of movement for European Economic Area (EEA) nationals. There have also been concerns raised about the scope and impact of bail conditions.

ECHR issues Challenges in this area have centred on matters of 'fear of return to the destination state', whether in terms of the death penalty or the risk of torture, inhuman or degrading treatment contrary to Art. 3 ECHR: that is, the *Chahal* principle whereby Art. 3 precludes absolutely a State returning someone to a country where there are substantial grounds for believing that if returned to that country there is a real risk that he or she will be subjected to torture, inhuman or degrading treatment or punishment at the hands of state or non-state actors. The United Kingdom Government is intervening in a case before the European Court of Human Rights Court in which an individual is contesting the human rights compliance of a decision of the Netherlands to deport him on security grounds.[100] The Government's objective here is an aspect of its wider strategy of trying to secure a change in one of the 'rules of the game', namely a modification of the absolute preclusion of deportation afforded by the *Chahal* principle. In effect, the Government is seeking to have adopted the view of the minority in *Chahal*.[101]

It is thought unlikely that the Court will resile from the principle it has reaffirmed many times since it would eat into a fundamental principle, the absolute nature of Art. 3 ECHR. The Government would argue that the nature of the modern terrorist threat is such as to require change, a view with some support from a European Commission document on combating terrorism.[102] But the Court in *Chahal* in 1996 made clear that it was

---

[100] *Ramzy* v *Netherlands* Application no. 25424/05.
[101] JHRC 3rd (2005): para. 148.
[102] Bonner (2004): 99.

... well aware of the immense difficulties faced by States in modern times in protecting their communities from terrorist violence. However, even in these circumstances, the Convention prohibits in absolute terms torture or inhuman or degrading treatment or punishment, irrespective of the victim's conduct. Unlike most of the substantive clauses of the Convention and of Protocols Nos. 1 and 4, Art. 3 makes no provision for exceptions and no derogation from it is permissible under Art. 15 even in the event of a public emergency threatening the life of the nation.[103]

And, as this book has argued, it is misleading to characterize the post-9/11 threat as significantly different from earlier manifestations of terrorism with which the Court has had to deal.

Were the Court to modify the principle, this would have effects on United Kingdom courts since there is a strong presumption that their HRA duty to take account of ECHR jurisprudence will result in them following the Strasbourg Court's lead. Assuming, as is likely, that the *Chahal* principle remains intact, the core issue of SIAC is whether the existence of a Memorandum of Understanding with the destination state (a no-maltreatment agreement), probably coupled in each case with specific assurances with respect to the individual concerned, obviates or reduces below the requisite level any risk of ill-treatment contrary to Art. 3 or secures the removal of the risk of subjection to the death penalty. That question is one that can only be answered in the light of all the circumstances of the individual case, including the terms of the agreement, its monitoring arrangements, and the specific assurances in the context of that state's record on torture. There was from the Indian government in *Chahal* a formal assurance to the effect that, if Chahal were to be deported to India, he would enjoy the same legal protection as any other Indian citizen, and that he would have no reason to expect to suffer mistreatment of any kind at the hands of the Indian authorities.[104] The Court found his deportation precluded by Art. 3 ECHR:

Although the Court is of the opinion that Mr Chahal, if returned to India, would be most at risk from the Punjab security forces acting either within or outside state boundaries, it also attaches significance to the fact that attested allegations of serious human rights violations have been levelled at the police elsewhere in India. In this respect, the Court notes that the United Nations' Special Rapporteur on torture has described the practice of torture upon those in police custody as 'endemic' and has complained that inadequate measures are taken to bring those responsible to justice. The NHRC has also drawn attention to the problems of widespread, often fatal, mistreatment of prisoners and has called for a systematic reform of the police throughout India. Although the Court does not doubt the good faith of the Indian Government in providing the assurances ... , it would appear that, despite the efforts of that Government, the NHRC and the Indian courts to bring about reform, the violation of human rights by certain members of the security forces in Punjab and elsewhere in India is a recalcitrant and enduring problem.

---

[103] (1997) 23 EHHR. 413, para. 79.
[104] (1997) 23 EHRR 413, para. 37.

Against this background, the Court is not persuaded that the above assurances would provide Mr Chahal with an adequate guarantee of safety. The Court further considers that the applicant's high profile would be more likely to increase the risk to him of harm than otherwise. It is not disputed that Mr Chahal is well known in India to support the cause of Sikh separatism and to have had close links with other leading figures in that struggle. The respondent Government has made serious, albeit untested, allegations of his involvement in terrorism which are undoubtedly known to the Indian authorities. The Court is of the view that these factors would be likely to make him a target of interest for hard-line elements in the security forces who have relentlessly pursued suspected Sikh militants in the past.[105]

Whether the *Chahal* test is met in any particular case is both situation- and individual- specific. The matter is one of weighing the credibility of any Memorandum of Understanding (MOU) or other diplomatic exchanges and of other specific assurances in respect of the particular individual in order to assess in the light of information about the destination State the level of risk, if any, should that individual be returned. In three cases (Y, BB and G), SIAC (differently composed in each case) considered that the *Chahal* principle did not operate to preclude their deportation to an Algeria much changed since 2001 and, indeed, in the last two years (at the time of writing). SIAC considered material from the FCO, the United States State Department, from NGOs (including Amnesty), oral testimony from FCO representatives and from an academic expert on North Africa. In particular it focused on the moves towards reconciliation in Algeria, attempts to draw a line under the past by a President democratically elected and a Government thought less subject to control by the military. Important here were the terms and applicability to the individuals of an effective 'amnesty' in respect of relevant offences in a Charter and *Ordonnance* and also the release of many terrorist prisoners. Also of weight were the circumstances of others who had earlier returned to Algeria. That there was no formal MOU was immaterial, given the nature of the diplomatic exchanges and correspondence between the two Governments. Nor, given the low level of risk to the individuals, was the lack of explicit formal monitoring structures a problem, given the mutual interests of the two Governments in making the return process work, given ongoing scrutiny by NGOs both within and outside Algeria, and given that Algeria seemed committed to signing the Optional Protocol to UNCAT.[106] A similar approach was taken in *Abu Qatada* against the backdrop of the MOU with Jordan.[107] That country might torture other Islamist extremists but was unlikely, because of the diplomatic co-operation and the attention focused on the case, to maltreat Abu Qatada. The decision was controversial and an appeal is pending. SIAC found that deporting W,

---

[105] (1997) 23 EHRR 413, paras 104–6.

[106] SC/36/2005 (Y: 24 August 2006); SC/39/2005 (BB: 5 December 2006); SC/02/2005 (G: 8 February 2007).

[107] SC/15/2005, Judgment 26 February 2007.

U and Z to Algeria would not be contrary to ECHR obligations.[108] In contrast, it found deporting DD and AS to Libya would violate Art. 3 ECHR; despite the MOU with Libya, the mercurial nature of its government meant that while there was no probable risk of ill treatment, there was still a real risk.[109]

Issues under Art. 8 ECHR were considered by SIAC in respect of Y, BB, G and Abu Qatada. In no case was the inference with rights (impact on personal integrity, health or family life) it protected found disproportionate. Indeed in *G*, SIAC thought it difficult to envisage circumstances in which 'deportation on proven national security grounds would not be justified' under Art. 8(2).[110]

Another ground of challenge has been in respect of Art. 5(1)(f) ECHR. This permits detention for purposes of deportation, but only where deportation is a feasible prospect and the length of detention is reasonable given the nature and complexities of the case. On 13 March 2006, SIAC held that the length of detention of three Algerians while negotiations of memoranda of understanding were ongoing with Algeria did not fall foul of that principle.[111] It could not be said in such circumstances that the three could show certainty of success on the Art. 3 issues and that the Secretary of State had no arguable case in that respect. SIAC also noted that 'reasonable time' was not a matter of mechanics, but

> ... depends on the circumstances. Six months might be excessive in one case, but three-and-a-half years reasonable in another case. A very much more prolonged period than experienced here, for example, was held in *Chahal* by the European Court of Human Rights not to breach Art. 5.1 of ECHR.[112]

EU law This was considered by SIAC in respect of MK, a French national. SIAC held that deportation which would disrupt rather than eliminate terrorism was proportionate for the purposes of the public policy exception to free movement rights. Community law as exemplified in *Adoui and Cornuaille v Belgium* and in *Minsistere de L'Interieur v Olazabal* enabled deportation, a measure not applicable to United Kingdom nationals, because other concrete action (control orders, criminal prosecution) could be undertaken in respect of nationals engaging in the conduct grounding MK's deportation. Neither Community law nor comity required the United Kingdom to prosecute MK instead or to use a control order rather than deportation.[113]

Bail conditions Another concern was the imposition of bail conditions comparable to those only imposable through a derogating control order (with all its safeguards)

---

[108] SC/34/2005 (W); SC/32/2005 (U); SC/37/2005 (Z) (judgments 14 May 2007).
[109] SC/42/2005 and SC/50/2005 (judgments 27 April 2007).
[110] SC/02/05, judgment 8 February 2007.
[111] SC/13/22/31/33/38/2005 (*A and Others*).
[112] Ibid., paras 19–20.
[113] SC/29/2004 (19 May 2006).

under the PTA 2005. It may be arguable whether all of the conditions imposed are consonant with the terms of the power to admit to bail if that power is interpreted in terms of the purpose of conditions being to guard against absconding (removal of computers, searches of premises).[114] The problem is, however, that neither primary or secondary legislation provides detailed criteria on the terms of the power and the discretion to admit to bail.[115] That legislation merely states that the power can *include* conditions relating to that end.[116]

Detention in Iraq: Judicial Review and Human Rights

Art. 1 ECHR provides that the obligation to protect ECHR rights covers all persons within the jurisdiction of the contracting State. Since it is not limited to the territory of the State but, embraces places where the State has effective jurisdiction,[117] it extends to cover those detained by British forces in Iraq. So, in *R (Al-Skeini)* v *Secretary of State for Defence*,[118] the Court of Appeal held that ECHR protection extended to someone actually detained by British forces (one appellant who died in British custody) but not to others said to have been killed in encounters with British troops in Basra City in Iraq (five appellants). Although the United Kingdom was one of the occupying powers in the coalition that invaded Iraq, the majority of the Court did not regard it as being in effective control of Basra City at the material times or as being in the position of the civil power there. Rather it was there to maintain security, and in other ways to support the civil administration in Iraq. In *R (Al-Jedda)* v. *Secretary of State for Defence*, Mr Al-Jedda, a 48-year-old dual British citizen and Iraqi national, challenged his internment by British forces in Iraq as a breach of Art. 5 ECHR, of the equivalent but claimed to be 'free-standing' Convention Rights in HRA 1998, Sch. 2, and of common law.[119] He had been arrested, at the request of British intelligence authorities in October 2004. The detention was thus effected after a transfer of power from the Coalition Provisional Authority to the interim Iraqi government, a transfer seen by the UN Security Council as vesting Iraqi sovereignty in that interim government. The legal base for the detention rested on a range of Security Council Resolutions and agreement between the interim government and the United States as the commander of the multi-national force (MNF), authorized by those resolutions to 'take all necessary measures to contribute to the maintenance of security and stability in Iraq'. This was seen as extending the original ability of a belligerent power under international customary law to order internment when deemed necessary for imperative reasons of security. The mandate enabled that to

---

[114] JHRC 12th (2005–06): 41–3 (Campaign Against Criminalizing Communities).

[115] Blake and Husain (2003): para. 3.89.

[116] Immigration Act 1971, Sch. 2, para. 22.

[117] Ovey and White (2006): 24–7.

[118] [2005] EWCA Civ 1609.

[119] [2006] 3 WLR 954.

continue beyond the one year set out in Geneva Convention IV until 31 December 2006, unless revoked earlier or renewed. Mr Al-Jeddah traveled widely in the Middle East, he claimed on business (import and export of motor vehicles). He remained in regularly reviewed detention because the British authorities considered that his trips and presence in Iraq were for other purposes. He was under suspicion of membership of a terrorist group involved in weapons smuggling and explosive attacks in Iraq, and it was believed that he was personally responsible for: recruiting terrorists outside Iraq with a view to the commission of atrocities in Iraq; facilitating the travel into Iraq of an identified terrorist explosives expert; conspiring with him to conduct improvised explosive device (IED) attacks against coalition forces in the areas around Fallujah and Baghdad; and conspiring with that person and members of an Islamist terrorist cell in the Gulf to smuggle high-tech IED detonation equipment into Iraq, for use in attacks against Coalition forces. As a result of Art. 103 UN Charter, giving primacy to UN obligations in the hierarchy of legal obligations other than those that are *jus cogens*, the Court held that UN-imposed obligations to maintain Iraqi security, by internment if necessary, overrode obligations under Art. 5 ECHR. Moreover, Convention Rights in the HRA 1998 were not free-standing but coterminous with those under the ECHR itself, so that an individual could gain no greater rights under the HRA in a United Kingdom court than under the ECHR in the European Court of Human Rights at Strasbourg.[120] Standard Conflicts of Laws principles meant that common law could not be applied here; the applicable law was that of Iraq which, in present context, had sanctioned internment.

Diplomatic Protection and Guantanamo Detainees: Individuals, the Courts and the Executive

Under international law a State has the right of diplomatic protection of its citizens enabling it to deal with and claim reparation in respect of their maltreatment by another State. How far the United Kingdom Government should go in acting on behalf of British citizens detained by the United States in Guantanamo Bay has been acutely controversial. Some saw in its public silence, acquiescence or complicity in Guantanamo, although Government would point out that its quiet diplomacy eventually procured the release of all British citizens held there. Persons acting on behalf of those detainees had, however, resorted to the courts in an attempt to pressure the Government and, more recently, an attempt has been made to use court challenge to oblige the Government to intervene similarly in respect of foreign nationals, long-standing residents of the United Kingdom, detained at Guantanamo.[121] Both attempts at judicial review failed. Judicial review lies at the

---

[120] Applying the decision of the House of Lords in *R (Quark Fishing Ltd) v Foreign Secretary* [2005] 3 WLR 837.

[121] On the controversy, see the following reports of the FAC: HC 196 (2002–03) paras 228–39; HC 257 (2002–03), paras 19–23; HC 405 (2002–03), paras 244–46; HC 389 (2003–

application of those seeking to protect a right or a legitimate expectation that a particular course of action or procedure will be followed. In *Abbasi*, an application by a British citizen, the Court of Appeal held that international law had not yet recognized that a state was under a duty to intervene by diplomatic or other means to protect a citizen who was suffering or threatened with injury in a foreign state. Nor could Abbasi properly be said while in Guantanamo to be within the jurisdiction of the United Kingdom for the purposes of Art. 1 ECHR which could not apply simply on the basis that every state enjoyed a degree of authority over its own nationals. Neither the ECHR nor the HRA afforded support to the contention that the Foreign Secretary owed a duty to exercise diplomacy on Abbasi's behalf and so recognized no correlative right to that protection. However, the proposition that there was thus no scope for review of a refusal to render diplomatic assistance to a British subject who was suffering violation of a fundamental human right as the result of the conduct of the authorities of a foreign state was not correct either. The mere fact that the power was prerogative did not preclude review; that depended on the subject matter involved. Policy statements issued by the Foreign Office on diplomatic protection showed governmental recognition of a role in protecting the rights of British citizens abroad in respect of miscarriage or denial of justice. This gave rise to a limited legitimate expectation of some response by Government in respect of a British citizen victim. But the exact nature of that response was very much a matter within the discretion of the Foreign Secretary. The court through judicial review would step in if, contrary to its stated practice, the Foreign Office refused even to consider whether to make diplomatic representations. But that was not the case as regards Abbasi and the other British citizen detainees. The Foreign Office had considered A's request for assistance. British detainees were the subject of discussions between this country and the United States both at Secretary of State and at lower official levels. The court could not order that specific representations be made as that would involve the courts to an inappropriate degree in the conduct of foreign policy, more properly a matter for an executive responsible to Parliament. In *Al Rawi*,[122] a case brought in respect of foreign nationals, detained and maltreated at Guantanamo Bay, who were long-standing residents of the United Kingdom, no such legitimate expectation, neither because of that long-standing residence nor refugee status in the United Kingdom, could arise since it had never been Foreign Office policy to act on behalf of non-citizens. Obligations under UNCAT did not impose a duty to act as the applicants required. Nor did Art. 8 ECHR do so. The different treatment of non-nationals as opposed to nationals with respect to policy on diplomatic protection was not discrimination contrary to the Race Relations Act 1976 or under

---

04), paras 52–8; HC 36–I (2004–05), paras 53–61; HC 109 (2004–05), paras 71–79; HC 573 (2005–06), paras 32–36; HC 574 (2005–06), paras 34–9.

[122] *Al Rawi and Others (R on the application of) v Secretary of State for Foreign and Commonwealth Affairs and Secretary of State for the Home Department* [2006] EWCA Civ 1279.

Art. 14 ECHR read with Art. 8 ECHR. While the applicants had a strong moral case assertable in the field of political debate, judicial reluctance to interfere with the exercise of the prerogative in foreign affairs meant that the court should not require the Foreign Office to make a formal request to the United States on the applicants' behalf. The question of what representations should be made was a matter of prerogative discretion and the Foreign Office decision not to make representations at a high level on the basis that they would be 'ineffective and counterproductive' was not one with which the court should interfere. The *Wednesbury* 'abuse of discretion' arguments sought to take the court into territory marked as 'forbidden' by *Abbasi*. As the Divisional Court put it,

> In diplomatic relations it may not always be sensible to express judgments, at least openly, about the legality or otherwise of the actions of a friendly State if that could affect discussions, particularly in related areas. As the Court of Appeal said: 'in particular, if the Foreign and Commonwealth Office was to make any statement of its views of the legality of the detention of the British prisoners, or any statement as to the nature of the discussions held with US officials, this might well undermine those discussions'. That seems to us to be particularly apposite in the present case. ... But the court simply does not have, for the reasons that have already been given, the means to make a proper evaluation of that bearing in mind all the ramifications which are clearly involved in this delicate area.[123]

As the Court of Appeal saw it, the

> ... courts have a special responsibility in the field of human rights. It arises in part from the impetus of the HRA, in part from the common law's jealousy in seeing that intrusive State power is always strictly justified. The elected government has a special responsibility in what may be called strategic fields of policy, such as the conduct of foreign relations and matters of national security. It arises in part from considerations of competence, in part from the constitutional imperative of electoral accountability. ... This case has involved issues touching both the Government's conduct of foreign relations, and national security: pre-eminently the former. In those areas the common law assigns the duty of decision upon the merits to the elected arm of government; all the more so if they combine in the same case. This is the law for constitutional as well as pragmatic reasons, as Lord Hoffmann has explained. The court's role is to see that the government strictly complies with all formal requirements, and rationally considers the matters it has to confront. Here, because of the subject matter, the law accords to the executive an especially broad margin of discretion. This conclusion betrays no want of concern for the plight of the appellants. At the outset we described the case as acute on its facts, and so it is. But it is the court's duty to decide where lies the legal edge between the executive and judicial functions.[124]

---

[123] [2006] EWHC 972 (Admin), para. 97.
[124] [2006] EWCA Civ 1279, paras 147–8.

Another Guantanamo Connection: Challenging Refusal to Grant British Citizenship

In 2005, David Hicks, an Australian national, held in Guantanamo, sought to assert his entitlement to register as a British citizen because his mother was born in the United Kingdom but at a time when women could not automatically transmit citizenship to their children. He wished to do so to obtain the same sort of consular protection from the United Kingdom which he perceived as resulting in the more favourable treatment by the US authorities of British citizens detained with him at Guantanamo. The Home Secretary's refusal to do so was quashed by the High Court,[125] since the then-applicable law gave no power to refuse registration to someone who met the requisite conditions, which did not then embody a test of good character. Nor would the court use public policy 'to close what is now regarded as an unfortunate gap'. The Court accepted that the Home Secretary, having granted citizenship, could in principle then use the legally available means to deprive the person of it. He has now done so. However, the more limited means of deprivation in the transitional rules governing the case only permitted reference to conduct after registration, 'disloyalty' and 'disaffection' grounds covering only citizens owing allegiance to Her Majesty. The applicable law has since been changed so that applicants for registration as well as naturalization must satisfy a 'good character' requirement.[126]

Fair Trial: Procedural and Evidentiary Issues

Compatibility of the SIAC/High Court Processes with Art. 6 ECHR: the 'Fair Hearing' Aspect and the Scope of Review of Non-derogating Control Orders

It is very clear from the examination in the last chapter of the nature of proceedings before SIAC (national security immigration and citizenship matters, ATCSA detention) and the Administrative Court (the division of the High Court responsible for control orders under the PTA 2005) that their use of 'closed' sessions, albeit in the presence of a Special Advocate, and denial of certain relevant material to the individual and legal team, places the individual and that team at the very least 'under a grave disadvantage'.[127] The question whether such proceedings provide a fair hearing at common law (rules of natural justice or duty to act fairly in a procedural sense) has traditionally been left to the Home Secretary as the best

---

[125] *Hicks (R on the application of)* v *Secretary of State for the Home Department* [2005] EWHC 2818 (Admin).

[126] See chapter 7.

[127] *M* v *Secretary of State for the Home Department* [2004] 2 All ER 863, para. 13 (Lord Woolf CJ). In *A and Others* v *Secretary of State for the Home Department (No. 2)* [2005] UKHL 71, para. 58.

judge of the extent to which national security interests must in any case trump due process rights (see chapter 4). However, such cases precede the HRA era and the question now must be whether proceedings comply with the 'fair hearing' dictates of the ECHR. Whether particular proceedings are in this sense compatible with ECHR rights is less simple than might appear, because of the variable applicability and content of those rights and the plain fact that, as regards the executive measures examined in this Part of the book, as was seen in the last chapter, the courts in question have widely varying jurisdictions. Each of the schemes under scrutiny accords the judiciary markedly different powers ranging from an apparently mere supervision of the executive decision (for example, non–derogating control orders) to (in effect) an ability to make its own judgment on the merits of the question (for example, whether there are reasonable grounds to certify and detain a suspected terrorist under ATCSA, or whether, with respect to a derogating control order under the PTA 2005, the court is satisfied on the balance of probabilities, that the controlled person is an individual who is or has been involved in terrorism-related activity).[128] The Court of Appeal has in *MB* narrowed the gap between these and review of non-derogating control orders.

As regards ECHR rights, the matter is complicated, first of all, because, while its main 'fair hearing' provision (Art. 6) applies to all criminal proceedings (the determination of a criminal charge against a person), its guarantee of a fair hearing in respect of 'civil rights and obligations' by no means applies to a full range of legal proceedings other than criminal ones. The jurisprudence, thankfully, no longer draws a crude dichotomy in terms of private law (covered) and public law (not covered). But the European Court of Human Rights has since the turn of this century held that the term does not cover the immigration field.[129] In addition, as a complicating factor, whether particular proceedings in respect of other executive measures examined in this book qualify as criminal or civil for purposes of Art. 6 is not clear. Each of those terms in Art. 6 has an autonomous Convention meaning, not tied to the particular classification of the scheme at issue by the State. That classification is relevant but not determinative. The Council of Europe Commissioner for Human Rights thought it arguable that control order proceedings under the PTA 2005 could be characterized as 'criminal'. So did the JHRC. In *A and Others (No. 2)*, dealing with SIAC and ATCSA detention, the characterization issue was avoided: a deprivation of liberty was subject to the right in Art. 5(4) to have the legality of the deprivation determined by a court and it was 'well-established that such proceedings must satisfy the basic requirements of a fair trial'.[130] In addition, where the right to respect for family life protected by Art. 8(1) is at issue, this is a 'civil right' for purposes of Art. 6. But in any event, the terms

---

[128] See further the detailed examination in chapter 8.

[129] *Maaouia v France* (2001) 33 EHRR 42.

[130] [2005] UKHL 71, para. 25 (Lord Bingham), citing: *Garcia Alva v Germany* (2001) 37 EHRR 335; *R (West) v Parole Board, R (Smith) v Parole Board* [2005] 1 WLR 350 (HL).

of legitimate State restriction of that right enshrined in Art. 8(2) provide another vehicle for requiring proceedings to meet certain fair hearing standards. That 'permissible limitation' clause requires that the restriction in question be 'in accordance with law'. The jurisprudence of the Court of Human Rights now stresses that this requires an ability to challenge the restriction in some adversarial 'court-like' proceedings, attracting a degree of fair hearing protection, in which an independent body can review the reasons for the decision and relevant evidence, if need be with appropriate procedural limitations on the use of classified information.[131] Where national security is invoked, the individual must be able before that body to challenge that assertion.[132] The independent body must be able to react in cases where invoking that concept has no reasonable basis in the facts or reveals an interpretation of 'national security' that is unlawful or contrary to common sense and arbitrary. That is also true in respect of Articles 9 (freedom of religion and conscience), 10 (expression) and 11 (assembly and association), as well as Art. 1 of the First Protocol.

The SIAC regime was created as a result of the decision of the European Court of Human Rights in *Chahal* v *United Kingdom*,[133] in which that Court held that neither judicial review in the High Court nor proceedings in the Adviser system satisfied the Articles 5(4) or 13 ECHR.[134] The Court there contrasted those regimes with one version of a Canadian model brought to its attention:

> The Court recognises that the use of confidential material may be unavoidable where national security is at stake. This does not mean, however, that the national authorities can be free from effective control by the domestic courts whenever they choose to assert that national security and terrorism are involved. The Court attaches significance to the fact that, as the intervenors pointed out in connection with Art. 13, in Canada a more effective form of judicial control has been developed in cases of this type. This example illustrates that there are techniques which can be employed which both accommodate legitimate security concerns about the nature and sources of intelligence information and yet accord the individual a substantial measure of procedural justice.[135]

The Court set out the main facets of the Canadian regime later in the decision.[136] The Government (hardly unreasonably) clearly acted on the basis that this was a strong hint that such a regime would satisfy the dictates of the ECHR. Indeed, in evidence to the CAC examining the use of Special Advocates before SIAC, the Attorney General claimed that the system had been promoted in *Chahal* and subsequently approved.[137] The explanatory memorandum accompanying the rules

---

[131] *Al-Nashif* v *Bulgaria* (2003) 36 EHRR 37, paras 119–129, at 123.

[132] (2003) 36 EHRR 37, para. 124.

[133] (1997) 23 EHRR 413.

[134] See further chapter 4.

[135] (1997) 23 EHRR 413, para. 131.

[136] (1997) 23 EHRR 413, para. 144.

[137] CAC 7th (2004–05a): para. 49.

of procedure for the High Court when considering control orders contains a similar statement.[138] Lord Woolf CJ (as he then was) saw the Court in *Chahal* as encouraging the use of a Special Advocate procedure.[139] As the JHRC recently concluded, however,

> The question of the compatibility of the system of closed hearings with the Convention's guarantees of a fair hearing, and in particular whether it accords 'a substantial measure of procedural justice', ... remains an open one in Strasbourg.[140]

Crucially, at no point in *Chahal* did the Court expressly hold that such a regime *would* satisfy ECHR requirements on 'fair hearing'. In *Al-nashif* v *Bulgaria*,[141] where the deportation regime lacked any real mode of challenge, the Court, noting the SIAC system, specifically declined to give an opinion on its conformity with the ECHR.[142] Instead, it noted that there were means to balance national security and due process interests, and reiterated that

> While procedural restrictions may be necessary to ensure that no leakage detrimental to national security would occur and while any independent authority dealing with an appeal against a deportation decision may need to afford a wide margin of appreciation to the executive in matters of national security, that can by no means justify doing away with remedies altogether whenever the executive has chosen to invoke the term 'national security'. Even where an allegation of a threat to national security is made, the guarantee of an effective remedy requires as a minimum that the competent independent appeals authority must be informed of the reasons grounding the deportation decision, even if such reasons are not publicly available. The authority must be competent to reject the executive's assertion that there is a threat to national security where it finds it arbitrary or unreasonable. There must be some form of adversarial proceedings, if need be through a special representative after a security clearance. Furthermore, the question whether the impugned measure would interfere with the individual's right to respect for family life and, if so, whether a fair balance is struck between the public interest involved and the individual's rights must be examined.[143]

Yet SIAC and the High Court processes would arguably meet all those criteria.

Special Advocates are increasingly used in a variety of contexts in the United Kingdom's legal order.[144] One of those contexts, involving deprivation of liberty, concerns the powers and processes whereby the Parole Board decides whether a prisoner sentenced to life imprisonment can be released into the community on licence. A key question here is the future risk posed to the public by the prisoner.

---

[138] JHRC 12th (2005–06): para. 73.

[139] *Roberts* v *Parole Board* [2005] 2 A.C. 738, para. 58.

[140] JHRC 12th (2005–06): para.77.

[141] *Al-Nashif* v *Bulgaria* (2003) 36 EHRR 37.

[142] (2003) 36 EHRR 37, para. 97.

[143] (2003) 36 EHRR 37, para. 137.

[144] CAC 7th (2004–05a): paras 50, 51.

Sometimes information which it is important for the Parole Board to have to decide on that question will only be provided to it in circumstances where the Board can ensure that the identity of the source will not be disclosed (directly or indirectly) to the prisoner or his/her legal team. In *Roberts v Parole Board*,[145] the House of Lords held that whether such proceedings satisfied the fair hearing requirements of Art. 5(4) could only be decided after examining on the facts of the individual case, the process as a whole, including any appellate proceedings. Whether those requirements would be satisfied by a full hearing of the Parole Board involving a specially appointed advocate could not be decided in advance, as a matter of principle. By a majority of 3:2, the House decided that the Board had power to operate in this manner and that neither the nature of the proceedings nor the extent of the non-disclosure to the individual and his legal team necessarily abrogated his common law or ECHR/HRA fair hearing rights. Similar modifications of procedure to protect sensitive material or witnesses at criminal trial, were upheld by the House of Lords in *R v H, R v C*,[146] in the context of public interest immunity applications, and, more recently, by the Court of Appeal in *R v Davis, R v Ellis*,[147] in the context of protecting from identification by the accused or his lawyer witnesses at a criminal trial. In each of those cases, the courts undertook a detailed analysis of Strasbourg jurisprudence on the issue of a fair trial in criminal proceedings and the ability of a court to prevent disclosure to the accused and their lawyers of the identity of the witness, so long as cross-examination was permitted, either by the accused's lawyer or (as extended by the House and the Court of Appeal) a Special Advocate.

Somewhat surprisingly, the issue of due process compatibility has not been litigated in the course of challenges to SIAC and national security deportation. It has also barely been touched on in the context of challenges to SIAC and ATCSA. In the Court of Appeal during the derogation litigation, Lord Woolf CJ held that such proceedings were not criminal for the purposes of Art. 6(1). They were, however, civil proceedings within the ambit of that provision. He then merely noted that the ECHR right to a fair hearing embodies a 'national security' exception.[148] This comment is puzzling since Art. 5(4) contains on its face no such exception. Art. 6(1) does, but only as regards the public character of the proceedings in that it permits exclusion of the press and public. Presumably, like the Government, the comment proceeds on the basis, questioned above, that the European Court of Human Rights implicitly endorsed a SIAC-type system as compatible with the Convention's 'fair hearing' strictures. He considered in specific context that the use of the Special Advocate to probe the evidence that was withheld from the detainee and his/her lawyers, provided 'a substantial degree of

---

[145] [2005] 2 A.C. 738.

[146] [2004] 2 A.C. 134.

[147] [2006] EWCA Crim 1155.

[148] *A and Others v Secretary of State for the Home Department* [2003] 1 All ER 816, at 836 (para. 57).

protection'. Looking at the proceedings as a whole, including the appellate ones, he was satisfied that there had been no breach of Art. 6(1). The matter was not considered when the case went to the House of Lords. In *M* v *Secretary of State for the Home Department*,[149] one detainee (M) was released when the Court of Appeal upheld SIAC's decision to allow his appeal against certification and cancel the certificate. Giving the judgment of the Court, Lord Woolf CJ accepted that SIAC processes placed appellants at a grave disadvantage, but one mitigated to some degree by the role of the Special Advocate looking after the interests of the appellant.[150]

> Having read the transcripts, we are impressed by the openness and fairness with which the issues in closed session were dealt with by those who were responsible for the evidence given before SIAC. We feel the case has additional importance because it does clearly demonstrate that, while the procedures which SIAC have to adopt are not ideal, it is possible by using special advocates to ensure that those detained can achieve justice and it is wrong therefore to undervalue the SIAC appeal process.[151]

The matter of the compatibility with ECHR 'fair hearing' requirements of SIAC type procedures in the Administrative Court (the branch of the High Court dealing with non-derogating control orders) has now been decided by the Court of Appeal, but may yet go to the Lords. On 12 April, 2006, in *Re MB*,[152] Sullivan J considered the matter when conducting the adversarial hearing in respect of the non-derogating control order made against the respondent on 5 September 2005 by the Home Secretary with the permission of Ouseley J given in a 'without notice' hearing under PTA 2005, section 3. Sullivan J characterized the court's role at the adversarial stage as the supervisory one of judicially reviewing the Secretary of State's decision to seek an order. It could only quash that decision if it was 'obviously flawed' in light of applicable judicial review principles, deciding that as at the date of the Secretary of State's decision to go for an order.[153] Since MB's Art. 8 rights (private life and home) were engaged, Art. 6(1) applied as regards a determination of a civil right.[154] The ability of the court in its supervisory role at the permission stage was very limited and the standard of proof applied to the decision-maker very low, even though the allegation against him is a very serious one and breach of an order without reasonable excuse attracts quite serious criminal penalties. In short, the court's role here was more limited than that of SIAC under ATCSA and much less far-reaching than that of the High Court with respect to a derogating control order, where

---

[149] [2004] 2 All ER 863.
[150] [2004] 2 All ER 863, para. 13.
[151] [2004] 2 All ER 863, para. 34.
[152] [2006] EWHC 1000 (Admin).
[153] [2006] EWHC 1000 (Admin), para. 28.
[154] [2006] EWHC 1000 (Admin), paras 30–32. See also the characterization of ASBOs in *R (McCann)* v *Manchester Crown Court* [2003] 1 AC 787 (HL).

... the court itself decides, on all the evidence available as at the date of the hearing, and on the balance of probabilities, whether the controlee is or has been involved in terrorism-related activity and whether the imposition of obligations on him is necessary for purposes connected with protecting members of the public from a risk of terrorism.[155]

For there to be a 'fair hearing' the court reviewing the decision of the non-independent decision-maker (here the Home Secretary), had to have 'full jurisdiction', that is one sufficient to deal with the nature and requirements of the case.[156] The controlee cannot effectively challenge the basis on which the Home Secretary sought the order, and as regards the matter of what conditions could be imposed, the position was even more fettered since that power was framed subjectively, not objectively.[157] In conclusion, Sullivan J castigated the decision-making process as a denial of a 'fair hearing':

> To say that the Act does not give the [controlee] in this case ... a fair hearing in the determination of his rights under Art. 8 of the Convention would be an understatement. The court would be failing in its duty under the [HRA], a duty imposed by Parliament, if it did not say, loud and clear, that the procedure under the [PTA 2005] whereby the court merely reviews the lawfulness of the Secretary of State's decision to make the order upon the basis of the material available to him at that earlier stage are conspicuously unfair. The thin veneer of legality which is sought to be applied by section 3 of the [PTA 2005] cannot disguise the reality. That controlees' rights under the Convention are being determined not by an independent court in compliance with Art. 6.1, but by executive decision-making, untrammeled by any prospect of effective judicial supervision.[158]

The PTA 2005 did not enable him to conclude that, on the basis of the one-sided information then available to the Home Secretary, his decision to go for a control order against MB was flawed in the light of the principles of judicial review. The control order was thus valid and remained in force. Sullivan J, however, issued a declaration of incompatibility with ECHR rights of fair hearing in respect of the decision-making process for non-derogating control orders found in section 3 of the PTA 2005. On 1 August 1 2006, the Court of Appeal, however, held that Sullivan J had been wrong to find the process in breach of Art. 6 ECHR and refused MB leave to appeal to the House of Lords.[159] The Court held that Sullivan J had underestimated the degree of judicial scrutiny possible and had been wrong

---

[155] [2006] EWHC 1000 (Admin), para. 29.

[156] [2006] EWHC 1000 (Admin), para. 42, citing *Bryan v United Kingdom* (1995) 21 EHRR 342; *Runa Begum v Tower Hamlets LBC* [2003] 2 AC 430.

[157] [2006] EWHC 1000 (Admin), para. 84.

[158] [2006] EWHC 1000 (Admin), para. 103.

[159] *Secretary of State for the Home Department v MB* [2006] EWCA Civ 1140. See also, Travis (2006); Morris (2006).

to make the declaration of incompatibility. He (and counsel at that stage) 'astonishingly' had ignored section 11(2) PTA 2005 which makes the High Court the appropriate tribunal for HRA issues in respect of control orders.[160] Given that, and interpreting the court's powers under that section and section 3 of the PTA in accordance with the interpretative obligation in section 3 of the HRA so as to secure compatibility with Convention Rights, the Court held that this produced an enhanced level of judicial scrutiny. Section 11(2) so read 'requires the court in so far as it is able, to give effect to MB's Convention rights having regard to the state of affairs that exists at the time that the court reaches its decision' and a 'purposive approach to section 3(10) must enable the court to consider whether the continuing decision of the Secretary of State to keep the order in force is flawed'.[161] That accorded with the normal approach on judicial review in general.[162] Proceedings for a control order do not attract the criminal charge aspect of Art. 6 ECHR. However, involvement in terrorism–related activity is likely to constitute a serious criminal offence, although it will not necessarily do so. Hence, when reviewing a decision by the Secretary of State to make a control order, 'the court must make up its own mind as to whether there are reasonable grounds for the necessary suspicion'.[163] Doing so

> ... may involve considering a matrix of alleged facts, some of which are clear beyond reasonable doubt, some of which can be established on balance of probability and some of which are based on no more than circumstances giving rise to suspicion. The court has to consider whether this matrix amounts to reasonable grounds for suspicion and this exercise differs from that of deciding whether a fact has been established according to a specified standard of proof.[164]

The court is also required to review the decision of the Secretary of State that it was necessary, for purposes connected with protecting the public from a risk of terrorism, to make the control order and to consider his decision on each one of the obligations. This raised different issues and a degree of deference to the Home Secretary was appropriate here:

> Whether it is necessary to impose any particular obligation on an individual in order to protect the public from the risk of terrorism involves the customary test of proportionality. The object of the obligations is to control the activities of the individual so as to reduce the risk that he will take part in any terrorism-related activity. The obligations that it is necessary to impose may depend upon the nature of the involvement in terrorism-related activities of which he is suspected. They may also depend upon the resources available to the Secretary of State and the demands on those

---

[160] [2006] EWCA Civ 1140, para. 4.

[161] [2006] EWCA Civ 1140, paras 40, 44, 46.

[162] [2006] EWCA Civ 1140, para. 45.

[163] [2006] EWCA Civ 1140, para. 58.

[164] [2006] EWCA Civ 1140, para. 67.

resources. They may depend on arrangements that are in place, or that can be put in place, for surveillance. The Secretary of State is better placed than the court to decide the measures that are necessary to protect the public against the activities of a terrorist suspect and, for this reason, a degree of deference must be paid to the decisions taken by the Secretary of State. That it is appropriate to accord such deference in matters relating to state security has long been recognised, both by the courts of this country and by the Strasbourg court, … Notwithstanding such deference there will be scope for the court to give intense scrutiny to the necessity for each of the obligations imposed on an individual under a control order, and it must do so. The exercise has something in common with the familiar one of fixing conditions of bail. Some obligations may be particularly onerous or intrusive and, in such cases, the court should explore alternative means of achieving the same result. The provision of section 7(2) for modification of a control order 'with the consent of the controlled person' envisages dialogue between those acting for the Secretary of State and the controlled person, and this is likely to be appropriate, with the assistance of the court, at the stage that the court is considering the necessity for the individual obligations.[165]

The 'closed' session processes of scrutiny of the security material with the aid of a Special Advocate were compatible with ECHR requirements on 'fair trial'. Taking on board the comments of the European Court of Human Rights in *Chahal* and of other United Kingdom courts examined earlier in this section, the Court of Appeal stated:

> The present case is concerned with powers conferred on the executive to interfere with individual rights in order to protect the public against the risk of terrorism. The PTA empowers the Secretary of State to impose obligations, which fall short of infringing Art. 5, in order to prevent or restrict the risk that someone who is suspected of having been involved in terrorism will take part in terrorism in the future. Such obligations are likely to interfere with human rights other than those under Art. 5 and questions will arise as to whether such interference can be justified. If one starts with the premise that the *risk* of terrorism *may* justify such measures, we consider that it must follow that Art. 6 cannot automatically require disclosure of the evidence of the grounds for suspicion. Were this not so, the Secretary of State would be in the invidious position of choosing between disclosing information which would be damaging to security operations against terrorists, or refraining from imposing restrictions on a terrorist suspect which appear necessary in order to protect members of the public from the risk of terrorism. If one accepts, as we do, that reliance on closed material is permissible, this can only be on terms that appropriate safeguards against the prejudice that this may cause to the controlled person are in place. We consider that the provisions of the PTA for the use of a special advocate, and of the rules of court made pursuant to paragraph 4 of the Schedule to the PTA, constitute appropriate safeguards.[166]

The matter of the validity of the order itself will have to be decided by Sullivan J applying the enhanced powers of review identified by the Court of Appeal.

---

[165] [2006] EWCA Civ 1140, paras 63–5.
[166] [2006] EWCA Civ 1140, paras 85–6.

Sullivan J's judgment could have been read as giving by implication a 'fair hearing' seal of approval as regards 'fair hearing' issues to the fuller jurisdiction enjoyed by the High Court in respect of derogating control orders and by analogy that of SIAC with respect to ATCSA. SIAC's jurisdiction in the immigration law sphere, even after *Rehman*, might also be thought closer to that more ample jurisdiction end of the decision-making spectrum. He did, however, rather pointedly preface his remarks on what fairness required (the court's own appraisal of all the evidence as at the time of the hearing) with an assumption that a fair procedure was possible using open and closed sessions and a Special Advocate. The Court of Appeal decision that the lesser standard of review applicable in non–derogating cases and the processes used ('open' and 'closed' sessions', Special Advocates) satisfied ECHR requirements on 'fair trial' clearly means that the higher standard applied by the High Court for derogating control orders using those same processes would on that basis be ECHR compliant.

Compatibility of the Decision-making Process with Art. 6 ECHR: the Right to an Unbiased Adjudicator

A number of individuals have been moved from one security regime to another: from national security deportation to ATCSA detention, and from there to a non–derogating control order which was then rescinded with the person again being detained for purposes of deportation to a country entering a 'no ill-treatment' agreement with the United Kingdom. Such an individual might already have been the subject of a judgment by SIAC (deportation and /or ATCSA detention) or by the Administrative Court. The question thus arose as to whether a judge who has made findings in respect of the particular individual in other proceedings against him, or at an earlier stage in the same proceedings (for example, the initial *ex parte* grant of permission for a non-derogating control order under the PTA 2005), should recuse himself from sitting in other proceedings or at a later stage of the same proceedings (for example, the adversarial hearing stage in respect of that non-derogating control order). The Administrative Court, in contested control order proceedings, held that there was no automatic requirement to recuse.[167] The ordinary principles in respect of actual, presumed or apparent bias applied: actual bias would automatically disqualify; so would direct pecuniary or personal interest; and a judge should stand down (or his/her decision be nullified) if, looking at all the circumstances, a reasonable bystander would think there was a real possibility of bias. In the context of adversarial control order proceedings the judge set to hear it had to look at all the circumstances of the case in the light of those principles. Relevant questions would be: what part had the judge played in the other or earlier proceedings; what previously had the judge decided in them and on what material?

---

[167] *A and Others* v *Secretary of State for the Home Department (In re a Matter of a Control Order)* [2005] EWHC (Admin) 1669, paras 18–24.

The Evidentiary Aspects

For parties to them, torture is prohibited by Art. 3 ECHR, its ICCPR counterpart, and by UNCAT. But its prohibition is now more extensive. It has now attained in international law the status of a peremptory norm; that is, a prohibition enjoying a higher status in that legal order's hierarchy of rules than treaty obligations and 'ordinary' international customary law. As such it imposes on all States obligations with respect to the prohibition of torture which each State owes to all other members of the international community, so that any State can properly insist on another State fulfilling that obligation or calling for its breach to be discontinued. It is, however, equally clear, that torture is widely practised by State officials seeking intelligence or information from suspects. British officials, both at home and in the former Empire, have been guilty of what would now, under ECHR case law, be characterized as torture rather than merely inhuman and degrading treatment. The practice of extraordinary rendition – where one State moves its suspects to another State for interrogation through torture or other maltreatment, away from the risk of undue scrutiny of other arms of government, effective NGOs and an investigative media – represents in modern jargon an 'outsourcing of torture'.[168] All responsible authorities stress the need for international co-operation against terrorism. Part of this involves the intelligence agencies of one State sharing its intelligence with other 'friendly' states. The distinct possibility – some would say probability – is that some of the material passed on may be the product of torture, either by or (in the case of extraordinary rendition or outsourcing) on behalf of the State passing on the intelligence. A question litigated all the way to the House of Lords was whether such material obtained in that context (one in which torture *may* have been used) was admissible before SIAC to support certification and detention without trial of a foreign national under ATCSA. As regards criminal proceedings, of course, PACE section 76 precludes the admission of inculpatory statements (confessions) by the accused obtained through oppression, defined to include the use of torture. But in such proceedings the issue of the use of evidence obtained through torture of a third party would not arise because of the evidentiary rules on hearsay. In contrast, however, as we have seen, a key reason for using the executive measures considered in this book is that for variety of reasons – among them difficulties with the evidentiary standards of the criminal process – criminal proceedings cannot successfully be brought. The establishment of SIAC-type processes to monitor the propriety and legality of the use of such executive measures has perforce had to recognize that a different evidentiary regime is required to govern those processes; otherwise one merely transfers the problem from the criminal process. Hence neither SIAC (dealing with national security immigration or citizenship decisions or with ATCSA detention) nor the Administrative Court are bound by the strict rules of evidence applicable to other civil and criminal courts. The Rules of Procedure for SIAC empower it to receive

---

[168] See further FAC 4th (2005–06): paras 47–58; Marty (2006).

evidence that would not be admissible in a court of law.[169] Those for the High Court similarly stipulate that 'the court may receive evidence that would not, but for this rule, be admissible in a court of law'.[170] Unlike the criminal trial or civil proceedings, the processes of 'closed' session used both by SIAC and the High Court enable (at no little cost to the rights of the 'defence') the protection of informants, intelligence agents and operatives, other witnesses fearful of reprisals, and the secrecy or security methods of investigation. Consequently, as regards both courts the statutory restriction on non-admissibility of communications intercept material is lifted. The complexities of whether such processes afford a fair hearing have been examined above. Consideration is given here to whether material produced by torture can properly be considered by SIAC or the High Court in reaching their decisions or whether such material is, despite the width of the rules stated above, inadmissible. Also considered is whether the Home Secretary is precluded from acting on such material. These particular issues were litigated as regards SIAC and ATCSA detention all the way to the House of Lords. The view adopted here is that the principles laid down by their Lordships precluding the use of such material by SIAC in that context are applicable equally to decision-making by SIAC in its other 'security' jurisdictions and to the High Court when dealing with control orders. The Home Secretary and other executive authorities (the police, the Security Service (MI5) and the Secret Intelligence Service (MI6)) can act on such material. As regards SIAC and the High Court, the preclusion covers statements obtained through torture, but not physical evidence, probative in itself, obtained as a result of statements so obtained. Moreover, the absolute preclusion covers statements obtained through torture. Statements obtained as a result of inhuman and degrading treatment prohibited by Art. 3 ECHR are not automatically ruled inadmissible.

Between May and July 2003, SIAC heard the merits appeals under ATCSA of ten of the individuals detained as international terrorist suspects posing a threat to national security. SIAC heard evidence in 'open' session when the appellants and their legal representatives were present and in 'closed' session when they were excluded but Special Advocates were present. On 29 October 2003 'open' judgments on the general and the specific issues, and 'closed' judgments were given dismissing all the appeals. On the specific question of the admissibility before it of material obtained by torture, SIAC held the fact that evidence had, or might have been, procured by torture inflicted by foreign officials without the complicity of the British authorities went to the weight of the evidence but did not render it inadmissible.

On 11 August 2004, the Court of Appeal by a majority (Pill and Laws LJJ, Neuberger LJ in part dissenting) upheld SIAC's decision: the Secretary of State could rely on evidence which might have been obtained by torture, so long as

---

[169] Special Immigration Appeals Commission (Procedure) Rules 2003 (SI 2003/1034), r. 44.

[170] Civil Procedure Rules, r. 76.26(4).

neither he nor any of his agents were implicated in the torture, when determining whether to detain a suspected foreign terrorist under ATCSA.[171] This majority decision was criticized as being at odds with obligations under UNCAT,[172] and possibly fair trial under Art. 6 ECHR. Moreover requiring SIAC (and thus in reality also the Secretary of State) to be satisfied of the propriety or otherwise of the provenance of evidence is an important element in evaluating its reliability. *The Independent* newspaper commented, 'Thank goodness for the Law Lords'.[173] Thanks are certainly due to all of them as regards the principle of excluding from court proceedings material obtained through torture. It may be thought, however, that the majority of the House cannot properly be thanked for the admissibility test it propounded. This, while having an air of the practical about it from the perspective of the Home Secretary, sets the threshold too high for individuals, their lawyers and the Special Advocates.

On further appeal, the issue before the House of Lords was this:

> May the Special Immigration Appeals Commission ('SIAC'), a superior court of record established by statute, when hearing an appeal under section 25 of the Anti-terrorism, Crime and Security Act 2001 by a person certified and detained under sections 21 and 23 of that Act, receive evidence which has or may have been procured by torture inflicted, in order to obtain evidence, by officials of a foreign state without the complicity of the British authorities?[174]

It was properly characterized as one of constitutional principle, and not a mere argument about the law of evidence.[175] The Home Secretary accepted as inadmissible material obtained through the perpetration of torture by the British authorities or by a foreign government at their behest or with the complicity of those authorities.[176] While denying any legal obligation to do so, he further stated that he did not intend to rely on or present to SIAC or to the Administrative Court any evidence which he knew or believed to have been obtained through torture by a third country.[177] On 8 December 2005 a unanimous seven-member House of Lords held that non-physical or 'statement' evidence ('the raw product of interrogation under torture')[178] obtained through torture of anyone anywhere in the world was not admissible in a court in the United Kingdom, save to prove an

---

[171] *A and 9 Others* v *Secretary of State for the Home Department* [2004] EWCA Civ 1123.

[172] JHRC 18th (2003–04): paras 26–9; JHRC 10th (2004–05): paras 18–21.

[173] Cited in Thienel (2006): 408.

[174] *A and Others* v *Secretary of State (No.2)* [2005] UKHL 71, para. 1 (Lord Bingham).

[175] [2005] UKHL 71, para. 51 (Lord Bingham); para. 66 (Lord Nicholls); paras 81–3 (Lord Hoffman)

[176] [2005] UKHL 71, para. 1 (Lord Bingham).

[177] Ibid.

[178] [2005] UKHL 71, para. 88 (Lord Hoffman).

offence against the torturer.[179] The decision, as submitted above, thus goes wider than the specific context of ATCSA and SIAC. It is, moreover, one which differentiates between material which can be admitted before SIAC and that on which the Home Secretary or (in other circumstances) the police may take action (for example, to certify or detain a suspect or to effect an arrest or search premises for a bomb). In taking action, those executive authorities can proceed on the basis of material which may have been obtained through torture. If the torture was administered by or on behalf of United Kingdom authorities, that would breach Art. 3 ECHR (and thus the executive authorities would have acted unlawfully), but not the fair processes provisions of the ECHR.[180] The job of SIAC is to decide whether at the time of the hearing before it there are reasonable grounds for suspecting the appellant to be an international terrorist and for believing him/her to be a risk to national security. As Lord Nicholls put it:

> The executive and the judiciary have different functions and different responsibilities. It is one thing for tainted information to be used by the executive when making operational decisions or by the police when exercising their investigatory powers, including powers of arrest. These steps do not impinge upon the liberty of individuals or, when they do, they are of an essentially short-term interim character. Often there is an urgent need for action. It is an altogether different matter for the judicial arm of the state to admit such information as evidence when adjudicating definitively upon the guilt or innocence of a person charged with a criminal offence. In the latter case repugnance to torture demands that proof of facts should be found in more acceptable sources than information extracted by torture. ... in forming its own view on whether reasonable grounds exist SIAC is discharging a judicial function which calls for proof of facts by evidence. The ethical ground on which information obtained by torture is not admissible in court proceedings as proof of facts is applicable in these cases as much as in other judicial proceedings.[181]

The decision founded this welcome preclusion on a variety of legal bases: on the long-standing common law prohibition against torture; on the powers of a court to prevent abuse of its process and thus uphold the integrity of the administration of justice; and on Art. 3 ECHR read in the light of UNCAT and principles of public international law. The common law, to its pride and the admiration of continental commentators whose countries' legal orders permitted torture, had long set its face against the use of torture. Its sanction by the conciliar or prerogative

---

[179] [2005] UKHL 71, paras. 51–2 (Lord Bingham),76–9 (Lord Nicholls), 88, 94–7 (Lord Hoffman), 113 (Lord Hope); 148–150 (Lord Carswell), 160–164 (Lord Brown). For express statements permitting the use of physical evidence (the fruits of the poisoned tree) see paras 88 (Lord Hoffman), 161 (Lord Brown). Art. 15 UNCAT refers only to use of statements. Lord Rodger's opinion focuses purely on statements.

[180] [2005] UKHL 71, para. 47 (Lord Bingham).

[181] [2005] UKHL 71, paras 71, 76. See also paras 47–8 (Lord Bingham); 92–7 (Lord Hoffman).

Court of Star Chamber in the seventeenth century was one reason for the many common lawyers siding with Parliament rather than the King in the constitutional conflicts of that century, and Star Chamber was abolished in 1641. Art. 3 ECHR enshrines the right to be free from torture. UNCAT characterizes torture as an offence to human dignity, a denial of the purposes of the UN Charter and a violation of human rights. It prohibits States from permitting or tolerating it, even in times of war or other public emergency. States are required to take effective measures (legislative, administrative, judicial or other) to prevent its practice within their jurisdiction, and to criminalize acts of torture. Art. 15 of UNCAT provides that

> Each State Party shall ensure that any statement which is established to have been made as a result of torture shall not be invoked as evidence in any proceedings, except against a person accused of torture as evidence that the statement was made.

The prohibition of torture is not merely a treaty obligation binding the parties to the relevant Conventions. It has acquired the status of a peremptory norm of international law (*jus cogens*), thus enjoying a higher status in that legal order's hierarchy of rules than treaty obligations and 'ordinary' international customary law. As such it imposes on all States obligations with respect to the prohibition of torture which each State owed to all other members of the international community, so that any State can properly insist on another State fulfilling that obligation or calling for its breach to be discontinued.

While the preclusive rule recognized by all in this seminal decision of the House of Lords could be removed by Parliament through an enactment (a further demonstration of parliamentary sovereignty) it would require very clear words to do so. The statement in the SIAC Procedure Rules that SIAC 'may receive evidence that would not be admissible in a court of law' did not suffice to remove such a fundamental preclusion.[182]

The preclusive rule, however, is limited to exclusion of statements (non-physical material). It does not cover physical evidence probative of itself which may have been obtained as a result of statements procured by torture. This is stated explicitly only by two of the Law Lords in *A and Others*. As Lord Hoffman put it,

> As for the rule that we do not necessarily exclude the 'fruit of the poisoned tree', but admit relevant evidence discovered in consequence of inadmissible confessions, this is the way we strike a necessary balance between preserving the integrity of the judicial process and the public interest in convicting the guilty. And even when the evidence has been obtained by torture – the accomplice's statement has led to the bomb being found under the bed of the accused – that evidence may be so compelling and so independent

---

[182] [2005] UKHL 71, paras 51 Lord Bingham), 79 (Lord Nicholls), 94–7 (Lord Hoffman), 114 (Lord Hope), 137 (Lord Rodger).

that it does not carry enough of the smell of the torture chamber to require its exclusion.[183]

Lord Bingham had referred to this rule as the common law's 'pragmatic compromise'.[184] Lord Brown, endorsing that, pointed out the rationale: 'whereas coerced statements may be intrinsically unreliable, the fruits they yield will have independent evidential value'.[185] As for the others, their broader comments must be taken in the context of the case which, as Lord Hoffman stressed, was concerned only with statements, with 'the admissibility of the raw product of interrogation under torture'.[186] Moreover, Art. 15 UNCAT on which all drew deals only with statements: 'it creates no bar to the use of coerced statements as a basis for executive action [and] says nothing whatever about the fruits of the poisoned tree'.[187]

To ground automatic exclusion of a statement, the mode of obtaining it must constitute 'torture'; lesser maltreatment, albeit contrary to Art. 3 ECHR, its ICCPR counterpart or other provisions of UNCAT, does not produce automatic exclusion.

The question then arises of who must prove what and to what standard in terms of having material claimed to be procured by torture sought to be admitted allowed in or excluded: the admissibility test. The House, however, divided 4:3 on the precise admissibility test to be applied by SIAC. Government had been concerned that the House would set the admissibility test as high as that in PACE – where, once the issue has been raised by the suspect, it then falls to the prosecution to establish beyond reasonable doubt that the confession was not obtained through torture.[188] Neither majority nor minority in the House of Lords set the test so high.[189] For the majority, the question was whether SIAC was satisfied that it was more probable than not that the information/intelligence had been obtained by torture.[190] If it was so satisfied, that information/intelligence had to be excluded as inadmissible. If SIAC was not satisfied of that, the information/intelligence should be admitted but any doubts SIAC had about its procurement would then be relevant to the weight to be attributed to the material.

Lord Hope recognized that a conventional approach to the burden of proof in this context would be inappropriate. Since the detainee is very much in the dark concerning the information to be used against him/her, it would be 'wholly unrealistic' to expect him/her to prove anything, to do more than raise the issue and ask SIAC to consider it, essentially by pointing out that the information may have

---

[183] [2005] UKHL 71, para. 88.
[184] [2005] UKHL 71, para. 16.
[185] [2005] UKHL 71, para. 161.
[186] [2005] UKHL 71, para. 88.
[187] [2005] UKHL 71, para. 162 (Lord Brown).
[188] s. 76.
[189] For comment and analysis, see Grief (2006).
[190] Lords Hope, Rodger, Carswell and Brown.

come from any one of the countries in the world practising torture. It is then up to SIAC to examine the information and the facts in detail.

> It must decide whether there are reasonable grounds to suspect that torture has been used in the individual case that is under scrutiny. If it has such a suspicion, there is then something that it must investigate as it addresses its mind to the information that is put before it which has been obtained from the security services.[191]

SIAC must refuse to admit the material if it concludes that on the balance of probabilities it was obtained by torture. If left in doubt about whether it was obtained in that way, the material should be admitted but it must bear that doubt in mind when evaluating the material. He put the test that way (positively rather than negatively) because of the broad range of material that rule 44(3) enables SIAC to rely on, 'far removed from what a court would regard as the best evidence', and the practicalities of the world of intelligence within which the security and intelligence services, the Home Secretary and, most importantly, SIAC have to operate.

> SIAC may be required to look at information coming to the attention of the security services at third or fourth hand and from various sources, the significance of which cannot be determined except by looking at the whole picture which it presents. The circumstances in which the information was first obtained may be incapable of being detected at all or at least of being determined without a long and difficult inquiry which would not be practicable. So it would be unrealistic to expect SIAC to demand that each piece of information be traced back to its ultimate source and the circumstances in which it was obtained investigated so that it could be proved piece by piece, that it was *not* obtained under torture. The threshold cannot be put that high. Too often we have seen how the lives of innocent victims and their families are torn apart by terrorist outrages. Our revulsion against torture, and the wish which we all share to be seen to abhor it, must not be allowed to create an insuperable barrier for those who are doing their honest best to protect us. A balance must be struck between what we would like to achieve and what can actually be achieved in the real world in which we all live. Arts 5(4) and 6(1) of the European Convention ... must be balanced against the right to life that is enshrined in Art. 2 of the Convention.[192]

He thought this approach entirely consistent with the express terms of Art. 15 UNCAT and that taken by the Hanseatic Court of Appeals, Criminal Division in Hamburg in a case raising identical issues in the context of a criminal trial of a terrorist suspect charged with conspiracy in respect of the 9/11 attacks.[193] It was also consonant with the difficulties faced as much by the United Kingdom authorities as by the German, to which that case referred, difficulties presented to

---

[191] [2005] UKHL 71, para. 116.

[192] [2005] UKHL 71, para. 119.

[193] [2005] UKHL 71, para. 122. The case is *El Motassadeq*, 14 June 2005, NJW 2005, 2326.

the House in a statement by the Director General of MI5.[194] Lord Rodger, concurring, considered it not enough that there was a suspicion that the country from which the material emanated used torture. 'To trigger the exclusion, it must be shown that the statement in question has been obtained by torture'.[195] He supported his approach not only through the German case noted above, but with the approach of the European Court of Human Rights in terms of ascertaining whether there were substantial grounds for believing that there was a real risk that someone was returned to a particular country where they would face torture: generalized information about a country did not suffice; rather the specific allegations of the claimants had to be corroborated by evidence.[196] He noted that the Home Office carefully checked the material it proposed to put to SIAC for anything suggesting that torture had been used and that the Home Secretary regarded himself as duty-bound to place before SIAC any such material indicating that. Lord Rodger was confident that 'with the aid of the relevant intelligence services, doubtless as much as possible will be done. And SIAC itself will wish to take an active role in suggesting possible lines of investigation, just as the Hamburg court did'.[197] Lord Brown agreed with Lord Hope.[198] His difficulties in supporting the minority test would substantially have been lessened had it merely meant SIAC shutting out a statement whenever it simply could not decide one way or the other whether torture had been used. Given the expertise of SIAC, he thought that would be a rare case and in any event preferred the majority test.[199] Lord Carswell proved the key vote. Initially he had been minded to favour the minority (Bingham) test, but finally decided that the Hope test – which Lord Carswell's opinion thus made the majority test – had fewer practical problems and struck the better balance between fair hearing/due process issues and the right to life which the Home Secretary and associated authorities were charged under the ECHR to protect.[200]

The minority[201] espoused the Bingham test. SIAC had to exclude the material if satisfied that there was a real risk that the material had been obtained through torture. On this test, SIAC should refuse to admit the evidence 'if it is unable to conclude that there is not a real risk that the evidence has been obtained by torture'.[202] In exercising its tasks, SIAC should be guided by the prohibition of

---

[194] [2005] UKHL 71, para. 125.

[195] [2005] UKHL 71, para. 138.

[196] [2005] UKHL 71, para. 139. He cited the judgment of the Grand Chamber of the European Court of Human Rights in *Mamatkulov and Askarov v Turkey*, (2005) 41 EHRR 25, paras 71–3. The case concerned extradition from Turkey to Uzbekistan.

[197] [2005] UKHL 71, para. 143.

[198] [2005] UKHL 71, para. 172.

[199] [2005] UKHL 71, para. 173.

[200] [2005] UKHL 71, para. 158.

[201] Lords Bingham, Nicholls and Hoffman.

[202] [2005] UKHL 71, para. 56.

torture under Art. 3 ECHR, by the terms of Art. 15 UNCAT, by the due process demands of Art. 5(4) ECHR, and by the procedural handicaps imposed on the detainee and their lawyers by the procedures which SIAC, to protect sensitive security information, is obliged to adopt, procedures which very much place the detainee and their legal team in the dark.[203] Art. 15 UNCAT uses 'established', a term which normally places the burden of proving the truth of an allegation on those who make it. For Lord Bingham, however, the term had to be read differently in the far-from-ordinary context of SIAC procedures and their effect, both substantive (indefinite detention) and procedural (not knowing the detail of the case against him or her), on the detainee.[204] He saw the Hope (majority) test as one undermining the practical efficiency of UNCAT and as denying the detainee the standard of fairness which was their entitlement under the relevant due process/fair hearing provisions of the ECHR: Articles 5(4) and 6(1).[205] He supported this, characterizing very clearly the Hope test as one

> … which, in the real world, can never be satisfied. The foreign torturer does not boast of his trade. The security services, as the Secretary of State has made clear, do not wish to imperil their relations with regimes where torture is practised. The special advocates have no means or resources to investigate. The detainee is in the dark. It is inconsistent with the most rudimentary notions of fairness to blindfold a man and then impose a standard which only the sighted could hope to meet. The result will be that, despite the universal abhorrence expressed for torture and its fruits, evidence procured by torture will be laid before SIAC because its source will not have been 'established'.[206]

He thought the point even better put by his fellow dissenter, Lord Nicholls, for whom the Hope test

> … would place on the detainee a burden of proof which, for reasons beyond his control, he can seldom discharge. In practice that would largely nullify the principle, vigorously supported on all sides, that courts will not admit evidence procured by torture. That would be to pay lip-service to the principle. That is not good enough.[207]

Lord Hoffman, the other member of the minority, expressed entire agreement with the opinion of Lord Bingham.[208] He further saw 'honour' as underlying the legal technicalities of the appeal before the House.[209] As regards 'torture', Parliament intended SIAC to act as a court.[210] He agreed with Lord Bingham's approach to the

---

[203] [2005] UKHL 71, para. 59.
[204] [2005] UKHL 71, para. 58
[205] [2005] UKHL 71, para. 62.
[206] [2005] UKHL 71, para. 59.
[207] [2005] UKHL 71, para. 80.
[208] [2005] UKHL 71, para. 99.
[209] [2005] UKHL 71, para. 82.
[210] [2005] UKHL 71, para. 95.

term 'established' in Art. 15 UNCAT, a provision which could never have contemplated SIAC type procedures in which the individual had no idea either of the terms of a statement against him or the identity of its maker.[211] He gave short shrift to the Home Secretary's stated policy of non-reliance on material where he knew or believed it to have been obtained by torture:

> It leaves open the question of how much inquiry the Secretary of State is willing to make. It appears to be the practice of the Security Services, in their dealings with those countries in which torture is most likely to have been used, to refrain, as a matter of diplomatic tact or a preference for not learning the truth, from inquiring into whether this was the case. It may be that in such a case the Secretary of State can say that he has no knowledge or belief that torture has taken place. But a court of law would not regard this as sufficient to rebut real suspicion and in my opinion SIAC should not do so.[212]

The majority simply saw the Bingham approach as placing too high a burden on the Home Secretary and associated authorities with the responsibility of protecting the national security and the lives of the public. It is suggested by this author, however, that, for the reasons they gave, the Bingham test espoused by the minority better recognizes the relatively helpless position of the detainee and their lawyers, the limitations on Special Advocates and the policy behind both treaty and customary international law prohibitions on torture. It places a burden where it properly should lie; on those with the facilities (and claimed desire) to investigate matters. It gives better effect to Art. 15 UNCAT and the jurisprudence of its Committee against Torture.[213] Insofar as the Bingham 'real risk' test has an air of looking to the future rather than the past, Nicholas Grief, one of the counsel for the interveners in the case, advanced an adaptive formulation from Lord Bingham's earlier judicial experience (a 'complete confidence' test) which might have commanded more assent: 'unless SIAC can with complete confidence conclude that a statement was not obtained by torture, it should exclude it'.[214]

The opinions give an interesting coverage of the relevant law on torture and its historical development both nationally and internationally. Moreover they show that the 'irregular rendition', said to be used by the CIA to have terrorist suspects interrogated other than in the USA,[215] is nothing new. Charles II deployed it during his reign (1660–85), sending suspects from England, where torture was unlawful, to his other realm, Scotland (then a separate country), where torture could be used without breaching the law.[216]

---

[211] [2005] UKHL 71, para. 98.

[212] Ibid.

[213] Grief (2006).

[214] Grief (2006).

[215] See further FAC 4th (2005–06): paras 47–58; Marty (2006).

[216] [2005] UKHL 71, para. 107 (Lord Hope).

Evidentiary Issues: Use of SIAC Open Judgments in Control Order Proceedings

A number of individuals have been moved from one security regime to another: from national security deportation to ATCSA detention, from there to a non-derogating control order which was then rescinded with the person again being detained for purposes of deportation to a country entering a 'no ill-treatment' agreement with the United Kingdom. Such an individual might already have been the subject of a judgment by SIAC (deportation and/or ATCSA detention) or by the Administrative Court. To what extent can the Home Secretary or the relevant court rely in one set of proceedings on the judgment of another court in respect of the same individuals or as evidence of the links between, or the threat posed by, particular terrorist groups? The question arose in *A and Others* v *Secretary of State for the Home Department (In re a Matter of a Control Order).*[217] There the Administrative Court characterized its role in relation to a non-derogating control order as supervisory, as applying the principles of judicial review to a Minister not confined by the rules of evidence in terms of the material to which he or she may properly have regard. Its role was more limited than that of SIAC which, under ATCSA, had to reach its own conclusion on whether there were reasonable grounds for certification.[218] The court agreed with counsel's view that 'the way in which the Secretary of State could properly have regard to SIAC judgments must depend on the issues being addressed and the circumstances of each individual case'.[219] The Home Secretary was thus required by the court to indicate to the individuals and their lawyers on how he took account of each of those SIAC judgments (which parts he relied on and for what purposes).[220] Where some material which had been omitted from an otherwise public judgment because of its possible impact on pending or ongoing criminal proceedings (in this instance the so-called ricin trial) was with the Crown Prosecution Service, the Home Secretary was given just over two weeks to get it.[221]

---

[217] [2005] EWHC (Admin) 1669.

[218] [2005] EWHC (Admin) 1669, paras. 15, 16.

[219] [2005] EWHC (Admin) 1669, para. 15.

[220] [2005] EWHC (Admin) 1669, para. 14.

[221] [2005] EWHC (Admin) 1669, para. 13.

PART IV

Conclusion

Chapter 10

Retrospective and Reflective

This book has examined the use, in the period since 1905, of executive measures of internment, restriction of movement, exclusion and deportation as methods of managing terrorism and protecting national security. It has done so in a variety of contexts: dealing with the 'enemy' at home in the two World Wars; the 'Irish' and 'Northern Ireland' questions; and in refusing entry to or removing or deporting undesirable 'aliens'. Such measures were used both at home and in the establishment of and withdrawal from colonial empire. Initially eschewed (apart from the immigration control option) and thus given much reduced significance in the creation of permanent legislation to combat terrorism at the start of the twenty-first century, after 9/11 and 7/7 they again became a central feature of the State's legal armoury in what has misleadingly been called the 'war on terror'. Whatever the specific context these executive measures have been deployed to manage terrorism or threats to national security, in a variety of situations and for a variety of reasons, to supplement or to provide an alternative to a 'pure' or more often a 'modified' criminal prosecution approach (arrest and extended detention without charge; charge; trial; conviction; and sentence – initially death or imprisonment, now purely the latter, in part because of human rights obligations). That pure or modified criminal process, so often the State's central means of suppressing deviant behaviour, had for a number of reasons significant problems in coping with deviant criminality in the form of threats to national security, insurgency and terrorism. These problems were ones such as intimidation of witnesses or their reluctance to come forward to give evidence or information for fear of reprisals and/or a degree of tacit support for the insurgent or terrorist group with which the accused was connected. They could also be the difficulties posed in protecting in an adversarial system the identity of informants and security sources or methods of detection in a context in which a fair trial demands full disclosure of material which might establish innocence. As with the exile/deportation of Archbishop Makarios in Cyprus, however, the problems might stem not from the difficulties of getting a conviction, but rather from those which would arise if a conviction was obtained.

This admixture of either type of criminal prosecution approach and the 'security' approach exemplified by the executive measures on which this book has focused, has not operated in a vacuum. Each context – other than perhaps the two World Wars – has had its constitutional, political or 'hearts and minds' dimension, although this last term seems to have been coined in the Malayan emergency of the late 1940s and the 1950s. This dimension is particularly obvious and striking in the responses to the Irish and latterly Northern Ireland questions and in the emergencies that marked the withdrawal from colonial empire. Those broader aspects of those responses operated alongside and often in tension with the security powers which are the main subject of this book. They involved – whatever the initial public stances of non-negotiation – talking to and reaching an accommodation with those previously condemned by Government as terrorists, rebels, malign elements, or subversive or seditious agitators. Ireland, Northern Ireland, Cyprus and Kenya are, of course, the prime examples in this book. But we have seen them featured also in Malaya. Former rebels or terrorists on taking power as the new democratic government have not been slow to use the same or analogous security powers the British deployed against them to deal with perceived threats to the new State or their own hold on political power. This constitutional, political or 'hearts and minds' dimension has been seen not to be wholly absent from the so–called post 9/11 'war on terror', but the nature of the threat has been perceived to make that dimension much more problematic than dealing with irredentist or nationalist terrorism. Constitutional and political solutions are not so readily apparent; the causes which serve to feed the threat are among the most intractable, their resolution not readily lying in the hands of States facing the threat; the demands of the 'opposition' or 'enemy' are more diffuse or rightly seen by the threatened as areas which are simply 'non-negotiable'.

In varying degrees, each of the executive, security powers treated in this book impacts significantly on the fundamental rights and freedoms of individuals: liberty and security of person (freedom from arbitrary arrest and detention and its dangers of torture or other maltreatment); fair trial and due process; respect for private and family life, home and correspondence; freedom of religion or conscience, expression, assembly and association; rights of residence and freedom of movement.

Internment, viewed as preventative by governments and punitive by those subjected to it, most obviously has the same direct impact as imprisonment after criminal conviction, with the added impact (not usually felt by the convicted prisoner) of no legitimate expectations about a likely release date ascertainable in accordance with predetermined and relatively transparent rules. The 'house arrest' enabled should derogating control orders be deployed, is internment by another name, albeit in what may be pleasanter surroundings. But, as was shown, exclusion to Northern Ireland might transfer individuals from a secure to a hostile environment, tainted with the finding of 'terrorism', move them from employment to unemployment, from good housing to bad, and place them at risk of death or serious bodily harm from paramilitaries on the other side of the sectarian divide, acting as 'pro-State terrorists or even 'proxy' terrorists for the security forces. The same could well be true of refusal of entry or deportation on security grounds (especially ones conferring a stigmatizing badge of involvement in terrorism) to the State of which the exclude/deportee is a national or some other willing receptor State, even where there is no real risk of death, torture or other inhuman or degrading treatment or punishment.

It is, of course, tempting to dismiss the range of restrictions imposed under non-derogating control orders as minor inconveniences (especially when contrasted with the danger they are there to prevent), as mere restrictions on movement, not, legally speaking, one of the fundamental human rights binding the United Kingdom. Closer examination in chapter 7 of those actually imposed, however, reveals very significant degrees of interference with rights to respect for home, correspondence, private and family life, with freedom of thought, conscience and religion, and with associated and intertwined freedoms of expression, assembly and association, central to a liberal democracy, and central to the individual as a social animal.

Those impacts run through all the situations examined in this book. But for almost half the period under study – until 1953 – those rights and freedoms found their expression mainly in the political arena and only in a common law and its 'implied Bill of Rights' much muted by the power of statute and the willingness of the judiciary to accede to executive claims of 'emergency' and 'national security', something exemplified most graphically by *R v Halliday, ex parte Zadig* in the First World War and by *Liversidge v Anderson* in the Second World War. The voice of key rights and freedoms was more muted in that legal arena than in some other States since, generally, neither within the United Kingdom nor abroad in its colonial Empire did they find expression in a constitutional instrument or even a statutory Bill of Rights. Until 1948, moreover, they found no real expression in an international legal order founded as now on the sovereignty of States, but one in which the treatment by a State of its own nationals was a matter of domestic jurisdiction, and generally not regarded as the proper concern of other States. Not so, of course, the position of foreign nationals in respect of whom their national State might invoke its right of diplomatic protection. That possibly benefited Eamon De Valera, who escaped execution for his part in the 1916 Easter Rising. But both in the expansion of colonial empires and the German expansionism which lead up to and formed a central part of World War Two, concern for how another State treated one's nationals produced military aggression motivated by less lofty concerns.

After 1945, the international perspective underwent a sea change, in part motivated by the need to limit that danger of aggression and by guilt on the part of the victors at having stood idly by for too long in the face of Fascism. Human rights concerns were a key part of the UN Charter, and its General Assembly – the international community – proclaimed its Universal Declaration of Human Rights in 1948. The Cold War and the division between the developed and developing worlds made it difficult to secure agreement on binding international human rights standards at UN level. In contrast, the greater cohesion of a Western Europe, with vivid memories of one totalitarianism and fearful of a real threat from another in the form of Soviet expansionism, saw the creation of the Council of Europe and the speedy drawing up and adoption of the ECHR. That entered into force in 1953 with enforcement machinery, with roles for legal and political institutions – the Commission and Court of Human Rights, in the former category, and the

Committee of Ministers of the Council of Europe in the latter. The individual, under the ECHR, was thus very much the subject of that part of international law. Nor was the impact of the ECHR confined to Europe and thus to a relevance in our context to the Cyprus and Northern Ireland questions. Powers used to combat terrorism connected with those questions have, of course, produced many of the landmark ECHR cases of the Commission since *Greece* v *United Kingdom* (the first and second Cyprus cases) in 1957 and of the Court since *Lawless* v *Ireland* in 1961.[1] Almost on first adhering to the ECHR, the United Kingdom surprisingly chose to extend ECHR protection to its colonial empire, despite the states of emergency in many of those colonial entities. The potential and actual impact of the ECHR, however, was significantly blunted by the United Kingdom's failure to make the right of individual application available, whether to those at home or in its empire, until 1966. But the ability of one State party to bring an application against another was not optional, and the United Kingdom appreciated its impact both as regards Cyprus and the Northern Ireland question, with petitions in each case brought by States Parties with wider political interests in the underlying conflicts – Greece and Ireland, respectively. The period since acceptance of the ECHR right of individual petition in 1966 produced a range of individual challenges to a variety of the executive measures surveyed in this book. Some, like *Chahal* v *United Kingdom* (national security deportation and freedom from torture, inhuman and degrading treatment) imposed very significant and, for Government, irritating restrictions on ability to deploy them. The incorporation of the ECHR into United Kingdom law through the HRA, operative since October 2000, has very much changed the rules of the judicial game as was evidenced in *A and Others* (ATCSA detention without trial of foreign national terrorist suspects), *A and Others (No. 2)* (non-admissibility of material obtained through torture), *MB* (non-derogating control orders and denial of fair trial) and *Re JJ* and *E* (the limits of restrictions imposable by a non-derogating control order). Lord Steyn, a retired Law Lord and Chairman of *Justice*, thought *A and Others* a decision going to the 'very heart of our democracy' which anchored our constitutional system on the rule of law, making crystal clear that the United Kingdom 'has become a constitutional state'. He characterized the last 25 years as a period when

> ... the power of the executive over the affairs of the nation and the lives of individuals grew inexorably, [and] the role of judges has also changed. The European Union and the Human Rights Act 1998 contributed to this process. But there has been a general expansion of the power and influence of the judiciary in Britain as discontent with the working of our democracy increased. What Lord Hailsham called the elective dictatorship played a decisive role in this process. Moreover, Britain has become a multi–cultural society in which the need to protect the rights of minorities has become ever more important. Generally the need to protect individual rights has come centre

---

[1] See *Ireland* v *United Kingdom*; *Donnelly* v *United Kingdom*; *Brogan* v *United Kingdom*; *Brannigan and McBride* v *United Kingdom*.

stage. The public is now increasingly looking not to Parliament, but to the judges to protect their rights. In this new world, judges nowadays accept more readily than before that it is their democratic and constitutional duty to stand up where necessary for individuals against the government. The greater the arrogation of power by a seemingly all-powerful executive which dominates the House of Commons, the greater the incentive and need for judges to protect the rule of law.[2]

The United Kingdom is a state committed to respect for the Rule of Law, something it would cite as a positive benefit for those countries which formed part of its colonial empire and something reflected in its extension to them of protection under the ECHR. As has been seen in this book and other histories of colonial empire and the Irish/Northern Ireland questions, the extent to which its security laws and policies matched up to the rhetoric of the Rule of Law can legitimately be questioned. Its sense of fair play and due process forming part of that ideal, has meant that governments have shown concern to adhere to the strict forms of the law. This was shown graphically in respect of a number of deployments of martial law in the nineteenth century British Empire.[3] It is also reflected in the creation in respect of each of the executive security powers examined in this book of administrative review machinery enabling their subjects to make representations on the adverse decision made in respect of them. For most of the period surveyed, the administrative means of challenge consisted of representations in an advisory system of review (to one or more advisers or an Advisory Committee). On two occasions, however, regimes capable of making a binding decision were deployed: in practice in Malaya because of the workload involved;[4] and with respect to internment in Northern Ireland under the DTO 1972 and NIEPA 1973.[5] Human rights' litigation under the ECHR produced in *Chahal* as regards national security deportation, condemnation by the Court of Human Rights of both the adviser system and attenuated judicial review as not consonant with Art. 5(4) ECHR (right to effective review of detention by a court) and Art. 13 ECHR (right to an effective remedy). The lawmakers responded in the Special Immigration Appeals Commission Act 1997 with a new appellate expert body, the Special Immigration Appeals Commission (SIAC), empowered to subject to very close scrutiny the Home Secretary's decisions on security grounds as regards immigration issues and to make a binding decision on the matter. For a while, it appeared that SIAC could become a specialized national security court. Its jurisdiction embraces not only national security decisions in the immigration law context (refusal of entry, revocation of leave to remain, deportation and refusal to revoke a deportation order). Its remit also extends to revocation of British citizenship. Under ATCSA it embraced certification decisions in respect of the indefinite detention without trial

---

[2] Steyn (2006): 247.
[3] Kostal (2005); Hussain (2003).
[4] See chapter 5.
[5] See chapter 3.

of foreign national terrorist suspects. In addition, Home Secretary Blunkett floated the idea of SIAC-type criminal trials of terrorist suspects, a proposal thankfully not adopted. However, after the declaration of incompatibility in respect of ATCSA detention issued in *A and Others*, the law-makers chose not to give SIAC a role in respect of control orders, the replacement for indefinite detention without trial. The task of issuing control orders on the application of the Secretary of State was instead given to the High Court, which would also consider appeals against his refusal to revoke one and challenges to those the scheme permitted him to make without prior judicial involvement. But the High Court operates SIAC-type procedures to try to balance the individual's and public interest in due process with the wider public interest in protecting sensitive material from disclosure: the use of 'open' and 'closed' sessions and the role of the Special Advocate. It has been seen that the High Court's remit is more extensive with respect to derogating control orders, not as yet deployed. Its powers in respect of non-derogating control orders have been criticized as scant and in *MB* Sullivan J found them incompatible with ECHR fair trial rights, a finding reversed by the Court of Appeal which gave them more substance. Nonetheless, administrative or specialist challenge mechanisms have in consequence of the ECHR become more sophisticated and judicialized, embodying an appellate role from SIAC or the High Court, albeit on law only. But, despite all the litigation to date, a central question remains definitively unanswered: do these SIAC-type processes for protecting sensitive evidence meet ECHR requirements on fair hearing?

Throughout the period under study, typically the ordinary courts have never formally been closed to victims of the executive measures examined in this book. Some attempts have been made to limit the range of questions they can deal with, occasionally after the emergency actions may be protected by an Indemnity Act and, on occasion, a Law Officer's permission might be needed to bring some proceedings. But generally the subject matter has not been the subject of an ouster clause. For most of the period, the case law has afforded ringing judicial statements on the courts' role in protecting individual liberties, mainly in celebrated dissents. The traditional role of the courts in these fields, however, has rather been that of deference to executive knowledge and expertise, and to appear at times more executive-minded than the executive when the red flag of national security or emergency was waved. Despite ringing rhetoric, they did not use the powers available to them with appreciable effect. Traditionally, judicial review in these security areas was attenuated. The HRA era has seen changes in that approach with judicial action beginning to match ringing rhetoric. The post-*Chahal* creation of SIAC, and the powers of a High Court deploying SIAC-type processes with respect to control orders under the PTA 2005, have been accompanied, under the alternative remedies rule, by the withdrawal from this particular stage of the application for judicial review. The involvement of the Court of Appeal and the House of Lords instead stems from statutory appeals on a point of law, that of the former under the specific provisions of these post-1997 schemes, that of the latter flowing from the standard generalized rights of appeal to their Lordships' House.

The HRA era has witnessed a more empowered and less deferential judiciary – witness most markedly the approach of the House in *A and Others* and of other courts with respect to control orders.

Such enhanced judicial scrutiny has been characterized as both proper and welcome. It has, nonetheless, attracted criticism from politicians within and outside the Government.[6] Reflecting impatience at the constraints on 'effective anti-terrorist action' perceived to be set by a HRA so boldly introduced in 1998 as part of a package of imaginative constitutional reforms, Government frustration has produced headline-seeking calls for repeal or amendment of the HRA and even withdrawal from the ECHR, with the Lord Chancellor/Secretary of State for Constitutional Affairs appearing with emollient words to explain that the Prime Minister really meant no such thing, but merely to express concern at judicial misuse of the tools and particularly to reiterate criticism of the *Chahal* principle precluding deportation as some sort of misapplication of the ECHR and Art. 3.

Government has made full use of appellate mechanisms to endeavour to overturn victories won by individuals, with mixed success. It has, moreover, sought in a number of ways to change the rules of the game for the courts. Here one can point to the limited nature of the High Court's powers in respect of non-derogating control orders (something expanded by the Court of Appeal using the HRA), litigation in respect of which is ongoing. More directly and of great concern in a society committed to the rule of law, is the sweeping ouster clause sought to be inserted into the NIAA 2002 by the Asylum and Immigration (Treatment of Claimants) Bill.[7] Thankfully narrowed as a result of the legislative process, it limits recourse to the courts to error of law and sets strict time-limits. Lord Steyn characterized the original attempt as

> ... an astonishing measure ... contrary to the rule of law ... contrary to the constitutional principle on which our nation is founded that Her Majesty's courts must always be open to all, citizens and foreigners alike, who seek just redress of perceived wrongs. ... a wholly disproportionate approach to the undoubted abuses in the immigration system. Instead of addressing those abuses, the section by and large abolishes justice and due process. If such legislation is effective in this corner of the law – not even involving the endless war against terrorism – what are the portents for our democracy? Why should the [provision] not serve as a model in other areas?[8]

Fortunately, that has not happened and recent dicta in the House of Lords in *Jackson* indicated that the courts, deploying the rule of law, might even modify the central tenets of parliamentary sovereignty and reject such legislative attempts 'to subvert the rule of law by removing governmental action affecting the rights of the

---

[6] HC Library Research Paper 06/44 (2006): 35–7.

[7] Steyn (2006): 251.

[8] Ibid.

individual from all judicial powers'.[9] Having threatened direct amendment of the *Chahal* principle in terms of legislative amendment in respect of United Kingdom courts, government is instead trying to have that principle re-thought by the European Court of Human Rights by intervening, with a number of other States Party to the ECHR, in a national security deportation case brought by a putative deportee against the Netherlands.[10]

All agree that the current international terrorist threat is unlikely quickly to diminish. That continued threat of terrorism and other threats to national security mean that the use of the types of executive measure surveyed in this book will remain a prominent feature of the United Kingdom's attempts to manage these threats. This arena will remain one in which, in their justified concern to protect human rights central to their vision of our democratic society, judges will continue to map out the contours of the new constitutional settlement effected by the HRA. The first step on the road to that settlement was the United Kingdom's bold acceptance of the ECHR, a human rights instrument seen to be of prime importance in our analysis, in ways in which the Governments of both political persuasions which helped create and ratify it could probably never have imagined. It is important that the courts show vigilance and imagination in so mapping those contours. The types of powers examined in this book may well be necessary when the State faces great threat. The also impact significantly on the rights of individuals in ways similar in many cases to imprisonment following conviction, but through processes that lack the transparency and safeguards of the criminal prosecution approach to which they both provide an alternative and a supplemental means of dealing with threats to national security, whether through terrorism or otherwise. The rules of the game have indeed changed since 9/11, but arguably less so in the way in which the Prime Minister puts it. In this HRA era, it is rather the rules of the judicial game that have changed to the benefit of all in our democratic society. When courts and others attempt to uphold human rights and civil liberties against government, they are acting neither foolishly nor illegitimately, but rather fulfilling a proper role in a civilized society founded on the rule of law. This book has amply illustrated the dangers of neglecting that ideal, whether at home or in colonial empire, and its dictates are just as vital in current context. As Feldman has put it, 'we need to think about the sort of society in which we want to live, not just the risk from particular threats to life or health'.[11] Faced with grave danger, it is tempting to be 'better safe than sorry', to fall back on 'necessity', to be prepared to countenance illegality or tear down long-standing legal or constitutional safeguards blocking the way to 'effective action'. But if our response to any significant threat to our security or safety is without proof of a criminal offence to lock away or seriously disrupt the lives of those merely thought to be a threat, this represents a

---

[9] *R (on the application of Jackson)* v *Attorney General* [2006] 1 A.C. 262, para. 159 (Baroness Hale). See also paras 107, 120 and 126 (Lord Hope).

[10] *Ramzy* v *Netherlands*.

[11] Feldman (2006): 379.

grave danger to the nature of our liberal society. A US Marine in Vietnam is said to have justified destruction of a village saying 'we had to destroy it in order to save it'. Are we, like that Marine, in danger of destroying our liberal 'village' in order to save it? In considering such matters, it is constitutionally proper that there be tensions between organs of government, that Government and judges disagree, that they are not necessarily on the 'same side'.[12] It is the job of the courts in terms of human rights and threats to the nation to be willing to speak truth to power, regardless of popularity. As the Lord Chancellor put it recently:

It is a part of the acceptance of the rule of law that the courts will be able to exercise jurisdiction over the executive. Otherwise the conduct of the executive is not defined and restrained by law. It is because of that principle, that the USA, deliberately seeking to put the detainees beyond the reach of the law in Guantanamo Bay, is so shocking an affront to the principles of democracy. ... Without independent judicial control, we cannot give effect to the essential values of our society. To give effect to our democratic values needs the participation of executive, legislature, and judiciary together. How well they do it, as in every endeavour, depends on the quality of the individual decisions each branch of the state takes. The ability to give effect to these values is not just the morally correct position to take ... It is also a vital part of providing security for our peoples. The rule of law and the protection of human rights provide the setting in which innovation, and economic prosperity occur. As we see countries applying to join the EU, they do so in the full knowledge that the economic benefits come only with subscription to the democratic and human rights values of the EU. The identification of these underpinning values is vital in the context of the fight against terrorism. For us to succeed in a battle which seeks to undermine our very way of life we must win, not just by the strength and effectiveness of the coercive and security apparatus of the state, but also because of the superiority of the values of our society over the values of those who attack us. Without these values what we are fighting for can get lost in the way we fight.[13]

---

[12] Steyn (2006): 248.
[13] Falconer (2006).

Bibliography

Allen C (1965), *Law and Orders* (London: Stevens).

Anderson D (1994), 'Policing and Communal Conflict: the Cyprus Emergency, 1954–60' in R. Holland (ed.), *Emergencies and Disorder in the European Empires after 1945* (London: Frank Cass), 177–207.

Anderson D (2005), *Histories of the Hanged: Britain's Dirty War in Kenya and the End of Empire* (London: Weidenfeld and Nicholson).

Andrew C (1985), *Secret Service: the Making of the British Intelligence Community* (London: Guild Publishing).

Baddiel D (2005), *The Secret Purposes* (London; Abacus).

Baker J (2002), *An Introduction to English Legal History* (London: Butterworths, 4th ed.).

Baker Review (1958), *A Review of the Cyprus Emergency April 1955–March 1958 by Brigadier G Baker, Chief of Staff to the Governor of Cyprus 1955–57* in National Archives Ref CO 968/690.

Barber N. (1971), *The War of the Running Dogs: the Malayan Emergency 1948–1960* (London: Collins).

Barnard, C (2004), *The Substantive Law of the EU: the Four Freedoms* (Oxford: Oxford University Press).

Bayly C and Harper T (2007), *Forgotten Wars: the End of Britain's Asian Empire* (London: Allen Lane).

Bevan V (1986), *The Development of British Immigration Law* (London: Croom Helm).

Bingham, Lord (2006), 'The Rule of Law', The Sixth Sir David Williams Lecture, Faculty of Law, University of Cambridge found at <http://cpl.law.cam.ac.uk/Media/THE%20RULE%20OF%20LAW%202006.pdf>

Bishop P and Mallie E (1988), *The Provisional IRA* (London: Corgi).

Blake N and Husain R (2003), *Immigration, Asylum and Human Rights* (Oxford: Oxford University Press).

Bonner D (1982), Combating Terrorism in Great Britain: the Role of Exclusion Orders' (1982) *Public Law* 262.

Bonner D (1985), *Emergency Powers in Peacetime* (London: Sweet and Maxwell).

Bonner D (2002), 'Managing Terrorism While Respecting Human Rights? European Aspects of the Anti–terrorism Crime and Security Act 2001' (2002) 8 *European Public Law* 497.

Bonner D (2004), 'Porous Borders: Terrorism and Migration Policy' in B Bogusz and R Cholewinski et al (eds), *Irregular Migration*, (Netherlands, Koninkliijke Brill NV 2004), 93.

Bonner D (2006), 'Responding to Crisis: Legislating against Terrorism' (2006) 122 *Law Quarterly Review* 602.

Bonner D and Cholewinski R (2006), 'The Response of the United Kingdom's Legal and Constitutional Orders to the 1991 Gulf War and the Post–9/11 "War" on Terrorism' in E Guild and A Baldaccini, *Terrorism and the Foreigner* (Leiden: Martinus Nijhoff).

Boyle K, Hadden T and Hillyard P (1975), *Law and State: the Case of Northern Ireland* (London: Martin Robertson).

Boyle K, Hadden T and Hillyard P (1980), *Ten Years On in Northern Ireland: the Legal Control of Political Violence* (London: Cobden Trust).

Butler L (2002), *Britain and Empire: Adjusting to a Post-Imperial World* (London: I B Tauris).

Bruce S (1992), *The Red Hand: Protestant Paramilitaries in Northern Ireland* (Oxford: Oxford University Press).

CAC 7th (2004–05a), House of Commons Constitutional Affairs Committee, Seventh Report of Session 2004–05, *The Operation of the Special Immigration Appeals Commission (SIAC) and the Use of Special Advocates*, HC 323–I (London: TSO).

CAC 7th (2004–05b), House of Commons Constitutional Affairs Committee, Seventh Report of Session 2004–05, *The Operation of the Special Immigration Appeals Commission (SIAC) and the Use of Special Advocates*, HC 323–II (London: TSO).

Campbell C (1994), *Emergency Law in Ireland* (Oxford: Clarendon Press).

Carlile, Lord (2003), *Anti-Terrorism, Crime and Security Act 2001 Part IV Section 28 First Review* (London: Home Office).

Carlile, Lord (2005), *Anti-Terrorism, Crime and Security Act 2001 Part IV Section 28 Review 2004* (London: Home Office).

Carlile, Lord (2006), *First Report of the Independent Reviewer Pursuant to Section 14(3) of the Prevention of Terrorism Act 2005* (London: Home Office).

Carlile, Lord (2007), *Second Report of the Independent Reviewer Pursuant to Section 14(3) of the Prevention of Terrorism Act 2005* (London: Home Office).

Carruthers S.L (1995), *Winning Hearts and Minds: British Governments, the Media and Colonial Counter–Insurgency 1944–1960* (London: Leicester University Press).

Carvel J (1991a), 'War in the Gulf: Suspect Iraqis taken to prison', *The Guardian*, 17 January 1991.

Carvel J (1991b), 'War in the Gulf: Jail prepared for terror suspects' *The Guardian*, 18 January 1991.

Carvel J (1991c), 'War in the Gulf: Baker curbs immigration' *The Guardian*, 19 January 1991.

Chappell C (1984), *Island of Barbed Wire: the Remarkable Story of World War Two Internment on the Isle of Man* (London: Corgi).

Churchill W (2000), *The Second World War Vol. 5: Closing the Ring* (London: the Folio Society).

Clarke P (1996), *Hope and Glory: Britain 1900–1990* (Harmondsworth: Penguin)

Clough M (1998), *Mau Mau Memoirs: History, Politics and Memory* (Boulder: Lynne Riener).

Clutterbuck R (1966), *The Long Long War: the Emergency in Malaya, 1948–1960* (London: Praeger).

Cm 3420 (1996a), *Inquiry into Legislation against Terrorism Vol. I* (London: TSO).

Cm 3420 (1996b), *Inquiry into Legislation against Terrorism Vol. II* (London: TSO).

Cm 3782 (1997), *Rights Brought Home: the Human Rights Bill* (London: TSO).

Cm 4178 (1998), *Legislation Against Terrorism: A Consultation Paper* (London: TSO).

Cm 6147 (2004), *Counter–Terrorism Powers: Reconciling Security and Liberty in an Open Society: a Discussion Paper* (London: TSO).

Cm 6469 (2005), *Intelligence and Security Committee, The Handling of Detainees by UK Intelligence Personnel in Afghanistan, Guantanamo Bay and Iraq* (London: TSO).

Cm 6593 (2005), *Government Reply to the Sixth Report from the Home Affairs Committee Session 2004–05: Terrorism and Community Relations* (London: TSO).

Cm 6596 (2005), *Government Response to the Constitutional Affairs Select Committee's Report into the Operation of the Special Immigration Appeals Commission (SIAC) and the Use of Special Advocates* (London: TSO).

Cm 6785 (2006), *Intelligence and Security Committee, Report into the London Terrorist Attacks on 7 July 2005* (London: TSO).

Cm 6888 (2006), HM Government, *Countering International Terrorism: the United Kingdom's Strategy* (London: TSO).

Cohen M (2007), 'Judicial Activism in the House of Lords: a Composite Constitutional Approach' (2007) *Public Law* 95.

Coogan T (1988), *The IRA* (London: Fontana).

Costello F (2003), *The Irish Revolution and its Aftermath 1916–1923* (Dublin: Irish Academic Press).

Cox M (2006), *A Farewell to Arms?: beyond the Good Friday Agreement* (Manchester: Manchester University Press).

Crawshaw N (1978), *The Cyprus Revolt: An Account of the Struggle for Union with Greece* (London: Allen and Unwin).

Cumberbatch J (1991), "Prisoner of war – Can a suburban computer salesman be seen as a threat to national security? He can if he's Palestinian", Women's Page, *The Guardian*, 30 January 1991.

David S (2000), *The Indian Mutiny* (London: Penguin Books).

Defence 6th (2004–05), House of Commons, Defence Select Committee, Sixth Report of Session 2004–05, *Iraq: an Initial Assessment of Post–Conflict Operations*, HC 65–I (London; TSO).

Defence 1st (2005–06), House of Commons, Defence Select Committee, First Special Report of Session 2005–06, *Iraq: an Initial Assessment of Post–Conflict Operations: Government Response to the Committee's Sixth report of Session 2004–05*, HC 436 (London: TSO).

Defence 5th (2005–06), House of Commons, Defence Select Committee, Fifth Report of Session 2005–06, *The UK Deployment to Afghanistan*, HC 558 (London: TSO).

Defence 6th (2005–06), House of Commons, Defence Select Committee, Sixth Special Report of Session 2005–06, *The UK deployment to Afghanistan: Government Response to the Committee's Fifth Report of Session 2005–06*, HC 1211 (London: TSO).

Diplock, Lord (1972), *Report of the Commission to consider Legal Procedures to Deal with Terrorist Activities in Northern Ireland*, Cmnd. 7497 (London: HMSO).

Director of Operations Malaya (1957), *Review of the Emergency in Malaya, June 1948–August 1957 by the Director of Operations Malaya* WO 106/5990 TNA.

Director of Operations Malaya (1958), *The Conduct of Anti–Terrorist Operations in Malaya*, 3rd ed. in WO 279/241 TNA.

Dolan A (2006), 'Killing and Bloody Sunday, November 1920' (206) 49 *The Historical Journal* 789.

Donohue L (2001), *Counter–Terrorist Law and Emergency Powers in the United Kingdom 1922–2000* (Dublin: Irish Academic Press).

Dummett A and Nicol A (1990), *Subjects, Citizens, Aliens and Others: Nationality and Immigration Law* (London: Weidenfeld and Nicholson).

Eagles I (1982), 'Evidentiary Protection for Informers – Policy or Privilege?' (1982) 6 *Criminal Law Journal* 175.

Elkins C (2005), *Britain's Gulag: the Brutal End of Empire in Kenya* (London: Jonathan Cape).

English R (2003), *Armed Struggle: a History of the IRA* (London: Macmillan).

Erskine, Gen W (1955), *The Kenya Emergency (June 1953–May 1955)*, WO 236/18, TNA.

Evans J (1983), *Immigration Law* (London: Sweet and Maxwell, 2nd ed.).

Ewing K and Gearty C (2000), *The Struggle for Civil Liberties: Political Freedom and the Rule of Law in Britain 1914–1945* (Oxford: Oxford University Press).

FAC 4th (2003–04), House of Commons Foreign Affairs Select Committee, Fourth Report of Session 2003–04, Human Rights Annual Report 2003, HC 389 (London: TSO).

FAC 6th (2004–05), House of Commons Foreign Affairs Select Committee, Sixth Report of Session 2004–05, *Foreign Policy aspects of the War against Terrorism*, HC 36–I (London: TSO).

FAC 4th (2005–06), House of Commons Foreign Affairs Select Committee, Fourth Report of Session 2005–06, *Foreign Policy Aspects of the War against Terrorism*, HC 573 (London: TSO).

Falconer, Lord (2006), 'The Role of Judges in a Modern Democracy', Magna Carta Lecture, Sydney, Australia, 13 September 2006, found at <http://www.dca.gov.uk/speeches/2006/sp060913.htm>.

Federation of Malaya, Paper No. 33 (1952), *Resettlement and the Development of New Villages in the Federation of Malaya, 1952*, CO 1022/29, TNA.

Federation of Malaya Paper No. 59 (1953), *Criminal Procedure Committee Report*, in CO 1022/491, TNA.

Feldman D (2006), 'Human rights, Terrorism and Risk: the Roles of Politicians and Judges' (2006) *Public Law* 364.

Fenwick H (2002), 'The Anti–Terrorism, Crime and Security Act 2001: a proportionate response to 11 September?' (2002) 65 *Modern Law Review* 724.

Ferguson N (2004), *Empire* (London: Penguin).

Fisk R (1975), *The Point of No Return: the Strike which Broke the British in Ulster* (London: Times Books; Deutsch).

Foley C (1964), *Legacy of Strife: Cyprus from Rebellion to Civil War* (Harmondsworth: Penguin).

Ford R (2006), 'Judges deal blow to 'draconian' anti–terror laws', *The Times*, 2 August 2006.

Forster, Lt. Col J (1957), *A Comparative Study of the Emergencies in Malaya and Kenya* (Operational Research Unit Far East Report No. 1/57), WO 291/1670, TNA.

Franck T (1968), *Comparative Constitutional Process: Cases and Materials: Fundamental Rights in the Common Law Nations* (London: Sweet and Maxwell).

Fraser A (1996), *The Gunpowder Plot: Terror and Faith in 1605* (London: Weidenfeld and Nicholson).

French D (1978), 'Spy Fever in Britain, 1900–1915' (1978) 21 *The Historical Journal* 355.

French T (1979), 'Lord Bryce's Investigations into Alleged German Atrocities' (1979) 14 *Journal of Contemporary History* 369.

Gardiner, Lord (1975), *Report of a Committee to Consider, in the Context of Civil Liberties and Human Rights, Measures to Deal with Terrorism in Northern Ireland*, Cmnd. 5847 (London: HMSO).

Gatrell V (1996), *The Hanging Tree: Execution and the English People, 1770–1868* (Oxford: Oxford University Press).

Ghai Y and McAuslan P (1970), *Law and Political Change in Kenya* (Oxford: Oxford University Press).

Goldenberg S and Dodd V (2006), 'British Shoe Bomber "part of fifth 9/11 plot"', *The Guardian*, 28 March 2006.

Goss O and Ní Aoláin F (2001), 'From Discretion to Scrutiny: Revisiting the Application of the Margin of Appreciation Doctrine in the Context of Article 15 of the European Convention on Human Rights' (2001) 23 *Human Rights Quarterly* 625.

Grant S (1991), 'A Just Treatment for Enemy Aliens' (1991) 141 *New Law Journal* 305.

Greer D (1973), 'Admission of Confessions and the Common Law in Time of Emergency' (1973) 25 *Northern Ireland Legal Quarterly* 199.

Greer D (1980), 'The Admissibility of Confessions Under the Northern Ireland (Emergency Provisions) Act 1973' (1980) 31 *Northern Ireland Legal Quarterly* 205.

Grief N (2006), 'The Exclusion of Foreign Torture Evidence: a Qualified Victory for the Rule of Law' (2006) *European Human Rights Law Review* 201.

Griffith J (1977), *The Politics of the Judiciary* (London: Fontana).

Griggs J (1997), *The Young Lloyd George* (London: Harper Collins).

HAC 6th (2004–05), House of Commons Home Affairs Select Committee, Sixth Report of Session 2004–05, *Terrorism and Community Relations*, HC 165 (London: TSO).

Harris T (2006), *Revolution: the Great Crisis of the British Monarchy* (London: Penguin).

Hart P (2005a), *The IRA at War 1916–1923* (Oxford: Oxford University Press).

Hart P (2005b), *Mick: The Real Michael Collins* (London: Macmillan).

Hayes–McCoy G (1966), 'The Conduct of the Anglo–Irish War' (January 1919 to the Truce in July 1921' in D Williams (ed.), *The Irish Struggle 1916–1926* (London: Routledge and Kegan Paul).

HC 1087 (2006), *Report of the Official Account of the Bombings in London on 7th July 2005* (London: TSO).

HC Library Research Paper 06/44 (2006), Horne A and Berman G, *Judicial Review; a Short Guide to Claims in the Administrative Court* found at <http://www.parliament.uk/commons/lib/research/rp2006/rp06-044.pdf>.

Hennessy P (2006), *Having It So good: Britain in the Fifties* (London: Allen Lane).

Hepple B (1969), 'The Immigration Appeals Act 1969' (1969) 32 *Modern Law Review* 668.

Hepple B (1971), 'Aliens and Administrative Justice: The Dutschke Case' (1971) 34 *Modern Law Review* 501.

Hiebert J (2005), 'Parliamentary Review of Terrorism Measures' (2005) 68 *Modern Law Review* 676.

Hoffman B (1999), *Inside Terrorism* (London: Indigo).

Hogge A (2005), *God's Secret Agents* (London: Harper Collins).

Holland R (1998), *Britain and the Revolt in Cyprus 1954–1959* (Oxford: Clarendon Press).

Holmes C (1988), *John Bull's Island: Immigration and British Society 1871–1971* (London: Macmillan).

Home Office (1991), *Control of Immigration: Statistics 1990*, Cm 1571 (London: HMSO).

Home Office (2001), *Control of Immigration: Statistics 2000*, Cm 5315 (London: HMSO).

Home Office (2004), *Control of Immigration: Statistics 2003*, Cm 6263 (London: HMSO).

Hussain N (2003), *The Jurisprudence of Emergency: Colonialism and the Rule of Law* (Ann Arbor: Michigan University Press).

Jackson J and Doran S (1995), *Judge without Jury: Diplock Trials in the Adversary system* (Oxford: Clarendon Press).

James L (1998), *The Rise and Fall of the British Empire* (London: Abacus).

Jenkins R (1991), *A Life at the Centre* (London: Macmillan).

Jenkins S (2006), 'Blair is wildly exaggerating the threat posed by terrorism', *The Guardian*, 22 November 2006.

Jessberger F and Gaeta P (2006), 'Introduction' (2006) 4 *Journal of International Criminal Justice* 891.

JHRC 18th (2003–04), House of Lords/House of Commons Joint Select Committee on Human Rights, Eighteenth Report of 2003–04, *Review of Counter Terrorism Powers*, HL 158/HC 713 (London: TSO).

JHRC 9th (2004–05), Ninth Report of Session 2004–05, *Prevention of Terrorism Bill: Preliminary Report*, HL61/HC389 (London: TSO).

JHRC 10th (2004–05), House of Lords/House of Commons Joint Select Committee on Human Rights, Tenth Report of Session 2004–2005, *Prevention of Terrorism Bill*, HL 68/HC 334 (London: TSO).

JHRC 3rd (2005), House of Lords/House of Commons Joint Select Committee on Human Rights, Third Report of Session 2005–06, *Counter–Terrorism Policy and Human Rights: Terrorism Bill and Related Matters*, HL 75–I/HC 561–I (London: TSO)

JHRC 12th (2005–06), House of Lords/House of Commons Joint Select Committee on Human Rights, *Counter–Terrorism Policy and Human Rights: Draft Prevention of Terrorism (Continuance in force of sections 1 to 9) Order 2006*, HL 122/HC 915 (London: TSO).

JHRC 19th (2005–06a), House of Lords/House of Commons Joint Select Committee on Human Rights, Nineteenth Report of Session 2005–06, *The UN Convention Against Torture (UNCAT)*, HL 185–I/HC701–I (London; TSO).

JHRC 19th (2005–06b), House of Lords/House of Commons Joint Select Committee on Human Rights, Nineteenth Report of Session 2005–06, *The UN Convention Against Torture (UNCAT)*, HL 185 II/HC 701 II (London: TSO).

Jowell J (2003), 'Judicial Deference, Servility or Institutional Capacity' (2003) *Public Law* 592.

Jowell J (2004), 'The Rule of Law Today' in J Jowell and D Oliver (eds), The Changing Constitution (Oxford: Oxford University Press, 5th ed).

Kautt W (1999), *The Anglo–Irish War 1916–1921: A People's War* (London: Praeger).

Kavanaugh K (2006), 'Policing the Margins: Rights Protection and the European Court of Human Rights' (2006) 4 *European Human Rights Law Review* 422.

Keay J (2000), *India: a History* (London: Harper Collins).

Kee R (1989), *Trial and Error: The Maguires, the Guildford Pub Bombings and British Justice* (Harmondsworth: Penguin).

Keir D and Lawson F (1979), *Cases in Constitutional Law* (Oxford: Clarendon Press, 6th ed.).

Kitson F (1960), *Gangs and Counter–Gangs* (London: Barrie and Rockcliff).

Kitson F (1971), *Low Intensity Operations* (London: Faber).

Kochan M (1983), *Britain's Internees in the Second World War* (London: MacMillan).

Kostal R (2000), 'A Jurisprudence of Power: Martial Law and the Ceylon Controversy of 1848–51 (2000) 28 *Journal of Imperial and Commonwealth History* 1.

Kostal R (2005), *A Jurisprudence of Power: Victorian Empire and the Rule of Law* (Oxford: Oxford University Press).

Lafitte F (1988), *The Internment of Aliens* (London: Libris).

Lathbury Lt Gen (1956), *The Kenya Emergency* (May 1955–November 1956), WO 236/20, TNA.

Legomsky S (1987), *Immigration and the Judiciary : Law and Politics in Britain and America* (Oxford: Clarendon Press).

Leigh I (1991), 'Gulf War Deportations' (1991) *Public Law* 331.

Leigh I and Lustgarten L (1994), *In From the Cold: National Security and Parliamentary Democracy* (Oxford: Clarendon Press).

Lomas O (1980), 'The Executive and the Anti–Terrorist Legislation of 1939' (1980) *Public Law* 16.

Louis W (1999), 'The Dissolution of the British Empire' in J Brown and W Louis (eds), *The Oxford History of the British Empire, IV: The Twentieth Century* (Oxford: Oxford University Press), 329–355.

Lowry D (1977), 'Terrorism and Human Rights: Counter–Insurgency and Necessity at Common Law' (1977) 53 *Notre Dame Law Review* 49.

McBarnet D (1981), *Conviction: Law, the State and the Construction of Justice* (London: MacMillan).

Macdonald I and Blake N (1991), *Macdonald's Immigration Law and Practice*, (London: Butterworths, 3rd ed.).

McEldowney J (2005), 'Political Security and Democratic Rights' (2005) 12 *Democratization* 766.

McGuffin J (1973), *Internment* (Tralee: Anvil Books).

McKittrick D and McVea D (2001), *Making Sense of the Troubles* (London: Penguin, rev. ed).

Marks S (1995), 'Civil Liberties at the Margin: the UK Derogation and the European Court of Human Rights' (1995) 15 *Oxford Journal of Legal Studies* 69.

Marty D (2006), Council of Europe Parliamentary Assembly, Committee on Legal Affairs and Human Rights, *Alleged Secret Detentions and Unlawful Inter–State Transfers of Detainees involving Council of Europe Member States*, rapporteur Dick Marty), Doc. 10957, 12 June 2006 (Strasbourg: Council of Europe).

Mathews A (1988), *Freedom, State Security and the Rule of Law* (London: Sweet and Maxwell).

Mitchell A (2002), 'Alternative Government: "Exit Britannia" – the Formation of the Irish National State, 1918–21' in J Augusteijn (ed.), *The Irish Revolution 1913–1923* (Basingstoke: Palgrave), 70.

Morris N (2006), 'Appeal judges attack control orders for terror suspects', *The Independent*, 2 August 2006.

Mullin C (1987), *Error of Judgment: the Truth about the Birmingham Bombings* (Swords, Co. Dublin: Poolbeg).

Nash D (1999), 'The Boer War and its Humanitarian Critics' (1999) 49 *History Today* 42–49.

National Commission (2004), *The 9/11 Commission Report: Final Report of the National Commission on Terrorist Attacks Upon the United States* (New York: Norton and Company).

Nelson, S (1984), *Ulster's Uncertain Defenders: Protestant Political, Paramilitary and Community Groups and the Northern Ireland Conflict* (Belfast: Appletree Press).

Newton Committee (2003), Privy Councillor Review Committee, *Anti–Terrorism, Crime and Security Act 2001 Review: Report*, HC 100 (2003–04) (London: TSO).

OASA Review (2002), *Report of the Committee to Review the Offences Against the State Acts 1939–1998 and Related Matters* (Dublin: Government Publications).

O'Higgins P (1962), 'The Lawless case' (1962) *Cambridge Law Journal* 234.

O'Higgins P (1964), 'Disguised Extradition: the Soblen Case' (1964) 27 *Modern Law Review* 523.

Oscapella I (1980), 'A Study of Informers in England' (1980) *Criminal Law Review* 136.

Ovey C and White R (2006), *Jacobs and White: European Convention on Human Rights* (Oxford: Oxford University Press, 4th ed.).

Pakenham T (1966), *The Year of Liberty: the Story of the Great Irish Rebellion of 1798* (London: Abacus).

Pakenham T (1979), *The Boer War* (London: Weidenfeld and Nicholson).

Pakenham T (1992), *The Scramble for Africa* (London: Abacus).

Palley C (1972), 'The Evolution, Disintegration and Possible Reconstruction of the Northern Ireland Constitution' (1972) 1 *Anglo–American Law Review* 368.

Palley C (2005), *An International Relations Debacle: The UN Secretary–General's Mission of Good Offices in Cyprus 1999–2004* (Oxford: Hart Publishing).

Patkin B (1979), *The Dunera Internees* (Walnut Creek, California: Benmir Books).

Peers S (2003), 'EU Responses to Terrorism' (2003) 52 *International and Comparative Law Quarterly* 227.

Phillips, Lord Chief Justice (2006), 'Terrorism and Human Rights', text of a lecture delivered to Singapore Academy of Law (August 2006) and as the University of Herfordshire Law Lecture (19 October 2006), accessed at

<http://www.judiciary.gov.uk/publications_media/speeches/2006/sp191006.ht m.>.

Police Ombudsman (2007), *Statement by the Police Ombudsman for Northern Ireland on Her Investigation into the Circumstances Surrounding the Death of Raymond McCord Junior and Related Matters*, found at <http://www.policeombudsman.org/publicationsuploads/BALLAST%20PUBL IC%20STATEMENT%2022-01-07%20FINAL%20VERSION.pdf>.

Poole T (2005), 'Harnessing the Power of the Past? Lord Hoffman and the *Belmarsh Detainees* case' (2005) 32 *Journal of Law and Society* 534.

Prebble J (1967), *Culloden* (Harmondsworth: Penguin).

Preston D (2003), *Wilful Murder: The Sinking of the Lusitania* (London: Corgi Books).

Primoratz I (1995), 'What is Terrorism?' in C Gearty (ed.), *Terrorism* (Aldershot: Dartmouth).

Quinault R (2005), 'Underground Attacks' (2005) 55 *History Today* 16.

Quinlivan P and Rose P (1982), *The Fenians in England* (London: John Calder).

Radcliffe, Lord (1956), *Proposals for Cyprus: Report submitted to the Secretary of State for the Colonies by the Rt. Hon. Lord Radcliffe*, GBE Cmnd. 42 (December 1956).

RAND (1999), *Countering the New Terrorism* (Washington DC: RAND).

Richardson L (2006), *What Terrorists Want: Understanding the Terrorist Threat* (London: John Murray).

Roberts A (2000), *Salisbury: Victorian Titan* (London: Phoenix/Orion Books).

Rowntree Report (2006), Blick A, Choudury T and Weir S, *The Rules of the Game: Terrorism, Community and Human Rights* (York: Joseph Rowntree Reform Trust).

Rubin G (1994), *Private Property, Government Requisition and the Constitution 1914–1927* (London: Hambledon Press).

SACHR (1976–77), *Annual Report for 1975–76*, HC 130 (1976–77) (London: HMSO).

Sandhu K (1964a), 'The Saga of the "Squatter" in Malaya' (1964) 5 *Journal of Southeast Asian History* 143.

Sandhu K (1964b), 'Emergency Resettlement in Malaya' (1964) 18 *Journal of Tropical Geography* 157.

Schmid A, (1984), *Political Terrorism: a Research Guide* (New Brunswick, NJ: Transaction Books).

Schmid A and de Graaf J (1982), *Violence as Communication: Insurgent Terrorism and the Western News Media* (London: Sage).

Schmid A and Jongman A (1988), *Political Terrorism: a New Guide to Actors, Authors, Concepts, Data Bases, Theories and Literature* (Amsterdam; Oxford: North–Holland).

Scrutton T (1918), 'The War and the Law' (1918) 34 *Law Quarterly Review* 116.

Sharpe R (1976), *The Law of Habeas Corpus* (Oxford: Clarendon Press).

Sharpe R (1989), *The Law of Habeas Corpus* (Oxford: Clarendon Press, 2nd ed.).

Shennan M (2004), *Out in the Midday Sun: The British in Malaya 1880–1960* (London: John Murray).

Short K (1979), *The Dynamite War; Irish American Bombers in Victorian Britain* (New Jersey: Atlantic Highlands).

Simpson A W B (1994), *In the Highest Degree Odious: Detention without Trial in Wartime Britain* (Oxford: Clarendon Press).

Simpson A W B (1996a), 'The Exile of Archbishop Makarios III' (1996) *European Human Rights Law Review* 391.

Simpson A W B (1996b), 'Round up the Usual Suspects: The Legacy of British Colonialism and the European Convention on Human Rights' (1996) 41 *Loyola Law Review* 629.

Simpson A W B (2004), *Human Rights and the End of Empire* (Oxford: Oxford University Press).

Spjut R (1986), 'Internment and Detention without Trial in Northern Ireland 1971–1975: Ministerial Policy and Practice' (1986) 49 *Modern Law Review* 712.

St Clair Mackenzie V (1918), 'Royal Prerogative in War–Time' (1918) 34 *Law Quarterly Review* 152.

Steinberg J (1966), 'The Copenhagen complex' (1966) 1 *Journal of Contemporary History* 23.

Stent R (1980), *A Bespattered Page? The Internment of 'His Majesty's Most Loyal Enemy Aliens'* (London: Andre Deutsch).

Stephenson D (2004), *1914–1918: The History of the Great World War* (London: Allen Lane).

Stevens D (2004), *UK Asylum Law and Policy: Historical and Contemporary Perspectives* (London: Sweet and Maxwell).

Stevens, Lord (2005), *Not for the Faint Hearted: My Life Fighting Crime* (London: Weidenfeld and Nicholson).

Steyn, Lord (2006), 'Democracy, the Rule of Law and the Role of Judges (2006) 3 *European Human Rights Law Review* 243.

Stone R (1990), 'National Security versus Civil Liberty' in F Patfield and R White (eds), *The Changing Law* (Leicester: Leicester University Press), 119–137.

Strachan H (2003), *The First World War: Volume I: To Arms* (Oxford: Oxford University Press).

Taylor A (1973), *English History 1914–1945* (Harmondsworth: Pelican)

Thienel T (2006), 'Foreign Acts of Torture and the Admissibility of Evidence' (2006) 4 *International Journal of Criminal Justice* 401.

Thompson D (1963), 'The Committee of 100 and the Official Secrets Act, 1911' (1963) *Public Law* 201.

Thompson E (1982), *The Making of the English Working Class* (Harmondsworth: Penguin).

Thornberry C (1963), 'Dr Soblen and the Alien Law of the United Kingdom' (1963) 12 *International and Comparative Law Quarterly* 414.

Tomkins A (2002), 'Legislating Against Terror: The Anti–Terrorism, Crime And Security Act 2001' (2002) *Public Law* 205.

Townshend C (1983), *Political Violence in Ireland: Government and Resistance since 1848* (Oxford: Clarendon Press).

Townshend C (1986), *Britain's Civil Wars: Counterinsurgency in the Twentieth Century* (London: Faber).

Townshend C (1988), 'British Policy in Ireland 1906–1921' in D G Boyce (ed.), *The Revolution in Ireland 1879–1923* (Basingstoke: MacMillan)

Townshend C (2006), *Easter 1916: The Irish Rebellion* (London: Penguin).

Travis A (2006), 'Reid's curfew orders on six terror suspects are illegal, say judges', *The Guardian*, 2 August 2006.

Travis A and Gillan A (2006), 'New blow for Home Office as judge quashes six orders', *The Guardian*, 29 June 2006.

Travis A and Norton Taylor R (2006), 'Iraqis in anti–terror row are "Al Qaida agents"', *The Guardian*, 30 June 2006.

Tudsbery, Capt. F (1916), 'Prerogative in Time of War' (1916) 32 *Law Quarterly Review* 384.

Wade H and Forsyth C (2004), *Administrative Law* (Oxford: Oxford University Press, 6th ed.).

Walker C (1992), *The Prevention of Terrorism in British Law* (Manchester: Manchester University Press, 2nd ed.).

Walker C (2002), *Blackstone's Guide to the Anti–Terrorism Legislation* (Oxford: Oxford University Press).

Walsh D (1982), *The Use and Abuse of Emergency Legislation in Northern Ireland* (London: Cobden Trust).

Walsh O (2002), *Ireland's Independence 1880–1923* (London: Routledge).

Ward A (1969), *Ireland and Anglo–American Relations 1899–1921* (London: LSE and Weidenfeld and Nicholson).

Wardlaw G (1989), *Political Terrorism* (Cambridge: Cambridge University Press, 2nd ed.).

Williams, G (1953), *Criminal Law: the General Part* (London: Stevens)

Williams B (1960), *The Whig Supremacy 1714–1760* (Oxford: Clarendon Press).

Wilson Committee (1967), *Report of the Committee on Immigration Appeals* Cmnd. 3387 (London: HMSO).

Winder R (2005), *Bloody Foreigners: The Story of Immigration to Britain* (London: Abacus).

Wright L (2006), *The Looming Tower: Al Qaeda's Road to 9/11* (London: Allen Lane).

Index

.